The Taoiseach

Also by Iain Dale

The Prime Ministers, 1721–2020: Three Hundred Years of Political Leadership
The Presidents, 1789–2021: 250 Years of American Political Leadership
Kings and Queens: 1200 Years of English and British Monarchs
Dictators: 64 Dictators, 64 Authors, 64 Warnings from History
British General Election Campaigns, 1830–2019: The 50 General Election Campaigns That Shaped Our Modern Politics
Why Can't We All Just Get Along
On This Day in Politics: British Political History in 365 Days
Margaret Thatcher

The Taoiseach

A Century of Political Leadership

Iain Dale

First published in Great Britain by Swift Press, 2025

9 8 7 6 5 4 3 2 1

The Taoiseach © Iain Dale 2025
Individual chapters © contributor's own 2025

All rights reserved

The right of Iain Dale to be identified as the
Author of this Work has been asserted in accordance with the
Copyright, Designs and Patents Act 1988.

Printed and bound in Great Britain by CPI Group (UK) Ltd,
Croydon CR0 4YY

A CIP catalogue record for this book is available from the British Library

We make every effort to make sure our products are safe for the purpose for which they are intended. Our authorised representative in the EU for product safety is Easy Access System Europe, Mustamäe tee 50, 10621 Tallinn, Estonia gpsr.requests@easproject.com

ISBN: 9781800754249
eISBN: 9781800754256

Contents

Notes on contributors   4
List of abbreviations   7
Length of service   8
Preface by Micheál Martin   9
Introduction by Iain Dale   14

1. The office of Taoiseach *by* Eoin O'Malley   16
2. W. T. Cosgrave *by* Ciara Meehan   26
3. Éamon de Valera *by* David McCullagh   41
4. John A. Costello *by* Charles Lysaght   69
5. Seán Lemass *by* Bryce Evans   93
6. Jack Lynch *by* Stephen Collins   112
7. Liam Cosgrave *by* Deirdre Foley   137
8. Charles Haughey *by* Gary Murphy   153
9. Garret FitzGerald *by* Eoin O'Malley   180
10. Albert Reynolds *by* Martin Mansergh   197
11. John Bruton *by* Matthew Dempsey   224
12. Bertie Ahern *by* Mick Clifford   237
13. Brian Cowen *by* Theresa Reidy   257
14. Enda Kenny *by* Harry McGee   278
15. Leo Varadkar *by* Philip Ryan   296
16. Micheál Martin *by* Gavan Reilly   312
17. Simon Harris *by* Pat Leahy   339

For Deborah and Mike Slattery

'We, of our time, have played our part in the perseverance, and we have pledged ourselves to the dead generations who have preserved intact for us this glorious heritage, that we, too, will strive to be faithful to the end, and pass on this tradition unblemished.' – Éamon de Valera

'You know, I have a theory about Charlie Haughey. If you give him enough rope, he'll hang you.' – Leo Enright

'That's fine in practice, but will it work in theory?' – Garret FitzGerald

'The public are entitled to have an absolute guarantee of the financial probity and integrity of their elected representatives, their officials and above all of ministers. They need to know that they are under financial obligations to nobody.' – Bertie Ahern

'Geographically, we are at the periphery of Europe, but I don't see Ireland in that way. The way I see us is as an island at the centre of the world.' – Leo Varadkar

'I want to bring new ideas and new energy and, I hope, a new empathy to public life. Time is certainly short, and there's a lot to do.' – Simon Harris

Contributors

Mick Clifford is Special Correspondent with the *Irish Examiner* newspaper and co-author, with Shane Coleman, of *Bertie Ahern and the Drumcondra Mafia* (2010).

Stephen Collins is a columnist with, and former political editor, of the *Irish Times*. He is the author of numerous books, notably *The Power Game: Ireland Under Fianna Fail* (2001), co author with Ciara Meehan of *Saving the State, Fine Gael from Collins to Varadkar* (2020) and *Ireland's Call: How Brexit Got Done* (2023).

Matthew Dempsey was Editor and Chief Executive of the *Irish Farmers Journal* until 2013, has been President of the Royal Dublin Society, was awarded an honorary Doctorate from University College Dublin and contested the recent Senate (Seanad Eireann) elections.

Bryce Evans is Professor of Modern World History at Liverpool Hope University. Among his books are a biography of Seán Lemass, *Seán Lemass: Democratic Dictator* (2011), and *Ireland during the Second World War: Farewell to Plato's Cave* (2014).

Deirdre Foley is a historian of modern Ireland and has published widely on the social, legal and economic status of women. She is a Research Ireland fellow at the Department of History, Trinity College Dublin.

Pat Leahy is Political Editor of the *Irish Times*. His books include *The Inside Story of Fianna Fáil in Power* (2009) and *The Price of Power: Inside Ireland's Crisis Coalition* (2013).

Charles Lysaght is an Irish lawyer, biographer, obituarist and occasional columnist. He contributes entries to the *Dictionary of Irish Biography* and has written a biography of Brendan Bracken (1979).

David McCullagh is an award-winning Irish journalist, author and news presenter with RTÉ. He has written several books including *A Makeshift Majority: The First Inter-party Government, 1948–51* (1998); a biography of John A. Costello, *The Reluctant Taoiseach* (2010); and a two-volume biography of Éamon de Valera. The first volume was titled *Rise, 1882–1932* (2017) and the second, *Rule, 1932–1975* (2018).

Harry McGee is political correspondent of the *Irish Times* and the author of *The Murderer and the Taoiseach* (2023).

Martin Mansergh is a former Fianna Fáil politician who served as a Minister of State from 2008 to 2011. He served as a Teachta Dála (TD) for the Tipperary South constituency from 2007 to 2011. He was a Senator (Agricultural Panel) from 2002 to 2007. He played a leading role in developing Fianna Fáil policy on Northern Ireland. He is the author or editor of several books including *The Legacy of History for Making Peace in Ireland* (2003).

Ciara Meehan is Dean of Students at the University of Galway. Her books include *The Cosgrave Party: A History of Cumann na nGaedheal, 1923–1933* (2010), *A Just Society for Ireland? 1964–1987* (2013) and *Saving the State: Fine Gael from Collins to Varadkar* (2020), which she co-wrote with political journalist Stephen Collins. Most recently, she authored *A Woman's Place? Challenging Values in 1960s Irish Women's Magazines* (2023).

Gary Murphy is Professor of Politics at Dublin City University and an expert on Irish electoral history. He is the author of the definitive biography of Charles Haughey, *Haughey* (2021).

Eoin O'Malley is Associate Professor of Political Science at Dublin City University. He has co-edited six books on Irish politics. The most recent book is *Charlie vs Garret: The Rivalry that Shaped Modern Ireland* (2025). He is a weekly columnist with the *Sunday Independent*.

Theresa Reidy is a political scientist at University College Cork and Co-editor of the *International Political Science Review*. She has given expert evidence to parliamentary committees, the Constitutional Convention and the Citizens' Assembly and is a regular contributor to radio, television and the print media.

Gavan Reilly is a political journalist and presenter at Virgin Media Television in Dublin, and is the author of *Enda the Road: Nine Days that Toppled a Taoiseach* (2019) and *The Secret Life of Leinster House* (2025).

Philip Ryan is a journalist with the *Irish Independent* and co-author of a biography of Leo Varadakar, *Leo* (2018).

Abbreviations

AIB	Allied Irish Banks
AG	Aktiengesellschaft (public limited company)
BSE	bovine spongiform encephalopathy
CBS	Christian Brothers School
CGT	capital gains tax
CIÉ	Córas Iompair Éireann
EC	European Community
EEC	European Economic Community
EFTA	European Free Trade Area
ETA	Euskadi Ta Askatasuna
EU	European Union
FDI	foreign direct investment
GAA	Gaelic Athletic Association
GDP	gross domestic product
GPA	Guinness Peat Aviation
GPO	General Post Office
HSE	Health Service Executive
IDA	Industrial Development Authority
IFSC	International Financial Services Centre
IMF	International Monetary Fund
IRA	Irish Republican Army
MEP	Member of European Parliament
NAMA	National Asset Management Agency
NATO	North Atlantic Treaty Organization
NFA	National Farmers Association
NGO	non-government organisation

NPHET	National Public Health Emergency Team
PD	Progressive Democrats
R&D	research and development
RTÉ	Raidió Teilifís Éireann
SDLP	Social Democratic and Labour Party
SJ	Society of Jesus
TD	Teachta Dála
UCD	University College Dublin
UN	United Nations
UNRWA	United Nations Relief and Works Agency
UTV	Ulster Television
UVF	Ulster Volunteer Force
VAT	value added tax

Length of service

Éamon de Valera	21 years, 2 months, 1 day
Bertie Ahern	10 years, 10 months, 11 days
Jack Lynch	9 years, 9 months, 12 days
W. T. Cosgrave	9 years, 3 months, 4 days
Seán Lemass	7 years, 4 months, 17 days
Charles Haughey	7 years, 2 months, 2 days
Enda Kenny	6 years, 3 months, 5 days
John A. Costello	6 years, 3 days
Garret FitzGerald	4 years, 11 months, 3 days
Leo Varadkar	4 years, 5 months, 3 days
Liam Cosgrave	4 years, 3 months, 25 days
Albert Reynolds	2 years, 10 months, 2 days
Brian Cowen	2 years, 9 months, 30 days
John Bruton	2 years, 6 months, 12 days
Micheál Martin	2 years, 5 months, 20 days (as at 23 January 2025)
Simon Harris	9 months, 14 days

Preface

An Taoiseach

Micheál Martin

If you look at a map of Europe from December 1922, you will find newly independent states stretching in one continuous stripe from the Arctic Circle to the Adriatic – from Finland down to the short-lived Kingdom of Serbs, Croats and Slovenes. On the far left of the map, you will see on the island of Ireland the only other new state, founded during what was the greatest period of state formation in the history of Europe.

Partitioned – against the will of the majority – into uneven parts, one part bore a curious name: it was not a 'republic' nor a 'kingdom' but a 'free state'. It was the only new state to emerge from the lands of a power on the winning side of the First World War. It was also the only state to retain any form of connection to the state that formerly controlled it – a connection that was central to the civil war still underway in December 1922.

The new Irish state also drew on a very specific nationalist and republican history which distinguished it from the others. While it stood physically apart, it shared many of the same issues such as legal and administrative continuity, economic crises, civil conflict, evolving state symbols, nationals living outside the state border and insecure minorities living within the state border. One of the poorest independent states in the world, and with few natural resources or developed industries, the new Irish state faced quite dramatic hurdles. Yet, if you were to look at that same map of Europe in 1942, the now unambiguously republican Irish state was the only new state that remained intact and democratic.

Ireland is today one of the world's longest continuous democracies. It has the first constitution adopted through a free referendum. It has dramatically reversed its economic fortunes, and its population has risen significantly. We have many social, economic, political and environmental challenges that confront us and an urgent need to show that we retain the ability to deliver sustained progress. However, no one can seriously question the scale of the progress achieved and sustained since Independence. In this populist age, where so many people would rather undergo torture than admit that governments and political leaders can make a positive contribution, the facts of modern Irish history show the central role that politics played in securing progress.

I don't believe in trying to personalise everything to 'great men' over time. This is a form of history writing that has rightly fallen out of fashion. However, I think that we have been lucky in the remarkable leadership we have often seen from Taoisigh. For me, certain moments of leadership from Taoisigh still resonate. Éamon de Valera's actions in the 1930s, in particular, remain almost breathtaking for the assertion of sovereignty involved and the complete rejection of the extremism of the time. He not only faced down those who were inspired by European fascism, he took a path of democratic republicanism that remains the dominant political attachment of people irrespective of party allegiance.

De Valera's governments of the 1930s saw the only recorded example in Europe of a defeated revolutionary group coming to power and then introducing new and rigid limits on its own powers. The 1937 Constitution removed the ability of a governing majority to decide the fundamental law of the country, reserving that right to the people through referendums. It strengthened judicial independence and extended protections to all groups. At that time, and in the context of dramatically rising international tensions, for any state to include in its basic law a requirement that the state respect international law remains inspiring.

While many achievements by leaders can reflect the luck of being in office at the right time, the archives show the direct personal leadership of de Valera in drafting this new constitution. The first draft, written out in pencil on squared mathematical paper, is in de Valera's handwriting and involves all of the major decisions subsequently adopted by the people in a free referendum.

I have also always been inspired by Seán Lemass's time as Taoiseach. A man who had fought in the 1916 Rising, and who had been central to the republican cause, ended his career 50 years later driving forward a new modernising energy and the effort to root Ireland fairly within what is now the European Union. Above all others, he was a leader in the cause of Irish independence who had a broad conception of national sovereignty. He saw joining Europe as securing Irish sovereignty not threatening it.

I know that there are those who are impatient with the idea of Lemass changing the national mood. I think they are quite simply wrong and that the evidence for this is overwhelming. Leaving aside the facts of radical new policies in fundamental areas like trade and education, I think the reflections of Heinrich Böll, the German Nobel Prize for Literature laureate, make the case very well.

Böll published his *Irish Journal* in 1957, just before Lemass became Taoiseach. It presented a picture of Ireland so downbeat and depressing that Böll was banned from attending receptions at the Irish embassy in Bonn. Ten years later, Böll published a second edition of what had been a very successful book. This time, he added an extra chapter in which he explained that in his visits to Ireland in the 1960s he had noticed a new spirit in the country – one that was becoming more international, confident and optimistic.

The period in which Lemass held the office of Taoiseach was a lesson to all about the role of political leadership. In practical terms, membership of the European Union has meant that Taoisigh spend a very large amount of time on matters which are of little interest to those who focus instead on the issues of the current news cycle. However, this in-depth engagement with European leaders is central to the ability of our small and geographically peripheral state to influence a wide range of issues.

This engagement with Europe has been a two-way process, which has included a range of substantive achievements during Irish presidencies of the Council. For example, during Liam Cosgrave's term, he, together with his Minister for Foreign Affairs and successor Garret FitzGerald, began the holding of regular European Council summits, with the first official Council meeting taking place in Dublin in 1975. During the 1990 presidency, Charles Haughey played a central role in helping the German Chancellor, Helmut Kohl, to secure support for German reunification – a fact generously and repeatedly acknowledged by Kohl. During the 2004 presidency, Bertie Ahern's skill in leading the enlargement process and a series of tricky negotiations was reflected in him being asked to lead the Commission – an offer which he turned down.

Significant and positive actions can be seen in every Irish presidency, and this speaks to the role of the Taoiseach in giving Ireland the ability to be an important participant in critical debates. Also significant is that the leader of the Irish government spends more time in the national parliament answering questions and speaking in debates than any other European leader. In contrast to Westminster, for example, the Taoiseach handles business questions and is expected to answer questions in depth at least twice a week. This has evolved over time, but it means that the Taoiseach is very closely engaged with the issues of the moment.

Unfortunately, this can have a distorting impact on the nature of political coverage and debate. Over time, the amount of political content in the media has grown steadily, but the breadth of that coverage has significantly narrowed. Most of the time it seems that the bulk of political news is focused on the opening of each parliamentary day when the leaders of the opposition set the agenda through a series of opportunities to raise questions on any issue. Over time, the role of detailed speeches and initiatives in political coverage – or even non-partisan discussion – has declined quite dramatically.

My staff have for many years tried to persuade me out of accepting invitations to give speeches on policy or history, arguing that the most effective way of staying out of the media is to give a substantive speech. I think they are exaggerated in this, but there is no doubt that political discourse in Ireland has moved overwhelmingly to a more aggressively partisan and short-term framing. This is particularly evident when you look at how much of what we know about the intentions of Taoisigh of the first half of our independence comes from speeches rather than political commentary.

Ireland today is a diverse European democracy. We have a multi-party system which will always require coalitions to be built before a government can be formed. As such, the work of the Taoiseach has and will continue to evolve. You must both hold a diverse government together and work to ensure that it addresses both immediate and longer challenges effectively. This requires standing against broader tendencies in politics where public debate increasingly tends towards trying to impose a binary – for or against, us or them – framing.

The role and importance of the office of Taoiseach has evolved constantly over the past century, and I have no doubt that it will continue to evolve. One thing that will never change is that to hold the office of head of government of a free, democratic and liberal republic is a deep honour.

Introduction

Iain Dale

Back in 2021, I edited a book called *The Prime Ministers*. It was a collection of 55 essays, each written by a different historian, politician or journalist, on the 53 men and two women who had held the office of British Prime Minister in the 300 years since Sir Robert Walpole came to power in 1721. I followed it up with a similar book on American Presidents, one on English and British Kings and Queens and, in 2024, a collection of essays on 64 of the world's most infamous dictators.

So what next, I thought to myself? I considered Australian Prime Ministers, French Presidents and German Chancellors, but then I thought about looking at the (then) 15 men who had served in the office of Irish Taoiseach. Initially, I assumed that someone in Ireland would have beaten me to it, but a quick Amazon search showed that no one had.

In recent years, I had become a little bit obsessive about learning more about Irish history and contemporary politics. It had always been a mystery to me that people in Britain know comparatively little about their nearest neighbour, despite a shared history and language. I remember watching the RTÉ drama *Rebellion* a few years ago and thinking about the fact that the Easter Rising and the War of Independence did not feature in the core history curriculum in UK schools. From then on, I started reading more about the history of Britain and Ireland. I tried to buy autobiographies of leading Irish politicians. That proved to be more difficult than I thought. In Britain, it is almost a constitutional duty for ex-Prime Ministers to write their memoirs. In Ireland, only Garret FitzGerald, Albert Reynolds, Bertie Ahern and now Leo Varadkar have put pen to paper.

I will also be honest and admit that I barely knew anything about several of the 16 Taoisigh (pronounced *Teeshig*, the plural of 'Taoiseach'), but then again I knew nothing about some of the earlier British Prime Ministers before embarking on recruiting authors for that book.

My agent tried to find a publisher for the book in Ireland, but not a single Irish publisher was interested. I was astonished. Was it because I was a Brit, with no immediate links to Ireland? If so, they were too polite to say. I don't give up that easily, though. I then decided to launch a podcast called *The Irish Taoiseach* (still available from wherever you get your podcasts) and set about contacting potential interviewees for the 16 episodes. They included a Senator, several biographers of Taoisigh and political journalists. The interviews were very conversational and lasted between 30 and 90 minutes. The episodes were recorded and released in 2023 to some excellent reviews.

It was then that I met the then commissioning editor for Swift Press, George Owers, who instantly saw the potential for the book. We agreed terms very quickly, and this book is the result. Thanks to the editor, Lucie Ewin; copy-editor, Liz Hudson; and publicists Rachel Nobilo and Declan Heeney.

I wanted this book to appeal to the general reader and asked the contributors to write in an accessible manner and to avoid the usual academic niceties, such as footnotes. Each author was encouraged to be opinionated while outlining the personal and political lives of the Taoiseach they were writing about. I am grateful to the Royal Irish Academy's *Dictionary of Irish Biography* for permission to reproduce its entry on Albert Reynolds by Martin Mansergh.

If you spot any errors, please do let me know at info@iaindale.com, and they will be corrected in any future edition. I hope you enjoy reading this book as much as I have enjoyed editing it.

Iain Dale
Tunbridge Wells, August 2024

The office of Taoiseach

Eoin O'Malley

Not long before she became UK Prime Minister, the then British Foreign Secretary, Liz Truss, wished to 'strongly encourage the Irish *tea sock* to discuss [the Northern Ireland Protocol] with the EU'. Her mispronunciation of the title Taoiseach was hardly new – for some in Northern Ireland, it is almost a point of principle. Truss's was no doubt a genuine attempt to pronounce it correctly: many others in her position would merely state the 'Irish Prime Minister'. The unusual title gives the office a romantic air, a sense of exceptionalism, and suggests an ambiguity about the nature of the office that needs to be decoded. But as much as some find the term unpronounceable, the office is certainly not unusual compared to other European heads of government.

Before adopting the title Taoiseach, Ireland used phrases like 'Executive Council' for the government or cabinet and 'President of the Executive Council' for the head of the government or Prime Minister. The decision to not use these terms, common in other decolonised countries formerly under British control, might not have been a deliberate rejection of the British practice. The adoption of President for the head of government appears to have been done during Éamon de Valera's – or Dev's, as he was known – tour of the USA in an attempt to relate better to US audiences. In fact, the functioning of the cabinet and the role of the President were more similar to the British practice than that of any other European country. The rest of the political system adopted Gaelicised names, such as Dáil Éireann and Oireachtas (parliament), but these too adopted the norms and practices learnt from the Houses of Parliament in London.

It was hardly a surprise, then, in the mid-1930s, when a new constitution was mooted, that the drafters would reconsider the title of the President of the Executive Council. There was a shift to the title 'Prime Minister' at this time. The introduction of new Irish titles to the draft English editions of the Constitution was clear in 1936, but still these were direct translations, with *An Priomh Aire* for Prime Minister and *An Leas-Phríomh Aire* for Deputy Prime Minister. It was only in the final draft in February 1937 that the titles *An Taoiseach* and *An Tánaiste* were introduced. These were then standardised in following (substantially unchanged) copies. Still, in debates on the Constitution, many speakers referred to the proposed office of 'Prime Minister'.

Given the times, and the suspicion over de Valera's democratic credentials, there was an assumption that *An Taoiseach*, which can be translated as 'The Chief', was reflective of something like *Der Führer* in Germany or *Il Duce* in Italy. It would also have been entirely within the Irish political culture, where mass movements were often sustained by charismatic individuals – Daniel O'Connell and Charles Stewart Parnell – leading personalist political organisations.

The revolutionary period in Ireland from around 1912 to when the state was founded in 1922 had revealed some remarkable leaders and had buried some others. Of those who emerged, most of the leaders of the 1916 Rising were executed, and the remaining political leaders all came from the revolutionary tradition. Constitutional nationalists were largely discredited, or at least Irish politics had passed them by. De Valera, Michael Collins and Arthur Griffith were the clear leaders left on the field as the new state was being formed. De Valera lost out as the Anglo-Irish Treaty was accepted by Dáil Éireann. The deaths in quick succession of Griffith and Collins left W. T. Cosgrave as a third- or even fourth-choice leader for the pro-Treaty side. Cosgrave was not a charismatic leader, and he did not try to be when he took over as the first head of government or President of the Executive Council in the newly independent Ireland.

He retained the government team he inherited and in Richard Mulcahy and Kevin O'Higgins had significant colleagues who could rival him for the job.

By comparison, de Valera – commonly addressed as 'Chief' well before the title Taoiseach was suggested – was the undisputed leader of his party. Opposition politicians at the time feared Dev had ambitions to concentrate power in the office. But while Dev did see the Taoiseach as a leader of the government, who spoke for and acted for the government as a whole, he did not have totalitarian ambitions, even if he gave the head of government a name that might have connoted these.

In a famous book on the office of Taoiseach, Brian Farrell distinguished between 'Chairman or Chief'. He argued that some holders of the office were instinctively chairmen and others chiefs. But the analysis of the holders showed that those instinctive chiefs behaved as chairmen. Later holders, such as Charles Haughey and Garret FitzGerald, who were temperamentally chiefs, were forced by their political circumstances to resign themselves to chairing their governments. Still, the office is often seen as one of the more powerful head-of-government positions in the democratic world. It is usually ranked with the UK and former British colonies such as Canada and Australia in having an exceptionally powerful head of government. We might expect that that power emanates from political institutions: the Constitution and the Department.

The main change that the new constitution proposed in 1937 was that the Taoiseach, unlike the President of the Executive Council, could hire and fire his ministers and could dissolve the Dáil, that is, call an election. The earlier version, the Irish Free State Constitution, did not give these powers to the President. But de Valera appeared to be a 'chief' in selecting his cabinet; he did not depend on the Constitution for that power before 1937. The changes made no discernible difference to the way a Taoiseach was selected. Before and after 1937, the Taoiseach was usually the leader of the largest party that could command a majority in Dáil Éireann, either by itself or in coalition with others.

A key question, then, should be whether the power of the Taoiseach stems from the office or do the holders of the office bring a power to the office? When John A. Costello took on the office of Taoiseach, it revealed a great deal of the nature of the office. Costello was not the leader of Fine Gael, the largest party in that government. Nor was he even selected as Taoiseach before the parties had agreed the formation of the government. So, although the Constitution gave him that power, the selection of ministers was something effectively held by party leaders.

In the early iterations of the state, when names and titles were fluid, the Department of Finance was where power lay. This might have been a result of Michael Collins's energy and focus as a minister building up that department. When he was briefly the chair of the Provisional Government, he both held that office and kept the Finance portfolio. Finance retained this power and centrality to all government decision throughout the history of the state.

By contrast, the Department of the President of the Executive Council, and later the Department of the Taoiseach, was really just a secretariat, a glorified private office for the Taoiseach. The department that supports the Taoiseach is not very large. In 1938, there were about 20 people employed there, excluding messengers and cleaners, 10 of whom were clerical staff. The office provided a coordinating function and kept the Taoiseach abreast of the activities of all the departments and their ministers, but it did not control them. The coordination function was primarily and legally held through the operation of cabinet meetings. The Department of the Taoiseach, then, was the 'post office' that took in information for cabinet to consider and sent out decisions once taken.

The Secretary to the Department was also Secretary to the Government, and one holder took pride that he was there to serve the government as a whole and not an individual Taoiseach. Any new issues not already assigned a department automatically ended up in the Department of the Taoiseach, and Taoisigh could assign themselves any issue they wanted to. Still, most ministers saw the Taoiseach as a consensual, coordinating figure rather than a dominating one. The Taoiseach consulted and advised ministers but did not direct them.

Even though a story has Seán Lemass explaining Dev's power to a British minister that if Dev was in a minority in cabinet, 'the cabinet then takes its decision by a minority of one', this was true of 'chiefs' like de Valera as well as the less obviously dominant Taoisigh. Dev did not always get his way, and Lemass was much more forceful in contrast to de Valera, who tended to proceed at the pace of the slowest man.

If one of a Taoiseach's roles is to facilitate government decisions, they also have to lead a party in parliament and in the country, to maintain the confidence of the Dáil by holding the party together. This might have seemed easy: government Teachtaí Dála (TDs) – members of the Dáil – rarely if ever rebelled. It was not necessary to be a great orator to hold your government together: indeed, none of the holders of the office can be identified as exceptional public speakers. This might also have been because of the conservative nature of the political leaders. But this was hardly true of Lemass, who introduced some radical changes of policy in the 1960s in spite of scepticism within his party. His position as a leader came at a time when there was a changing of the guard from the revolutionary generation. 'Ordinary' political leaders took over from nation-building leaders, and his cabinet was predominantly made up of a generation without first-hand experience in the revolution. With them came a willingness to challenge the Taoiseach – even within Fianna Fáil. Though we see the new generation leaders, Jack Lynch at the forefront, being challenged within their party, the political culture still exalted the leader. Fianna Fáil's 1969 campaign centred on 'Let's back Jack'. Liam Cosgrave, who led a cabinet 'of all the talents', was still the most recognised and respected leader in that government.

Another role of a Taoiseach is to communicate with the public, and in Ireland there was a vast difference in coverage devoted to Taoisigh compared to other ministers. Even if their parties thought of Taoisigh as ordinary politicians, the public still treated them with respect and expected them to have solutions to emerging social problems. By the 1970s, those problems were growing, or at least more prominent.

There was something of a change in the office in the 1970s. Jack Lynch had commissioned a report on the prime-ministerial office in Belgium from the Irish Ambassador. When Lynch asked whether he could get an economic adviser, his secretary responded that that was what the Department of Finance was for. But Lynch, a former minister in that department, said that was exactly why he needed separate advice. The Department, almost as small as it had been in the 1930s, now started to expand its policy-analysis role. The European Economic Community (EEC) necessitated a more visible Taoiseach, and the emergence of the Troubles meant that Northern Ireland could no longer be ignored. There was an expansion of the Department, and civil servants such as Dermot Nally were brought into senior roles. The Government Information Service was expanded, giving the Department a greater role in the relationship with a more assertive media covering politics.

A sea change occurred from 1979 when Charles Haughey took over. If anyone was temperamentally a chief, it was Haughey. A keen student of government and an exceptionally efficient administrator, Haughey closed an economic planning department and merged much of it into the Department of the Taoiseach. He created the first explicit sections within the Department, including an expanded private office. By 1980, there were 45 staff (115 including clerical staff, messengers and cleaners). Within a year, that 115 rose to 187. These numbers fail to reveal that the Department was by now also heavily laden with senior staff who had policy functions. This reflected Haughey's desire for policy control and for the Taoiseach to be more directive than ever before. If there had been fears of the 'presidentialisation' of the office in the 1930s, we saw it in the 1980s. Haughey assumed many new functions and even informally took on the budgetary negotiations with line ministers instead of the Minister for Finance.

Haughey's successor, Garret FitzGerald, was as active as Taoiseach, with an interest in all policy areas and opinions on all of these. The two men, who dominated politics in the 1980s, expanded the Department, including, by 1990, the refurbishment and expansion of the building that it had occupied since Independence. This enabled it to house the growing department in more appropriate surroundings.

The expansion of the Department probably took place in response to the increasing complexity of policy-making, the greater constraints on political leaders as a result of a more globalised and more sophisticated economy, the membership of the European Union (EU) which controls a large number of policy areas, the increased willingness of the courts to involve themselves in policy-making, and a more aggressive, attentive and insatiable media. All these have possibly made Taoisigh less powerful than they once were. Certainly, Taoisigh do not tend to last as long in office as they once did. While just five men held the office in the first 50 years of the state, 10 did so in the 50 years that followed. Taoisigh no longer seem to be the big beasts that dominate the political scene.

The expansion of the Department continued under the successors to Haughey and FitzGerald. When Albert Reynolds formed a coalition with the Labour Party under Dick Spring, a new innovation was the introduction of 'programme managers'. These were appointed to each department by their line minister with the purpose of pushing the Programme for Government agreed by the two parties. It freed up time for the Taoiseach since many easier decisions that used to take up time at cabinet no longer needed to be discussed there. Where a Taoiseach's job might once have been to lead or mediate discussions to generate a decision, now the role was becoming one where the Taoiseach was just one of the actors negotiating their position. That is not to say that the Taoiseach does not have significant structural advantages. Being able to control the agenda of the cabinet meetings still affords them important control.

Another significant change was the increased use of cabinet committees under Bertie Ahern. There had been suspicion of cabinet subcommittees because of their uncertain role in the Arms Crisis scandal in 1970, but by the 1990s it was found that cabinet meetings alone were insufficient to provide coordination function and that some agreed plans got stalled in departmental silos. More recently, crises saw the setting up of powerful subcommittees. The Great Recession and its aftermath led to an Economic Management Council of the two main economic ministers, Michael Noonan and Brendan Howlin, with Taoiseach Enda Kenny and Tánaiste Éamon Gilmore (both coalition party leaders) and some officials. A similar committee was used again during the COVID-19 pandemic, which some complained curtailed the authority of cabinet.

These changes were introduced in part as a result of the normalisation of coalition government. From 1989, there were no longer any single-party governments, and the prospect of a single-party government in Ireland is remote. The party system has been upended, especially since 2011. There are no longer large parties that can command 40 per cent of the vote. As a result, Taoisigh are no longer like the UK Prime Minister, on which the office was modelled. Having to satisfy the needs of coalition government essentially redrafts the role of the Taoiseach. If before a Taoiseach was the 'captain of the team', now they have a powerful co-captain, who controls a group of players that can walk off the pitch at any time. One Taoiseach, John Bruton, did not see his role to drive Fine Gael policy through government but to achieve, support and maintain a government policy.

The sense that the Taoiseach was no longer the chief became most pronounced by the time of the coalition government between Fianna Fáil, Fine Gael and the Green Party. The similar size of the first two parties meant that neither party had an obvious claim to the office of Taoiseach. The two parties agreed to share it by rotating who held the offices of Taoiseach and Tánaiste between Micheál Martin and Leo Varadkar halfway through the lifetime of the government. (Technically, of course, it was a new government.) For the first time, someone who had served as Taoiseach was now a minister in the government. Although it is hard to tell from this juncture, it must have changed the relationship between Taoiseach and Tánaiste and the way civil servants treated each of them. Although both were conscious not to step on each other's toes, both were party leaders holding senior executive office and so the Tánaiste at either time was not going to limit himself to his departmental responsibilities. It is likely to have temporarily developed into a dual premiership. That the rotation of the office continued after the 2024 election might mean this is a more permanent norm.

As well as the dilution of the authority of the office of Taoiseach as a result of coalition, there has arguably been an abandonment of political power by the political elites. Though the idea of social partnership – a mechanism to agree pay rates and industrial policy between unions, employers and government – was an example of political authority, over time it lost much of this, becoming instead a mechanism for government to buy off the trade-union movement. It was later extended to include other social groups and policy in more areas. This was later criticised as reducing the authority of cabinet to set policy.

Other forums were set up that removed from politics certain functions that were once inherently political. The accountability function of the Oireachtas has been eroded by court decisions, and tribunals of inquiry are now seen as the preferred route to inquire into significant policy failures. These have been slow, expensive and indecisive, often reporting only well after the issue has lost its relevance. What might have been once part of day-to-day politics is also shifted to a host of other accountability bodies including, for instance, the Ombudsman, a Fiscal Advisory Council, a Media Commission, etc. Other bodies, non-governmental organisations (NGOs), have received increased state funding and now actively lobby the state, setting a policy agenda in ways that the Taoiseach and government used to do. These depoliticise policy-making in ways that might not be good for Irish democracy.

There has also been a shift to making decisions by referendum. Most of these are necessitated by the Irish Constitution, but their increased use in areas untested by the courts might indicate an unwillingness on the part of the executive, and the Taoiseach as its head, to directly take on issues. Another innovation in Irish democracy that has won plaudits is the use of citizens' assemblies. However, again, it might be seen as an abdication of political leadership to outsource to a small group of people the testing and even sourcing of new policy ideas.

Looking back at the office of the Taoiseach over the past century, we are seeing it at a time of decline in power. Having taken control of Ireland's policy-making through achieving independence, one generation successfully built a state and a relatively settled, peaceful nation. The path to economic prosperity and the solutions to the tragedy of Northern Ireland were probably put in place in the 1980s and 1990s, which might be seen as the apogee of political power for the Taoiseach. Since then, the office's power has diminished. It might take a new generation of political leaders to 'take back control'.

W. T. Cosgrave

1922–32

Ciara Meehan

Full name: William Thomas Cosgrave
Date of birth: 5 June 1880
Place of birth: Dublin
Education: St Joseph's School, Marino, Dublin
Date of death: 16 November 1965
Site of grave: Goldenbridge Cemetery, Inchicore, Dublin
Married to: Louisa Flanagan (m. 1919)
Children: Liam and Míceál
Assumed office: Formally elected President of the Executive Council, 6 December 1922
Date of resignation: 9 March 1932
Length of tenure: 9 years, 2 months, 23 days
Quotation: 'I feel intensely proud to be the first man called to preside over the first government which takes over the control of the destiny of our people.'

In the newly official corridors of power in Leinster House, W. T. Cosgrave emerged in August 1922 as the steady hand who would guide the nascent Irish Free State through its formative years. By the time he was elected the first President of the Irish Executive Council – the forerunner of the office of the Taoiseach – in December that year, the country had endured the Easter Rising and War of Independence, leading to a treaty with Britain after centuries of conflict, and it was in the midst of a civil war. The 'natural' leaders, Arthur Griffith and Michael Collins, had died within 10 days of each other in August, and so the task of state-building fell to the 42-year-old Cosgrave. The *Irish Times* described him as having a 'thoroughly conservative face' and noted how his tendency to wear clothes in sombre hues, accompanied by a bowler hat, made him look like 'the general manager of a railway company'. This depiction implied a certain level of stability and adherence to tradition without conveying much dynamism. The article also recognised him to be the 'most capable man' in the parliament. Anyone who harboured doubts about his abilities soon had them dispelled.

Born in Dublin on 5 June 1880, William Thomas – typically referred to as W. T. throughout his political career – was the second of Thomas and Bridget Cosgrave's six children. Following Thomas's death at the age of 33, Bridget married Thomas Burke and had two additional children. W. T. was educated by the Christian Brothers, and, not unlike other boys of his age in the 1890s, he left school just before his 15th birthday. Though this early exit from formal education was not unusual, his experience did contrast with such future cabinet colleagues as Kevin O'Higgins and J. J. Walsh who were graduates of University College Dublin (UCD).

The Cosgrave family owned two pubs and a grocer's shop on James's Street, and, shortly after leaving school, W. T. went to work in the family business, harnessing his aptitude for figures. Speaking at the unveiling of a commemorative plaque at the site of one pub in October 2013, his son Liam observed, 'he made a good job of it', helping to improve the pub's financial fate. Born in 1920, Liam was W. T.'s first-born child, resulting from his marriage to Louisa Flanagan on 24 June 1919. The couple had a second son, Míceál, in 1922.

W. T. was a devout Catholic, and his deep religious faith was engrained in him as a child. He carried this with him throughout his life, even having a private oratory in his marital home. He served Mass in retirement right up to the day before he died. The influence of this profound faith on his thinking can be seen in his approach to policy-making while in government. In the area of divorce, for example, he took advice from the bishops, subsequently introducing a motion that would prevent applications for divorce, which had been possible under British rule, in the Free State.

Politics was part of the Cosgrave household before W. T.'s involvement. His father was active in local politics and was a member of the Board of Guardians of the South Dublin Union. While W. T. attended the first meeting of Sinn Féin in 1905, his formal political journey began when he was elected as a councillor on the party ticket to Dublin Corporation in 1909. To appreciate why the *Irish Times* could so confidently describe Cosgrave as the 'most capable man' in government in September 1922, it is essential to go right back to this point when he began developing and refining his skills as a politician. He earned a reputation as an active councillor, advocating for the working classes, especially in the area of housing, and he was well regarded. Though he did not know it at the time, local government was the training ground that prepared him for political leadership.

Like many of his contemporaries, he had a dual involvement in political life and physical fighting. He joined the Irish Volunteers – founded in response to the establishment of the Ulster Volunteers, which had been created to protect against any forced imposition of Home Rule – in 1913. The following year, he participated in the Howth Gunrunning, in which arms and ammunition were imported for use by the Volunteers. The Irish Republican Brotherhood, which predated the Volunteers, coexisted with this new movement and even shared some members. Cosgrave, however, never sought membership, despite being invited to join. As his biographer Michael Laffan explained, like many Catholics, he did not approve of secret oath-bound societies.

Cosgrave participated in the Easter Rising, taking his place alongside the Volunteers who occupied the South Dublin Union under the command of Éamonn Ceannt. In many ways, though, he was a reluctant Volunteer, considering such action to be 'little short of madness'. Any symbolic strike against Britain was, in his view, pointless. Cosgrave was arrested for his part and was sentenced to 'death by being shot', which was later commuted to life imprisonment. 'Life imprisonment' translated into a temporary prison stay, and Cosgrave was released in 1917.

Thereafter, his focus was solely on politics. His victory in a by-election in Kilkenny City in August 1917 was part of a series of by-elections held in 1917 and 1918 that saw Sinn Féin triumph in most, foreshadowing the party's routing of the Irish Parliamentary Party at the 1918 general election. Cosgrave was elected to Kilkenny North at that election, and he was returned at every subsequent election he contested until his retirement in 1944.

In the aftermath of the general election, Sinn Féin abstained from Westminster and instead set up the Revolutionary Dáil in which Cosgrave was Minister for Local Government, and where he built on his experience in local politics. He was assisted in the Department by Kevin O'Higgins, later to be his Vice-President after Independence. Like all the revolutionary departments, Cosgrave's operated under difficult circumstances, and he was often on the run, but his still earned a reputation as one of the most successful. He garnered support for Sinn Féin across the county and borough councils so that the majority recognised his department almost a year and a half before the Treaty was signed. Central to his achievements was a successful undertaking to redirect rate payments to his department instead of to Britain. Such recognition and activity helped legitimise the Revolutionary Dáil. As Diarmaid Ferriter has noted, by mid-1920 even Southern unionists were impressed by the Department's efforts, even if their cooperation was sometimes coerced by fear.

This work was taking place against the backdrop of the War of Independence. When a ceasefire was eventually declared and a team of Irish plenipotentiaries was assembled to travel to London for negotiations, Cosgrave was not considered. He was critical of Éamon de Valera's decision not to directly participate, and a rift between the two men would emerge during the debates when Cosgrave took a more pragmatic line, to the disappointment of de Valera. The rift was never healed, and when the two men passed one another in the corridors of Leinster House after Independence, it is said they would not acknowledge each other.

The Anglo-Irish Treaty was signed on 6 December 1921. The benefits, as presented to the Dáil, did not garner unanimous acceptance, and Sinn Féin split. The Treaty was approved, however, and Cosgrave played a critical role in this, further demonstrating his leadership abilities. Tragically, the split in Sinn Féin was mirrored in a split in the armed republican movement, and in this acrimonious environment Ireland was drawn into civil war. By the time the Free State came into formal existence on 6 December 1922, how or when the fighting might end could not be easily predicted. Furthermore, in August, Arthur Griffith had died unexpectedly, and, 10 days after his death, Michael Collins was killed in an ambush in his native Cork. Cosgrave became Chairman of the Provisional Government.

When the Dáil gathered on 6 December 1922, exactly one year after the Anglo-Irish Treaty had been signed, to mark the first formal meeting of the Free State, there was no fanfare or pageantry. Protestors might have added some colour to the event, but road barriers ensured that those who would demonstrate their opposition were unable to gather in the vicinity. The only indication that the new state had been born manifested in a muted symbol of Independence: a Tricolour flew above Leinster House. Inside, as politicians meandered through the corridors with an air of anticipation, en route to the Dáil chamber, the mood was sombre.

The *Irish Times* reported that 'the opening meeting of the Free State was a very dull affair'. The first hour was consumed by tedious formalities. The official record recounts that Michael Hayes, explaining he had been authorised by the Governor General, administered the Oath individually to those 79 TDs present. Cosgrave was the first to adhere to the requirement. Although one of the most controversial elements of the Treaty, even that process of complying with the Oath did not inject any drama into the proceedings as anti-Treaty TDs continued to apply the policy of abstention from Westminster to the Free State Dáil.

Although those who opposed the Treaty were not physically present in the chamber, their presence could be felt in the government speeches. Nominating Cosgrave to be President of the Executive Council, Peter Hughes, TD for Louth, suggested, 'He is going to have during his term of office, perhaps, a troublesome, and perhaps a stormy time.' Cosgrave would experience that stormy time personally when his home in Beechpark was targeted and burnt down by republicans in January 1923.

Cosgrave's first official words as the inaugural President of the Executive Council are worth recalling in full:

> On this notable day when our country has definitely emerged from the bondage under which she has lived through a week of centuries, I cannot deny that I feel intensely proud to be the first man called to preside over the first government which takes over the control of the destiny of our people, to hold and administer that charge, answerable only to our own people and to none other; to conduct their affairs as they shall declare right without interference, not to say domination, by any other authority whatsoever.

These remarks were a continuation of the arguments that had been advanced in favour of the Treaty when the document was being debated in the weeks after it was signed. Cosgrave also used his speech to criticise the 'mad efforts' of those who opposed the Treaty.

The threat of danger hung in the air. The following day, fears became a reality when Seán Hales, a government TD, was shot dead and Pádraig Ó Máille, the Leas Ceann Comhairle (Deputy Chairperson), was wounded in an attack by anti-Treaty supporters. Remaining resolute and calm, Cosgrave's leadership was crucial in steadying the nerves of panicked colleagues.

The attack on its own was shocking, but the unfolding aftermath proved equally astounding. Four republican prisoners – Rory O'Connor, Liam Mellows, Joe McKelvey and Dick Barrett – were taken from their cells in Mountjoy Prison and executed in retaliation for Hales's death.

Since all four of the men had been imprisoned in July 1922, they could not, in any way, have been responsible for the murder. The government had clearly stepped outside the rule of law. But Cosgrave was defiant. He told the Dáil there was a 'diabolical conspiracy afoot' that needed to be crushed. This theme of being tough on law and order became a central tenet of Cumann na nGaedheal's identity and one that was a mainstay also of its successor party, Fine Gael.

The four Mountjoy prisoners are the most famous of those executed, but they were not the only individuals to face such a fate. Executions, often carried out without trial, were the government's favoured method to break the republican campaign. The government presented these executions as necessary and justifiable acts, carried out in defence of the state during wartime. But no matter the threat to the state, real or perceived, executions were not easily accepted as a legitimate tactic to bring the Civil War to an end. Tom Johnson, leader of the Labour Party, was damning in the Dáil, telling Cosgrave, 'You have killed the new state at its birth.' He may have overstated his case, but he was certainly correct that the creation of the state had been marred. The memory of those executed cast a long shadow, informing propaganda and fuelling demands in the intervening years for a state apology.

As fighting, reprisals and intimidation punctuated life during the Civil War, the *Roscommon Herald* reported that Cosgrave's physician had recommended he give up the Presidency and retire to the South of France for health reasons, estimating that he would die within the year if he failed to do so. This obviously did not happen – he lived to the age of 85 – and Cosgrave is alleged to have said, 'They will call me a coward if I give up now. My work is in Ireland.'

Under his leadership, the government embraced the practical task of building the new state. Simultaneously, a new political infrastructure had to be built around the pro-Treaty faction of the Sinn Féin split that now occupied the government benches. Cumann na nGaedheal was inaugurated on 7 December, and Cosgrave saw it as a party of 'nation builders, who would rear the new Ireland in the light of the old ideals'.

This description, coupled with the choice of name, firmly and deliberately positioned Cumann na nGaedheal in the tradition of the 'old ideals' of Gaelic Ireland.

As an in-depth analysis is beyond the scope of this chapter, Cumann na nGaedheal, in summary, can be described as having functioned as a government first and a party second. This ordering would especially put it at a disadvantage after Fianna Fáil emerged in 1926 and focused energies on building an extensive branch network that would become legendary.

The statute books for the first few years of Independence document a flurry of activity. Though some structures, including the civil service, were retained from British rule, there was much about the functioning of the state that had to be decided and implemented. This included the creation of an unarmed police force, a risky move at a time of civil war, and a revision of the army to better represent peacetime conditions.

Cosgrave's government faced significant financial challenges. The Easter Rising, the War of Independence and the Civil War all did financial damage. The physical fighting that impacted the landscape had a knock-on effect for businesses and for the economy in general. Easily the most famous of the austerity measures was Ernest Blythe's decision to cut the old-age pension by one shilling in 1923. Although it was reinstated in 1924, the cut went into political folklore, doing significant damage to Cumann na nGaedheal and handing opponents a potent tool to periodically assail the party's successor, Fine Gael, in the decades that followed.

Because of the constraints on spending, there was little room for creativity. There were two very notable exceptions that demonstrated that, when needed, the government could take risks and think big. The first of these was the Tailteann Games, an Irish version of the Olympics, that brought together more than 5,000 entrants competing for 1,000 medals across 23 different categories over 16 days in August 1924. The presence of some of the world's biggest sporting names, who travelled on to the Free State after the Paris Olympics, lent prestige to the event and brought the attention of international journalists. *The Times*, the *New York Times* and the *Sydney Morning Herald* were among those newspapers that reported favourably on the proceedings.

The Shannon electrification scheme was the other major financial investment of this period. The government resisted pressure from the opposition benches to refine the scheme to focus instead on the River Liffey in Dublin, deciding on the bolder option of harnessing the River Shannon as the scale of the project had the potential to deliver a cheap supply of electricity across the Free State rather than the capital alone. Advocating for the scheme in the Dáil, Patrick McGilligan, Minister for Industry and Commerce, spoke of how economic freedom was as important as political freedom.

These flagship projects were part of an image-building strategy, intended to affirm that the Irish were capable of self-government and that the new state was a success. The state's successful application to join the League of Nations was also part of that strategy. The basic requirement for membership was that the applicant had to be an autonomous state; that the Irish application was approved served as international recognition of the new state's status.

As they were driven by various ministers, such achievements cannot be solely attributed to Cosgrave. But, as President of the Executive Council, his legacy is closely intertwined with that of the governments he led. Cosgrave should receive credit for the way in which he managed his cabinet, empowering those around the table. To use Brian Farrell's classic characterisation of Irish leaders, he was a chairman rather than a chief. This meant that he delegated authority, providing the space for his ministers to develop projects. Later in life, Blythe recalled that Cosgrave never hurried a decision at cabinet meetings, allowing ministers time to voice their various opinions, but once he reached a conclusion, it was usually accepted by the rest of the cabinet. Indeed, Cumann na nGaedheal would come to be referred to as 'the Cosgrave party' by the late 1920s by both the national and regional newspapers – a clear indicator of the strong association in the public mind of the party with his leadership and of his significant influence.

His handling of the Army Mutiny is a pertinent case study of how he asserted that influence. In brief, Major General Liam Tobin and Colonel Charles Dalton – representing the Irish Republican Army Organisation, a faction within the Free State Army that was loyal to Michael Collins's legacy – issued an ultimatum in March 1924 in response to the restructuring of the army. They wanted the Army Council, including Minister for Defence Richard Mulcahy, removed and for the government to do more to achieve a republic. The 'mutiny' did not amount to anything (although Mulcahy did resign), but the episode showed that civilian control had been firmly established.

Cosgrave was physically absent from cabinet for part of this episode due to an unspecified illness. Speculation emerged, and persisted in the years after, that he simply took to his bed rather than deal with the situation. Consequently, the crisis is sometimes presented as a low point in his career. However, a closer examination is needed. Cosgrave physically missed only five cabinet meetings between 18 and 21 March 1924. While the minutes of these meetings are dry and succinct – typical of such records – there is a strong sense, nonetheless, that his presence could be felt. Memos and letters from him were read aloud. The minutes record his insistence and expectation that all decisions be passed by him before any official announcements were made and that he also received visits from ministers to his home.

A telling amendment was made to a statement intended for the press following Mulcahy's resignation. The draft version, submitted to Cosgrave at his home for approval, read, 'The President has decided, subject to the approval of Dáil Éireann, to take up the duties of the Ministry of Defence. During the illness of the President, the Vice-President [Kevin O'Higgins] will act for him in that Ministry.' The version issued to the press did not include the final line. Practicalities meant that O'Higgins would have to take up the acting role, but the omission of this fact in the official statement was symbolic – Cosgrave was not relinquishing control. There is no space here to tease out the true extent to which O'Higgins had ambition to replace Cosgrave as President, as many suspected at the time, but if he did aspire to the leadership, his untimely death denied him the opportunity.

Kevin O'Higgins, considered the strong man of the cabinet, was murdered on 10 July 1927. A poem written by a reader of the *Donegal Democrat* depicted Cosgrave 'alone on the ship with his helmsman lost' and posed the question, 'can he guide me alright?' Facing the biggest challenge to the state since the murder of Seán Hales, the government responded decisively, using legislative change rather than retaliatory execution to address the situation. The year before O'Higgins's murder, Éamon de Valera, who had parted ways with anti-Treaty Sinn Féin, had formed his own party, Fianna Fáil. Abstention was also observed by its elected members. The package of legislation introduced in the summer of 1927 forced de Valera's hand, manoeuvring him and his supporters from the margins to the heart of democratic political life. Whatever his private reservations, Cosgrave publicly welcomed the development, observing it to be the 'best thing that has happened during the last five years'.

When Fianna Fáil TDs finally entered the Dáil, the parliamentary arithmetic changed significantly, and for the first time the Cumann na nGaedheal government was faced with a substantial opposition. The immediate consequence was a motion of no confidence, tabled by the Labour Party. Although it was unsuccessful, it precipitated a general election in September 1927, which returned Cosgrave to power for the last time. Over the next five years, the Dáil, in its fuller state, settled comfortably into the rhythm of conducting the business of politics.

By the time of the 1932 general election, Cumann na nGaedheal appeared jaded, and continued references to the 1921 Treaty implied that it lacked new ideas. That election saw a transfer of power from the winners to the losers of the Civil War. Éamon de Valera replaced Cosgrave as President of the Executive Council. Though clearly a disappointing blow to Cosgrave's party, the peaceful transition was tangible evidence that democracy had been firmly embedded in the new state – contrasting sharply with the fate of many of the other new nation-states that had emerged from the break-up of empires after the First World War.

When the 1933 snap election returned Fianna Fáil for a second term, Cosgrave's party was forced to accept that its place on the opposition benches was more than a temporary arrangement. As Fianna Fáil's critics became increasingly concerned about de Valera's politics, a new political party was born. Although Cumann na nGaedheal made up the largest component, Cosgrave was not chosen to lead Fine Gael. Although he had proven his abilities, he was the face of a party and a government that had stagnated. Appointing him to the leadership would have created continuity with Cumann na nGaedheal, therefore undoing the purpose of creating a new party (although, arguably, this is ultimately what happened). Instead, Eoin O'Duffy became the party's first president. At the time, he was both respected and trusted by many of his peers, although, tellingly, Cosgrave could not be counted among them.

The contrast between the two men was striking. Cosgrave was sociable yet unassuming while O'Duffy was charismatic and arrogant, self-styling himself as the third most important man in Europe. He had been the leader of the Blueshirts, one of the other two components that made up Fine Gael; the third was the National Centre Party. As his descent into fascism gathered pace, he was the type of leader that a democratic political party – one that prided itself on commitment to law and order – could not afford. Prominent Fine Gael members, some of whom had been Blueshirt members themselves, strategically guided him towards resignation in September 1934.

As O'Duffy was not a TD, Cosgrave had been the de facto Fine Gael leader in the Dáil, and since Cosgrave was the most experienced politician in the parliamentary party, his return to the helm seemed logical. But Fine Gael was not quick to fill the vacancy, delaying installing a successor until the Ard Fheis (party conference) in March 1935. The delay either implies a lack of enthusiasm for Cosgrave's return or it is a commentary on the availability of alternatives. Whatever the case, when the party gathered for the Ard Fheis, Cosgrave was unanimously selected as O'Duffy's replacement. Behind the scenes, there was some unease, with one prominent member writing that Cosgrave's return 'quite blasts all chances of beating Dev in any measurable time'.

Indeed, Cosgrave would spend the rest of his career in opposition. In the same way that achievements in government cannot be attributed to Cosgrave alone, Fine Gael's long stay on the opposition benches, which continued after Cosgrave's retirement until the formation of the First Inter-party Government in 1948, is not solely his fault. Persistent challenges in organisation and party financing remained unresolved. Nevertheless, as the party leader, he must bear some responsibility for the string of electoral defeats.

As Cosgrave entered the final months of his political career, the general election of 1943 delivered a highlight of his experience. His 23-year-old son Liam was elected for Dublin County, meaning that the two men shared the opposition benches for a short period of time. Liam would follow in his father's footsteps, becoming leader of Fine Gael in 1965 and Taoiseach in 1973. While family dynasties have been a characteristic of Irish politics, they are the only father and son to have both served as head of government.

When Cosgrave announced his departure from politics in 1944, colleagues were unsurprised though some still urged him to reconsider. But after more than two decades in the Dáil, during which more time was spent in opposition than in government, he slipped away into quiet retirement. The Fine Gael Senator Jim Dooge once observed that Cosgrave's absence from a funeral was like dying without the rites of the Church, and attendance was the sole aspect of a typical Irish politician's activities that he retained; Mass, in general, remained a constant in his life. Otherwise, Cosgrave steadfastly refrained from commenting on politics, setting a template that his successors, until Garret FitzGerald, also observed. He did, however, bring his considerable skills to the Racing Board, to which he was appointed by a Fianna Fáil government in 1946. This role allowed him to further embrace his lifelong love of horses.

W. T. Cosgrave died in November 1965. He lived long enough to see his son Liam become Fine Gael leader earlier that year. The tributes flowed. James Dillon, who had led the party from 1959 to April 1965, observed wisdom and integrity to have been W. T.'s most striking qualities. These traits were echoed across other expressions of remembrance. Especially noteworthy was the generous acknowledgement paid by Fianna Fáil's Seán Lemass, then Taoiseach, in the Dáil:

> For, although William T. Cosgrave has left us, the work he has done for Ireland endures. The generosity of his youthful response to the call to serve Ireland, the privations and the sacrifices which he endured so that national freedom might be ours, the capacity he displayed in presiding over the administration while responsibility was his, the grace with which he handed over responsibility when the people so willed.

His speech continued in that vein. He was followed by John A. Costello, who had served under Cosgrave and who had twice been a Fine Gael Taoiseach himself. In his opening comments, he expressed his view that it was possible for them to be in the Dáil because of W. T. Cosgrave. Essentially, both men, from either side of the political divide, were united in honouring Cosgrave's legacy of democratic state-building.

Despite receiving such contemporary acknowledgements and endorsements of his legacy, Cosgrave, and indeed the wider Cumann na nGaedheal party, remained somewhat overlooked in Irish historiography until relatively recently. It was not until Michael Laffan wrote *Judging W. T. Cosgrave* in 2014 that he was the subject of a substantial, scholarly biography. Prior to that, Anthony J. Jordan had produced a general history, and Stephen Collins had written a joint study of father and son. Other contributions focusing on Cumann na nGaedheal have been made by John M. Regan, Mel Farrell, Jason Knirck and myself. Cosgrave did not deserve the years of neglect.

Like all political leaders, his legacy, and that of the governments he led, is complex. He eschewed populism and made difficult decisions, often at the expense of votes. He was a man of government, interested in exercising power rather than concerned with its trappings. Criticisms have lingered through the decades over contentious decisions, such as the use of executions to end the Civil War and the reduction of the old-age pension, symbolic of broader societal inequalities left unaddressed. His government perpetuated traditional gender roles, thus limiting the role of women in society; that women were forbidden from serving on juries in this period is just one example. Yet, amidst these shortcomings and failings, a tremendous amount of work went into building and crafting the infant state. Geography alone does not explain why democracy flourished in the Irish Free State when it crumbled in many comparable new states in Central and Eastern Europe in the interwar period.

When evaluating W. T. Cosgrave's standing among past Taoisigh, it is perhaps best to reference Lemass and Costello. Their recognition that the democratic parliament they were standing in existed because of Cosgrave and his colleagues positions him as one of the most important leaders of independent Ireland.

3

Éamon de Valera

1932–48, 1951–4, 1957–9

David McCullagh

Full name: Éamon de Valera
Date of birth: 14 October 1882
Place of birth: New York City
Date of death: 29 August 1975
Site of grave: Glasnevin Cemetery, Dublin
Education: Christian Brothers School, Charleville; Blackrock College
Married to: Sinéad Ní Fhlannagáin (m. 1910)
Children: Vivion, Máirín, Éamonn, Brian, Ruairí, Emer and Terry
Assumed office: (1) 9 March 1932; (2) 13 June 1951; (3) 20 March 1957
Date of resignation: (1) 18 February 1948; (2) 2 June 1954; (3) 23 June 1959
Length of tenure: 21 years, two months, one day
Quotation: 'They would have to wade through Irish blood, through the blood of the soldiers of the Irish government, and through, perhaps, the blood of some of the members of the government in order to get Irish freedom.'

No Irish person is ever likely to serve longer as head of government than did Éamon de Valera, and few could aspire to match the scale of his achievements. As Taoiseach, he extended Irish sovereignty, introduced a new constitution and kept Ireland out of the Second World War. He dominated Irish politics for a generation, charted a new economic course and set the social and cultural tone for society at large.

And yet his tenure as Taoiseach is deeply controversial. While he gave his name to an era, the term 'de Valera's Ireland' is now a shorthand for a despised conservative backwater. And, judged by the aims he set out to achieve – unity, restoration of the Irish language, economic self-sufficiency – his term of office might appear to have been a failure.

He was almost 50 when he became President of the Executive Council (the job he later renamed Taoiseach), and he had been shaped by his first half century: by his upbringing, by his introduction to politics and, above all, by the crucible of the Civil War. Much of his behaviour in office can only be explained by these formative experiences, the first being the circumstances of his birth.

De Valera was always bothered about the question of his paternity. His mother, Irish emigrant Kate Coll, claimed to have married a Spaniard, Juan de Valera, in 1881; their son, Edward, was born the following year in Manhattan. According to Kate, her husband subsequently died somewhere in the American West, where he had gone for the sake of his health. However, no record of their marriage has been found, nor of Juan de Valera's existence or death. This left question marks over young de Valera's paternity, questions that greatly troubled him and which he went to great, though unsuccessful, lengths to try to answer. The unanswered questions led to jibes from political opponents in the future. More importantly, they left him uncertain of his identity and perhaps more open to identifying closely with institutions and causes that could give him a sense of belonging: Blackrock College, the Irish language, the nationalist cause.

But young de Valera was to suffer worse than an absent father: the parent who definitely was present in his early years, his mother, chose to put an ocean between them, sending him home to Ireland at the age of just two and a half, to be raised by her own mother. While he never expressed his feelings about this directly, his correspondence with his mother certainly hints at his resentment of her decision. The Colls were not well-off, living in a labourer's cottage in Bruree, Co. Limerick, and young Eddie de Valera was expected to do his full share of chores on the family's half-acre holding. While not out of the ordinary for the time and place, it was a harsh enough upbringing, and he seemed destined to be an agricultural labourer.

That he managed to escape that fate was entirely due to his own determination and hard work. He wanted to go to secondary school, rare at that time for people from his background, and had a stiff battle to persuade his Uncle Pat (his guardian since the death of his grandmother) to agree. But eventually he succeeded, an essential step for his future. At the Christian Brothers School (CBS) in Charleville, Co. Cork, de Valera did brilliantly in his exams, coming 50th in the entire country and winning a scholarship that transformed his life, allowing him to transfer to the exclusive Blackrock College in South Co. Dublin.

This was a new world, as he later recalled: 'No more long trudges over the interminable distance … from Charleville … No more chopping of turnips for the cows, or the drawing of water, or the attempts to do my lessons in the intervals.' On his first night there, he heard boys in the dormitory crying with homesickness, and he could not understand why they were upset. As far as he was concerned, this was heaven: no chores and unlimited time for study. De Valera would identify strongly with Blackrock for the rest of his life, choosing to live and die in the vicinity of the college, sending his sons there and attending its events almost obsessively.

But attending the school did not remove his insecurities; in a sense, they intensified them, largely due to the fact that he did not do as well in his exams as he expected. While he did brilliantly in his first year there, winning a further scholarship, his results disimproved after that, culminating in a very disappointing pass degree in his BA. This left him in a quandary: a pass degree was not enough to get him the university job he had anticipated, leaving him scrabbling to find work in Dublin, picking up part-time teaching jobs where he could. It was an unsettled, and unsettling, existence that magnified his insecurities. He described in a letter to his mother the 'hard battle' which he had to fight.

Eventually, he managed to make a career, securing a permanent post at the teacher-training college in Carysfort Avenue, Blackrock, Co. Dublin, in September 1906, which allowed him to call himself 'professor' – a title he appears to have been delighted with. He was still teaching there, along with a number of other places, when he was gaoled in 1916.

Teaching also led him to the Irish language, which was useful for his career and which gave him a new cause to identify with. It also gave him a new name – Éamon rather than Edward – and even introduced him to his wife, Sinéad Ní Fhlannagáin, who had been his teacher in a Gaelic League class. So, by the time he turned 30, in October 1912, he was married with two small children and another on the way; he was firmly ensconced in the middle class with a teaching job in Carysfort and a temporary university post in Maynooth; and he had a consuming interest in Irish, which gave him a cause to pursue. And he had got there thanks to determination and self-reliance, character traits strongly reinforced by his background. These characteristics would be important because de Valera was not destined to live his life in obscurity.

Everything changed, for him and for Ireland, thanks to the Home Rule Crisis, which brought de Valera into public life as a member of the Irish Volunteers. He joined on the night the Volunteers were formed in November 1913 and rose through the ranks thanks to his drive, his ambition and his single-mindedness. He was one of four battalion commandants in Dublin during the 1916 Rising, commanding the garrison at Boland's Bakery, a position that gave him a prominence that enabled his political career. De Valera's performance during the Rising was less stellar than his admirers claimed but considerably more assured than his critics would allow.

Arguably, the most important thing he did in 1916 was to survive, which was entirely due to luck and had nothing to do with being born in America. By the time he was court-martialled and sentenced to death, a public backlash against the executions had set in, and he and others tried at the same time had their sentences commuted to life imprisonment. Being a leading figure in the Rising helped make him the leader of the prisoners in Dartmoor and later Lewes gaols (although this was not quite the automatic process his supporters liked to claim – he fought to make himself leader). Being leader of the prisoners made him a natural candidate for the East Clare by-election when the convicts were released in June 1917.

Winning East Clare made him the perfect candidate to become leader of the new Sinn Féin party in October 1917 – it included Arthur Griffith's original Sinn Féin as well as many Volunteers and republicans of various kinds and was in essence a coalition between advanced republicans and more moderate nationalists. De Valera's unique contribution to this coalition was the formula that Sinn Féin would seek a republic and then the Irish people could decide afterwards what form of government an independent Ireland should have. That kept everyone – from Griffith to hard-line republican Cathal Brugha – in harness and working together. For the time being.

His efforts to make Sinn Féin the leading force in Irish nationalism were immeasurably helped by the British government. It first threatened to introduce conscription to Ireland in the wake of the devastating German spring offensive of 1918. De Valera skilfully used the crisis to outflank the Irish Parliamentary Party, incidentally forging an alliance with the Catholic hierarchy that was to prove useful. Having failed to conscript the manpower required from Ireland, the British government then decided to arrest de Valera and other leading Sinn Féiners on transparently trumped-up charges of conspiring with Germany.

Warned in advance of his impending arrest (by the increasingly influential Michael Collins), de Valera decided to allow himself to be caught, on the assumption that the resulting propaganda would be helpful. Sinn Féin subsequently swept the boards in the December 1918 general election, winning 73 seats to 26 seats for unionists and six for the Irish Parliamentary Party. Another propaganda victory followed when, in February 1919, a few weeks after the first meeting of Dáil Éireann, de Valera managed to escape from Lincoln Prison.

After some months at large, de Valera decided to travel to the USA in an effort to secure recognition of Irish independence, raise funds and generate publicity for the Irish cause. While he failed in the first aim, he was hugely successful in his financial and propaganda efforts, which were crucial to the eventual success of the War of Independence. His absence for 18 months of the struggle raised some eyebrows, then and since, but it can certainly be argued that his work in America was more important than anything he could have done at home.

Some thought his time in the USA changed him – Griffith allegedly described him as 'a good man who has been ruined by America'. He was certainly the subject of unprecedented adulation, which must have been a huge boost to his ego, although he also faced opposition from some Irish-American leaders, which had the opposite effect, accentuating the insecurity of his youth and leaving him prone to regard opposition as underhand and malicious. He returned to Ireland in December 1920, partly because tentative peace feelers had been coming from London.

The following six months were the most intense of the entire war but eventually led to a truce and to the talks in London that led to the Treaty. Having met British Prime Minister David Lloyd George in London immediately after the truce, de Valera knew the likely shape of an eventual deal. Partition was already a reality and would have to be accepted, at least in the short term. So would some form of connection with the British Empire: this was seen as essential in London. De Valera's strategy was to come up with a future relationship that would satisfy British demands while also being acceptable to republicans. His solution was what he called 'External Association': Ireland would be outside the Empire but would voluntarily associate with it, without giving allegiance to the Crown. This had the advantage that it was acceptable to republicans, such as Cathal Brugha, and the disadvantage that it was not acceptable to Conservative opinion in Britain. This was the fundamental error in de Valera's strategy: in order to maintain the unity of the Independence movement, he had committed himself to an outcome that was not achievable.

De Valera made three further mistakes in handling the talks. Most importantly, he refused to go to London himself. While there were sound tactical reasons for his decision to hold himself in reserve – reasons which are rarely acknowledged – it was, on balance, an error. A related mistake was to believe he could control the delegation from Dublin, which was impossible given the inevitable communication delays of the period. Finally, he sent the delegates back to London for the final round of talks without a clear idea of what they were seeking. A cabinet meeting on 3 December lasted a full day and appears to have been chaotic. There was disagreement within the negotiating team about what exactly had been decided at cabinet and what form of words would be acceptable. It is not surprising there were bitter recriminations afterwards.

De Valera's response to the Treaty was to argue that it should be rejected, in the hope that the British could be persuaded to accept external association. But further unpleasant surprises loomed. First, to his shock, he was outvoted in cabinet, by four votes to three; then the Dáil voted to accept the Treaty, by 64 votes to 57. He had lost narrowly – but he had lost, and as a result he resigned as President. He was well aware that public opinion supported the Treaty, not as an ideal solution but as a way of ending conflict and returning to normal life.

While Michael Collins argued that the Treaty gave Ireland 'the freedom to achieve freedom', de Valera believed it would prevent further progress towards full independence. Infamously, he argued in a speech in Thurles on St Patrick's Day, 1922, that future efforts to free the country would involve the use of violence against the government established by the Treaty: 'They would have to wade through Irish blood, through the blood of the soldiers of the Irish government, and through, perhaps, the blood of some of the members of the government in order to get Irish freedom.' He always insisted this was a warning rather than a threat, but his opponents understandably viewed his remarks as an incitement to violence, with many holding de Valera personally responsible for the Civil War that would break out in June. In truth, there would have been a civil war with or without de Valera – the militants paid very little attention to him – but the point is it would have been much smaller, and much shorter, without his support.

De Valera himself acknowledged that he was a reluctant leader of the extremists, describing himself as a 'fish out of water' in the role, and, from an early stage, he argued for an end to hostilities. He was ignored, until Irish Republican Army (IRA) Chief of Staff Liam Lynch was killed in action in April 1923, at which point the anti-Treaty side ceased hostilities, without formally ending the war or surrendering weapons. De Valera was arrested on an election platform in Clare and languished in gaol for a year, much of it in solitary confinement.

He was released in July 1924, with the Free State government understandably viewing him as a spent political force. Understandably – but wrongly. Éamon de Valera had risen from obscurity to political leadership once; now he was about to rise again, this time against even greater odds, given the opprobrium heaped on him because of the Civil War. His first step was to attempt to rebuild the Sinn Féin party. In the latter stages of the Civil War, he had insisted on retaining the name, despite opposition from republican purists who felt it did not imply commitment to their maximum demands. That, in de Valera's view, was precisely why they should retain it: he wanted to reach as broad a swathe of opinion as possible. 'Our aim is not to make a close preserve for ourselves, but to win the majority of the people again. I understand the difficulties but we must teach our people to be broad in this matter.' He wanted to cast the net as widely as possible, to win over as many people as possible; this was not a man who would be content with leading a die-hard rump. But that is where he found himself.

Sinn Féin was abstentionist; when he suggested that once the Oath was gone, attending the Dáil was a matter of tactics rather than principle, he found more opposition than he liked. When his policy change was narrowly defeated at the Sinn Féin Ard Fheis in March 1926, he announced his resignation. De Valera always claimed that as he walked out of that Sinn Féin Ard Fheis, he was walking away from politics, until he was persuaded by Seán Lemass that he could not turn his back on his life's work. It is highly unlikely that it took much persuasion for de Valera to stay on the political stage, and almost immediately he set about establishing his new party, Fianna Fáil.

Within a matter of days, he was operating out of a new office in

O'Connell Street with, as he put it, 'no furniture, no light, no money'. That did not last long: money started to flow in from his loyal supporters in America. But what was he going to do? Was he going into Dáil Éireann? Was he going to take the Oath? His opponents who remained in Sinn Féin believed that was his intention all along, but he denied that and continued to give hostages to fortune. 'Neither I, nor any member of Fianna Fáil will ever take that oath. That is final, and I hope it is clear.' It was clear, but, as it turned out, it was not final.

After the murder of Kevin O'Higgins, new laws made it mandatory for election candidates to agree to take the Oath. W. T. Cosgrave was offering de Valera a choice: swallow your words or give up politics. De Valera characteristically dithered before deciding that in fact the Oath was not an oath at all but was 'merely an empty political formula which deputies could conscientiously sign without becoming involved, or without involving their nation, in obligations of loyalty to the English Crown'. Before he signed the book signifying that he accepted the Oath, he read out a statement in Irish: 'I am not prepared to take an oath. I am not going to take an oath. I am prepared to put my name down in this book in order to get permission to go into the Dáil, but it has no other significance.' He then took the Bible off the table and left it on a couch by the door, covered the text of the Oath with papers he was carrying and signed his name, stating that one day he would have the book burnt.

Why did he do it? There was the legislation introduced by Cosgrave; there was pressure from within Fianna Fáil; and there was a possibility of joining forces with Labour and the National League to vote Cosgrave's government out. But there had also been a change in the way the Oath was administered. Back in 1922, TDs had to stand up in the Dáil chamber and recite the Oath in public; now, it only required a signature in a private room – maybe it really *was* only an empty formula.

In any event, de Valera was now inside the Free State parliament that he had taken up arms to oppose. And while W. T. Cosgrave had succeeded in forcing de Valera into the Dáil, he had also signed his own political death warrant because once Fianna Fáil was inside the system, it would at some stage come to power. De Valera continued to build up the party and, equally importantly, established his own newspaper, the *Irish Press*, which played a huge part in his election victory in 1932. Exactly 10 years and two months after he resigned the presidency following the Treaty vote, de Valera was elected back to power as President of the Executive Council, at the head of a Fianna Fáil minority government with Labour support. He was now finally in a position to show what he could do as head of government.

Before considering de Valera's actions in government, it is worth looking at his leadership style. Reading over Dáil and newspaper reports from the 1930s, one word comes up again and again in descriptions of de Valera: dictator. The assumption was that de Valera's party, and his ministers, did whatever he told them. But, in fact, Fianna Fáil was not the monolith presented to the world. There were real divergences and fierce disagreements, although in de Valera's time those divisions were kept private. In government, de Valera insisted on unanimous decisions, no matter how long it took. Seán Lemass said he kept debate going 'until those who were in the minority, out of sheer exhaustion, conceded the case made by the majority'. He got his way by persuasion rather than diktat. This insistence on getting consensus appears to have been at least partly due to the Treaty split. He had been shocked then to discover opposition where he had assumed agreement. He had learnt his lesson: he now wanted his colleagues not just to acquiesce but to wholeheartedly agree.

The other reason cabinet meetings went on for hours was that de Valera could be very indecisive, as he admitted:

> I wonder whether the people who get things done are those who are a little blind to every side of a question but the one side. Some of us are always wasting time and breaking our hearts, wondering whether the other fellow's way may not be right, going into his point of view, trying to meet him – trying to do the impossible.

He did not sound like a dictator, and, when it counted, he did not act like one, either. In the mid-1930s, he had an overall majority in the Dáil; he had abolished the Seanad; he had a tame Governor General; and the Free State Constitution could be amended by a simple majority vote in the Dáil. In other words, he could do whatever he wanted. It was, as Seán MacEntee pointed out, 'the most absolute government in Europe'. But at a time when many countries were becoming dictatorships, de Valera introduced a new and impeccably democratic constitution, and, instead of simply voting it through the Dáil, he put it to the people in a risky referendum, proof of his commitment to majority rule – at this point in his career anyway.

Another aspect of de Valera's leadership style was his pragmatism and his flexibility – again, not qualities that go with his public image. De Valera liked to be seen as consistent in all things, as completely wedded to principle, as unchanging in his views. But while he never changed his priority of seeking to extend Irish sovereignty, his way of achieving his aims changed all the time – entering the Dáil in 1927 being a prime example. Flexibility was hard-wired into Fianna Fáil. The aims which de Valera gave to his party were so widely defined that they could comfortably accommodate massive changes in direction.

The same was true of the 1937 Constitution. Again and again, he would state a principle and then add a caveat that made the principle almost meaningless. 'As far as practicable' was a favourite qualifier, and who knew what that meant? Articles 2 and 3 were a good example: Article 2 laid claim to the territory of Northern Ireland, so no one could accuse de Valera of abandoning republican principle, while Article 3 admitted that Dublin's writ would not run north of the Border, 'pending the reintegration of the national territory'. It was an ingenious example of de Valera's dexterity – or, as opponents would claim, of his trickiness. Labour leader Bill Norton once said that de Valera was 'a most skilful gentleman. He can throw a somersault on the edge of a razor blade and, when you express amazement, he will say there are heaps of room for everybody to do it.'

When de Valera came to power in 1932, some people expected him to be revolutionary, but he moved cautiously. While he released IRA prisoners locked up by Cosgrave, he did not sack Garda Commissioner Eoin O'Duffy, as many of his supporters expected, nor did he purge the civil service. And, while he suspended the operation of Cosgrave's emergency anti-IRA legislation, Article 2A, he did not repeal it – keeping it, in case he might need it later. Again and again, he said that once the Oath of Allegiance was removed, nobody would be blocked from taking part in politics and therefore nobody would have any excuse for resorting to physical force. It was a warning the IRA should have heeded.

De Valera's top priority in government was to assert Irish sovereignty and to dismantle the remaining features of the Anglo-Irish Treaty. His first targets were the Oath and the Land Annuities, the repayments of money lent to Irish farmers to buy their land. De Valera claimed that the money was not legally due to Britain and refused to pay it over. The British were predictably unimpressed (though they admitted in private that they were on shaky legal ground – an independent arbitrator might well have found for de Valera, which is why London made sure the case did not go to arbitration).

Prime Minister Ramsay MacDonald viewed him as an extremist, saying he was 'absolutely impossible … Unless we gave him everything he wanted … he would agree to nothing.' The British also seemed to view him as unhinged. They considered enlisting the help of a doctor from Leopardstown Hospital in Dublin, who claimed to have the 'medical knowledge … essential for dealing with the psychological problem presented by Mr de Valera's mind'. David Lloyd George, who had negotiated with him a decade before, made a rare appearance in the House of Commons to say that de Valera was 'perfectly unique, and I think this poor distracted world has a good right to feel profoundly thankful that he is unique'. But he went on to make a more important point, which showed that de Valera was being perfectly rational, and perfectly consistent. Lloyd George said that what de Valera was looking for in 1932 was exactly what he had been looking for in 1921: 'He has not changed one iota from that position … He is that type; he will never change right to the end.'

In retaliation for de Valera keeping the Land Annuities, the British put special duties on Irish goods, which devastated cattle exports, and de Valera in turn put extra tariffs on British goods. This became known as the Economic War, though it was entirely political in origin and in ultimate settlement. In the first full year of the Economic War, de Valera withheld £4.9 million from the British, the British collected £4.4 million in special duties, and the Irish government paid out £2.5 million in export bounties. As time went by, Dublin spent more on bounties while the British collected more in duties, so, in effect, the Irish government was using the withheld annuities to subsidise exports from which the British recouped their losses. After massive disruption to the cattle export trade, the two governments ended up about even.

J. H. Thomas, the British Dominions Secretary, was convinced that the electorate would remove de Valera as soon as they got the chance, particularly because of the impact of the Economic War. But the 1933 election proved him wrong: Fianna Fáil improved its position, winning an overall majority for the first time, and it became clear that de Valera was there to stay.

While de Valera viewed sovereignty and undoing the Treaty as his top priority, the dispute it caused with Britain was only one of the problems facing the government: the economy was, of course, still dealing with the effects of the Great Depression, and Fianna Fáil did its best to protect the worst-off. In his first budget, Seán MacEntee balanced the books by increasing taxation and cutting civil-service salaries while protecting social welfare and finding money for housing. The housing drive was particularly impressive. Between 1923 and 1932, fewer than 2,000 houses a year had been built with state aid, but between 1932 and 1942, the average annual figure was 12,000.

The other main thrust of Fianna Fáil's economic policy was protection: foreign goods were kept out with tariffs, and foreigners were prevented from owning companies in Ireland. Without these measures, given the international depression and the effects of the Economic War, both unemployment and emigration would have been much worse than they were, although protected industry remained small-scale, relatively inefficient and reliant on imported raw materials.

The Economic War also led to the rise of the Blueshirts, under the leadership of General Eoin O'Duffy, who was sacked as Garda Commissioner after de Valera was returned to power in the 1933 election. As has been mentioned, many Fianna Fáil supporters had expected O'Duffy to be removed in 1932, but de Valera's innate caution made him hold back. The irony is that if Cosgrave had been re-elected in 1932, he was planning to dismiss the increasingly volatile O'Duffy, which makes Cosgrave's decision to merge his party, along with the Centre Party, with the Blueshirts to create Fine Gael, under the leadership of the self-same O'Duffy, baffling. The only explanation is that the opposition genuinely believed that de Valera was planning to outlaw them and assume dictatorial powers.

O'Duffy is now seen as something of a buffoon, but he did not seem like a joke at the time. He had a brilliant War of Independence record and had done a magnificent job in establishing An Garda Síochána as an unarmed force in the middle of the Civil War. When he announced a Blueshirt parade past Leinster House in August 1933, the government was so worried by parallels with Mussolini's March on Rome a decade before that de Valera banned the parade. A quarter of a century later, he looked back on the ban, along with the Constitution, as his greatest achievement because many in the Army and the Gardaí sympathised with O'Duffy, and if they had refused to follow de Valera's orders, democratic government would have been at an end.

Of course, the Blueshirts were not the only ones making trouble; de Valera's allies in the IRA were enthusiastically breaking heads as well. Indeed, their violence was one of the main driving forces behind the establishment of the Blueshirts in the first place. De Valera now positioned himself as an honest broker, warning in the Dáil that if the violence by both sides continued, 'By heavens! We will come out and ask the sane people of the country to knock the heads of both parties together.' Despite his initial closeness to, and reliance on, the IRA, de Valera was now able to position himself as the representative of the 'sane people of the country', occupying the middle ground between two extremes. And he turned on the IRA, as figures for convictions by the Special Powers

Tribunal show. Once the Blueshirts had been cut down to size, attention turned back to the IRA in 1935.

Partition had been a big theme for de Valera in opposition; not so much in government. He admitted in the Dáil in May 1935:

> We have no plan ... by which we can inevitably bring about the union of this country ... Our present policy is that we here intend to go along in our own way, always leaving the door open ... for those who are separated to come along and join with us.

He firmly believed that the route to a united Ireland lay through London. The British government had partitioned Ireland, and, he believed, it had the power to undo it; he tried unsuccessfully to persuade the British government to put pressure on Stormont. One of the problems with resolving the dispute with London was that the British insisted on treating the economic and political questions together; there could be no end to the Economic War until de Valera committed to staying in the Commonwealth and recognising the King as head of state, which de Valera, of course, refused to do.

Then he got lucky, thanks to King Edward VIII's relationship with American divorcee Wallis Simpson. British Prime Minister Stanley Baldwin refused to allow Edward to marry Mrs Simpson; at which point, Edward said he would abdicate. Which was all well and good; Westminster could be relied on to legislate for the succession of his brother. But each dominion, which at the time included the Irish Free State, had to agree to the change, and if de Valera were to refuse, Edward would remain King in Ireland while George was King in the UK and the rest of the dominions.

De Valera turned out to be surprisingly tolerant on the King's difficulty, being the only dominion prime minister who thought Edward should be allowed to marry Mrs Simpson:

> It was true that divorce was not recognised in Catholic countries but King Edward was a Protestant and in Protestant countries the attitude

to divorce was different ... many ... would, in these democratic days, be attracted by the idea of a young King ready to give up all for love.

But that solution would not fly, and, with London desperate to have the Dáil agree to the change of King, de Valera skilfully used the situation to introduce constitutional change. The King was removed from the internal affairs of the Free State by deleting all reference to him in the Constitution, but he retained a role in external affairs: the King would formally appoint diplomats and approve treaties, on the advice of the Irish government. This allowed the British to say that Ireland was still in the Commonwealth while de Valera could claim to be completely independent but voluntarily linked to the Commonwealth. It was his idea of 'External Association', first advanced during the Treaty negotiations of 1921, and he managed to get it through the Dáil in just two days and accepted by the British, thanks to Edward VIII.

This resolved one of the key difficulties facing his new constitution, which was published the following May. It is not clear when de Valera decided to introduce an entirely new constitution, but he had always regarded the original Irish Free State Constitution as suspect because it was drafted under British supervision and had not been put to the people for their express approval. In any event, both he and Cosgrave had made a mockery of it with constant amendment. While many articles of the old constitution would be incorporated into the new one, the overall ethos of the new document would be recast by de Valera to be both more Catholic and more republican.

The Constitution achieved de Valera's aim, expressed in 1933, of establishing 'a Republic in fact' so that 'when the time comes, the proclaiming of the Republic may involve no more than a ceremony of formal confirmation of a status already attained'. He did not declare the state a republic in 1937 because he believed it would be wrong to do so while Partition remained. The Irish Free State was gone, replaced with a new name: 'Éire, or in the English language, Ireland'. Ireland would have a president as head of state. While the new office had little real power – the

President was in the main only to act 'on the advice of the government' and had limited discretionary powers – it was an important symbol of sovereignty.

The new post led to opposition criticism of de Valera's alleged dictatorial tendencies, as some claimed he could use the presidency to undermine democracy. Similar claims were made about the changes he made in the role of head of government. The President of the Executive Council was to be renamed 'Taoiseach', with enhanced powers. Many powers previously exercised by the Executive Council as a whole were now given to the Taoiseach, who was also to have the power to sack ministers. While the criticisms were overdone, there was no doubt that de Valera had further strengthened the office he held.

There has been criticism (more pronounced in recent decades than at the time) of the Catholic ethos of the Constitution, evident in the preamble, the articles on social policy and the article on religion. De Valera was assisted in his drafting by several Catholic clerics, including John Charles McQuaid, then the President of Blackrock College and later Archbishop of Dublin. McQuaid's influence was apparent on the articles on social policy, which incorporated the latest Catholic thinking on issues such as the rights of parents and the role of women in the home. The latter references incensed feminists and remain controversial.

But McQuaid did not get everything he wanted, particularly in the article on religion, which he hoped and expected would recognise the Catholic Church as the 'one true church'. While in an early draft de Valera had included such a recognition, he quickly realised it would be politically unacceptable (not least to his cabinet colleagues) and backtracked. The furthest he could go was to recognise the 'special position' of the Catholic Church, due to it being the church of the vast majority of the population. The clause also recognised the other faiths then present in the state, including the Jewish religion – not an insignificant gesture in the Europe of the late 1930s.

The reference to the Catholic Church's 'special position' was later criticised as giving it too much influence, but at the time it was criticised for not going far enough. The Vatican, the hierarchy and John Charles McQuaid were among those opposed to the religion clause, although they refrained from doing so publicly, to de Valera's great relief. In the event, the Constitution was adopted by a narrow enough margin, 56.5 per cent in favour to 43.5 per cent against. (Almost 10 per cent of the votes cast were spoiled, which probably also reflected hostility or at least doubt about the Constitution.) A public row over religion would probably have scuppered the whole project.

With constitutional questions resolved for the time being, one of the main stumbling blocks to the resolution of the Economic War had been removed. Another change that helped get an agreement was the appointment of a new Dominions Secretary, Malcolm MacDonald, the son of former Prime Minister Ramsay MacDonald, who was far more impressed than his father by de Valera, who he later described as a 'transparently honest and sincere man ... I learnt to have a high respect and indeed affection for this austere, impassioned old Sinn Féiner.'

Even more important was the new British Prime Minister, Neville Chamberlain, who decided, before talks even began, that the three Treaty ports of Cobh, Berehaven and Lough Swilly – occupied by the British under the terms of the Treaty – should be handed over to de Valera, without any commitment that they would be available to Britain in time of war. This decision made Irish neutrality possible – giving Chamberlain a strong claim to be the man who kept Ireland out of the Second World War. The other matters in dispute were also resolved, with the Land Annuities being waived in return for a £10 million lump sum and a new trade agreement reached, which tied the Irish economy back into the British economy again. The agreement more or less ended Fianna Fáil's attempt to fundamentally recast the Irish economy.

In a Dáil speech in July 1939, de Valera acknowledged the continued flight from the land and the decline of the small town and village and admitted that there was little enough he could do about it. 'There is no use in hoping that we can put back the clock.' That sentiment coming from Éamon de Valera would surprise many Irish people. If he is remembered for one phrase, it is for 'comely maidens dancing at the crossroads' – despite the fact that he never actually said it. The speech in question was broadcast on St Patrick's Day in 1943 to mark the 50th anniversary of the Gaelic League. De Valera spoke of that

> ideal Ireland that we would have ... the home of a people who valued material wealth only as the basis of right living; of a people who were satisfied with frugal comfort and devoted their leisure to the things of the spirit, a land whose countryside would be bright with neat and cosy homesteads, whose fields and villages would be joyous with the sounds of industry, with the romping of sturdy children, the contests of athletic youths, and the laughter of happy maidens ...

In his script, the maidens were 'comely' rather than 'happy', but he changed it just before the broadcast. There was no dancing mentioned, either at crossroads or anywhere else.

Much scorn has been heaped on that speech, but a couple of things should be taken into account. First of all, de Valera was not describing Ireland as it was, or as he wished it to be. He was talking about the Ireland the founders of the Gaelic League a half century before had imagined. Second, he was not using the term 'frugal comfort' to advocate a life of dreary subsistence for the Irish people: he was advocating the sharing of the nation's wealth. In August 1940, he told the Dáil that 'a small community such as ours will have to be content with frugal comfort, if that comfort is to be universal'. In other words, to ensure a minimum for everyone, the better-off would have to accept a lower standard of living.

That speech was made during the Second World War, in which Ireland, of course, was neutral, a policy that had been foreshadowed by de Valera throughout the 1930s. During this decade, he was a leading light at the League of Nations, encouraging member states to live up to their responsibilities. He was critical of the failure to stand up to Japan over its invasion of Manchuria and even more of the failure to stop Mussolini's invasion of Ethiopia. It was, he said, 'the final test of the league and all that it stands for'.

And the League failed the test. Speaking with 'a feeling of bitter humiliation', de Valera said they had to admit that 'we must abandon the victim to his fate … Is there any small nation represented here which does not feel the truth of the warning that what is Ethiopia's fate today may well be its own fate tomorrow?' Given the failure of the League to protect a member state, the only thing that small countries could do, he said, was to avoid becoming the tools of any great power and to resist with all their strength every attempt to force them into a war against their will.

Neutrality was the ultimate expression of Irish sovereignty. Ireland was one of only five European nations that managed to remain neutral, the others being Switzerland, Sweden, Spain and Portugal. And it was the only dominion that refused to declare war along with Britain. Winston Churchill denied the legitimacy of Irish neutrality: 'Legally I believe they are at war but skulking.' Churchill thought Ireland should be treated differently to the other neutrals, which proved the importance of neutrality – it was the only way to demonstrate to London that Ireland was an independent state.

In the summer of 1940, with France overrun by the Germans, Churchill desperately wanted the Treaty ports back, and he was prepared to bribe de Valera to get them. The bribe was action on Partition. In return for allowing British forces into Irish territory, de Valera was offered a firm guarantee of a united Ireland. He rejected it – in part because he did not trust the British to actually deliver, by forcing Stormont into a united Ireland. As mentioned earlier, his Partition policy rested on the assumption that the only way to secure unity was through British pressure, so this decision undermined that policy. He was also, rightly, worried that Irish cities would be defenceless against German bombing. And, of course, there was the very real possibility, even the probability, that Britain would lose the war.

But there was another reason. The price of unity would be to dilute the sovereignty he had carefully built up over the previous decade. He told the Fianna Fáil Ard Fheis in September 1943: 'We have a right to the unity of our country and we have a right to the independent action of our people also. We are not going to sacrifice one of these rights in order to obtain the other. Both are due to us.' He was not prepared to trade sovereignty for unity, a demonstration of where his priorities lay, despite all the rhetoric on Partition.

So, Ireland continued neutral, promising to fight whoever invaded. There was thought to be a real threat of a German invasion, though the strength of the Royal Navy and the Royal Air Force put the German high command off, and there was always the possibility that Churchill, and later Roosevelt, would approve the seizure of the ports if the Battle of the Atlantic demanded it.

De Valera thought that moment had come when he was woken up in the middle of the night in December 1941, after Pearl Harbor, to be told the British representative, Sir John Maffey, had an urgent message for him from Churchill. De Valera had the Chief of Staff of the Army alerted to prepare for a possible invasion. But all Churchill sent was another encouragement to enter the war: 'Now is your chance. Now or never."A Nation once again." Am very ready to meet you at any time.' De Valera – correctly – decided that Churchill had been celebrating American entry into the war a bit too enthusiastically and went back to bed.

American pressure on Ireland to enter the war was particularly resented because the USA only entered the war after itself being attacked. On the other hand, America, unlike Ireland, was not dependent on the supply line across the U-boat-infested Atlantic; to American eyes, Irish refusal to help in the Battle of the Atlantic seemed both wrong and self-defeating.

The tension between de Valera and the land of his birth was most obvious in his relationship with David Gray, the American Minister to Ireland during the war. Gray was a very well-connected political appointee; his wife was an aunt of Eleanor Roosevelt, which gave him a direct line into the White House that he used frequently. He came to detest de Valera, and the feeling was mutual. Gray's most famous manoeuvre was the American Note in February 1944, demanding the removal of the German and Japanese legations prior to D-Day, in the confident expectation that the demand would be refused. He asked for something he knew he would not get so that he could put de Valera on record for refusing to help so that if he came to the USA after the Second World War he would not be able to influence American politics as he had after the First. And Gray got what he wanted: after de Valera said no, an opinion poll showed that 71 per cent of Americans were aware of his refusal, with 66 per cent thinking the USA should take further action, including 4 per cent who believed war should be declared.

Even more effective than the American Note was Gray's goading of de Valera towards the end of the war with a demand to hand over the German legation before hostilities had formally ended. This led directly to de Valera's infamous visit to the German Minister, Eduard Hempel, to express condolences on the death of Hitler. This provoked a storm of protest from Americans, particularly Irish Americans, who wrote to de Valera condemning his actions. One expressed regret that the British hadn't shot de Valera when they had the chance; another suggested that 'the Irish people should tar and feather you, you dirty bum'.

De Valera's reputation in America and Britain was severely damaged, and it would have been severely damaged at home as well if it had not been for Winston Churchill, who famously took a swipe at de Valera in his victory broadcast at the end of the war, complimenting himself on his restraint in not invading Ireland and seizing the ports. De Valera replied a couple of days later, calmly and with his trademark dignity, pointing out that Ireland had not stood alone against aggression for a year or two, like Britain, but for several hundred years.

The Allied diplomats in Dublin, who had gone to such trouble to put de Valera in the wrong, were furious at Churchill's speech. The Canadian envoy, John D. Kearney, said, 'We had him on a plate. We had him where we wanted him. But look at the papers this morning!' So, thanks to Churchill, de Valera had snatched a late victory and his reputation – in Ireland at least – was restored.

But there was a price to be paid for neutrality, in terms of post-war isolation, in the loss of American support and in the deepening of the gulf with Northern Ireland. Neutrality can be, and has been, criticised on all those grounds and on the grounds of morality. But in September 1939, the moral issues did not seem so clear; de Valera did what most small countries in Europe did: he tried to stay neutral. And, thanks to geography and luck, he succeeded.

The biggest criticism was of his refusal to allow the Treaty ports to be used, especially because Ireland was just as threatened by the U-boat blockade as was Britain. But, with the French coast in German hands, Cobh and Berehaven would not have been much use, while Lough Swilly was made superfluous by a major navy base in Derry. And he had, of course, done plenty to help the Allied cause, supplying food to Britain as well as volunteers for the armed forces and workers for war industries, allowing overflights, releasing crash-landed Allied aircrew and sharing intelligence. But, because he wanted to maintain his public image as an unwavering neutral, he could not admit that after the war, and the true extent of Irish assistance to the Allies was not known for many years.

At the end of the Second World War, de Valera, now 62, was in an unassailable position: he had a secure majority in the Dáil, a united and loyal government and a new-found stature as the man who had kept Ireland neutral. What followed came almost as an anticlimax: another 14 years as either Taoiseach or leader of the opposition, which added little to his reputation. He soldiered on until the age of 76, when he 'retired' to the presidency. Seventy-six is certainly old, but de Valera was not that old among his contemporaries; de Gaulle left office at 78, Churchill at 80, Konrad Adenauer at a quite remarkable 87 years of age.

And he was not the only one who had grown stale in office. One Fianna Fáil backbencher, M. J. Kennedy, observed that, 'The cabinet through long office have lost their moorings.' Another, Erskine Childers, said, 'the people are tired of some of the old faces'. Fianna Fáil finally met its match in 1948, when a 16-year period in office ended when all the other parties – and some independents – clubbed together to vote de Valera out. The *Irish Independent* headline the following day was 'Mr Costello is Taoiseach'; that, of course, would not do for the *Irish Press*, which had no doubt about the most important point, headlining its story, 'Mr de Valera is no longer Taoiseach.'

De Valera was convinced that he had been defeated by trickery and the vagaries of proportional representation. No effort was made to work on policies to present to the voters or to revamp the party organisation. While Seán Lemass was left to do the work in the Dáil, de Valera went off on a round-the-world anti-Partition tour which he enjoyed immensely, visiting the USA, Australia and India, where he and Jawaharlal Nehru traded notes on the various British prisons in which they had been incarcerated.

Fianna Fáil's assumption that all it had to do was wait and it would be returned to office was vindicated – just about – in 1951, when de Valera scraped back into power with the support of Noël Browne and some other independents. It was undoubtedly the worst government led by de Valera and arguably the worst in the history of the state. Part of the reason was that de Valera's eyesight had deteriorated very significantly. He had to spend five months, from August to December 1952, in Utrecht in the Netherlands for treatment. He had a total of six very painful operations and wrote home to Lemass: 'I hate to be a lame duck like this, but of course I can't help it.' The operations were only partially successful, and from this point on he had to memorise all his speeches.

The other problem was that this government was extremely conservative, a tone set by the Minister for Finance, Seán MacEntee. MacEntee's 1952 budget was one of the most controversial, and most politically damaging, in Irish history. Worried about a balance-of-payments deficit, he ramped up tax and cut food subsidies to choke off demand. In fairness, he also increased social welfare and children's allowances to compensate people, but these increases got little attention at the time and none since. MacEntee gets the blame for the 1952 budget, but, of course, de Valera knew exactly what he was getting when he appointed him. Fianna Fáil had fought the election on the basis that the inter-party government's spendthrift economic ways would lead to disaster. De Valera appointed MacEntee to Finance precisely because of his conservative fiscal views.

The government's popularity never recovered from that budget, and in 1954 it was booted out of office to be replaced by the second inter-party government which, unfortunately, was almost as bad. But this second spell in opposition was somewhat different because Seán Lemass finally began inching the party towards a more modern economic policy, though he did it very carefully, saying that all policies were open to change, 'subject to the preservation of the party's aims'. Luckily, as was mentioned earlier, de Valera had defined those aims so broadly that they could be stretched to cover a change from protection to free trade, from self-reliance to international involvement.

What Lemass was up against was revealed in July 1956, when de Valera said he was against foreign loans: 'I would rather go short of the things that would be got by an external loan than have an external loan. The policy of self-reliance is the one policy that will enable our nation to continue to exist.' That appeared to suggest that nothing had changed; so did the make-up of de Valera's last government in 1957. Five of the members had been in the first Fianna Fáil government a quarter of a century before: de Valera himself, James Ryan, Frank Aiken, MacEntee and Lemass. Another three had fought in the Civil War, and three more were the sons of former political colleagues. This extraordinary continuity obviously strengthened the cohesion of de Valera's governments; whether it was good for the country is another matter.

However, this was the government that introduced the First Programme for Economic Expansion, prompted by Ken Whitaker and with the full support of Seán Lemass and Jim Ryan, the Minister for Finance. In retrospect, though not at the time, the First Programme has been seen as a turning point. Its success lay not in meeting its targets (which were so modest that they were easily surpassed) but in the psychological effect of offering some hope that the economy could be turned round and that the state had a future. While Lemass, Ryan and Whitaker deserve credit, it should not be forgotten that de Valera was still Taoiseach, and while he was not at this point very active, he could certainly have blocked the change had he wanted to. But he managed to convince himself – or allowed Lemass to convince him – that what was being done was entirely consistent with Fianna Fáil policy. He even told Whitaker at one point that 'free trade had been his policy from the beginning', which was very much not in accordance with the facts.

In any event, de Valera's time at the helm was coming to an end. There has been a lot of speculation about whether he jumped or was pushed. From looking at the press coverage at the time, it seems clear that he had decided by the end of 1958 that he would not contest the next general election, though he had not set a date for departure. The end of Seán T. O'Kelly's term in the Áras gave him a suitably dignified exit strategy, and some of his colleagues encouraged him to consider taking it. Had he not already accepted that his days as Taoiseach were numbered, it is highly unlikely that his ministers would have had the desire, or the ability, to force him out. The Presidency provided decent cover for the inevitable.

The 14 years in the Presidency needn't concern us greatly. The role was a lot less active back then, and de Valera performed it with great dignity but not much energy. In fact, he very nearly lost his re-election bid in 1966, beating Tom O'Higgins of Fine Gael by just 10,000 votes.

There were two great political issues towards the end of his political life, which of course he could not comment on publicly. The first was entry into the EEC, as it then was. De Valera had always been wary of European integration, and, while it is not known how he voted in the referendum on membership, he may well have been in the minority that voted against. On New Year's Eve, hours before Ireland became a member, he said to his family that 'I am the first and last elected President of an independent Ireland.'

The other great issue was the outbreak of the Troubles, and the Arms Crisis that threatened to rip apart Jack Lynch's government and the Fianna Fáil party. Again, de Valera could not say anything publicly, but he did play a role behind the scenes, persuading Kevin Boland not to resign from cabinet over Northern policy in August 1969. Whether that was actually helpful from Lynch's point of view is open to question, but it certainly could be seen as a breach of the convention that a president should not interfere in politics. Throughout the Arms Crisis, de Valera steadfastly supported Lynch and opposed efforts to involve the state in military action to resolve Partition. He had supported non-violence for half a century, and he was not about to change now.

To sum up, de Valera did more than any other individual to define the parameters of Ireland's development between 1932 and his death in 1975. He spent 21 years as head of government, six years as leader of the opposition, 14 years as President of Ireland and just two years in retirement. But there are limits to his influence. 'De Valera's Ireland' is talked about as if he created the social and economic conditions of an entire country. Of course he was more influential than others, and of course he set a tone. But if he had never been sent home from America, how different would Ireland have been? The politics would certainly have worked out differently, but the forces that shaped society would have done much of their work without him.

He dominated because he was a master tactician as was shown by his astute calling of snap elections in 1933, 1938 and 1944 to secure a Fianna Fáil majority when the voters had been so misguided as to leave him in a minority in the previous election. But he also dominated because he represented better than other leaders what the voters wanted. He combined an unwavering belief in the sovereignty of the Irish people with the tactical skill to achieve his aims. He claimed to articulate an unchanging set of beliefs but altered them whenever the situation demanded.

The economic performance of independent Ireland up to the end of the 1950s was disappointing to say the least and in some eyes undermined the argument for Independence. Although external factors played a part, and other politicians had a role, de Valera's was the dominant presence, and so he attracts the lion's share of the blame. But he gave his backing to Seán Lemass when it counted and helped prepare the ground for a change of policy of which he did not really approve or which he probably did not understand fully.

His governments have rightly been credited with a number of achievements on the social and economic fronts: pensions for widows and orphans, the jobs created by protection (limited though they were), the housing drive, the semi-state companies. But while his government did more for the underprivileged than its predecessor, it did not usher in a social revolution. This is not surprising: de Valera did not try to change Irish society because he did not wish to see it change. The social conservatism of rural Ireland shaped him, and it would continue to exert a powerful hold on the country he led. Economic growth and wider education were required before the horizons of Ireland could widen.

He provided decisive leadership on the linked questions of Independence, sovereignty and national identity. Without the advances he made for Irish sovereignty, neutrality would have been impossible in the Second World War, and neutrality was the greatest assertion of Irish sovereignty. But while he enhanced the sovereignty, the unity and the identity of the Irish state, it was a 26-county state. Neutrality strengthened the Border and accelerated the divergence of the two parts of the island. It is not clear if de Valera really grasped this, but even if he did it was unlikely to have changed his approach. Throughout his career he gave priority to the state while talking about the nation.

Inevitably, Éamon de Valera's record as head of government is mixed. But in terms of his longevity in office, in terms of his dominance of Irish politics, in terms of the scale of his achievements on sovereignty, in terms of his impact on an era, he has a strong claim to be the most significant holder of the office of Taoiseach.

4

John A. Costello

1948–51, 1954–7

Charles Lysaght

Full name: John Aloysius Costello
Date of birth: 20 June 1891
Place of birth: Cabra, Dublin
Date of death: 5 January 1976
Site of grave: Deansgrange Cemetery, Dublin
Education: St Joseph's, Fairview; O'Connell School; UCD; King's Inns
Married to: Ida Mary O'Malley (m. 1919)
Children: Wilfred, Grace, Declan, Eavan and John
Assumed office: (1) 18 February 1948; (2) 2 June 1954
Date of resignation: (1) 13 June 1951; (2) 20 March 1957
Length of tenure: Six years, three days
Quotation: 'Even Irish unity may be bought at too high a price if bought at the price of sin and shame.'

Although I would have been aware of John A. Costello as Taoiseach twice between 1948 and 1957 while I was growing up in his Dublin constituency, my first real recollection of him was when I was a student in UCD and he presided at a meeting of its Literary and Historical Society. Recalling that he had twice been defeated in elections for auditor before the First World War, he waxed eloquent on how he, a Christian Brothers boy, lost because those voting for his posher opponents were better able to pay the subscription. I was puzzled that so many years later, after a successful life, he should still be so irked by this reverse.

Not long afterwards, in December 1961, when I was auditor of the Law Students Debating Society at King's Inns, he kindly agreed at short notice to preside at the inaugural meeting where I was to give an address. 'I'm not climbing into tails', he told me, declining to follow the usual practice at such meetings. He got most of the other guest speakers to follow his lead. In my inaugural address, I rehashed some theories on economics and law I had picked up from my reading but may not have understood fully. One was the superiority of natural law over positive law, an idea being espoused at the time by reputable champions of the Constitution and human-rights conventions. A Jesuit mentor had persuaded me to argue that lawyers needed to be trained in scholastic philosophy so as to know what the natural law ordained. This was too much for the practical common-sense lawyer that was Jack Costello; in his summing-up, he recalled a judge who was a philosopher and remarked that the experience of appearing before him was one that had to be undergone to be believed.

My address touched on trade-union law; he had just won an important case in which a split Supreme Court had decided that picketing to force an employer to operate a closed shop was a breach of the right to association in the Constitution. Costello waxed eloquent, attacking the behaviour of the trade union that had authorised the picket. This was reported in the newspapers, and the union concerned complained that it was unprofessional for a barrister to comment on a case in which he had been involved. He was prone to lose the run of himself and blurt out things when he got to his feet.

At my behest, the Law Students Debating Society decided to honour him by electing him a Vice-President. I wrote to him asking him to accept and recalling that he won the society's prize for an essay on the Brehon Law when he was a student in 1915. I received a reply stating that 'in reply to your blandishments, you may take it that I accept the office to which the Law Students Debating Society have elected me.' It was more brusque than I had expected.

Whenever I met him in the succeeding decade at social occasions, he was very friendly, generally asking why I was not practising at the Bar. He could not believe that a person would forgo practising at the Bar to have any other kind of legal job, even a judgeship. He had a tale he told me several times that amused him greatly; it concerned a nationalist barrister called Muldoon who went to canvass for the Liberal Party in Britain before the First World War. He was asked to dinner by the local Whig grandee, whose wife, upon learning that Muldoon came from Dublin, sought to establish common ground by asking him whether he knew their friend Lord Iveagh. 'No', muttered Muldoon defensively, only to be reassured by his hostess, 'Of course not; they are only brewers.'

I recall seeing Costello in church, his lips moving, verbalising his prayers silently and devoutly. He had lived his faith with charitable acts, one of which, I recall, was to send the chauffeur-driven car he had at his disposal as an ex-Taoiseach to take shopping a widowed cousin, who lived near our house in Merrion. 'What a kind man', was the response of my parents or any neighbours who knew about it. It would not have occurred to anybody to question its propriety.

A few years before his death, in 1974, *The Times* in London asked me to prepare an advance obituary of him. It remained the fullest account of his life written until Anthony Jordan's short biography in 2007. I returned to the subject, writing an entry of 8,000 words for the *Dictionary of Irish Biography* in 2009, having examined his papers lodged in UCD. A full biography by David McCullagh appeared in 2010.

John Aloysius Costello, as he was christened, was unusual, if not unique, among heads of government in independent Ireland in that he did not seek the office, but accepted it reluctantly only when pressurised to do so by political colleagues when the first inter-party government in the history of the State took office in 1948.

He was also the only one among the four heads of government in the first 40 years of the State's existence not to have fought in, or even supported, the 1916 Rebellion and the later guerrilla war that culminated in the foundation of the Irish Free State in 1922. A leading barrister, he was also unique among all Irish heads of government in not being primarily a politician. His eminence in his profession of barrister gave him a unique cachet among politicians.

It was through this profession that Costello became involved in politics. Born on 2 June 1891, at home in 13 Charleville Road, Cabra, he was the younger of two sons of a Clareman, also John Costello, who was a staff officer in the Registry of Deeds, and one of many Catholics from rural Ireland who at that time found employment in the civil service and settled in the new suburbs on the northside of Dublin. His wife, Rose Callaghan, was from Westmeath. Young John, always called Jack, went to school with the Christian Brothers at St Joseph's Fairview and O'Connell School, from which he won a scholarship for the sons of civil servants to UCD. He became a keen debater in the college's Literary and Historical Society. Having taken a first-class degree in modern languages (including Irish), he turned to law and was called to the Bar in November 1914.

He did not follow into service in the First World War his medical-doctor brother (who won the Military Cross) and many contemporaries, nationalist as well as unionist. Instead, he applied himself single-mindedly to practise at the Bar, joining the Munster Circuit, where he was briefed mainly by solicitors in Clare. He felt he was resented by fellow barristers in the Law Library on account of his background. 'They would bridle', he recalled, 'when they saw me, an Irish Catholic, getting a brief.' In fact, half of those in what was then an all-Ireland profession were Catholic. However, his grievance that Catholics were treated unfairly in a country ruled, as he saw it, by the Protestant Ascendancy did not divert him into political involvement in the years of ferment that followed. Hugh Kennedy, who had been his master, took him on as a 'devil' to assist with conveyancing work, and Costello acquired a sufficient practice by 1919 to marry Ida O'Malley, the daughter of a medical practitioner in Galway and herself a teacher at the Dominican Nuns' school at Eccles Street.

In June 1921, one month before the truce that brought armed hostilities between the IRA and Crown Forces to a halt, Costello was briefed by an Ennis solicitor to appear with Hugh Kennedy for John Egan, who had been sentenced to death by a military court for the possession of ammunition. At a hearing held shortly after the truce in July 1921, Charles O'Connor, Master of the Rolls, defied precedent and decided that the military court lacked jurisdiction to try an offence punishable with death. The case created a sensation because the judge had to threaten to commit the Commander-in-Chief of the army in Ireland to prison to secure Egan's release. The judgment called into question the legality of other executions and was under appeal when the conclusion on 6 December 1921 of the treaty for the establishment of the Irish Free State intervened to make it irrelevant.

Although, during his political life, Costello sometimes praised the efforts of those who had achieved independence by the use of force, he never claimed that he had supported them or their political wing, Sinn Féin; always a devout and obedient Catholic, his attitude at the time may have been influenced by the views of the church authorities who had consistently condemned the IRA campaign of assassination. He did claim that he had appeared in the courts set up under the aegis of the administration established by the Sinn Féin members returned in the 1918 general election. There is, however, no record that he was among the few barristers who did so before the truce in July 1921. After that, many barristers appeared in these courts, even if they had never been Sinn Féin supporters, and Costello was among them.

Hugh Kennedy advised the Irish delegation that negotiated the Treaty and was appointed law adviser to the Provisional Government, chaired by Michael Collins, to whom the British government handed over the administration of Southern Ireland early in 1922. Kennedy appointed Costello as a part-time assistant, a post he continued to hold when John O'Byrne succeeded Kennedy as Attorney General in June 1924. Costello provided opinions on a wide range of complicated legal issues arising from the changeover between the two administrations.

He retained his private practice and was briefed on behalf of the Native American widow of the Tammany boss Richard Croker, upholding a bequest to her that was disputed by the family of his earlier marriage; she invited her counsel to a celebration dinner and made them gifts of 1,000 guineas (£1,050) apiece. This helped Costello to buy 20 Herbert Park, where his family of three boys and two girls grew up and which remained his home for the rest of his life. He also represented the State in litigation and was nominated as Standing Counsel to the Revenue.

In May 1925, Costello was called to the Inner Bar. In January 1926, he succeeded as Attorney General when John O'Byrne was appointed a judge. 'His industry, ability and energy are very great', reported the *Irish Law Times*; 'he is a good lawyer and an excellent advocate.' As Attorney General, he gave up private practice and did not appear in court even on behalf of the State, preferring to brief barristers supportive of the government such as Charles Bewley, Cecil Lavery, Basil McGuckin and Thomas Finlay to do so.

It was a time when legal issues such as public-safety legislation, the maritime boundary with Northern Ireland, payment of annuities due to the British government under the Land Purchase Acts and the independence of the Dominions were to the forefront in political debate, so adding to his routine work as Attorney General directing prosecutions, some of which, such as the prosecution of the Fianna Fáil deputy leader Seán T. O'Kelly for contempt of court, were also politically controversial. 'Costello has done wonderful work', noted his old mentor Hugh Kennedy in his diary. Costello, who regarded himself as non-aligned politically, kept a low profile and abstained from public statements.

He was engaged as legal adviser at imperial conferences and at the League of Nations, where the Irish Free State was asserting its right to act more independently of the British government. He was part of the Irish delegation at the negotiation of the Statute of Westminster 1931, which recognised the full sovereignty and equality of the Dominions within the Commonwealth.

Although he had regarded his position as Attorney General as apolitical, Costello did speak on behalf of government candidates at the general election of February 1932 at which the Cumann na nGaedheal government, led by W. T. Cosgrave, was defeated by Fianna Fáil under Éamon de Valera. Within a year, in January 1933, de Valera, whose government had been dependent on support from the Labour Party, called a snap election at which Fianna Fáil won an overall majority. Costello, who had returned to practise at the Bar, was adopted as a candidate in the eight-seater Dublin County constituency and came second, after ex-unionist Henry Dockrell, among four Cumann na nGaedheal deputies elected. From 1937 until 1948, with a break between the 1943 and 1944 general elections, he represented the three-seat Dublin Townships constituency carved out of the former Dublin County one and comprising the generally more affluent southside suburbs. In the political world, he was John A., not Jack.

Costello's legal expertise and experience in government made him a formidable contributor to Dáil debates. A slight, dapper man without an especially commanding presence, he imposed himself by a belligerence and fluency that were his hallmark as a barrister. One of his first interventions was to defend Eoin O'Duffy, the Commissioner of An Garda Síochána, with whom, as Attorney General, he had worked closely, and who was peremptorily dismissed in March 1933. Later that year, O'Duffy became his political leader when Cumann na nGaedheal joined with the Centre Party and O'Duffy's National Guard (the Blueshirts) to form the new Fine Gael party. Early in 1934, Costello acted for O'Duffy in the High Court and in the Supreme Court, securing his release when an attempt was made to charge him before a military tribunal.

On 28 February 1934, when opposing the Wearing of Uniforms Bill outlawing the wearing of the blue shirt, Costello told the Dáil, 'The Minister ... carefully refrained from drawing attention to the fact that the Blackshirts were victorious in Italy and the Hitler Shirts were victorious in Germany as, assuredly, in spite of this Bill and in spite of the Public Safety Act, the Blueshirts will be victorious in the Irish Free State.' Made before the full horrors of these Continental regimes were apparent, the remarks were symptomatic of Costello's love of a rhetorical flourish rather than any fascist leanings.

Proud to have helped to achieve the Statute of Westminster, one aspect of which was that the King had to act solely on the advice of the Irish government on Irish matters, Costello believed that the Free State should honour its undertaking in the founding Treaty to remain within the Commonwealth. Accordingly, he opposed in December 1936 de Valera's proposed Bill removing the King from the Constitution, describing it as 'a political monstrosity' that left it uncertain whether the state was a republic or in the Commonwealth. It dishonoured, he argued, obligations 'to those Dominions which helped the representatives of the Irish people to achieve their freedom in the Imperial Conferences'.

Costello was unimpressed by the Constitution proposed by de Valera's government and enacted by referendum in 1937, which did not declare a republic but provided for a president without making the incumbent the head of state and envisaged using the King for external purposes, such as signing treaties or credentials for Irish ambassadors. This practice, given effect by the External Relations Act, 1936, was enough for the British government to regard Éire (as the state was renamed in 1937) as still within the Commonwealth and for them to have the new monarch King George VI crowned as King of Ireland.

In these circumstances, and noting the absence of Irish delegates from Commonwealth conferences, Costello came to doubt if Irish membership of the Commonwealth still subsisted; he also came to believe that British acceptance of de Valera's actions undermining the Treaty settlement of 1921 released from their undertakings those who had pledged to observe and defend it. Listening to constituents on the canvass, he overheard one say, 'Sure that fellah Costello is only an ould Englishman'; this kind of reaction convinced him that Fine Gael lost support because it was regarded as pro-British.

Fine Gael supported de Valera's declaration of neutrality in the Second World War, which broke out in 1939. Costello joined in his party's call for a national government. When Fianna Fáil showed no interest in this, he felt free to make common cause with members of other parties in questioning the authoritarian use of the emergency powers that had been granted to government over a wide range of activities. This made future cooperation in government with such people less unthinkable, especially as hopes receded that Fine Gael would ever have enough support in the Dáil to form a government on its own.

However active Costello was in politics, the main focus of his life after 1932 was his legal practice. Many of his early reported cases were challenges to the government of one kind or another and even involved him, as in *The State (Ryan) v. Lennon*, in questioning the constitutionality of legislation allowing internment without trial that had been enacted while he was Attorney General. In that case, he formulated the argument adopted by Chief Justice Hugh Kennedy in his minority judgment in the Supreme Court that the principles of natural law could override the strict terms of the Constitution. In rebuilding a more general practice, Costello was supported by his UCD contemporary Arthur Cox, a leading solicitor, who briefed him regularly for such important clients as the Electricity Supply Board. In cases arising from industrial injuries in which he appeared, Costello was usually on the side of the workman rather than the insured employer. He was also briefed on behalf of trade unions; in 1935, he represented the Irish Transport and General Workers' Union in a successful action to prevent a British union of the same name from using it in Ireland.

He was counsel in cases of a political nature such as the referral to the Supreme Court of the School Attendance Bill 1942, where he was successful persuading the court that the Bill, limiting the right of parents to choose their children's school, infringed the rights of the family under the Constitution. He was now in the front rank at the Bar, second in reputation only to Cecil Lavery, whom he looked up to as a legal genius and always insisted was the outstanding barrister of his time. Costello was more a workhorse admired for his thoroughness and total commitment to clients, apparently unable to conceive that they might be unmeritorious or in the wrong. Although inclined to be peppery, he was esteemed by fellow barristers for his integrity and accessibility as well as acts of kindness, contributing to collections for needy colleagues or visiting sick ones in hospital.

His large practice did not take him away from his family of three sons and two daughters; his concentration was so good that he was able to work at home on his briefs in the evenings sitting with his wife in the midst of them. He made no secret of giving priority to his practice and the needs of his family over his political career. Costello may have been fortunate that he was not overly dependent on constituency work to maintain his political popularity in a largely middle-class constituency.

At the general election called by de Valera in January 1948, his Fianna Fáil party lost seats to the newly formed radical republican Clann na Poblachta party led by Seán MacBride and was deprived of its overall majority in the Dáil. Although the Fine Gael share of the vote fell to an all-time low under 20 per cent, leaving it with less than half the number of seats required to form a government on its own, it remained the second largest party. Costello, who topped the poll in his constituency, had told party colleagues that he had no intention of abandoning his practice to become a minister or attorney general. But the Labour Party leader, William Norton, who had admired Costello's work as counsel for workmen and for trade unions as well as his stances in the Dáil on issues affecting them, was insistent that Costello rather than Fine Gael leader Richard Mulcahy should be Taoiseach in any inter-party government.

MacBride, who had been apprehensive about the readiness of republicans to serve under Mulcahy because of his role repressing them in the Civil War in the early 1920s, then agreed to Costello, with whom he had formed a friendly relationship at the Bar, although his initial preference had been for Sir John Esmonde, a barrister who had defended republicans being prosecuted. Mulcahy agreed readily, and a reluctant Costello was persuaded by close friends, such as Arthur Cox, as well as party colleagues, that his agreement to serve as Taoiseach was necessary to the formation of an inter-party government. He relented, although genuinely fearful that he would not be a success.

Costello's government began well with the negotiation in June 1948 of a trade agreement with the British government improving access for Irish agricultural exports. The warm relations established during these negotiations were consolidated when Prime Minister Clement Attlee took his summer break in the west of Ireland. However, they did not outlast the declaration by Costello, while on a visit to Canada in September, that it was intended to repeal the External Relations Act 1936, under which, as noted, the King signed the credentials of Irish ambassadors and treaty-makers.

Costello's statement was made in response to a report in the *Sunday Independent* predicting the repeal. There seems to have been no prior formal government decision authorising this action, although most ministers favoured it and ratified it readily on Costello's return. There had also been no prior consultation with the British government. Freddie Boland, the senior diplomat in the Department of External Affairs, was disgusted by the slapdash way it had all been managed. 'Jack Costello', he recalled, 'had as much notion of diplomacy as I had of astrology.'

When questioned in Canada, Costello also confirmed that this meant leaving the Commonwealth. The option of retaining Commonwealth membership as a republic, an arrangement shortly to be adopted for India, was not explored on either side. Instead, the British decided merely to refrain from treating the new republic as a foreign state and joined with the Dominions of the Commonwealth in retaining existing arrangements relating to trade and immigration.

The legislation repealing the External Relations Act stated that the description of the state was the Republic of Ireland, and the government celebrated its coming into force on Easter Monday 1949 as an acknowledgement that the state established under the 1937 Constitution was a republic – the word 'republic' had been deliberately omitted from the Constitution itself.

To emphasise that it was done with the full support of Fine Gael and not just to satisfy Seán MacBride's Clann na Poblachta party, Costello piloted the Republic of Ireland Bill through the Oireachtas. He predicted that the removal of the last formal link with the British Crown would end a provocation to republicans and so take the gun out of Irish politics. Privately, he hoped that it would ensure that Fine Gael was no longer damaged electorally by being branded the pro-British party and would fare better when, as he hoped, politics focused on bread-and-butter issues.

The declaration of the Republic alienated those who had taken at face value the commitment of Fine Gael to keep Éire in the Commonwealth. This alienation was most marked among the former unionist, largely Protestant, community, and was compounded when Costello referred to the 'so-called reformation' at a meeting in Trinity College and apologised to the Irish people in the Dáil for describing as an Irish newspaper the *Irish Times*, which was then the organ of that community. An ardent Catholic, whose friends were drawn almost exclusively from within his own Catholic world, Costello had little rapport with Protestant Ireland, North or South.

The departure from the Commonwealth also alienated a previously sympathetic British government, largely because it was done without prior consultation. They responded by enacting, without prior consultation with the Irish government, the Ireland Act 1949, with a provision that Northern Ireland would not cease, without the approval of its parliament, to be part of the United Kingdom. Although this did no more than restate Britain's long-standing support for the right of Northern Ireland to opt to remain in the United Kingdom, it was enough to spark off an all-party anti-Partition campaign in the Republic.

On 10 May 1949, moving a motion in the Dáil condemning the Ireland Act, Costello remarked with the kind of rhetorical flourish in which he rejoiced, 'We can hit the British government in their prestige and in their pride and in their pocket.' The absurdity of the successor party of the one that had agreed to Partition in the 1920s now challenging its legitimacy escaped him.

Less controversial in a country proud of its wartime neutrality was the government's rejection early in 1949 of an invitation to join NATO (the North Atlantic Treaty Organization), giving as a reason for doing so the occupation of Northern Ireland by Britain, a NATO member. The hope that this would persuade the USA to press for a united Ireland was not realised. An offer to President Truman to enter a bilateral defence pact with the USA fell on deaf ears.

Thereafter, responding to advice from his son-in-law and trusted adviser Alexis FitzGerald that he should not upset the traditional constituency of the Fine Gael party and should speak only from a prepared script, Costello toned down his own utterances on Partition and allowed Seán MacBride to make the running on it, one facet to which was the 'sore-thumb' policy getting Irish officials attending international meetings to raise the issue at every opportunity.

More constructively, agreements were reached with the government of Northern Ireland for joint action in relation to Lough Foyle, the Erne fisheries and the Dublin–Belfast railway. Commenting on these at a Fine Gael Ard Fheis in February 1951, Costello said that they had 'given some grounds for the belief that friendly relations can do much to achieve eventual unity more certainly than threats of bloody warfare'.

Meanwhile, the economy had thrived. Agriculture revived; houses were built; social welfare increased; and hospital services, especially those for tuberculosis patients, improved. In a broadcast at the end of 1949, Costello announced that 'Ireland is now entering the most prosperous period in her history.' The prosperity was fuelled by Marshall Aid from the USA and a decision emanating from Costello's personal economic adviser, Patrick Lynch, to introduce a capital budget, so ensuring that the accepted practice of having a balanced budget did not prevent borrowing for capital purposes. The establishment of the Industrial Development Authority (IDA) to encourage industrial investment, and of Córas Tráchtála to promote exports, were the first moves away from policies of self-sufficiency that had held sway since 1932.

By his supportive attitude, Costello won the confidence of ministers from other parties as well as his own and was content not to interfere with them. The collegiate nature of the government, which accorded with the views Costello had expressed in the debates on the Constitution in 1937, was one cause of the long and meandering cabinet meetings that became a feature of his government. While some ministers showed little sense of collective responsibility when disagreeing publicly with others, Costello won credit for the very fact that he had confounded expectations by holding together such a diverse crew. Personal loyalty to him was a factor in this. Those close to him recognised that beneath a veneer of gruffness and despite a quick temper he was an exceptionally compassionate, generous and loyal man. James Everett, a Labour minister whom he had supported in 1950 through an embarrassing confrontation arising from the appointment of a political crony as Postmaster of Baltinglass, described him as a saint.

Costello's reluctance to interfere with ministers, together with a laxity of cabinet procedures, contributed to a crisis about a scheme for free maternity services promoted by the Clann na Poblachta Minister for Health, Noël Browne, whose work combating the tuberculosis epidemic had been widely acclaimed. In 1950, a proposal to provide free 'Mother and Child' services without any means test was opposed publicly by the medical profession and privately by Dublin's Archbishop John Charles McQuaid on behalf of the hierarchy.

Costello had established a good relationship with Browne, whom he supported through an earlier difficulty in the Dáil. He now tried to act as an intermediary with the doctors, assuring them that there would be no question of a general state-financed health service replacing private practice if they would accept a 'Mother and Child Scheme' that was not means-tested. Browne took exception to such discussions taking place behind his back and accused Costello of treachery.

In March 1951, apparently under the impression that he had resolved outstanding differences with Archbishop McQuaid, and having broken off negotiations with the medical profession, Browne moved to introduce a scheme that was not means-tested, relying on an unrevoked forgotten government decision of 1948 accepting this. He had not notified Costello in advance. On receipt of renewed representations from the hierarchy stating that the scheme would be contrary to Catholic teaching, Costello called a meeting of the government at which all the ministers except Browne agreed that, in compliance with the wishes of the hierarchy, the scheme would be means-tested. Browne indicated that he would have to consider what he would do. Some days later, he issued a bulletin announcing that he was pursuing a compromise scheme, based on insurance contributions, that had been suggested by the executive of the Congress of Trade Unions. At this point, he was directed to resign by his party leader, Seán MacBride, with whom he was in more general contention. Browne complied and then released the correspondence with the hierarchy and with Costello to the *Irish Times*.

In the subsequent debate in the Dáil, Costello took exception to Browne issuing his bulletin without consultation with his cabinet colleagues and said that he would have asked for Browne's resignation if MacBride had not done so. Costello defended the stance taken by the government on the basis that he and his colleagues felt bound to accept the teaching of the bishops in matters of faith and morals. It was an attitude to be expected of a genuinely pious Catholic who, upon taking office, had led the government in sending a message to the Pope reposing themselves at his feet. But it needs to be set in the context that Costello's stance in relation to the intervention of the hierarchy evoked no dissent from other political leaders and Browne himself stated that as a Catholic he, too, felt bound by the ruling of the bishops. Costello was faulted by Browne in his resignation speech only for failing to convey his views to the bishops and to keep him informed of their reaction and that of his ministerial colleagues – charges that Costello refuted quite convincingly. Significantly, a non-means-tested scheme was never enacted subsequently.

Costello did not ask MacBride to nominate another minister in Browne's place but insisted on taking over the Department of Health himself. He blamed civil servants in the Department for fomenting the confrontation that had led to Browne's resignation and threatened stern action against them. Distrustful of their bias against the medical profession and in favour of socialised medicine, he insisted that the medical staff, who had been rather sidelined in the Department, should take over responsibility for negotiating with their fellow doctors to resolve the differences that had occurred. A professional man himself, Costello had an instinctive fellow-feeling for the medical profession and its desire to preserve its independence from state control. In the debate following Browne's resignation, he had paid tribute to the role of the profession in the whole negotiation when they had opposed the absence of a means test. That he had ever gone along with Browne's proposals and, at one point, personally made a case to the doctors to accept them, is testimony to how he saw his role in government as being a chairman rather than a chief.

The government's majority in the Dáil was now under pressure. Prone to reward personal rather than party allegiance, Costello appointed Charles Casey, a barrister who had helped him when he returned to the Bar in 1932, to succeed Cecil Lavery as Attorney General in preference to Sir John Esmonde, a long-standing member of the Fine Gael party in the Dáil. Esmonde, a survivor from the Centre Party, left Fine Gael and later resigned from the Dáil. Some previously supportive independents withdrew support. In May 1951, threatened with defeat in the Dáil on the agricultural estimates, Costello called a general election.

One of the last acts passed before the dissolution of the Oireachtas established an Arts Council, so realising what Costello described as 'a personal ambition going back many years'. He was an assiduous collector of paintings by Irish artists and had long been conscious that the neglect of design inhibited the competitiveness of Irish goods. The arts, bridge and golf (whether his regular Sunday fourball at Portmarnock Golf Club, of which he was captain in 1947, or an occasional round at Milltown Golf Club) were his interests outside politics, the law and his family.

Later focus on the manner in which he mismanaged the departure from the Commonwealth and succumbed to clerical pressure over Noël Browne's Mother and Child Scheme has obscured the high regard in which Costello was held after three years in office. The 1951 general election was the first in the history of the state not fought primarily on the national issue, which pleased Costello and seemed to some to vindicate his decision to sever the former link with the Commonwealth. The Fine Gael share of the national vote increased from under 20 per cent to almost 26 per cent, and Costello himself topped the poll in his constituency. Although other parties that had participated in his government lost ground, it looked as if Costello would be re-elected as Taoiseach when the Dáil assembled. In the event, he was defeated only because the Ceann Chomhairle resigned to vote with Fianna Fáil against him as did Noël Browne and fellow defectors from Clann na Poblachta. Éamon de Valera became Taoiseach again. Costello became leader of the opposition, making him the effective leader of Fine Gael, although Mulcahy retained his position as head of the party outside the Oireachtas.

Costello, who had returned to a busy practice at the Bar, was not all that active in opposition, but this mattered less because de Valera, too, was often absent. As it turned out, the country incurred its largest ever balance-of-payments deficit in 1951, and in early 1952 Fianna Fáil's Minister for Finance was compelled to bring in a harsh budget. The government lost popularity so completely that Costello assumed the standing of Taoiseach-in-waiting. In these circumstances, the offer to him by de Valera of a Supreme Court judgeship in 1953 was seen as a political stroke and rejected out of hand.

In that year, Costello was retained by Arthur Cox to act for Winston Churchill in a threatened libel action in the Irish courts arising out of his war memoirs. Former British Attorney General Sir Hartley Shawcross, who was advising Churchill informally, wrote to him having researched the merits of Irish barristers who might represent him: 'Costello is said to occupy easily the leading position at the Irish Bar and he impressed me as being undoubtedly a fighter.' However, Costello did not have to fight in this case as Shawcross negotiated a settlement directly with the prospective plaintiff, General Dorman O'Gowan, providing for the insertion in future editions of the memoirs of a footnote exculpating Dorman O'Gowan from any blame for military reverses suffered in the Desert War.

Costello became Taoiseach again in a coalition following a general election in June 1954 where the Fine Gael share of the national poll rose to 32 per cent, its highest since 1938. Costello polled so well in his Dublin South-East constituency that another Fine Gael deputy was elected on his surplus, so unseating Noël Browne, who had now joined Fianna Fáil. This time, Costello was in command of the distribution of portfolios among his own party and appointed some able ministers from a younger generation, notably Gerard Sweetman, Liam Cosgrave and Tom O'Higgins. Costello was more assertive as head of government in directing his ministers than he had been in his first term.

The government held its own initially. As Minister for Health, Tom O'Higgins defused the long-running dispute with the doctors over extended free health services by agreeing that the Mother and Child Scheme would be means-tested; he also promoted a state-sponsored insurance scheme that would ensure that middle-income patients were able to pay for private health care. Useful measures of law reform, a pet project of Costello's, were initiated or enacted.

In 1955, Ireland was admitted to the United Nations (UN). Costello made it clear that the Irish stance there would be pro-Western and anti-Communist. However, even in the wake of a triumphant visit to the USA, when he was feted by President Eisenhower, Costello turned a deaf ear to suggestions that his government should compromise Irish neutrality by allowing American military aircraft to use Shannon as a stopover.

As an uncompromising opponent of Communism, Costello was receptive to representations from Archbishop McQuaid opposing a visit of a soccer team from Communist Yugoslavia in October 1955; acting on the government's advice, President Seán T. O'Kelly did not attend their match. However, Costello showed himself capable of facing down the hierarchy when he rejected pressure from them to exclude Trinity College from participation in a proposed agricultural institute. He disregarded McQuaid's views in appointing the writer Seán Ó Faoláin as Chairman of the Arts Council. 'While I cannot expect Your Grace's blessing', Costello wrote to the Archbishop, 'I feel sure that I will have your prayers.'

Costello was prevented by opposition from the Labour leader, Tánaiste William Norton, from giving effect to Fine Gael plans to cut food subsidies and to facilitate foreign investment. As 1955 drew to a close, a record balance-of-payments deficit emerged, as a result of which finance minister Gerard Sweetman felt compelled to cut back government expenditure, raise taxes and impose import levies. Unemployment and emigration soared; national morale plummeted.

In April 1956, Costello suffered a severe personal blow when his devoted wife died quite suddenly. He battled on; in September, sensing serious unrest among supporters, he overruled Sweetman and adopted a programme for recovery based on export-led expansion, to be achieved by introducing export tax relief and shifting public investment away from housing and hospitals to productive purposes. It was received enthusiastically by deputies of all parties supporting the government, including Clann na Poblachta.

While occasionally reiterating his views on the injustice of Partition, Costello was noticeably less hard-line on the issue than during his first term; the sore-thumb policy of raising the issue abroad was abandoned. Then, in November 1956, the IRA launched a series of attacks across the Border, shattering Costello's hopes that he had taken the gun out of Irish politics. While his government called in the army to assist police in apprehending IRA activists, Costello had no real stomach to be involved in more drastic action against them; he was on record stating that he would never again take any part in a government that had to enforce law by extrajudicial processes.

This turn of events stifled the political boost Costello had got from the acceptance of his new economic strategy; on 3 December 1956, he wrote to Thomas Bodkin, whom he had just failed to entice back from England to head the Arts Council before offering the post to Seán Ó Faoláin: 'I have had so many frustrating disappointments that one more does not make any difference.' He was losing heart.

Worse was to follow. On the first day of 1957, two IRA men were killed in a border raid, and crowds turned out to mourn them. Responding to this and to pressure from the British government, Costello not only condemned the IRA violence but spelt out the impossibility of forcing unwilling unionists into the Republic. He focused on discrimination

Catholics suffered in Northern Ireland rather than Partition itself. It was a new emphasis, but, coming in the wake of so much anti-Partition rhetoric, it did not carry conviction as representing an alternative policy based on acceptance of Partition as long as a majority in Northern Ireland desired it.

The National Executive of Clann na Poblachta was unwilling to support a government that imprisoned republicans, even as a result of ordinary criminal prosecutions. At the end of January 1957, it directed the party leader Seán MacBride, against his own inclination, to withdraw the support hitherto pledged to the government and to put down in the Dáil a motion of no confidence. This action, which took Costello by surprise, eroded the government's committed parliamentary majority but would not necessarily have led to its defeat. Yet he called a general election, disregarding, in so doing, the advice of Fine Gael ministers such as James Dillon and Tom O'Higgins who wanted to contest the vote in the Dáil rather than appear to be fleeing from office.

At the general election held on 5 March 1957, Fianna Fáil won a record overall majority. Fine Gael suffered heavy losses, albeit that their share of the national vote had not fallen below its 1951 level. In Dublin South-East, Costello still topped the poll, but his share of the vote was much reduced. Fine Gael were demoralised in the wake of their crushing defeat as de Valera established himself as the man most able and willing to take on the IRA introducing internment without trial. Fine Gael got little credit when Fianna Fáil, under the influence of civil servant T. K. Whitaker, adopted policies close to what Costello had planned in October 1956. The only issue on which Costello succeeded in working up a head of steam was opposition to the action of Foreign Minister Frank Aiken breaking ranks with the USA to vote for the discussion of the admission of Communist China to the UN.

It did not help that Costello, who was rebuilding his practice at the Bar, now attended the Dáil only spasmodically. This led to dissatisfaction being voiced privately in his party. It was not quietened by a successful campaign in 1959 to defeat in a referendum a Fianna Fáil proposal to abolish proportional representation. When, at the end of 1959, Mulcahy announced his retirement as leader of Fine Gael, there was no longer any reason to have different leaders for the party and the parliamentary party. Most of the latter were against Costello becoming leader unless he was prepared to serve full-time and so take on the new Taoiseach, Seán Lemass, who was more active in the Dáil than de Valera had been.

It came to Costello as what he described as a hurtful shock. 'I tried', he wrote to a priest friend, Dr Patrick O'Carroll, 'not always with success to take it as God meant it to be taken by me.' He decided to stand down rather than give up his practice or split the party by standing for the leadership. A factor in his decision may have been the need to earn money again to meet the medical expenses of his eldest son, Wilfie, the deterioration of whose mental health was such that he was now permanently hospitalised.

James Dillon succeeded as leader of Fine Gael. He and his chief supporter, Gerard Sweetman, were committed to getting Fine Gael into government on its own. Dillon, a powerful orator, had charisma even if he attracted more hostility than Costello. In the 1961 general election, Fine Gael clawed back the losses suffered in 1957, depriving Fianna Fáil under Lemass of an overall majority in the Dáil. However, neither Fine Gael nor Labour had an appetite for coalition, and Lemass was able to soldier on with the support of independents.

Costello derided as futile waiting for Fine Gael to overtake Fianna Fáil and supported those (now led by his son Declan) who advocated policies that would make Fine Gael a natural ally for Labour. When, on finding his policies rejected by the front bench of the party, Declan Costello was minded to join the Labour Party, his father persuaded him first to put the matter before the Fine Gael parliamentary party. This led to the adoption by the party of the 'Just Society' document in advance of the 1965 general election. However, the Labour Party was still bent on going it alone in the hope that the two major parties would be driven together, allowing Labour to emerge as the main opposition. Fewer votes transferred between it and Fine Gael. Although Fine Gael increased its share of the national vote, it won no extra seats. Fianna Fáil gained two seats, so making its government secure. One of these gains was in Dublin South-East, where, although Costello topped the poll, the Fine Gael share of the vote was much reduced and the second Fianna Fáil candidate was able to unseat Noël Browne.

On the back benches, Costello felt free to depart from the party line on occasion, most famously when he dissented somewhat from their opposition to the Succession Bill 1964 giving a surviving spouse an automatic right to one-third of the estate of the deceased. His proposals improving the Bill in several respects on its passage through the Dáil were lauded on all sides.

His high standing within Fine Gael as the person who had revived its fortunes when it faced terminal decline endured. In 1966, he was suggested as a possible candidate at the Presidential election to oppose Éamon de Valera, who, at the age of 83, was seeking a second term. However, at a meeting of the front bench of the parliamentary party, a proposal that Costello should stand was quickly withdrawn when Gerard Sweetman asked how, on the fiftieth anniversary of Easter Week, the party could oppose the oldest surviving officer of the Rising with a man who had been old enough to have fought in the Rising and had not done so. Costello continued to contribute usefully to Dáil debates right up to the 1969 general election when he stood down as his party's candidate in Dublin South-East in favour of future Taoiseach Garret FitzGerald.

Although universally respected, Costello could never match the personal charisma and public appeal of Éamon de Valera, the political opponent whom he had to take on. He had not the state-building legacy of W. T. Cosgrave nor, unlike de Valera and Seán Lemass, could he claim to have led the country in a new direction. His major initiative, the declaration of the Republic and the withdrawal from the Commonwealth, turned out to make little difference in practice. He failed to direct his party to a more constructive policy on Northern Ireland focused on removing discrimination against Catholics rather than reunification of the island.

His major legacy, apart from some tentative initiatives to abandon misguided policies of economic self-sufficiency, was to have provided for two three-year periods stable government untouched by corruption. He revived his own party by moderating its conservative and less nationalist image, so ensuring that there was an alternative government to Fianna Fáil and that it was led by Fine Gael. As a result, new life was breathed into Irish democracy, the excesses of unbroken one-party government curtailed and a left–right or urban–rural polarisation of Irish politics avoided.

Costello remained busy at the Bar into his eighties, a purposeful figure bustling around the Law Library or poring intently over papers at his desk with a cigarette in his mouth, flicking a propelling pencil in the air as he read. Overall, his practice became more concentrated on personal injuries actions, the major form of litigation at the time, his chosen role in which was to fight cases in court when those briefed with him had failed to reach a settlement. He was effective in persuading juries who decided such cases, always addressing them as one of their own. He was not much involved in the ground-breaking constitutional litigation of that era. He viewed with astringency the active role then espoused by the Supreme Court; asked to comment by Brian Walsh, its most creative judge, on the bearing of one of his constitutional judgments on the argument being made by Costello in a case, he remarked bluntly, 'the longer I remain in the profession, the more I realise that nothing is certain, especially in this court'. In his last speech in the Dáil, in April 1969, criticising a rather illiberal Criminal Justice Bill, he proclaimed his belief that 'the greatest safeguard of citizens' liberties is this house, not the courts'.

The contentment of Costello's later life was marred by the death in 1971 of his daughter Grace, who was married to solicitor Alexis FitzGerald, to whom Costello was personally close, as he was to his other daughter Eavan's barrister husband, Ralph Sutton. Even so, neither man ever called him anything but 'Mr Costello'. His youngest son, John, was a successful architect in Dublin. There were 19 grandchildren to whom Costello never failed to send a gift for their birthdays.

In company with Éamon de Valera, Costello was granted the Freedom of the City of Dublin in 1975. When de Valera died later that year, Costello delivered himself of a frank assessment which, while not generally debunking, contained the statement that de Valera had left behind nothing of permanent value – a remark that gave offence. This was symptomatic of a compulsive directness rather than any malice, for, unlike many of his Fine Gael colleagues, Costello felt little or no personal hostility towards de Valera and was deeply appreciative of the courtesy and kindness de Valera had shown towards him at the time of his wife's death.

Costello was diagnosed with lung cancer soon afterwards and died at home on 5 January 1976. A state funeral was declined by his family. Whether or not this was in accordance with his own wishes, it was consistent with his view of himself more as a private man who had played a public role when called upon to do so rather than a career politician. It was also consistent with a disinclination ever to place himself on a pedestal. As was well said by the future Chief Justice Tom Finlay, a devoted younger colleague at the Bar and in the Dáil, when writing to Costello on his retirement from politics: 'You finally destroyed the myth, that great men must be aloof and unapproachable.' This may have been because Costello did not see himself as a great man nor aspire to be one; what he asked of himself was to be a good hard-working man, living a dutiful and honourable life among his own people; in that he did not fail.

Costello was buried in Deansgrange Cemetery beside his wife after Requiem Mass at his parish church in Donnybrook, where he had attended Mass daily for many years.

5

Seán Lemass

1959–66

Bryce Evans

Full name: Seán Francis Lemass
Date of birth: 15 July 1899
Place of birth: Ballybrack, Dublin
Date of death: 11 May 1971
Site of grave: Deansgrange Cemetery, Dublin
Education: O'Connell School, Dublin
Married to: Kathleen Hughes (m. 1924)
Children: Maureen, Noel, Peggy and Sheila
Assumed office: 23 June 1959
Date of resignation: 10 November 1966
Length of tenure: Seven years, four months, 17 days
Quotation: 'The historical task of this generation, as I see it, is to consolidate the economic foundations of our political independence.'

On 28 January 1916, Seán Lemass – the man generally acknowledged as the architect of modern Ireland and the nation's greatest ever Taoiseach – shot dead his 19-month-old brother, Herbert. The 16-year-old Irish Volunteer had been playing with a loaded revolver in the front room of the family home and accidentally discharged it into his baby sibling's head.

When we discussed this on the *Irish Taoiseach* podcast, Iain Dale asked, 'How would you ever get over something like that?' The answer it seems, for the young Lemass, was to throw himself headlong into the national struggle. Less than three months after killing Herbert, Lemass was taking potshots at the British Army from atop the roof of the General Post Office (GPO).

The revolutionary period in which Lemass came of age and that shaped him was one of violent and bitter turbulence that would later claim the life of another brother, his beloved Noel. It would be simplistic, therefore, to reduce his later life trajectory to the one horrific moment of Herbert's death. And yet it arguably imbued Lemass with a restless desire to atone – not in an overtly Catholic sense but in service to the nation. In the revolutionary period, this meant taking up arms in pursuit of the republican ideal. In the post-revolutionary period, this would take the form of a workaholic commitment to national regeneration exemplified by his responsibility for the two great economic transitions of independent Ireland in the 20th century: the construction and later dismantling of national protectionism. He remains, to quote another of his biographers, an 'enigmatic patriot'.

Whereas his dashing older brother Noel was shot in the hand, Lemass would survive the Easter Rising uninjured. In contrast to contemporaries who harped on endlessly about the derring-do of the struggle, Lemass rarely discussed his activities between 1916 and 1923. Interviewed, aged 70, about his memories of Easter Week, there was a humility to his recollections. 'I fired a few shots from the GPO, but whether they hit anybody I don't know.' The whole affair, he said, left him exhausted and hungry. Was it true that he had helped to carry the wounded James Connolly from the burning building? Yes, he had, but removing Connolly from the smouldering wreck of the post office was 'so slow and so frequently interrupted that almost everyone in the GPO helped in it at some stage'. There was a lingering boyish tinge, too, to his admiration for Patrick Pearse, still ardent 50 years later – 'very impressive ... his bearing and solemnity ... his wonderful oratory ... terribly calm, very much in control of himself' – and in his own readiness to give his life for 'the reawakening'.

Lemass was a laconic character, but the heady mood of Greek tragedy is unmistakeable in these reminiscences. His very involvement in the Rising bore a certain hubris. While walking in the Dublin Mountains just prior to the Rising, the two eldest Lemass brothers had come across Eoin MacNeill, Chief of Staff of the Irish Volunteers, who had issued the countermanding order cancelling the planned mobilisation of the Irish Volunteers and who informed them of developments, warning Noel and Seán off the entire doomed enterprise. They nodded and listened sympathetically like the good middle-class boys they were, but then, when out of sight of MacNeill, hurriedly scrambled down the mountainside and leapt onto the next tram into town to join the scrap.

Fitting the dramatic theme, after being released home post-Rising thanks to his youth and peripheral status, Lemass's next move was to co-found an acting troupe. All very removed from the sober businessman persona of later life, and all contrary to the telos of Lemass, 'the supreme pragmatist' underlying much of the biographical literature, which tends to write off the radical republican streak in the man as mere youthful quixotism.

The verdict of 'supreme pragmatist' becomes even harder to sustain when we come to Lemass's involvement, aged 21, in the execution of a one-legged British courts-martial officer as part of the IRA Dublin Brigade's Bloody Sunday killings and his later arrest and detention. Harder still when, just short of his 23rd birthday, he reacted to the electorate's endorsement of the Anglo-Irish Treaty by holing himself up in the Four Courts with the recalcitrant anti-Treaty IRA. By 1925, aged 26 and still refusing to recognise the legitimacy of the Irish Free State, Lemass had even ascended to the titular leadership of the IRA as Minister for Defence in Éamon de Valera's republican 'ghost government'.

Rather than youthful folly or marginal idealism, Lemass's early military and political career points to a consistent republicanism inherited, it is fair to speculate, more from a Fenian tradition on his mother's side than from the careful paternal petit-bourgeois Parnellism of his father, hatter John Lemass. His father's outfitters on Capel Street in Dublin's city centre provided a relatively comfortable upbringing for Seán (Jack) and his six siblings. While the nearby slums were some of the most unsanitary in Europe, when his mother Frances gave birth to him it was in the summer house in South County Dublin in the company of her own nurse. The family was also well-off enough to employ a domestic servant. Seán, a good student, was educated by the Christian Brothers. But as he became an adolescent, the swell of popular unrest was never far from the Lemasses' front door, whether the great Dublin Lockout of 1913 or the Bachelor's Walk Massacre of 1914, and in January 1915 he joined the Irish Volunteers.

Like de Valera, the man whose political lead he would follow for the best part of 40 years, Lemass inherited a 'funny name' from his father. Although since converted to Catholicism, the Lemasses were originally French Protestant Huguenots, and Seán's dark complexion would earn him the derisive nickname 'the Jewman'. The closeness to de Valera has also been downplayed by a historiography bent on juxtaposing Lemass, supposedly the frustrated liberal, with de Valerite medievalism; in reality, the political vision was much closer, particularly in the early years.

Lemass ought to have spent the Rising under the command of de Valera at Boland's Bakery, where his battalion was posted and where he would have served as personal aide. Instead, his comradeship with Dev would develop in the years following republican defeat in the Civil War (1922–3). Where Lemass distinguished himself, and where his early utility to de Valera lay, was in his organisational capabilities.

Unlike Dev, Lemass was not an inspirational orator. Elected as Sinn Féin TD for Dublin South in 1924, he refused to take his seat. As this principled abstentionism demonstrated, there was nothing lacking in his republican credentials: he had been 'out in '16' and the War of Independence; equally significant to his early political career was his status as the brother of republican martyr Noel Lemass (who was abducted and butchered by the Free State Army Intelligence Department in July 1923). And yet he lacked political charisma. He more than compensated for this, however, with an organisational nous and drive. As the anti-Treaty republican movement fragmented post-Civil War, it was Lemass who travelled tirelessly the length and breadth of the new state, moulding de Valera's supporters into what would become 20th-century Ireland's most effective political machine: Fianna Fáil, the Warriors of Destiny. And, at 11 a.m. on 11 August 1927, Lemass, as party whip, was among the first to sign the Dáil book binding deputies to the hated Oath of Allegiance to the British Crown as Fianna Fáil finally took their seats and set about reshaping the Irish political landscape.

As a constitutional radical, Lemass was keen to combat the charge from the Cumann na nGaedheal government that Fianna Fáil stood only for 'an idealist's paradise'. Instead, he insisted, the party would deliver 'real, concrete advantages for the common people'. As a Dubliner, Lemass stood apart from his fellow top brass in the party, most of whom came from backgrounds more in keeping with the pervasive ruralist streak in Irish political culture at the time. He was awarded the Industry and Commerce brief over Seán MacEntee, signalling the start of a rivalry that would last for decades to come. Tariff protection for Irish industry – a staple of nationalist economic policy for well over a century – would remedy emigration, it was assumed.

Often, political tribalism and populist politicking trumped pragmatism. Lemass, who would later become synonymous with big state-driven development, opposed the Shannon Hydroelectric Scheme, citing its cost. On the other hand, he could appear positively Keynesian, arguing for higher taxation and state spending to combat poverty and inequality. He remained critical of the state security apparatus and famously, in 1928, described Fianna Fáil as only 'slightly constitutional', but his early leftism was increasingly tempered by a growing social conservatism as Fianna Fáil ditched the anti-hierarchy radicalism and pursued a quiet but firm rapprochement with the Church. There remained an impatient and illiberal disdain for democracy which amounted to more than just rhetoric and which was further influenced by the political turmoil following the Wall Street Crash of 1929. From opposition, the outline of government minister was starting to form, his ministerial style – restless, brusque, relentless – beginning to take shape.

When Fianna Fáil came to power in 1932, the party's appeal was based around more meaningful sovereignty, self-sufficiency, industrial development and better employment opportunities. Economic protectionism would cure many of the historical ills inflicted upon Ireland-as-colony. Lemass, like de Valera, was motivated by a genuinely held historical mission of national regeneration. Against the backdrop of global depression and an economic war with Britain, still the largest export market, 'drastic action' was needed in the economic sphere, and there was no room for laissez-faireism.

Swiftly, Lemass's Department of Industry and Commerce set about centralising many economic functions. A consistent aim was the ending of economic dependence on the old colonial power, and Lemass did, presciently, sketch out some ideas that resemble aspects of future European integration as a means to circumvent the nagging persistence of reliance on the British market.

He professed a rather high-handed disdain for *aboulia*, or indolence, in the Irish national character. In a drive to spearhead national development, it is understandable that he was broadly motivated by a post-colonial desire to eliminate any vestiges of a servile mentality and to further foster a national (predominately Catholic) business class alongside older (largely Protestant) capital. It was increasingly evident, too, and to the chagrin of some of his cabinet colleagues, that Lemass's centralising, crusading, developmentalist tendencies were driving Industry and Commerce's growing ascendancy over the Department of Finance. Feathers were ruffled, and accusations of patronage inevitably arose. Lemass was frequently snapped opening factories up and down the country, factories protected by his tariff walls but often churning out inferior high-priced products. In 1937, Lemass defended his industrial policy in the following terms:

> Industrial progress has been so rapid in the last few years that mistakes were nearly inevitable, but I do not admit that they were either numerous or serious. During that time, I acted on the principle that the only way

to avert mistakes was to do nothing. As I did not intend to do nothing, I discounted the mistakes in advance.

Few quotes encapsulate Lemass so neatly: the restless patriotic desire to forge ahead, the vanguardism and self-belief, the focus – albeit patrician – on delivering for the common good of the nation. What it also betrays is the zero-sum mentality of Lemass the avid poker player and racegoer, and the pitfalls of a gambler's impatience whereby to do something mistakenly, even rashly, is better than doing nothing at all. By the time he became Taoiseach, these character traits had, thankfully, diminished. While Lemass's energy and vision in the 1930s was enviable, then, there were also strategic gaps: the failure to establish a viable national shipping line, the failure to properly develop the road network, the failure to establish fertiliser plants to aid the agrarian economy. With the coming of the Second World War, these problems would be thrown into sharp relief.

As a minister, Lemass was doggedly devoted to his brief. Questions of social or foreign policy were largely left to Dev. Every cabinet minister was encouraged to send in suggested amendments to de Valera's 1937 Constitution; Lemass's were very few and suggest moral values which were more Victorian than revolutionary. Lemass has been characterised by some historians as agnostic, or even privately atheistic, but publicly he was anything but, and privately he was a member of the Knights of Columbanus, retaining close links to the hierarchy. In 1939, he praised the Constitution as 'possibly the first attempt to translate into practical law the principles of social justice as laid down by Pope Leo XIII'.

The line was drawn at church interference not in the secular realm per se but on any matter that threatened his authority. He was capable of standing up to the formidable Catholic–conservative bloc in Irish society at the time, but only when its calls for the vocational organisation of society – which urged decentralisation in certain realms – encroached on his purview.

The restless moderniser was responsible for some notable successes.

Aviation is one such example. In 1936, he approved the use of Foynes as a base for flying boats, and in 1938, he gave the go-ahead for the construction of Dublin Airport. Something of a micro-manager in certain fields, elsewhere he was happy to let civil-service lieutenants like John Leydon lead. Relinquishing control did not come easy, but it was a tendency that improved with age and one which was most visible in his style as Taoiseach. He recognised the importance of turf as fuel, and industrial employment and wages grew, even if high levels of emigration persisted.

Lemass was sceptical about the banking sector if it did not serve the common good, yet his reformist agenda was repeatedly vetoed by the Department of Finance. He has been described in this phase of his career as a 'quasi-socialist', and flashes of that caricature are certainly apparent. On labour relations, he was responsible for progressive reforms establishing a basic welfare safety net such as unemployment assistance, children's allowance and the 1939 law guaranteeing all workers a week's paid holiday a year.

Like many of his fellow revolutionaries, Lemass was not a liberal in the modern sense of the word. In an effort to combat unemployment and emigration, he was an enthusiastic champion of labour camps, large-scale public works and the removal of 'surplus population' from the land. The latter conviction chafed most noticeably against de Valeran agrarianism and evoked uncomfortable memories of 19th-century evictions. He believed in order, stability, unity and, in governmental terms, ministerial prerogative. These were qualities that were arguably best suited to the exigencies of war. Although neutral, Ireland was not spared the privations of war, and Lemass would take on extraordinarily wide-ranging powers when the Emergency was declared in 1939.

With the coming of the Emergency, Lemass was made Minister for Supplies and assumed economic powers that were nothing short of dictatorial. The straitened wartime supply situation should be stressed: starvation was a tangible possibility for a non-aligned nation such as Ireland as normal trading conditions disappeared and the war at sea intensified. Consequently, as one historian has stated, he became 'economic overlord' of independent Ireland. Lemass's Ministry of Supplies was distinguished not only by its infectious buzz of efficiency but also by its expansionist desire to subsume other departments.

From his top-floor office in the brand-new art-deco department building on Kildare Street, Lemass busied himself with effectively running the country as the bureaucracy beneath him swelled. The most potent symbol of Lemass's new-found power was the ministry's inspectorate, the new policemen of the domestic economy and enemies of the booming black market.

Yet the failure to establish a merchant marine pre-war would complicate the supply situation. In the opening stages of the conflict, Lemass enjoyed cordial relations with Anthony Eden, Neville Chamberlain's Secretary of State for Dominion Affairs, but the British attitude was to harden dramatically when Winston Churchill took over as British Prime Minister in 1940 and subsequently subjected neutral Ireland to renewed economic warfare in an attempt to get the country onside.

In a dramatic escalation of the supply shortage, petrol pumps across the state ran dry between Christmas and New Year 1940/1. Lemass, wrong-footed, hastily founded Irish Shipping Ltd in 1941, but better planning and procurement in the pre-war period would have secured greater material rewards for the Irish public. As the war progressed, Lemass and his team were frequently involved in fraught barter arrangements with the British as the Irish economy limped through the crisis. Lemass, a teetotaller, possessed a rare trump card in supplies of Guinness, which he withheld from export in 1942, forcing Britain to release much-needed stocks of wheat, coal and agricultural machinery.

Domestically, during the Emergency years, Lemass came to personify an overbearing bureaucracy that bore down disproportionately on both ordinary business people and the common man. In his defence, the war against the gombeen and the spiv had to be fought in order to ensure fair shares during hard times. Nonetheless, the all-too-late introduction of a comprehensive rationing system, coupled with the mistaken belief that the public would adhere to maximum price orders in the form of ministerial fiats, compounded a difficult situation.

It was during the Emergency that Lemass really earned the sobriquet 'democratic dictator' given to him later by political journalist Bruce Arnold. In a long memorandum on full employment, he rued democracy itself for its negative effect on long-term planning. His penchant for camp labour intensified. He did not feel in the least sentimental or awkward about the eviction and dispossession of farmers considered unproductive, insisting they must be 'eliminated'. And yet his desire for 'regulation and control' did not extend to Archbishop of Dublin John Charles McQuaid who was permitted a remarkably indulgent personal allowance of 51 gallons of petrol per month at a time in which private motorists were restricted to a gallon per month, a decision that raised the eyebrows of his faithful subordinate John Leydon and that jars with other accounts of Lemass's near-puritanical adherence to his own rules.

The Emergency would prove not only the acid test of Irish Independence but also a watershed in Lemass's career. To his great credit, he had overseen Ireland's material survival amidst a world conflict in which 20 million people died of starvation. It would prove the high point of central state intervention in Ireland, surpassing the controls introduced during the COVID-19 pandemic of 2020–3. It provided an opportunity for Lemass to unleash strong central government in order to counter what he called the 'fissiparous tendencies' of the Irish public. At the same time, the malodour of quasi-authoritarianism had crept in and alienated Fianna Fáil's natural constituency – the so-called plain people of Ireland – who would vote out Lemass & Co. in the 1948 general election.

The loss of ministerial power after 16 years would witness Lemass turning the screw within the party, imposing greater discipline to the party hierarchy and the whip. His time in opposition between 1948 and 1951 saw him take on the reins of the *Irish Press* newspaper and launch ad hominem attacks on political rivals under the nom de plume 'Dáil Reporter'. He engaged in the sort of red-baiting that Fianna Fáil had suffered in the run-up to the 1932 election. Although bitchy, Lemass's accusations of Communist sympathies seem to have been born from a growing conviction that, in the unfolding Cold War between East and

West, Ireland would be placed firmly in the latter camp and that neutrality had its limits. He also redoubled his calls for a western European economic community.

Lemass's mounting revisionism around neutrality was suggestive of the fact that cracks were gradually yet tellingly starting to appear in his long-standing fidelity to de Valera. Lemass – or, rather, 'Dáil Reporter' – welcomed Taoiseach John A. Costello's declaration of the Republic in 1948 as a rationalisation of the constitutional position. This clashed with Dev's opposition to the legislation, which he saw as detrimental to attempts to end Partition. Publicly, though, he toed the line. There was no suggestion of any leadership challenge, and, in any case, Lemass found himself embroiled in damaging corruption allegations (resolved in his favour in 1949 following a tribunal).

Viewed with hindsight, Lemass's turn towards modernisation and the Western mainstream was well under way, but for a man later associated with catapulting Ireland towards capitalist modernity and foreign direct investment, Lemass could prove frustratingly tribalistic. He was lukewarm about Ireland joining the International Monetary Fund (IMF) in 1947, and in 1950 was trenchant in his criticism of the foundation of the Industrial Development Authority (IDA), a semi-state body composed of industry experts whose remit was to research export markets and assess the health of the nation's trade.

This raises the question of his political identity and direction at this difficult stage of his career. The 'shift to the right' (i.e. away from centralised state interventionism and towards the free market) was not pronounced by this stage, or was at least still in development, exemplified by the fact that in the same year Lemass, mischievously, declared himself in favour of 'full socialism' over the 'cock-eyed socialism' of the coalition government.

In 1951, Fianna Fáil's return to power was marred by the first episode of serious ill health Lemass would experience when surgery on his gall bladder put him out of action for several months. At turns, he appeared progressive and receptive to change – for example, in striking up relations with Northern Ireland's Minister for Commerce – a harbinger of things to come when, as Taoiseach, relations with the Northern statelet would markedly improve.

However, we must be careful in reading too much into the 'turn' towards a more liberal Lemass taking hold in this period: in 1952, he declared himself against equal pay for women, which might be the case in 'the United States or Scandinavia' but which, in Ireland, was 'contrary to our way of life'. The mature Lemass was a self-confessed 'creature of habit', inclining towards the familiar and the reassuring. He never had much time for the hackneyed staples of Gaelic identity – the round towers and wolfhounds, even the language – but he opposed attempts to make Irish non-compulsory in schools. He conformed in some ways to his political rival Kevin O'Higgins's remark on how the Irish rebels of the 1920s were 'the most conservative-minded revolutionaries in history'. Although he believed 'progress once it is properly started must accelerate all the time', believing this to be a 'law of life just as scientific invention', he also enjoyed his pipe, his slippers and the comforts of home life.

Where it mattered most, however, Lemass's thinking was clearly undergoing a big change. Since returning to government, he had been making noises about abandoning protectionism and allowing foreign capital into Ireland. This went against a central tenet of republican ideology and one he had spent the best part of 25 years personally implementing. Such 'economic treason' would face real opposition from within the party and large sections of Irish business. Yet Lemass was increasingly ready to dispense with his protectionist revolution and to embrace a second, and largely contradictory, one.

The stakes could not have been higher. But then came defeat in the 1954 election, and Lemass once more reverted to the dutiful role of party disciplinarian, armed for long car journeys around the country with his pipe, tobacco and several chocolate bars as he set about once more rallying the soldiers of destiny into an electoral force. In the present age of politics, there is something tremendously endearing about a titan of national politics – now in his mid-fifties and showing all the physical strain of years in high office and decades of heavy pipe-smoking – heading back to the parish pumps of the country, to dinners on the road of chicken and chips and the parochialism and pettiness of local political organisation. Part of his frustration with local political bickering came from his conviction that Ireland needed voting reform, with the multi-candidate system replaced with first-past-the-post. His willingness to tour the *cumainn* of the country in opposition speaks to that sense of service, of a humility more typical, but by no means universal, in politicians of his generation.

In keeping with the gendered standards of the time, Lemass was the breadwinner of the family and his wife the homemaker. His eldest daughter, Maureen, when asked about her father, admitted that they rarely saw him – such was his workaholic character – and accordingly, such were the times, he never learnt how to change a nappy, make a cup of tea or boil an egg. Naturally, therefore, while his views on Northern Ireland and foreign investment were undergoing a liberalisation in the 1950s, the same could not be said of his social outlook, and within the party he discouraged the notion that women could take on political careers.

Instead, Lemass wanted the party to look towards go-getters of the ilk of his new son-in-law, Charles Haughey, a UCD graduate who married Maureen in 1951. An accountant by trade, Haughey was looked upon as brash and opportunistic by the party old guard – a self-seeking upstart. Lemass, however, encouraged Haughey. After all, he represented the new ethic which Lemass was coming to value, the new embodiment of the anti-*aboulia*, the confident young man unabashed about cultivating business contacts and free of what he called 'the slave spirit and inferiority complex' that had plagued previous generations thanks to imperial subjecthood.

The misplaced championing of Haughey, whose brashness clashed with the respect for public office held by the revolutionary generation, was partly due to familial loyalty and partly due to a mounting nausea when it came to de Valera. Lemass later admitted that the Chief 'had long since ceased to be a leader in the full sense of the term'. 'After a time he became, as I suppose people of his age bracket always tend to become, a man to whom you brought ideas – he became the judge of other people's ideas rather than the initiator of them himself.'

Ironically, when Taoiseach, Lemass himself would have the good grace to stop trying to initiate everything himself and allow a younger generation to hatch ideas. Yet the contrast between the two men stands nonetheless: although Lemass was tired-looking, great bags under his eyes, when he became Taoiseach aged almost 60 in 1959, no one could ever have accused him of the detached and myopic figure Dev cut by the 1950s.

As director of organisation, Lemass deserves much of the credit for Fianna Fáil's electoral triumph in 1957. Back in government, he was now openly in favour of ditching the protectionism a generation had grown used to. Interestingly, he supported Irish membership of the new European Free Trade Area (EFTA) bloc, a British alternative to the emerging EEC. Whether this is seen as consistent or not with his desire to end dependence on the British market, it is at least evidence of a conviction now established that Ireland simply could not go it alone any more.

He now threw himself into aspects of modernisation that seem shortsighted in the long term, such as the closure of railway branch lines and the championing of the motor car, but which symbolised the modernisation drive of the period. The influence of his loyal senior civil servant, John Leydon, had also been replaced by that of the economist and top civil servant at the Department of Finance, T. K. Whitaker. It is at this juncture that the well-worn juxtaposition between Dev and Lemass holds the most weight. While Lemass was ripping up the pages of the economic rulebook he himself had written, turning increasingly towards the Western mainstream, de Valera was increasingly blind and increasingly, embarrassingly, irrelevant to modern Irish life. Dev announced his intention to retire in January 1959. Six months later, he was gone. The Fianna Fáil parliamentary party elected Lemass the new leader, and a day later the Dáil followed suit.

Lemass's achievements as Taoiseach can be summed up in three main themes: (1) economic liberalisation; (2) recognising Northern Ireland;

and (3) orientation towards Europe. The first was signalled by T. K. Whitaker's landmark 1958 *Economic Development*, which laid out a blueprint for the replacement of protectionism with free trade. The '1958 Turn' emphasised increasing outside capital investment, and this policy was affirmed by Lemass in his first speech as Taoiseach on 24 June 1959. Between 1932 and 1957, Lemass had been the prime force behind import substitution industrialisation (protectionism), but a new post-war world demanded a new approach. The IDA, which he had initially opposed, now set about attracting foreign investment and expertise. In Irish political culture, too, the businessman was replacing the idealist, with Charles Haughey and his cabal – 'the men in the mohair suits' – courting speculators and builders in fashionable Dublin clubs and restaurants.

This was the Swinging Sixties, but social liberalisation did not inevitably follow economic liberalisation. Lemass remained openly hostile to writers like Seán O'Casey and Brendan Behan whom he thought part of an anti-Irish propaganda campaign. He was nervous about the subversive potential of television and even privately hated the ostentatiousness of American comic-book hero Superman!

Lemass remained deferential to the Church, in awe of the popes and close to the Irish Catholic hierarchy. At the same time, he was liberal enough to allow space for younger men to forge change. In a notable example, in 1966, he allowed youthful Minister Donogh O'Malley to implicitly challenge the Church's role in education by announcing free secondary schooling. He had told the Dáil in October 1959 that his government aimed at educating all children until they were at least 15, but in the ensuing years let O'Malley and a young colleague, Patrick Hillery, go further in transforming the educational landscape.

He is to be commended for changing his leadership style when Taoiseach to one commensurate with the top role. Still peremptory in leadership style, he in fact allowed ministers greater scope to develop policy within their own departments. In contrast to his previous failure to widely consult before taking decisions, he would regularly telephone various people around the country to gauge their opinions on policy. As

Des O'Malley, one of the Young Turks fostered under Lemass, put it, 'When he wanted to know what the Irish people were thinking, he got on the telephone, unlike Dev, of course, who only had to consult his heart.' More broadly, this amounted to a greater willingness to allow experts to have their say, especially on economic reform, in contrast to a certain staid anti-intellectualism that had dogged Irish society in the 1950s.

Lemass's second significant reform was around Northern Ireland. In line with the theme of economic liberalisation, in a 1959 speech in Oxford, Lemass proposed a 32-county free-trade area for goods produced in both territories. He also oversaw a shift in official terminology, with 'six counties' replaced by 'Northern Ireland'. Ever the deft political operator, he could be ambiguous, using both terms in one speech, but nonetheless the departure from Dev, who refused to acknowledge Northern Ireland's existence, was marked. In subsequent speeches, he claimed to recognise the legitimate fear of unionists over the ending of Partition, and such overtures did not go unnoticed north of the Border.

The centrepiece of this new, more harmonious, coexistence was of course Lemass's visit North in 1965 to meet Northern premier Terence O'Neill. The meeting has been relayed by some historians with all the air of a literary romance: it took place in secret as snow fell on Stormont; neither man told his wife about the secret visit; and the occasion was marked with a glass of champagne. Although the visit ended with Lemass's black Mercedes being pelted with snowballs by a young Ian Paisley, it was a symbolic and courageous meeting which Lemass characteristically played down later in front of the Fianna Fáil Ard Fheis, claiming to be at pains to 'discourage any exaggeration of the significance of the meeting'. He remained aware of the 'second-class status' of Northern Catholics that would help fuel the subsequent Troubles and continued to regard Partition as 'an absurdity'. But the step-change had occurred. In light of the Peace Process of the early 21st century and the dynamics of the post-Brexit settlement, Lemass's Northern policy does indeed appear before its time.

The third key plank of Lemassian change was in his orientation of

Ireland towards Europe, something which was not only consistent with his long-term nationalist aim of ending dependence on Britain but which also anticipated the free-trade federal Europe that would later emerge. While Lemass was previously content to leave foreign policy to Dev, he in fact played an active role in the formulation of foreign policy as Taoiseach. While Ireland's delegation to the UN tended to lean towards the rights of small nations, nuclear non-proliferation and decolonisation, Lemass had by this stage committed to the pro-American viewpoint.

Increasingly pursuing realpolitik and coming across as inoffensive to the Americans, he sought to clip the wings of the Irish UN delegation, stressing that they consider economic priorities before moral ones and that they pipe down on issues such as Algerian independence and the South Tyrol so as not to cause offence to the French or the Italians. While much of this displayed a regrettable willingness to roll over in the face of American pressure, Lemass's premiership did coincide with the visit of John Fitzgerald Kennedy to his ancestral homeland in 1963, of whose symbolism and tourist value Lemass was keenly aware.

There was a certain cynicism – some might say hard-headed realism – to Lemass that occasionally bubbled to the surface and which is evident in his moving Ireland towards an uncritical and unquestioningly pro-American stance. When viewed in the zero-sum context of the Cold War and its nuclear-armed camps, however, Lemass envisioned common European defence as resolutely Western and unequivocally stated, 'In any conflict between East and West we will always be on the side of the West.'

This foreign-policy reorientation recognised new realities but was also part of the strategic march towards Europe. Although Lemass had flirted with the EFTA, membership of free-trade Europe was always the more attractive option, and he privately confided that he blamed the British 'imperial frame of mind' as initially bent on engaging with the common market only to 'destroy it' or 'slow it down'. But, frustratingly for a nationalist like Lemass, Ireland's very membership of the club rested on the success of Britain's application. Discussions took place between Lemass and British Conservative Prime Minister Harold Macmillan in 1961, with both men enjoying each other's company. Speaking in Brussels in 1962, Lemass presented Ireland's application to join the EEC. However, French President Charles de Gaulle, whom Lemass never personally warmed to, vetoed British and Irish entry.

Lemass was someone with whom successive British governments thought they could do business, a 1958 memo describing him as 'not dominated by the sense of grievance and frustration which characterises so many of the older generation of Irish politicians'. In a further move away from protectionism, he signed a free-trade deal in 1965 with Macmillan's successor, Harold Wilson of the Labour Party. Europe, however, remained the elusive prize. Despite the failure to gain admittance to the EEC, when viewed in the long run, this was the beginning of an Irish relationship with Europe which has, most would argue, proved tremendously beneficial.

Although Lemass was again returned to power following the general election of 1965, campaigning around the slogan 'Let Lemass Lead On!', there was a deterioration in his health that could no longer be ignored. By 1966, the health effects of smoking copious amounts of pipe tobacco for over 40 years were beginning to show. In 1963, he collapsed at a reception, an episode attributed to 'an allergy'. He was increasingly tired and started to suffer blackouts. He was also suffering from hoarseness, and throat cancer was suspected.

His resignation was taken in good grace by most within the party, yet it paved the way for what would become a civil war within Fianna Fáil. After retirement, Lemass suffered from lung problems, and during his last illness, in 1971, he suffered a collapsed lung. 'I've had enough', he was rumoured to have stoically remarked. He died on 11 May 1971.

Relative to de Valera, Lemass was a liberal and reforming Taoiseach. As Taoiseach, he changed leadership style and proved receptive to the great change of the 1960s. And yet, it would be anachronistic to trace the great social and cultural liberalisation of 21st-century Ireland as stemming from Lemass, who was, after all, a Victorian. In many ways, too, he was something of a 'lucky Taoiseach': his two terms coincided with the Swinging Sixties, and the Northern Ireland Troubles would come later. Moreover, his conversion to Whitakerian neo-liberalism was more conditional than some have allowed for. Despite the embrace of Americanisation and foreign capital, Lemass retained some traits of the dirigiste, and his gradual and conditional economic liberalisation was not as full-throttle as some have suggested.

Lemass, more than anyone, discouraged the intellectual laziness of hero worship. Nonetheless, he deserves his status as Ireland's greatest Taoiseach for the three key aspects of change – economic liberalisation, recognising Northern Ireland and orientation towards Europe – outlined above, all of which have proved, to varying degrees, to have paid off in the long term. His *Irish Times* obituary captured some of his paradoxes – 'He protected Irish industry with tariffs, and he lived to dismantle them; he fought the British, and didn't hesitate to trade profitably with them' – while coming to a verdict it is impossible to disagree with: 'Seán Lemass left, in the totality of his life, a stamp for good on his country.'

6

Jack Lynch

1966–73, 1977–9

Stephen Collins

Full name: John Mary (Jack) Lynch
Date of birth: 15 August 1917
Place of birth: Shandon, Cork
Education: Christian Brothers, Cork North Monastery
Date of death: 20 October 1999
Site of grave: St Finbarr's Cemetery, Cork
Married to: Máirín O'Connor (m. 1946)
Assumed office: (1) 10 November 1966; (2) 5 July 1977
Date of resignation: (1) 14 March 1973; (2) 11 December 1979
Length of tenure: Nine years, nine months and 12 days
Quotation: 'The government of Ireland can no longer stand by and see innocent people injured and perhaps worse.'

Jack Lynch is generally remembered as a hugely popular but somewhat indecisive Taoiseach who didn't leave a lasting impression on his country. That is to miss the importance of his actions in the dark days of 1969/70 when the island of Ireland teetered on the brink of chaos and wild men in his cabinet pressed for armed intervention in Northern Ireland.

Lynch held his nerve through months of intense political pressure that culminated in what became known as the Arms Crisis. Whether the drift of events was a result of indecision on Lynch's part or 'masterly inactivity' that gave his enemies enough rope to hang themselves is a matter for argument. One way or another, he ultimately outwitted his opponents at cabinet, firing some and forcing others to resign, and he pulled the country back from the brink of a potential catastrophe. The fairness of his actions has been questioned, then and since, but he managed, through a mixture of conviction and shrewdness, to save the state from the most serious challenge it had faced since the Civil War. That was a considerable achievement which can never be underestimated.

It took a high degree of political skill by Lynch to establish control of his government because significant elements in Fianna Fáil hierarchy never accepted him as the rightful leader. Wide elements of the party organisation never really took to him either. It was my impression from attending Fianna Fáil Ard Fheiseanna that Charles Haughey generated far more passionate loyalty from party members than Lynch ever achieved.

It was a different story with the public. Lynch was widely liked and admired by the Irish electorate and adored in Cork. Following his record election victory in 1977, he was generously described by his defeated Fine Gael rival, Liam Cosgrave, as the most popular Irish politician since Daniel O'Connell, the pioneer of constitutional nationalism who forced the British government to concede Catholic Emancipation in the 19th century. Given Lynch's electoral performance, it was hardly much of an exaggeration.

Jack Lynch was born in Shandon in Cork City in 1917, the fifth of seven children of a quiet hard-working tailor, Dan Lynch, and his wife, Norah. He was christened John Mary but as he grew up was commonly known as Jack. Lynch went to the local Christian Brothers' school, the North Monastery, where he proved a diligent student and a magnificent sportsman. His mother died when he was just 13, and his father took the six surviving children to live with his sister, who had six children of her own. His father was a shy man who spoke little unless he had a few drinks taken, and Jack inherited some of his father's quietness and reserve.

Having completed secondary school, Lynch obtained a much-sought-after post in the civil service and was given a position in the courts system.

He moved on to the Department of Justice, where he served for a time as Private Secretary to the Head of the Department, Stephen Roche, in Dublin. He also began to study for the Bar and qualified in 1945. He then took a big gamble and retired from his secure civil-service post to practise as a barrister.

At that stage, Lynch was a national figure because of his Gaelic Athletic Association (GAA) exploits. He joined the legendary Glen Rovers hurling club at the age of 10 and went on to captain the Cork senior hurling team at the age of 20. Lynch was one of the finest hurlers ever to play the game, winning All-Ireland medals with Cork in 1941, 1942, 1943, 1944 and 1946 and adding a football medal in 1945. The winning of six All-Ireland medals in a row in different codes was an incredible record which no one, before or since, has equalled.

On the evening of the Munster final of 1943, Lynch went to Glengarriff for a short holiday with some of his teammates. There he met Máirín O'Connor from Dublin who was to have such a huge influence on his life. Jack and Máirín married on 10 August 1946 and were extremely close until the day he died in October 1999. Their closeness was intensified by the fact that they did not have any children.

I had one long conversation with Lynch in 1986 when I was a political reporter with the *Irish Press* and was assigned to interview him for a special supplement to mark the 60th anniversary of the founding of Fianna Fáil. At that stage, he had retired from politics, and we sat down for a meeting at the Irish Distillers' office in Bow Street, Dublin. Lynch had been appointed to the Board of Directors of the company given his well-known partiality for whiskey, particularly the company's Cork brand 'Paddy'.

What was immediately striking about Lynch was that he was a big man, something that was not conveyed on television. In the course of a long conversation, he emphasised that he did not have the 'republican' credentials of many other Fianna Fáil politicians. Instead, he stressed that his family belonged to the parliamentary political tradition in Cork where his father was a follower of the charismatic William O'Brien who dominated the politics of the county in the decade before 1914. Lynch recalled his father's stories of the struggles between the followers of O'Brien and those of the Irish Parliamentary Party leader, John Redmond, for domination in Cork politics. It was a struggle the O'Brienite All for Ireland League won in the two general elections of 1910 when the party took eight out of the nine seats in Co. Cork against the official Irish Parliamentary Party.

The bitter feud between the two factions centred on O'Brien's effort to bring moderate unionists and nationalists together in 1905 on a policy of 'conciliation and consent'. It was no accident that Jack Lynch, as the inheritor of the O'Brienite tradition of Cork, chose to adopt a policy of 'conciliation and consent' in the dark days of 1969 and 1970, to the horror of the Fianna Fáil republicans who regarded the eruption of the Troubles as an excuse to pursue the first national aim of a united Ireland, by whatever means. Powerful ministers such as Neil Blaney and Kevin Boland made no secret of their view that Lynch was not a true Fianna Fáil man, and it was whispered in the party that his father, the tailor, had made uniforms for the British Army.

Lynch's political journey began when he was invited by the local Fianna Fáil organisation to stand as the party's candidate in a by-election. He turned down the chance to run because he knew that a friend of his, Pa McGrath, was interested. In the event, McGrath won the nomination and the seat. Lynch campaigned for McGrath and made his first recorded political speech in Blackpool on a platform he shared with the candidate and the Minister for Finance, Frank Aiken. Lynch was approached by Fianna Fáil not simply because of his sporting prowess but also because he was a clearly intelligent young man with serious prospects.

Another approach was made in 1948 when de Valera called a general election, and this time Lynch agreed to stand on the Fianna Fáil ticket with Pa McGrath. Both were elected, with Lynch the leading Fianna Fáil candidate on his first attempt.

A rumour later did the rounds that he had also been approached by Fine Gael and tossed a coin to see which party he would stand for. There was never any truth in this, but it was widely circulated by his internal opponents in later years. What actually happened was that Lynch and his wife, Máirín, discussed his misgivings about giving up a promising career at the Bar to enter politics. She urged him to do what he really wanted, and in the end they tossed a coin in the doorway of Cash's shop in Cork, and it landed in favour of politics.

The still-hesitant Lynch chose to go to a law dinner before the Fianna Fáil selection convention and arrived late after he had been formally nominated. Members of Glen Rovers were his power base, and against his express wishes they printed special polling cards and canvassed for him personally to the exclusion of the other party candidates.

He met de Valera for the first time during that campaign when the Taoiseach came to Cork for the final rally:

> I met Dev a couple of hours before the meeting. He was usually keen to find out at such meetings what the local issues were. He then went back outside the town to make a processional entry. I had a reverential awe for him but at that meeting I found him very human.

Lynch clearly made a strong impression on Dev because he was offered an influential position in his early days in Leinster House. The party decided to appoint a researcher and a secretary to the parliamentary party, and de Valera asked Lynch to take on both jobs along with his duties as a TD. Part of his job was to draft speeches for the party leader as well as to prepare briefs for front-bench members and to index Dáil debates and newspapers for his colleagues. Lynch did the job for a year but eventually he told de Valera that he would have to take more time to concentrate on his legal practice, and he scaled back his work.

He clearly made an impression on 'the Chief' because when Fianna Fáil was returned to power in 1951, the relatively inexperienced Lynch was surprised to find that he had been appointed Parliamentary Secretary to the Taoiseach. He had just retired from playing hurling and football that year. 'He informed me in Irish that he was appointing me to a new position, parliamentary secretary to the government, with roving responsibilities for the Gaeltacht and the congested districts, he told me. One of the reasons Lynch had established an immediate rapport with Dev was his fluency in the first national language. The party leader was deeply disappointed that so few of his TDs could speak the language, and most of his conversations with Lynch then and later were in Irish.

After the 1957 election, de Valera offered Lynch promotion to the cabinet as Minister for Education. Lynch initially refused the offer and, in a pattern that was to repeat itself again and again, only relented after intense pressure from Dev. This reluctance to push himself to the fore was remarked on by observers at the time and was noted in a *Business & Finance* profile of him in August 1965: 'One of his traits I noticed particularly was his meticulous attention to the words he used in public speeches. I used to help him on his speeches from 1948 to '49, and I learnt a lot of the need for precision in speech from Dev.'

Being at cabinet meetings was not a new experience for Lynch because he had attended them as Parliamentary Secretary, but he was now able to participate fully in decision-making:

> When I was in Education I had very little difficulty in getting things through cabinet. Dev, who had been Minister for Education at one time for a few months, was sympathetic to the demands I made. He used to ring up every now and again to enquire how things were going.

James Dukes, Lynch's Private Secretary in the Department of Education, described him to writer Bruce Arnold as the most calm man he had ever worked with, who 'hated anything that was done wrong' and who always planned his time well. 'He was immensely courteous to everyone. He didn't give his opinion easily. He liked to mull things over. He liked to consider every bit of evidence – a product of his legal training – and he was good on legislation.'

When Seán Lemass took over from de Valera in 1959, Lynch was promoted to the Department of Industry and Commerce. 'I was none too keen on the change', Lynch recalled later, but he was given no choice by

Lemass, who called him up to his old office in Kildare Street and snapped at him, 'I want you to sit at this desk.' Jack did as he was told and served for six years at the department that Lemass had built up into one of the most powerful in the government. The key task assigned to him was to effectively dismantle the policy of protectionism followed by Lemass at the Department for the previous 30 years in order to pave the way for the country's application for membership of the EEC.

Lemass told the Dáil in January 1962 that the conduct of negotiations in Brussels would be entrusted to Lynch, and Lynch accompanied the Taoiseach on his tour of the EEC capitals, canvassing support for the Irish application. With the backing of Lemass, he managed to overcome the reluctance of some of his more traditional cabinet colleagues, and he was able to develop a joint approach with the main opposition party, Fine Gael.

After the general election of 1965, Lemass promoted Lynch to Finance, the most senior department of all. The move marked the start of a close relationship with the Secretary of the Department, Ken Whitaker, who came to have a decisive influence for the rest of his political career. Lynch and Whitaker were contemporaries, and the two men quickly developed a deep mutual confidence with the civil servant feeling he could talk to his new minister with total freedom. Their relationship developed as they travelled together to international meetings.

The Anglo-Irish Free Trade Area Agreement, concluded in London in December 1965, represented a landmark shift in Irish economic policy, providing for the phased dismantling of the tariff barriers in existence between Ireland and Britain since the Economic War of the 1930s. While Lemass led the negotiations, it was Lynch and Whitaker who did the detailed work, and it fell to Lynch to defend the policy U-turn in the Dáil.

At this stage, speculation began to develop that the quiet Corkman might one day succeed to the Taoiseach's office. In August 1965, *Business & Finance* magazine remarked of Lynch: 'Of one Irish politician it is often said that he is too straight and honest for his calling. Yet this man's years in the Dáil have been highly successful. To date he has filled three cabinet posts and now holds the all important portfolio of Finance.' That same year, John Healy, in his 'Backbencher' column in the *Irish Times*, came to a similar conclusion despite his unabashed admiration for Haughey:

> Jack Lynch would win pulling up in a party vote tomorrow morning. He does everything right. When every other government Minister drives a Mercedes, Jack drives a Cork Ford. He smokes a thinking pipe. He likes the quiet little jar. He doesn't want anything, just the job. A nice fellow. A hell of a nice fellow.

Healy was being sarcastic, but his assessment of Lynch's support was accurate enough.

When Lemass shocked his party by resigning in November 1966, the succession was initially regarded as a battle between his son-in-law, Charles Haughey, and another rising star, George Colley. Lynch should have been an obvious candidate given his senior position as Minister for Finance, but his claims were initially obscured by his reluctance to seek the position, and it meant that media speculation centred on the Haughey–Colley rivalry.

In fact, about eight weeks before he retired, Lemass called Lynch into his office and enquired if he was interested in succeeding him, but the quiet, pipe-smoking Corkman was adamant that he was not. Some weeks later, Lemass summoned Lynch, Haughey and Colley to his office and told them they should be thinking about the future leadership of the party. Lynch recalled: 'I reminded him of my previous interview with him when I said I was not interested. I cannot precisely recall the response from the other two but they seemed to indicate that they were interested.'

Many TDs were unhappy that the only choice they were being offered was Haughey or Colley. 'There was a discontent in the party at that choice. People in the party didn't think much of what was offering', recalled Patrick Hillery, later President of Ireland, who was also a member of the cabinet.

At that stage, Haughey, who had been in the Dáil for just nine years, was a controversial Minister for Agriculture. He married Lemass's daughter in 1951, but he did not settle down to a life of quiet domesticity. He socialised with younger cabinet colleagues such as Donogh O'Malley and Brian Lenihan and enjoyed the good life. He became, in Tim Pat Coogan's oft-quoted phrase, 'the epitome of the men in the mohair suits'. The stories about their drinking exploits in the Fianna Fáil haunt of Groome's Hotel were legion. They also patronised the more upmarket Russell Hotel where Haughey consorted with financiers and builders and developed a taste for French cuisine and fine wine. In 1957 he bought a fine house, Grangemore in Raheny, on 45 acres of land, rode to hounds and behaved with a lordly arrogance.

George Colley was a very different person, one who was respected by the ageing founding fathers of the party like Frank Aiken and Seán MacEntee. Aiken in particular tried to pilot Colley towards the leadership and was annoyed that Lemass had stepped down before his protégé had time to build up significant support in the parliamentary party.

Before the two-horse race could develop momentum, a third candidate threw his hat into the ring. Neil Blaney was an experienced, dour, tough-talking Donegal man who had more ministerial experience than either Haughey or Colley and whose father had been a Fianna Fáil TD. He had the strong support of his cabinet colleague Kevin Boland, whose Fianna Fáil pedigree was even better. His father, Gerry, had been a minister in all of de Valera's cabinets until 1957, while his uncle, Harry Boland, was killed fighting for the republican side in the Civil War. Blaney and Boland represented the hard, nationalist wing of Fianna Fáil; arrogant in their belief about the party's divine right to rule, they despised some of their colleagues whom they regarded as going soft in the liberal 1960s.

Blaney's entry into the race changed its complexion and prompted a group of TDs from Cork to begin a 'Draft Jack' campaign, which rapidly snowballed. Fearful that the three ambitious contenders would split the party, Lemass again asked Lynch to let his name go forward, and he urged the three declared candidates to withdraw.

Lynch revealed what happened next in a piece he wrote for *Magill* magazine just after he retired in 1979:

Lemass again invited me to his room, informed me that several backbenchers wanted me to run and that the party generally favoured me as his successor. He pointed out that I owed the party a duty to serve, even as leader. He gave me to understand that the other contenders, to whom he had already spoken, were prepared to withdraw in my favour. I told him I would reconsider my position and would discuss it with my wife. We decided after a long and agonising discussion that I would let my name go before the party.

Colley, too, wanted to discuss with his wife the proposition that he withdraw from the contest. This allegedly prompted Lemass to remark, 'What kind of people have I got when one man has to get his wife's permission to run and the other has to get his wife's permission to withdraw?'

Under pressure from Lemass, Haughey and Blaney agreed to withdraw, but, to general surprise, Colley persisted with his bid even though he must have known it was doomed. When the parliamentary party gathered on 9 November 1966, Lynch easily beat Colley by 59 votes to 19 with the support of the Haughey and Blaney factions. The two ambitious ministers had reluctantly accepted Lynch in the belief that he would be an interim leader and that they would have another chance to contest the position in the not-too-distant future. The hard-core nationalist element of the party led by Blaney and Boland made no secret of the fact that they did not believe he was a true Fianna Fáil man. They assumed that because of this he would take direction from them. 'Let him in so long as he does what we tell him', said Boland to Blaney.

The contemptuous attitude of Boland, who successfully resisted Lynch's attempt to move him out of the Department of Local Government, was undisguised. During the Dáil debate on the nomination of the government, Lynch passed Boland a note as the latter made a typically long and acrimonious speech asking him to rein in the invective. Boland glanced at the note, crumpled it up, threw it on the floor of the chamber and continued speaking, unabashed.

Lynch appointed Haughey to take over from him at Finance, but he too was clearly waiting for the new Taoiseach to falter. Fine Gael leader James Dillon forecast that they would pursue their leadership ambitions relentlessly. 'There is not an hour, or a day, or a week until they break [Lynch's] heart, that the clash of knives will not be heard in the corridors of Fianna Fáil.'

When forming his first government, Lynch retained all of the ministers from Lemass's old cabinet. Writing for *Magill* magazine shortly after he retired in 1979, he explained that as Lemass had already effected the transition from one generation to another, he had little choice but to endorse the changes already made:

> While superficially this made life easier for me, it did cause problems for I was thereby deprived of one major strength every Prime Minister usually enjoys: the power of cabinet appointment. Of course I had that power formally, but, in effect, most ministers knew they owed their position to Seán Lemass, not to me.

He also found that because his reluctance to stand for the leadership was well known, it was widely assumed that he was merely an interim leader. He was irritated by people saying to him, 'Don't worry, you won't need to be there long – there is always the Park', meaning the Phoenix Park, where the President's residence is located. The journalist Desmond Fisher recalled meeting Lynch at the Irish Embassy in London after he had written a piece for the British magazine *The Statist* using the term 'interim Taoiseach'. Lynch approached him and whispered, 'Interim Taoiseach. I'll show you.' Yet he had only himself to blame for creating the impression of weakness by being such a reluctant candidate in the first place.

One consolation for the new Taoiseach was that he had the support of President de Valera. According to Fianna Fáil gossip, de Valera and Lynch had regular long conversations in Irish. When Lemass became Taoiseach in 1959, he kept his contact with Dev to the bare minimum and did not encourage the President to keep in touch with him. By contrast, Lynch was far more deferential to the President and welcomed Dev's desire to discuss political developments. This relationship was to prove crucial to Lynch when the Northern crisis developed.

Lynch's shaky authority suffered a blow when his government's proposal to amend the Constitution to abolish proportional representation was decisively rejected by the electorate in 1968. However, when he called a general election in June 1969, he surprised his colleagues as well as the opposition and the media by winning a decisive majority after a barnstorming campaign that showed how truly popular he was with the Irish public. The victory strengthened considerably his position within the party.

Unfortunately for Lynch, his new-found authority was quickly challenged during the crisis that erupted in Northern Ireland in August 1969 following a complete breakdown in law and order after an Apprentice Boys march in Derry. Violence spread across the North, and thousands of Catholics were driven from their homes in Belfast. There were nine stormy cabinet meetings in August 1969 when Blaney, Boland and Haughey attempted to push Lynch into a hard-line nationalist reaction. At one stage, the beleaguered Taoiseach agreed to deliver a strong statement to the nation on television, as demanded by his more hawkish ministers. Haughey and Blaney participated in drafting the speech and included a call for UN intervention and a demand that the British should immediately begin negotiations about the constitutional position of the North. The tone of the statement was calculated to exacerbate an already tense situation, but, in the circumstances, it was the minimum Lynch's more strident colleagues in government would accept.

A whole folklore subsequently developed about the background to Lynch's television address that night, particularly in relation to one passage where he said, 'The government of Ireland can no longer stand by and see innocent people injured and perhaps worse.'

The final draft that Lynch brought with him to RTÉ was riddled with insertions and deletions in pen all over the typed text. Desmond Fisher, the Deputy Head of News at RTÉ, provided Lynch with a room to work in and also fetched the Taoiseach a bottle of his favourite drink, Paddy whiskey.

> I could not help noticing that his script was badly typed, with corrections in ink scrawled all over it. I said he could not possibly go on air with a script in that state and immediately arranged to have it typed out in a large typeface with double spacing between the lines. He asked for a private telephone, and I overheard him telephoning his wife, Máirín, to consult her on changes he proposed to make.

Fisher's account shows how vulnerable Lynch was at the time. Isolated and browbeaten by the hard-liners at cabinet, the only trusted adviser he could rely on absolutely was his wife. Between them, they produced the final draft of what was probably the most fateful statement a Taoiseach has ever made on television. Still, the speech was substantially the same as the one forced on Lynch by his ministers. Blaney later boasted that it 'was composed word for word – every comma, every iota – as a collective cabinet speech … It was a cabinet speech, made by Jack Lynch.'

Another indication of just how isolated Lynch was emerged in a discussion before the broadcast with Fisher, a native of Derry and a vastly experienced journalist who had worked in London for many years.

> At one point he asked me what I thought would happen if he were to order the army into the North, as some of his advisers counselled. I said that I thought they would get about 20 miles into Down or Derry before they would be massacred in a fight with the British. He smiled wanly at my answer and said he had come to the same conclusion himself.

By this time, the atmosphere around the cabinet table was fraught. Lynch, confronted with the biggest crisis of his political life, consulted the wisest man he knew, Ken Whitaker, by now the governor of the Central Bank. Whitaker was on holiday in a house in Carna, Co. Galway, at the time, but the Taoiseach contacted him through the Gardaí.

A garda arrived at the house early on the morning of 15 August to tell Whitaker that the Taoiseach wished to speak to him urgently. Whitaker went back into Carna with the garda and phoned Lynch from the barracks. The two men had a long discussion about the political situation and the options facing the government. Returning to the holiday home, Whitaker put his advice in writing and posted it to the Taoiseach that afternoon.

In his written advice, Whitaker expressed his horror at the rioting in Derry and said no government could benefit by appearing to support it. He urged Lynch to avoid associating the government solely with the Northern nationalists and to reach out to unionists by stressing that the aim of a united Ireland would be a fair deal for all. He warned Lynch against allowing his government to appear as if it were 'driven before the emotional winds fanned by utterly unrepresentative organisations such as Sinn Féin', and he criticised the 'disproportionate publicity' they were getting from RTÉ. Whitaker's views reinforced Lynch's instinctive response to the crisis, but they ran counter to the demands for action being voiced by wilder elements of the cabinet.

There is no record of what was said at cabinet, but Lynch, probably emboldened by his conversation with Whitaker that morning, infuriated Boland so much that he threatened to resign. Boland stayed away from the cabinet over that crucial weekend even though he was put under huge pressure to return by Haughey and Blaney. Lynch also wanted Boland to return, fearing that a resignation at this stage could split his government apart.

The rebellious Minister was summoned to Áras an Uachtaráin the presidential residence, by President de Valera and asked not to go through with it. In his book *Up Dev*, published in 1977, Boland gave an account of what happened. 'The President talked of the constitutional crisis that would be caused by my resignation – particularly on this issue. He foresaw a change to a Fine Gael controlled government and pointed out the seriousness of this in the circumstances that existed.'

So much for the notion that the Presidency is above politics! It showed, though, that Dev was still backing his protégé. The records do not show whether or not Lynch discussed his political dilemma with de Valera, but, given the closeness of the two men, it is more than likely that the Taoiseach did rely on the President for advice. It is striking that the two people whose advice we *know* he sought were not Fianna Fáil politicians at all. One was his wife, Máirín, and the other was the most eminent public servant in the history of the state, Ken Whitaker.

One major concession Lynch made to his hard-line ministers was to agree to the establishment of a cabinet subcommittee to examine ways to relieve distress in the North. Haughey and Blaney were members of the subcommittee alongside two of Lynch's loyal supporters: Pádraig Faulkner from the border county of Louth and Joseph Brennan from Donegal. Faulkner recalled later that the subcommittee met once, but neither Haughey nor Blaney turned up for the scheduled second meeting and it never met thereafter. However, it did provide the cover for Blaney and Haughey to embark on a strategy of their own which ultimately involved the use of state funds for the purchase of arms to be given to nationalists in Northern Ireland.

Captain James Kelly, a member of Army Intelligence, emerged as the conduit between the Haughey–Blaney faction and the emerging Provisional IRA. Kelly organised a meeting with Northern republicans in Bailieboro, Co. Cavan, on 4 October. To their delight, Kelly told the leading IRA figures that £50,000 could be made available for the purchase of weapons. The meeting was monitored by the Special Branch, and alarm bells began to go off at Garda Headquarters about what Kelly was up to. It was known that he was reporting directly to Blaney, as well as to Minister for Defence Jim Gibbons, in flagrant disregard for the military chain of command.

The only clue available to the Irish public about the developing tensions in government came through a series of political speeches. In a major statement of policy on 20 September, in Tralee, Lynch was emphatic that the government had no intention of using force to end Partition:

> The unity we seek is not something forced but a free and genuine union of those living in Ireland based on mutual respect and tolerance

and guaranteed by a form or forms of government authority in Ireland providing for progressive improvement of social, economic and cultural life in a just and peaceful environment. Of its nature this policy – of seeking unity through agreement in Ireland between Irishmen – is a long-term one. It is no less, indeed it is even more, patriotic for that.

The speech was drafted for Lynch by Whitaker, and it restated in clear and unambiguous terms the fundamental doctrine that underpinned Irish government policy. Its impact was crystal clear as far as Patrick Hillery was concerned: 'I was away at the United Nations when Jack made the speech in Tralee. That was the most important speech that was made during the whole period. After it we knew where we were going and the Fianna Fáil policy of peaceful means was clearly set out.'

Lynch followed up his speech by laying down clear lines of policy. He endorsed a detailed memorandum from the Department of Foreign Affairs on the approach to the North. It stressed the need for cooperation with the British government to ensure that there were fundamental reforms in the North to benefit the nationalist community. It suggested that the long-term objective of a federal Ireland should be pursued through diplomatic channels but that fundamental changes in the Republic on issues such as divorce and contraception were required to push this policy forward. The memo also proposed the establishment of an Anglo-Irish Division in the Department of External Affairs to deal with the North which would work in tandem with the Taoiseach's Department. It set in place an approach that was to underpin Irish government policy for the following half century and more.

While Lynch, with the support of a majority in the cabinet, had set out the government's Northern policy in clear and unambiguous terms by the autumn of 1969, the hawks continued to go their own way by word and deed. Blaney used the occasion of a function in Letterkenny in early December celebrating his 21 years in the Dáil to nail his colours to the mast: 'I believe, as do the vast majority, that the ideal way of ending Partition is by peaceful means. But no one has the right to assert that force is irrevocably out. The

Fianna Fáil party has never taken a decision to rule out the use of force if the circumstances in the six counties so demand.' This was a straightforward defiance of Lynch's policy that earned newspaper headlines and Dáil jibes from the opposition about a split in Fianna Fáil.

The media predicted a showdown between Lynch and his enemies at the Fianna Fáil Ard Fheis of 20 February 1971. Blaney and Boland orchestrated opposition to the official line, but Lynch met the challenge head-on and received a standing ovation to the chant of 'We back Jack!' to the fury of Blaney and Boland. By contrast, Lynch's loyal ministers such as Hillery and Faulkner backed him to the hilt. They had no doubt he was following a policy which they understood clearly and which they believed was supported by the whole government.

Hillery was adamant that Lynch did not know what Blaney and Haughey were really up to:

> There was no winking or anything like that. Jack would not do that. Jack was so straight he was kind of innocent. I remember one time someone said the farmers would water the milk going into the creameries if it was not tested. Jack couldn't believe that people would do that. He was straight up all the time. I am quite clear about that.

The conspirators received a boost from a directive issued on 6 February by the Minister for Defence, Jim Gibbons, to the Chief of Staff of the Defence Forces, Sean MacEoin. The verbal instruction, delivered in the Minister's office, was that if there was a complete breakdown of law and order in the North and the British Army were unable to protect the nationalist population, the Irish Army should be ready to cross the Border and to bring arms and ammunition to distribute to the minority to use for their own protection. This directive was used by the anti-Lynch faction in cabinet to justify their plans to import arms and hand them over to the fledgling Provisional IRA.

It all came to a head in May 1970. On 5 May, Lynch persuaded his alcoholic and hospitalised Minister for Justice, Micheál Ó Moráin, to resign.

On 6 May, the country awoke to the news that Lynch had dismissed Blaney and Haughey because 'they do not fully subscribe to government policy' on Northern Ireland. On 7 May, Boland resigned from the government in protest and Lynch appointed Desmond O'Malley as Minister for Justice. Over the following days, he completed his cabinet reshuffle.

The episode is far too complex to detail here, and there are contradictions in the accounts later given by virtually all the participants. Tellingly, neither Lynch nor Haughey ever spoke about what happened and took their secrets to the grave. A raft of theories has swirled around the event which has become the 'grassy knoll' of Irish political history. A number of commentators then and since, the most recent being Michael Heney and David Burke, have put forward suggestions that Blaney and Haughey were acting with government authority and that Lynch was the one acting in bad faith.

Circumstantial evidence, including the contradictory diaries of the Secretary of the Department of Justice, Peter Berry, is cited as evidence that Lynch knew about the plan to import arms long before he claimed. The contingency plan for a doomsday scenario in the North is the other main plank of this argument. The problem with this theory, as historian Gary Murphy points out in his biography of Haughey, is that no one was clearly able to say when this doomsday point would be reached.

There was a wide expectation of a party revolt after the sackings, but Lynch handled his parliamentary party with consummate skill and finally took control of the government, four years after becoming Taoiseach. Contrary to expectations, there was no debate in the parliamentary party on Northern policy that might have exposed the deep divisions on the issue. Instead, Lynch put a motion to the meeting that referred solely to the right of the Taoiseach to hire and fire ministers. As there was no disputing the Taoiseach's constitutional right of appointment, the motion was passed overwhelmingly.

On 28 May, Blaney and Haughey were arrested on charges of conspiring to import arms and ammunition. On 2 July, Blaney was discharged. On 23 October, after two jury trials, Haughey was acquitted and, flushed with triumph, challenged Lynch, then at the UN in New York, from the steps of the Four Courts. But Lynch copper-fastened his control of the party at a press conference where, in an extraordinary show of solidarity, he was met at the airport by the entire cabinet – apart from two ministers who were out of the country: 50 TDs, 27 Senators and the two leading party elders, MacEntee and Aiken. Haughey swallowed his pride and marched through the Dáil lobbies to vote confidence in a Taoiseach he despised.

There will always be questions about why Lynch left it so late in the day to act decisively. The obvious answer is that he did not feel himself politically strong enough to move earlier. From the beginning of the crisis in August 1969, Lynch knew that he did not have majority support at cabinet for the moderate approach he favoured. He fought a rearguard action in August 1969, to blunt the demands of the hawks for direct intervention. He succeeded in diverting them by a series of measures, including the establishment of the subcommittee and by allowing Haughey to preside over the fund for relief. He must have known that it was a risky strategy but the alternative was to stage a direct confrontation with the hard men which could have led to his removal from office. Presented with this dilemma, Lynch successfully played for time and managed to get control first of his cabinet and then of his party, and ultimately brought the people of the country with him. The tactics did allow the Arms Crisis to develop, but only because Lynch had not reckoned on how far his opponents at cabinet were prepared to go in pursuit of their own strategy.

Having got rid of his troublesome ministers, Lynch was in a position to appoint a cabinet he could rely on. George Colley was promoted to Finance, and his young chief whip Desmond O'Malley took control of the Department of Justice where he had the responsibility for dealing with the escalating IRA campaign. Internment was mooted but dropped after the disastrous imposition of the measure in Northern Ireland. Instead, the non-jury, three-judge Special Criminal Court was established to deal with subversive activity. This provoked enormous protests from the republican movement, its fellow travellers and civil-liberties campaigners, but the court worked and was still in operation half a century later to deal with subversion and organised crime.

There was much more unity of spirit and purpose in the cabinet and no overt hostility to Lynch as the situation in Northern Ireland worsened in 1971. British disillusion with unionist rule prompted Edward Heath to invite Lynch to a hastily convened summit at Chequers on 6–7 September 1971. It was Lynch's first formal meeting with a British Prime Minister since October 1968. That led on to a tripartite meeting with Brian Faulkner, again at Chequers, on 27–8 September.

The events of Bloody Sunday on 30 January 1972, when British paratroopers shot dead 13 civilians in Derry, intensified the sense of crisis. They led to the burning of the British Embassy in Dublin by a mob led by IRA activists, but astonishingly did not result in a dramatic deterioration in British–Irish relations. This was mainly because Lynch stuck to a policy of conciliation and cooperation designed to maximise his influence with Heath, whom he had met in Brussels on 23 January after they had both signed the Treaty of Accession to the EEC. Lynch was concerned to prevent differences on Northern Ireland impinging on joining Europe.

Lynch met Heath three more times for discussions on a British White Paper on Northern Ireland. Shortly after Lynch lost office in 1973 Heath remarked that he 'had succeeded in making a lot of progress with Mr Lynch'. Heath's sentiments reflected the transformation in the relationship between Taoiseach and Prime Minister that remained a key factor in British–Irish relations in the subsequent decades.

In parallel with improving relations with the UK, Lynch and his Minister for External Affairs, Patrick Hillery, were engaged in one of the most important initiatives in the history of Irish Independence: the application to join the EEC, the precursor to the EU. In the middle of the Arms Crisis, Lynch approached Trinity College economist Martin O'Donoghue and asked him to become his special adviser. He told O'Donoghue that he wanted him to oversee his Department's handling of Ireland's entry application to the EEC and the main lines of economic policy as he had other matters to attend to.

With his cabinet finally sorted, Lynch focused the attention of the government on EEC entry. Over the next two years, Lynch and Hillery drove the campaign to gain entry to the EEC alongside the UK and Denmark. They had to overcome considerable doubts at a senior level in Brussels and in the capitals of the six member states about whether Ireland was ready for membership, given its poverty relative to the EEC and the other applicants.

Having convinced Europeans that Ireland was fit to join, the next challenge was to convince the Irish people. 'At this time', Hillery recalled, 'I was in charge of the negotiations about entry to the EEC which were in retrospect very important, but at the time it was difficult to get the party interested.' Reflecting back on what might have happened if Ireland had descended into civil war in 1969/70, he said in an interview with me in 2000, 'God if it had gone wrong there would have been death all over the place and we would never have got into Europe.'

The referendum campaign to join the EEC was held in May 1972. While the Labour Party, Sinn Féin and some trade unions campaigned for a No vote, the government had the backing of Fine Gael, as well as the business and farmers' lobbies, and the proposal won the backing of 83 per cent of the electorate. Later in the year, at Lynch's instigation, the government held a referendum to delete the special position of the Catholic Church from the Constitution, and the Yes vote was 84 per cent. Emboldened by his referendum success, and disarray in Fine Gael over O'Malley's anti-terrorist measures, Lynch called a snap general election in early 1973.

The gamble almost paid off, with Fianna Fáil increasing its share of the vote to 46.2 per cent, but the party lost power because for the first time in 16 years, Fine Gael and Labour came together with a voting pact and a joint programme. Leading the opposition for the first time, Lynch took a relaxed attitude to his role and allowed leading members of the front bench a lot of latitude. The Fine Gael–Labour coalition continued Lynch's Northern Ireland policy based on conciliation and consent, and the outcome was the Sunningdale Agreement of 1973.

On a personal level, Lynch suffered a setback when he shattered his right heel bone boarding a boat near his holiday home in West Cork. The injury never fully healed, and he walked with a limp thereafter. Hillery's appointment as Ireland's first European Commissioner deprived Lynch of a major ally, and he relied heavily on O'Malley and a team of backroom advisers led by Martin O'Donoghue. One controversial decision he did make in 1975 was to reappoint Haughey to the front bench against the advice of his strongest supporters. It was done as a nod to the party membership, among whom Haughey was still very popular, but it was a serious political miscalculation and a sign of weakness.

Jack Lynch led Fianna Fáil to one of its greatest ever victories in 1977 when the party won 51 per cent of the first-preference vote with an American-style campaign focused on the personality of the leader. With 84 seats out of 148, it was the biggest Dáil majority won by a party in the history of the state. With hindsight, the result is even more remarkable because no party has managed to obtain an overall majority since then, never mind win 20 more seats than all other parties combined. By comparison, the highest share of the popular vote Bertie Ahern achieved was 42 per cent. Only Éamon de Valera once, in 1938, won a slightly higher share of the popular vote than Lynch, but he never came near such an overwhelming Dáil majority in his 12 elections as party leader.

The astonishing scale of the election victory in 1977 was both a triumph and disaster for Lynch, and he knew immediately that it had paradoxically weakened his position in the party. A swathe of new TDs, most of them Haughey supporters, were elected, and, as soon as political difficulties manifested themselves, a group began plotting to oust Lynch. Another serious negative was that the 1977 election manifesto contained a host of giveaways like the abolition of domestic rates, the abolition of car tax and a range of spending commitments that undermined the public finances and created the conditions for the 'lost decade' of the 1980s when the economy shuddered to a halt. On the positive side, the breach in the link with sterling in March 1979, when Ireland joined the European Monetary System despite Britain staying out, was a significant move whose beneficial impact only became clear with time.

Overall, though, the government seemed directionless. The voters picked up on this, and the first direct elections to the European Parliament in June 1979 saw Fianna Fáil take just five of the 15 seats. Worse was to follow when the party lost two by-elections in the Taoiseach's home city of Cork in November 1979. It was a cruel blow to Lynch, and his time as Taoiseach was clearly coming to a close. He had already decided to step down some time during his term of office and hoped to do so early in 1980 after the Irish Presidency of the EEC. However, the election setbacks emboldened his enemies in the party, with the encouragement of Haughey, to start biting his heels.

A diffident performance at a press conference following a meeting with an angry Margaret Thatcher after the murder of Lord Mountbatten in August 1979 did not help. In a speech commemorating the Civil War republican leader Liam Lynch on 9 September, Síle de Valera, a Fianna Fáil backbencher elected in 1977 and the granddaughter of de Valera, criticised Lynch's abandonment of the party's traditional republican rhetoric.

The mutterings on the back benches grew while he was on an official visit to Washington in November 1979. The hard-drinking, fiddle-playing TD Bill Loughnane called him a 'liar' for denying a deal with the British for RAF overflights along the Border. George Colley tried to discipline Loughnane, but the parliamentary party rejected the move, and Lynch's authority was clearly undermined. On his return from the USA, he decided to bring forward his plans to step down and was encouraged to do so by Colley who assured him that Haughey was not strong enough to win the leadership. He resigned as Taoiseach and leader of Fianna Fáil on 5 December 1979, but, contrary to Colley's assurance, Haughey won the resulting leadership contest by 44 votes to 38.

Jack Lynch received no presentation from Fianna Fáil to mark his departure and did not attend any public party event of significance for the rest of his life. He did not contest the general election of 1981, and, in November 1993, he suffered a stroke that left him partially blind. He was in increasing pain from his shattered heel because he could no longer sustain the general anaesthetics necessary for further operations. He died on 20 October 1999 in the Royal Hospital, Donnybrook, Dublin. After a state funeral in the North Cathedral in Blackpool, Cork, he was buried on 23 October.

The politician chosen to deliver the oration at his graveside was Desmond O'Malley, Lynch's closest confidant in the 1970s, who had been expelled from Fianna Fáil in 1985 and who had gone on to found a new political party, the Progressive Democrats (PDs). Nothing better illustrated the relationship between Jack Lynch and Fianna Fáil than the fact that it was O'Malley, rather than the Fianna Fáil leader of the day, Bertie Ahern, who was asked to say the last words over his coffin.

Most leaders ultimately lose the support of their own parties, but Lynch was unique in Irish politics in that he was always regarded as a bit of an outsider by many at the highest level in Fianna Fáil. The fact that he was famous before he ever joined the party distanced him from his senior colleagues as did his lack of fervour when it came to partisan political debate. 'Softness of speech and manner, consideration for others, readiness to listen, absence of pomp, a sense of humour were elements of a most attractive personality which combined modesty and unpretentiousness with good judgement and a deep sense of responsibility and firmness of purpose', wrote Ken Whitaker after his death. 'I never saw him in a rage or heard him say anything disparaging or hurtful about others.'

An old political rival of Lynch, the Labour politician Barry Desmond, who also hailed from Cork, made a similar point after Lynch's death: 'Jack was a great Glen Rovers man; a great Corkman but he was never a real Fianna Fáil man and the country was all the better for that.' One of his successors as a Fianna Fáil Taoiseach, Brian Cowen, put it a bit differently when he said, in October 2008, that Jack Lynch always put country first, party second and himself a poor third.

His lifestyle was in tune with his public image and the antithesis of the flamboyance and arrogance personified by the 'men in the mohair suits'. On weekend visits home to Cork during his time as Taoiseach and in retirement, he liked nothing better than to spend a couple of hours on Saturday evenings in the Glen Rovers clubhouse playing the card game 25 and drinking a few whiskeys with his lifelong friends. The contrast with the lavish lifestyle indulged in by Haughey could not have been more marked.

Any assessment of Lynch's performance in the Taoiseach's office has to take account of the fact that his diffidence and innate courtesy were a political handicap at times. He allowed his internal enemies too much room for manoeuvre and let his allies foist an irresponsible general-election manifesto on him in 1977 when he would have won without it. Yet when all is said and done, the strength of character that compelled him to reject the aggressive policy towards Northern Ireland being advocated by his powerful cabinet colleagues in 1969/70 enabled him to steer the country safely through the most dangerous crisis it faced in a century of Independence. That paved the way for the country's entry into the EEC, a move that began the transformation of Ireland from one of the poorest and most backward countries in Europe to one of the richest and most progressive. It is a legacy for which he deserves the gratitude of the generations who came after him.

7

Liam Cosgrave

1973–7

Deirdre Foley

Full name: Liam Mícheál Gobbin Cosgrave
Date of birth: 13 April 1920
Place of birth: Beechpark, Rathfarnham, Dublin
Education: Castleknock College; Synge Street Christian Brothers School
Date of death: 4 October 2017
Site of grave: Goldenbridge Cemetery, Inchicore, Dublin
Married to: Vera Osborne (m. 1950)
Children: Mary, Liam T. and Ciarán
Assumed office: 14 March 1973
Date of resignation: 5 July 1977
Length of tenure: Four years, three months, 25 days
Quotation: 'Some of these commentators and critics are now like mongrel foxes; they are gone to ground, but I'll dig them out, and the pack will chop them when they get them.'

Liam Cosgrave's background and career are emblematic not only of Ireland's entrenched Civil War politics but also of the aspirations of the post-colonial Irish state, which was deeply Catholic and conservative for many years. His political career spanned more than four decades during which time he became known for his steadfast commitment to party principles, his personal integrity and his disciplined if subdued leadership of Fine Gael.

Cosgrave's 1973–7 term as Taoiseach is most strongly associated with both Ireland's new status as a member of the EEC and the Sunningdale Agreement. While his years in office can be seen as a time of sustained modernisation as Ireland settled into international alignment, this period was also fraught with economic difficulty, political fracture and the delicate diplomacy of addressing the Troubles. Moreover, the Cosgrave era bore the growing pains of a political party that had to grapple with increasing social liberalism, largely as a result of the feminist movement.

Liam Cosgrave's experience of leading in the shadow of his father, W. T. Cosgrave, and his reticence to engage with any kind of legacy or biographical project, arguably informed a somewhat shy public persona. In public engagement and discussion, he was more at ease discussing the career of his father rather than his own. Journalist Marian Finucane recalled that he was very reluctant to give interviews. In fact, she and her colleagues eventually realised that in order to engage him, it was preferable to begin a conversation about his father.

Liam was born in April 1920, in the middle of the War of Independence, to Louisa and William T. Cosgrave. His mother came from an old nationalist family; her father, Alderman Michael Flanagan, was a colleague of W. T. as an Irish Parliamentary Party member of Dublin Corporation.

It is difficult to disentangle Liam's life from that of his father. W. T. was present at the first meeting of Sinn Féin in 1905, elected as a councillor in 1909 and later became chairman of Dublin Corporation's finance committee. He took part in the 1916 Rising alongside his brother and stepbrother, who lost his life in the conflict, as part of the 4th Battalion of the Volunteers occupying the South Dublin Union (now St James's Hospital). After the Rising, he was imprisoned and sentenced to death (later commuted to a life sentence), elected as a Sinn Féin MP and, as Minister for Local Government, was a crucial part of the Revolutionary Dáil during the War of Independence. When his son Liam was born in April 1920, W. T. was a wanted man, spending time on the run and in disguise. In December 1922, W. T. was elected President of the first Executive Council of the Irish Free State – a position he held for a decade. He was also a founder member of Cumann na nGaedheal, the parent party of Fine Gael.

W. T. took the anti-Treaty side during the Civil War. Consequently, in 1923, the family home, Beechpark in south Dublin, where Liam had been born, suffered an arson attack in which most of the contents were destroyed. Owing to this incident, and the escalation of reprisal killings, the family had to live separately for some time. Liam, then three years old, was brought to stay with his paternal grandmother on James's Street in the inner city and later to the safety of the Curragh army camp, in Co. Kildare, where his father spent some time with the family when he was not at Government Buildings. The family home was later rebuilt, and Liam lived in or beside it for the rest of his life with his wife, Vera, whom he married in 1950, and their three children: Mary, Liam T. and Ciarán.

As a child, Liam was photographed with his family at the official opening of the Shannon Hydroelectric Scheme at Ardnacrusha, one of the biggest Cumann na nGaedheal success stories. In this sense, he watched the new state being built around him as he grew up. He was acutely aware and protective of his father and his party's legacy in this endeavour. Liam and his father also had a shared deep commitment to the Catholic faith.

Unsurprisingly, at the age of 17, in 1937, Liam joined his father's party. He spoke at a Fine Gael public meeting for the first time in the same year and evidently seemed intent on taking part in government from quite a young age. He had all the trappings of a typical politician in the new Irish state. In addition to the Cosgrave political legacy, his socio-economic situation was more than comfortable. He grew up in a large home in south Dublin and was educated by the Christian Brothers at Synge Street and at Castleknock College. Having finished school, he went on to UCD and the King's Inns to study law at a time when those in the 'professions' accounted for less than 3 per cent of the total Irish workforce. Upon his death, he left an estate of over €33 million. Cosgrave had an interest in equestrian pursuits from an early age and was a lifelong member of the South County Dublin Harriers Hunting Club. This social pedigree and remarkable wealth meant that he was hardly, as he has previously been described, 'an ordinary-seeming individual'.

From 1940, Cosgrave spent time in the army, having joined after the government appealed for recruits at a meeting in College Green after the fall of France. Interestingly, he looked back on this recruitment drive, backed by all parties, as the beginning of the end of hard-line Civil War divisions in Ireland, recalling the meeting as 'the first time that both sides had spoken off the same platform … it altered the whole attitude'. He liked army life, eventually rising to become a lieutenant, and living in the Curragh once again for a period.

Army aside, Liam's career path can be described as a popular political pipeline, especially for Fine Gael, which has been associated with Ireland's wealthier classes. He was called to the Bar in 1943 at the age of 23 and sought a Fine Gael nomination to Dáil Éireann in the same year. He recalled, 'It all happened together, you know, in the sense that I became a barrister and a TD together, having of course left the army.' Cosgrave represented the constituency of Dublin County, later known as Dún Laoghaire–Rathdown. He held this seat until his retirement from politics in 1981, when his son, Liam T., replaced him in the same constituency.

Until he retired, in 1944, W. T. was Liam's colleague in the Dáil. Asked whether he felt his father's legacy hung over him as he embarked on his own political career, Liam reflected:

> I got in through his good name in the beginning, but once I was elected, I knew I was on my own … I had a huge area to work. My constituency originally stretched from Balbriggan to Bray … it was a very big job to keep in touch with it all, but I did the best I could. In fact, there was an election within a year, and I put up my vote twelve hundred votes, while the party was going down. But that shows you how much I had to put in. Sure, I survived … I did the best I could … he [W. T.] retired a few months after I was elected, and that was it. I was on my own then.

By 1944, Liam was appointed to the front bench and the following year was made chair of the Committee of Public Accounts. Even with such rapid progression in Leinster House, he remained attentive to his local electorate and was known for his reliable presence at Fine Gael branch meetings in his constituency. This loyalty was rewarded; he topped the poll there in every election between 1948 and 1981.

During his first years in the Dáil, Cosgrave quickly established a reputation as a hard-working and dedicated public servant. His experience in the army led him to make frequent interventions from early on in favour of better welfare provision for those in the defence forces. He served in several capacities in the First Inter-party Government, including as Secretary to the Government and as Chief Whip.

These roles facilitated crucial insights for the future leader regarding the everyday dynamics of coalition and in particular the importance of placating backbenchers. He served as Parliamentary Secretary to the Minister for Industry and Commerce, Daniel Morrissey, attending negotiations that preceded the signing of the 1948 Anglo-Irish Trade Agreement. As Morrissey suffered from ill health in this period, Cosgrave made a significant contribution in guiding through the Dáil the legislation that established the IDA in 1950, which was staunchly resisted by Fianna Fáil.

While the opening up of the Irish economy is more commonly credited to the First Programme for Economic Expansion of 1958, these earlier developments can be understood as equally important anchors for Irish foreign trade. Cosgrave's experience under Morrissey in negotiating railway, fishery and hydroelectric projects with ministers in Stormont was also significant. The negotiations built his belief in cooperation with Northern Ireland through, in his own words, 'practical measures' over 'verbal patriotism'.

Cosgrave led Ireland onto the international diplomatic stage after he was made Minister for External Affairs in the Second Inter-party Government in 1954, at the beginning of a crucial period for Irish diplomacy and international alignment. The first aspect of this was his election as Chairman of the Committee of Ministers of the Council of Europe in 1955. Most significant, however, was Ireland's admittance as a member state of the UN in the same year. Cosgrave then led the first Irish delegation to a meeting of the UN General Assembly in 1956.

His address to the assembly denounced the Russian invasion of Hungary and the British and French invasion of Suez, and expressed sympathy and concern for Palestinian refugees in the aftermath of the Arab–Israeli war. Cosgrave also declared during this speech his determination that 'the unity of Ireland shall be achieved' through peaceful means. His contribution to the assembly was extremely well received and set the tone for Irish foreign policy for some years to come. The three principles of this policy were Irish commitment to the UN Charter, the non-association of Ireland with bloc voting and the preservation of Christian civilisation, resulting in Ireland's primarily pro-Western, pro-Christian and anti-Communist alignment in the General Assembly long beyond Cosgrave's tenure.

His first nomination to the leadership of Fine Gael at the age of 39 was credited by Cosgrave himself to divisions even older than the scars of the Civil War. As the other candidate and ultimate victor in 1959 was James Dillon, son of the last leader of the Irish Parliamentary Party, Cosgrave claimed that his own supporters expressed a preference 'that the old Sinn Féin tradition should lead the party'. Dillon's leadership saw a swing towards a more progressive policy for Fine Gael. Cosgrave's endorsement of this policy, and specifically the Just Society document, may have aided his eventual election as leader of the party in 1965.

While he set about revitalising the party by appointing a comparatively youthful front bench, Cosgrave remained canny when it came to party unity. Asked about the growing liberalisation of the party, he notably commented that 'a bird never flew on one wing'. However, his leadership was not fully secure for some years, with frequent threats from the liberal end of Fine Gael, intensifying in 1971–2. In 1971, Cosgrave played a key role in the Arms Crisis, which he described in the Dáil at the time of its unfolding as 'the greatest scandal that has hit this state since we won

Independence'. As leader of the opposition, he pressured then Fianna Fáil leader and Taoiseach Jack Lynch to take action against senior ministers who were involved in importing arms intended for the IRA. He had received a tip-off that Charles Haughey and Neil Blaney had alleged involvement in a conspiracy to import and provide arms to the IRA in Northern Ireland, for which they were ultimately dismissed.

There was widespread opposition within Fine Gael to Cosgrave's support for the Offences Against the State (Amendment) Bill, tabled by the Fianna Fáil government in November 1972. At the 1972 Ard Fheis, Cosgrave famously compared his opponents within the party to 'mongrel foxes'. At this time, Garret FitzGerald and Tom O'Higgins were Cosgrave's primary rivals for leadership.

After the 1973 general election, Cosgrave led a coalition government of Fine Gael and the Labour Party, known as the National Coalition, formed on 14 March. The joint election campaign was tight and well organised around a 14-point manifesto, the negotiation of which with Labour Cosgrave had largely delegated to his colleagues. He adhered as far as was possible to the programme on which the National Coalition was elected.

Cosgrave's somewhat unconventional style of leadership was apparent early in the life of his government. In December 1973, the Supreme Court declared the ban on the importation of contraceptives to be unconstitutional for married persons as part of the landmark McGee case. It was ruled that Mrs Mary McGee's marital privacy had been infringed when contraceptives intended for her personal use were confiscated by customs officials. Consequently, the government had to at least attempt to legislate for this ruling.

Patrick Cooney, the Fine Gael Minister for Justice, introduced legislation in 1974 to regulate and allow for married couples to obtain contraceptives under licence in pharmacies. Fianna Fáil were against any liberalisation of the law on contraception and opposed the Bill in the Dáil on grounds of protection of public morality and health. Cosgrave did not contribute to the debate of this Bill in the Dáil. When the time came for a vote, without warning, he crossed the floor along with six other Fine Gael colleagues to help defeat the Bill. While those who knew him well were not largely surprised due to Cosgrave's Catholicism, John Bruton, a 26-year-old Fine Gael TD at the time of this vote, later expressed the view that for the Taoiseach not to vote with his own government on this occasion was 'not collective responsibility'.

The National Coalition's economic ambitions were quickly scuppered by the first global oil crisis brought on by the 1973 Arab–Israeli conflict. The electorate had not experienced such high unemployment in about 20 years, inflation was rising, and the government's income-tax policy was particularly unpopular. A wealth tax was introduced in 1975, but it was levied at only 1 per cent of the value of assets in excess of £100,000. Most importantly, family homes, bloodstock, livestock and pension rights were exempt. Nevertheless, the tax was a political and financial disaster for the government as it was resisted strongly by the public, and it was ultimately impractical as it brought in less revenue than the old system of estate duties it had replaced. The wealth tax was abolished by Fianna Fáil in 1977.

Despite rising costs, the new benefits of EEC membership protected the objectives of Cosgrave's government in terms of expanding social-welfare measures. An extra £27 million in spending was available to the Minister for Finance, Richie Ryan, for the 1973 budget due to the substantial savings Ireland made on agricultural subsidies after joining the EEC. The resultant widening of the national safety net was transformative for many. In 1974, sickness and unemployment insurance were extended to all employees while earnings-related components were added to the basic flat-rate sickness, short-term occupational injury and unemployment benefits respectively. Pension insurance was extended to all employees, and a means-tested allowance for the wives of prisoners was introduced.

In terms of how these expansions pertained to women, Cosgrave was eager to highlight during a Seanad debate on the report of the first Commission on the Status of Women that the Social Welfare Act, 1973, provided several changes which were specifically recommended by this

Commission, whose report was deeply influential in terms of policy change. The Commission on the Status of Women's report was made available to the public in May 1973, and Cosgrave's coalition pledged to implement its 49 recommendations.

The Department of Social Welfare was largely responsive to aspects of the report for which it was responsible; it kept a list of the recommendations pertaining to social welfare and, having already furnished the Commission with estimates during the period in which the report was being prepared, was ready to respond at quite an early stage after the report was published. Therefore, it would be inaccurate to credit these changes solely to Cosgrave or his party. As Fianna Fáil deputies were frequently keen to highlight in Dáil debates, it was Jack Lynch who acceded to the formation of a Commission on the Status of Women back in 1969. Additionally, the majority of the Commission's recommendations were harmonious with Labour policy.

The Social Welfare Act, 1973, allowed married women to avail themsleves, for the first time, of their pre-marriage social-insurance contributions for various benefits. The Act also introduced a scheme of allowances for unmarried mothers who kept custody of their children. It was a means-tested allowance at the same rate as the rate of the widow's pension. While the allowance can be viewed as progressive in a society that had long ostracised single mothers, not all of the electorate were amenable to it. As Ciara Meehan outlines in her history of Fine Gael in this period, Cosgrave's government received many letters 'accusing it of condoning promiscuous behaviour by financially rewarding unmarried mothers'. Moreover, this legislation had conservative roots; such an allowance would not have been granted by the Irish state prior to the legalisation of abortion in Britain in 1967.

Another notable change occurred when children's allowance was made payable to mothers by default. Since its introduction in 1944, this payment was made directly to fathers. The allowance had to be signed over by them for mothers to be able to collect the money directly. Again, this was a change that had been recommended by the Commission on the Status of Women and lobbied for by many women's groups. In this sense, Cosgrave's government was essentially following the blueprint created before they came to power. This is not to say that this blueprint was followed to the letter. The Commission's study of the consequences of the future implementation of equal pay found that married couples on one (male) wage with three or more children would be among the worst-off in terms of net income. Accordingly, it was recommended that there should be an adjustment of social-welfare allowances on the introduction of equal pay, and a specific payment of £125 per year was recommended for certain families.

On foot of the struggle to introduce equal pay, no action was taken by the National Coalition on this specific recommendation. It could be stated that Cosgrave oversaw the implementation of equal-pay legislation, but the truth of the matter was that he resisted it due to intense lobbying from employers. The Anti-Discrimination (Pay) Bill was due to come into force on 31 December 1975, but Cosgrave attempted to delay its application until 1977. The coalition was long aware of its obligation to legislate for equal pay under the Treaty of Rome since Ireland became an EEC member state, in addition to its pledge to implement the recommendations of the Commission on the Status of Women. Additional pressure was applied with a new European Council Directive in February 1975.

Due to global economic decline, the Federated Union of Employers campaigned in 1975 to allow deferral of equal pay. Cosgrave made a televised appeal for a pay pause in December 1975. In the Dáil, he announced plans to amend the Equal Pay Bill to provide for 'the position of industries that would experience unemployment as a result of the implementation of equal pay', primarily manufacturing and retail, which relied on cheap female labour. Companies such as Magee clothing company and H. Williams supermarket had made repeated representations to the Taoiseach on the matter.

There was a widespread sense of disappointment and betrayal among the public after the announcement. Sentiments to this effect are visible in letters sent to Cosgrave thereafter. One woman's letter indicated that her patience with Cosgrave had run out in the quest for equal pay: 'Prior to the last general election, Fine Gael promised if they became the government, that they would abolish all discrimination against women. Deeds now, not words, please. Implement equal pay, NOW.'

For the government to delay the implementation of the Act, it had to apply to the EEC for a derogation from the European Equal Pay Directive. Irish women's organisations wrote to the President of the European Commission demanding an investigation, and, together with trade unions, they also organised a petition for equal pay which received over 36,000 signatures. The government's request for a derogation from the EEC's Equal Pay Directive was denied on 14 April 1976. The European Commission stated that Cosgrave's government failed to provide sufficient detail of the alleged financial difficulties and did not specify in sufficient detail which sectors were undergoing severe crisis and hence should be eligible from exemption from equal-pay measures. From this point, the Anti-Discrimination (Pay) Act had force.

While Cosgrave's coalition never succeeded in eliminating poverty as per their 14-point manifesto, they certainly had a successful housing policy. In a period where immigration surpassed emigration for the first time on record, the National Coalition built over 100,000 new houses, expanded tenant purchase legislation and raised the limit and income qualifications for housing loans.

A less successful plank of the coalition's endeavours was an attempt to introduce free hospital care, which was quietly set aside after resistance from the medical profession. The abandonment of a proposed national youth policy and the deferral of a census in 1976 due to high cost also arguably cost Cosgrave and his party key electoral insights prior to the 1977 election, at a time when Ireland had the youngest and fastest-growing population in western Europe.

In seeking a political solution to end the violence in Northern Ireland, a belief grew that if both the nationalist and unionist communities could be represented in a power-sharing government then the interests of all the people could be addressed in an inclusive way. This shift from the old view from the Republic that partition should be ended with or without the consent of unionists, towards a 'unity by consent' policy, nonetheless correlated with Cosgrave's wish for a united Ireland. In 1973, Cosgrave reconvened Jack Lynch's All-Party Committee on the Implications of Irish Unity 1973, renaming it to the All-Party Committee on Irish Relations, again indicating a new prioritisation of peace over reunification as the death toll of the Troubles increased.

After the fall of Stormont and the imposition of direct rule from Westminster in 1972, the British government published two White Papers in spring 1973 that proposed devolved power-sharing in Northern Ireland and the creation of an assembly at Stormont. Elections took place in June, and the Northern Ireland Assembly Executive met on 31 July, though negotiations for a power-sharing executive did not reach agreement until November. Tripartite talks between Northern Ireland, Irish and British political representatives took place in December in Sunningdale Park, Berkshire, to try to resolve difficulties that remained around setting up of a power-sharing government. On 9 December, the Sunningdale Agreement was signed. Cosgrave stated at the signing:

> There are no winners and no losers here at Sunningdale today. In signing the agreement, the Irish government fully accepted and declared that there could be no change in the status of Northern Ireland until a majority of the people of Northern Ireland want to change that status. The British government declared that it was, and will remain, their policy to support the wishes of the majority of the people of Northern Ireland. The current status of Northern Ireland is that it is part of the United Kingdom. If in the future the majority in Northern Ireland were to indicate a wish to become part of a united Ireland, that wish would be supported by the British government.

It was agreed that a Council of Ireland would be formed so that the Republic of Ireland would have jurisdiction regarding issues of joint concern with the North. A Council of Ministers was to be set up, consisting of seven members from the Northern Ireland Executive and seven from the Irish government. A consultative assembly, comprising 30 members from the Northern Ireland Assembly and 30 from Dáil Éireann, was to have advisory and review functions under the agreement.

Cosgrave welcomed the formation of the Council of Ireland. In his opinion, it would promote and encourage the growth of consensus politics throughout Ireland and the eventual elimination of violence. However, the Sunningdale Agreement ultimately failed to achieve its goals due to opposition from unionist politicians, trade unions and paramilitary groups.

Threats to national security grew in the Republic in 1974 with the murder in March of Billy Fox, a Fine Gael Senator, in Monaghan by the Provisional IRA, followed by the Dublin and Monaghan bombings by the Ulster Volunteer Force (UVF) in May that killed 33 people, one of whom was a pregnant woman.

Cosgrave was criticised for his government's response to the bombings. He asserted that 'everyone who has practised or preached violence or condoned violence must bear a share of responsibility for today's outrages'. The first large attack on the Republic by loyalists in this period provoked despair rather than outrage, however. A great deal of the media discourse ascribed as much blame to militant republicans as to the loyalist bombers. Disillusionment with the IRA was growing, and this was certainly bolstered by Cosgrave's leadership, which had long prioritised the retention of law and order at all costs. This was visible in his support of special-powers legislation and his ongoing toleration of the notorious 'Heavy Gang' within An Garda Síochána.

Cosgrave's characteristic refusal to engage with republicans in any capacity was again visible with the kidnap of Dutch businessman Tiede Herrema in 1975. The IRA attempted to demand the release of republican prisoners in Portlaoise in exchange for the return of the industrialist, but Cosgrave refused to reply, and the matter was subsequently resolved by the Gardaí.

Cosgrave greatly overestimated the popularity of his coalition government at the time of the 1977 election and certainly underestimated the readiness of Fianna Fáil. His decision to call this election is regarded widely as the biggest mistake of his career. Constituency borders had been controversially redrawn in 1974 to maximise the Fine Gael vote, particularly in Dublin. However, in the context of a deteriorating economic situation, Fianna Fáil pledged in a media-savvy campaign to abolish various rates and taxes. Their eventual victory had the largest majority ever gained by one party. Cosgrave resigned as Fine Gael leader a week after the 1977 election and was replaced by Garret FitzGerald, marking a victory for the younger, more liberal wing of the party. Cosgrave made no attempt to influence the appointment of the next leader. He remained in the Dáil until his retirement in 1981, when his son Liam T. was subsequently elected to the same Dún Laoghaire seat.

A comparatively subdued leader, Cosgrave made a concerted effort to delineate between his public and private life, refusing to make any kind of political comment after his retirement. In 2014, at the launch of Michael Laffan's book on W. T. Cosgrave, Liam stated that his father never wanted his life written about. He followed the same personal policy and refused several approaches about writing a memoir. While it is difficult to assess exactly how his family legacy in politics affected Liam personally, it is certain that Cosgrave, as Meehan and Collins emphasise in *Saving the State*, 'was fiercely loyal to the legacy of the state's founders and worshipped his father'.

His father's legacy may be seen as a guiding compass of sorts for Liam, particularly at difficult moments throughout his political career and in his perceived defence of the Republic against the IRA. A simultaneous strength and weakness of Cosgrave, according to Conor Cruise O'Brien, was his 'very strong emotional attachment to the institutions of this state, and his hostility to anything that might overthrow or damage them'. A taciturn speaker, his contributions to Dáil debates were typically judicious and concise. Rarely if ever prone to elaboration, Cosgrave can be seen as a relatively honest broker, especially in comparison to many future Taoisigh. He was certainly part of the moneyed Irish establishment, with a sustained interest in polo, racing and hunting throughout his life. Such interests proved useful during negotiations at Sunningdale, as he shared a passion for hunting with Ulster Unionist Party leader Brian Faulkner. Equally, south of the Border, the pastime helped him bridge the political divide as it was a pastime shared by Cosgrave and Lemass.

Cosgrave's period of leadership is often recalled as a time of transformative change in the Republic, and, equally, a period of flux and soul-searching for Fine Gael and its policies. A swathe of legislation created a more equitable situation for women, and the Troubles in Northern Ireland progressed with intensity with the Sunningdale Agreement offering a degree of hope for a brief period.

He is remembered for some famous gaffes. In addition to the 'mongrel foxes' incident, in 1977 Cosgrave addressed a Fine Gael Ard Fheis and attacked political commentators, referring to them as 'blow-ins' who could 'blow out or blow up'. Within the Fine Gael grass roots, particularly the old guard, the comments landed well, but they were less well received by wider political and media circles. Having started life as a politician long before Ireland had a national television station, Cosgrave was not generally confident or convivial in interviews on screen, and this probably added to the notoriety of his blunders. At his core, however, he was an unequivocal and congenial personality, described by a fellow TD as 'the most humane man I ever met in public life'.

Critics will associate Cosgrave with his failure to initiate a meaningful investigation into the Dublin and Monaghan bombings. The 2003 Barron Report noted that Cosgrave's government did not show much interest in the origin of the atrocities, despite allegations of British collusion with the UVF, and that the garda investigation failed to make full use of the information it had. No person was ever prosecuted for these bombings.

Equally, however, Cosgrave's contribution to Sunningdale should be acknowledged. While the Sunningdale Agreement ultimately failed to bring lasting peace to Northern Ireland, it laid the groundwork for future peace initiatives and ultimately the Good Friday/Belfast Agreement in 1998, which has wryly been described by Social Democratic and Labour

Party (SDLP) politician Seamus Mallon as 'Sunningdale for slow learners'.

Liam Cosgrave died on 4 October 2017, at the age of 97. His wife, Vera, had predeceased him in 2016. His long life could well be credited to his healthy routine: he ate with caution, kept fit and was not known to keep late hours or frequently drink to excess. During his time as Taoiseach, he habitually returned home to Beechpark daily from Leinster House for lunch with Vera.

His death was mourned by politicians from across the political spectrum, who praised his contribution to Irish politics and his commitment to public service. Described by Conor Cruise O'Brien as 'a cautious and rather gentle conservative personality', his life and his tenure as Taoiseach spanned a remarkable period in Irish state-building, consolidation and development. Cosgrave was one of very few politicians present at both commemorative events marking the 50th and 100th anniversaries of 1916 in 1966 and 2016 respectively.

The Cosgrave family declined a state funeral in line with his wish. However, owing to his profile, his Requiem Mass, held in his local parish at the Church of the Annunciation in Rathfarnham, was described by the *Irish Times* as 'a state funeral in all but name'.

8

Charles Haughey
1979–81, 1982, 1987–92

Gary Murphy

Full name: Charles James Haughey
Date of birth: 16 September 1925
Place of birth: Castlebar, Co. Mayo
Education: St Joseph's CBS; UCD
Date of death: 13 June 2006
Site of grave: St Fintan's Cemetery, Sutton Graveyard, Co. Dublin
Married to: Maureen Lemass (m. 1951)
Children: Eimear, Conor, Ciarán and Seán
Assumed office: (1) 11 December 1979; (2) 9 March 1982; (3) 10 March 1987
Date of resignation: (1) 20 June 1981; (2) 14 December 1982; (3) 11 February 1992
Length of tenure: Seven years, two months, two days
Quotation: 'We are living way beyond our means.'

At 5.43 p.m. on Friday, 23 October 1970, an immaculately dressed 45-year-old man took his seat in the dock of Courtroom No. 1 in Dublin's Four Courts to await his fate and discover his immediate future. As the accused settled himself, the foreman of the jury was asked by the clerk of the court to read out the verdict. Guilty meant gaol and the ruination of both a stellar political career and a seemingly idyllic family life. Not guilty, while an enormous relief, still spelt an uncertain future.

For the previous 17 days, the defendant had listened attentively to the proceedings in the criminal trial that had shocked the nation, brought ignominy to his family, put his liberty on the line and led to the greatest scandal in the half-century existence of the Irish state. Five days earlier, in giving evidence in his own defence, the man, in short, clipped tones suggesting a type of patrician hauteur, denied any wrongdoing and stated that all his actions were taken with the good of the state in mind. He was immutable in his insistence that what he was being accused of had no basis in fact.

At the end of an exhausting day in the witness box, where many of his answers consisted of the words *no* and *yes* and where he exercised what one observer called a gruesome control, he went home to the safety and security of his wife and four children. He was the last witness to testify in a bitterly fought trial, the first iteration of which had collapsed just a few weeks earlier when the presiding judge withdrew and the jury was discharged amidst fierce calls by the defence barristers for the trial to be abandoned altogether. On that occasion, when the judge, who also happened to be the President of the High Court, made his dramatic announcement, the defendant had hissed at him, 'Resign from the front bench.' The judge walked out of the courtroom without breaking stride or looking at the accused.

Now, less than a month later, that accused man rose from his seat when asked to do so by the clerk of the court as the jury foreman stood to deliver the verdict. The courtroom descended into silence as the foreman read out verdicts of not guilty on the charge that faced the accused and his three co-defendants of illegally importing arms into the state. As the packed courtroom erupted into cheers and journalists sprinted out the door to phone in their copy of the verdicts to their newsrooms, the defendant nodded at his family, supporters and the presiding judge, and gave a wry smile.

Minutes after the verdict was announced, chants of 'We want Charlie!' began to echo around the dome of the Four Courts. The Arms Trial, the most scandalous trial in the history of the Irish state, was at an end, and its most famous defendant, one of the most recognisable figures in the country, the former Minister for Justice, for Agriculture and for Finance, Charles Haughey, was free to go.

After accepting the boisterous well wishes of numerous supporters, Haughey eventually made his way to a press conference at the Four Courts Hotel. In angry but confident tones, he told the packed gathering that since he had been vindicated by 12 fellow citizens of Dublin, those responsible for the debacle of the trial had no option but to take the honourable course open to them. When journalists asked him what this course was, he replied cryptically that he thought it was pretty evident. The cryptic allusion was to the belief of many that the trial was essentially a political hit job and Haughey the political lamb sacrificed to ensure the Fianna Fáil government of Jack Lynch did not fall. The fact that he faced losing his liberty was a secondary consideration.

For many others, though, Haughey was no sacrificial lamb but rather a scheming, devious plotter who saw the emergence of violence in Northern Ireland the previous year as the perfect opportunity to force Lynch out of the office of Taoiseach. In that scenario, there was only one possible replacement: Haughey himself. Moreover, in his efforts to replace Lynch, those who saw Haughey as properly charged, and indeed guilty, were of the view that by dint of his reckless decision to assist in the illegal importation of arms to be used by republican terrorists in Northern Ireland, he had put the very stability of the Irish state at risk. To their way of thinking, he was more malignant traitor than sacrificial lamb.

The Arms Trial, with its famous protagonist, political machinations and bitter recriminations, enthralled the public. Charles Haughey went from political boy wonder, a minister at the age of 36 in 1961, to the disgraced betrayer of the state as alleged by the prosecution in his trial less than a decade later. In that heady decade of the 1960s, he had become Minister for Justice in 1961, Minister for Agriculture in 1964 and Minister for Finance in 1966, and he had masterminded Fianna Fáil's election victory of 1969 that saw the party win a comfortable overall majority. Yet, less than a year after that election triumph, Haughey was sacked from Lynch's cabinet as Minister for Finance and shortly afterwards charged with illegally attempting to import arms and ammunition into the country.

On his acquittal, Haughey reckoned that he had the support of the vast majority of the Fianna Fáil political party, and a quick political comeback was likely. If he reckoned his cryptic call for those responsible for the debacle of the trial would somehow force Lynch out of office, and him into it, he was badly mistaken. He found himself instead in the political wilderness for the next half decade as the parliamentary party rallied around Lynch. Yet, by December 1979, Haughey was in the office of Taoiseach as leader of Fianna Fáil, which itself was split down the middle after his election victory in a short but bitter contest against his arch-rival George Colley. Haughey had never lost the support of the so-called grass roots of ordinary Fianna Fáil members, and, indeed, the whiff of sulphur that emanated from him in the months and years after the Arms Trial gave him the aura of a man of destiny.

After his election as Taoiseach, Haughey became the dominant political figure of the 1980s. But, both in and out of office, he was dogged by controversy from allegations of phone-tapping of journalists to intimidation of political opponents. After his retirement, the scandal surrounding Haughey became even greater as revelations of a sexual affair and huge financial donations from private individuals emerged and ultimately ruined his reputation in both life and death.

Charles Haughey was unarguably the most talented and influential politician of his generation. Yet the very roots of his success – his charisma, his intelligence, his ruthlessness, his secrecy – have rendered almost impossible any objective evaluation of his life and work. Instead, he has been caricatured as a venal, shallow, one-dimensional character accused of little more than having nauseating or overvaulting ambition to the exclusion of anything else. His purchase of a James Gandon-designed mansion named Abbeville on the northside of Dublin city as his home and an island called Inishvickillane, off the Kerry coast, are viewed as symptomatic of a gauche empty character, obsessed with material things.

Such is his stock that he can be accused of almost any misdeed from subverting the state from within to behaving like some sort of Latin American dictator while Taoiseach. To some of his critics, he was a kept man who undermined and debased Irish democracy through a series of corrupt acts committed in return for huge sums of money to support his lavish lifestyle. His supporters, of whom there are few, say little about him.

Yet the real Haughey is a far more complex and nuanced character. There is the Haughey who rose from poverty on the northside of Dublin city to the Taoiseach's office. There is the Haughey of the Arms Trial and the Haughey at the beginnings of the Peace Process close to two decades later. There is the Haughey whose reckless public spending nearly bankrupted the state at the beginning of the 1980s, and the Haughey who ruthlessly cut national expenditure just a few short years later and resurrected the economy. There is Haughey on the international stage, engulfed in controversy over the Argentinian invasion of the Falkland Islands and the British military response, earning him the undying enmity of Margaret Thatcher. There is Haughey on the international stage as President of the EU Council of Ministers at the heart of the debate about the reunification of Germany and joining forces with Thatcher to rebuff further political integration in 1990. There is the defiant Haughey of the tribunal era when, in retirement, an organ of the state pored over his finances and his private life. He was arrested for the second time at the age of 74 and charged with obstructing the work of that tribunal. Ultimately there is Haughey at the centre of Irish politics for over three decades, whose legacy still casts a large shadow on the Irish state which was in its infancy when he was born.

Charles James Haughey was born in the early hours of 16 September 1925 in a small house in Castlebar, Co. Mayo. The house, named Mountain View, was Irish Free State Army property for the use of the commanding officer of the 4th Battalion, Western Command, 2nd Brigade. That man was Commandant Seán Haughey (known as Johnnie), and he lived there with his wife, Sarah (née McWilliams), and their growing family. Cathal, as Charles Haughey was known throughout his childhood and teenage years, was their third child and second son. Both Johnnie Haughey and Sarah McWilliams were veterans of the War of Independence and the Irish Civil War. They were born and reared practically next door to each other on two small farms in adjacent townlands: Knockaneill and Stranagone near Swatragh in Co. Derry.

The young Cathal Haughey had a rather peripatetic existence. He moved with his growing family from Castlebar to Mullingar, to Limerick, to Dunshaughlin before, ultimately, to Dublin, where his parents settled in 1933 into 12 Belton Park Road, in the working-class area of Donnycarney on the northside of the city. Their seventh and final child, Eoghan, was born in this house the following year.

Cathal Haughey's experience as a child of Donnycarney was to shape his whole life. His father was sick throughout his childhood, suffering from multiple sclerosis, and the young Haughey's entire existence revolved around that illness. He witnessed his mother physically lift his father up and down the stairs until he and his brothers became older and strong enough to do it themselves. They also fed their father as his wife did the housework in the morning. Raising seven children on an army pension in the end house of a terraced estate was difficult for his mother. Haughey was inspired by her struggle to make ends meet for her husband and children and was keen to enter the workforce as soon as possible to help with the family finances. His more far-sighted mother ensured he continued with his education.

Johnnie Haughey was officially diagnosed with multiple sclerosis in 1933 when the family moved to Dublin but was manifestly showing signs of the disease five years earlier, which forced him to leave the army. He had difficulty walking after 1934. By 1941, he was so incapacitated that he was completely bedridden. He was so affected by the disease that his pension statement had to be marked with an X as he was unable to write his own name.

In 1942, a doctor, who had examined him over the previous decade and a half, noted his fits of 'marked moroseness and depression' and that his gait was 'definitely spastic in character'. He died five years later, on 3 January 1947, leaving behind a devastated wife and seven children. His condition had been such for over a decade that it was considered to be 100 per cent debilitating. He was just over two weeks short of his 49th birthday.

So, the family home in which Charles Haughey grew up was one where the father figure was an invalid who was forced to lie in his bed all day and could only get out of it to go to the toilet. Charles and his siblings went to school while their father was in bed, and they came home to him in bed as well. But Haughey was immensely proud of his father and, as Taoiseach, instructed his private secretaries that any letter about his father was to be given directly to him. Haughey was equally as protective and proud of his mother.

Haughey's Northern heritage had a significant impact on his upbringing and later political life. Every summer once school was over, he was sent north on the train to Belfast with his three brothers from where they caught another train to Maghera, Co. Derry. At that small station, which ran until 1950, they were picked up by Sarah Haughey's brother, Owen McWilliams, who was a local cattle dealer. Their summer exodus was principally so Sarah Haughey could have a break from her rambunctious boys in her never-ending battle to cope with her husband's disability.

McWilliams took the Haugheys with him when visiting local marts all across south Derry and trained them in the art of cattle-dealing. They helped with his business, played GAA with the local teams, took part in athletics competitions and went to dances. The four Haughey boys were outstanding athletes in their youth and were of great benefit to the local GAA teams, but their victories in various races at the Maghera festival in the summer led to much resentment from locals, who initially took against these 'blow-ins' coming in and taking the glory. After a few years, the rage of the locals subsided, and the Haugheys were accepted as part of the fabric of the community.

Derry was not all idyllic summers for the Haugheys. Cathal Haughey witnessed sectarian riots in Maghera in 1935 when he was just 10 years old, which forged a lasting impression on him.

In 1939, as war broke out across Europe, Owen McWilliams bought new winter coats for Seán and Cathal, the eldest two of the Haughey boys, when they would have been 15 and 14 years of age. These were a farewell present from Derry and to wear throughout the winter to come. On the way home, the train was boarded by members of the Ulster Special Constabulary, or B-Specials, in Armagh, who took the two Haughey boys off the train and questioned them as to their new coats. They were held for the day and had their coats taken before being put on the last train to Dublin. The psychological impact on the teenage Haugheys can only be guessed at, but it was part of a reality that they put up with on their visits to Derry.

Beyond their prowess on the football fields, the Haughey children were also gifted academically. In August 1938, just a month shy of his 13th birthday, Cathal was placed first out of 500 in the Dublin Corporation scholarship secondary-school examination competition. His brother Seán had placed second the previous year. This scholarship allowed Cathal to enter the secondary-school system. Most of his friends at that time were not as fortunate because their families had not the means to allow them to attend secondary school. For Haughey, it was to be a formative experience. He forged a lifelong friendship with Harry Boland and was a classmate of George Colley who later became an embittered rival. Boland and Colley came from hard-core Fianna Fáil families whereas Haughey's father was a Michael Collins man, having fought with him during the War of Independence. This led to much suspicion of Haughey from many within Fianna Fáil and particularly those from the revolutionary generation who treated his membership of the party with some scepticism.

Haughey completed his Leaving Certificate examination in 1943 and won another scholarship that allowed him to enter UCD where he studied Commerce as a route to the financial security that he wanted for his mother, and himself. He started calling himself Charles rather than Cathal at UCD and had a spectacularly successful academic career, winning a number of internal scholarships that supported him in his studies and his extra-curricular pursuits. It was at UCD that he met Maureen Lemass, who was in the same class. She was the daughter of the Fianna Fáil Minister, and revolutionary veteran, Seán Lemass, and they began dating.

It was also at UCD that Haughey was involved in an infamous episode relating to the burning of the British flag on Victory in Europe Day in Dublin on 7 May 1945. He supposedly reached the top of the roof of Trinity College, tore down the Union Jack flag, burnt it and ran the Irish Tricolour to the top of the flagpole. But Haughey never did get to the top of Trinity to run the Tricolour up the flagpole and never did burn the Trinity Union Jack. He was certainly involved in street fighting between UCD and Trinity students on that evening outside Trinity, which was most likely fuelled by drink, and a Union Jack and an Irish Tricolour were both burnt. It was clearly a manifestation of Haughey's youthful nationalism. Ultimately the incident itself did no harm to Haughey's nationalist credentials when he was ascending through the ranks of Fianna Fáil and was indeed embellished by rumour over the years. He never did anything to quell those rumours.

Haughey graduated with first-class honours and placed second in the B.Comm. class of 1946. He then did something rather unusual and decided to train for both the accountancy and legal professions at the same time. By the time he was 24, he had been called to the Bar and qualified as a chartered accountant. His reasoning was that 'in a political career I felt that a knowledge of the law and naturally of legislation and all that whole area would be important and also that doing the Bar would be a natural adjunct to the accountancy profession'.

But it was clear that politics was Haughey's calling. After canvassing for Fianna Fáil in the 1948 election, he decided that he wanted to be a TD. Haughey proved to be a spectacularly disastrous candidate when he first ran for office in the March 1951 general election in the constituency of Dublin North-East. He received just 1,629 first-preference votes – under 3.5 per cent of the total poll. He married Maureen Lemass six months later.

While he was making his way in an accountancy practice he established with his old school friend Harry Boland what he really craved was a seat in the Dáil. He was chosen to run again in the 1954 general election but did no better, winning just under 4 per cent of the vote. He suffered further ignominy the following year when losing the Dublin Corporation seat onto which he had been co-opted in 1953. Haughey was the Fianna Fáil candidate in a by-election in the Dublin North-East constituency in 1956 but lost again and was by this time become increasingly downhearted about ever winning an election. There were also many in Fianna Fáil who considered him a serial loser who had been given enough chances.

But Haughey had the support of his father-in-law, Seán Lemass, and he was selected again to run in the general election of 1957. It was probably his last chance. At the fourth time of asking, he was eventually elected to the Dáil, taking the fourth of five seats with 4,168 first-preference votes – just over 10 per cent of the poll. Haughey would fight 10 more general elections. In every one, he topped the poll and took his seat on the first count.

On 20 March 1957, Haughey entered Leinster House as part of the 16th Dáil. Over the next 35 years, he would come to dominate its proceedings and become its most controversial figure. During his long career in the Dáil, Haughey lived by the dictum that a good TD 'should be approachable at all times, with a wide variety of tastes and interests, and a great deal of energy and enthusiasm'. His expertise in commerce marked him out in Fianna Fáil as someone the party could use in public debates not only in the Dáil but also on national radio and, later, television. He was very keen to be in the public eye but kept a close watch also on his constituency. Having tried for so long to be elected to the Dáil, he was keen to stay there.

In May 1960, Seán Lemass, elected Taoiseach the previous year, promoted Haughey to the position of Parliamentary Private Secretary in the Department of Justice. Lemass famously told Haughey, 'As Taoiseach it is my duty to offer you the post of parliamentary secretary and as your father-in-law I am advising you not to take it'. This was certainly said in jest. Lemass knew well that Haughey was ambitious but also extremely able. He was of the generation who believed wives should support their husbands, so it is unlikely he had any concerns about his daughter's future as the wife of someone on the rise politically.

For Haughey, the appointment as Parliamentary Secretary was the opportunity to make his mark on a larger scale. It would clearly do him no harm in the constituency and had the potential to offer him a quick route to a place at the cabinet table. That place came in the aftermath of the 1961 general election that saw Fianna Fáil retain office albeit in a minority government. Haughey had topped the poll in Dublin North-East with a massive 20 per cent of the vote and had brought in two running mates. He was rewarded with the position of Minister for Justice.

He was immediately faced with resolving a bitter dispute between rank-and-file members of the Gardaí and their management, which revolved around pay. With the help of the Archbishop of Dublin, who acted as an intermediary, Haughey was able to brook a resolution between the two sides. It gained him much respect within the garda representative bodies, and, politically, it won him the reputation of someone who got things done.

Haughey would prove to be an innovative and hard-working minister. With a group of talented officials, he drove through a quite remarkable series of legislative initiatives during his three-year period in Justice. This included legislation relating to the courts system, legal aid, intoxicating liquor, An Garda Síochána, coroners, extradition, adoption and the guardianship of infants, the death penalty, child offenders and, perhaps most famously, succession. The aim of the Succession Act was to safeguard the rights of widows and children on the death of a father.

Until Haughey's initiative, property was passed down from eldest son to eldest son through the generations. It was possible for a surviving wife and children to be left destitute on the death of their husband and father as family property could be sold against their interests. Haughey's aim was essentially to ensure that a man would have to provide for his wife and children after his death by, for the first time, giving women legal rights to their husbands' estates. A number of years later, the judge who heard the very first case deriving from the Act told Haughey that 'the provisions of the Act are imaginative, and will, I feel sure, be a great benefit to the community'.

Haughey was promoted to Minister for Agriculture in late 1964 in advance of the general election of 1965. It would prove a troubling experience. He was conscious of the fact that most farmers had relatively poor standards of living and low incomes, telling one Dublin city correspondent that very large numbers of farmers 'are living in remote areas with few facilities of any kind, inadequate houses often without water or sanitation and a whole lot of other things the city people take for granted'. Yet Haughey was constantly at war with the farming organisations during his tenure as Minister. He was of the view that no matter what he did, those organisations would never be happy and that he and his department were pawns in a power game played out by different farmer groups.

Fianna Fáil had been re-elected in 1965, and Haughey was reappointed to Agriculture. The signing of the Anglo-Irish Free Trade Agreement in December 1965, which came into effect the following July, did nothing to quell farmer resentment at what they continued to see as the sacrificing of rural interests to urban ones. The agricultural aspects of the Free Trade Agreement were among its most important provisions, but this did not suppress farmer anger about what they saw as declining farm incomes.

That anger finally spilled over in the form of a bitter protest by the main farmers' organisation, the National Farmers Association (NFA), in October 1966, when its leader Rickard Deasy set out on a 210-mile march from Bantry in West Cork to the Department of Agriculture in Dublin. Along the route, he was joined by some 30,000 farmers from all parts of the country. When they reached Dublin, nine farmers, led by Deasy, staged a 21-day sit-out on the steps of Government Buildings.

Fianna Fáil politicians viewed the NFA membership as being rock-solid Fine Gaelers and contemptuously referred to them as 'Nine Frozen Arses' due to the inclement weather facing the protestors. Haughey refused to negotiate with the NFA and displayed a serious amount of sangfroid in the face of their increasingly aggressive protests. This infuriated and antagonised the NFA even further and made the possibility of any breakthrough extremely remote.

The deadlock was eventually broken when Seán Lemass announced that he was going to retire as Taoiseach. In making the announcement, he announced that his health was quite good and that he wanted to leave to make way for a younger man. In reality, his health had deteriorated during his seven-year stint as Taoiseach, and he had had enough. At a meeting between the government and the NFA, it was agreed that the new Taoiseach and a potential new Minister for Agriculture would meet to chart a way forward.

Charles Haughey desperately wanted to be the new Taoiseach but quickly gauged that he did not have enough support among his parliamentary colleagues. He decided not to contest the leadership in which Jack Lynch decisively beat George Colley. Although no friend of Haughey's, Lynch appointed him as Minister for Finance. He disliked Haughey's brashness but recognised his ability and support among the grass roots of the Fianna Fáil party.

Haughey was Minister for Finance for three and a half years from November 1966 to May 1970. During this period, he was responsible for some innovative schemes that remain on the statute book to this day. These include providing state supports for pensioners in the form of free electricity and telephone usage and the introduction of a tax-free scheme for artists. This latter scheme led the broadcaster Eamonn Andrews to tell Haughey that it was a great idea: 'whether it can be worked out without spilling a lot of blood over a lot of statues, I don't know, but the principle is such a refreshingly civilised one in this materialistic world of ours that it must be applauded. I do so.'

Haughey's May 1969 budget saw the most comprehensive package of social benefits ever produced for the weaker sections of society and bore, as Michael Mills, the political correspondent of the *Irish Press*, put it, 'Mister Haughey's own personal stamp in his oft-expressed concern for those who are not in a position to provide for themselves.' The following month, Haughey masterminded a Fianna Fáil overall majority at the general election. He was reappointed Minister for Finance and seemed to have the political world at his feet. Within a year, he would be sacked and face a criminal trial at the Four Courts.

The backdrop to that criminal trial was the violence that erupted in Northern Ireland in August 1969. The period between the outbreak of the Troubles and Haughey's acquittal by the jury in October 1970 in his trial on conspiracy to import arms illegally into the state was the darkest of his life. The government was caught completely unaware by the crisis in Northern Ireland and had little idea of how to respond to it. In developing ad hoc contingency plans, the government decided that 'a sum of money – the amount and the channel of the disbursement of which would be determined by the Minister for Finance – should be made available from the exchequer to provide aid for the victims of the current unrest in the six counties'. Controversy still rages as to whether Haughey used that ministerial discretion to illegally import arms into the Irish state in spring 1970.

He was arrested at his home just before 10.30 a.m. on Thursday, 28 May 1970, and taken to Bridewell Garda Station where, along with his fellow Fianna Fáil TD Neil Blaney, he was charged with conspiring with John Kelly, Captain James Kelly, Albert A. Luykx and others unknown to import arms and ammunition into the country between 1 March and 24 April 1970.

A month earlier, on Wednesday, 22 April 1970, Haughey rose at 6 a.m. and decided to ride one of his horses around the grounds at Abbeville in order to clear his head for the busy day ahead in which he was due to present his budget. At the end of his ride, Haughey put his hand on a drainpipe at the back end of the house to jump off the horse, and the drainpipe broke. He fell heavily, suffering a number of injuries, including a fractured skull, a broken right collarbone, a torn right eardrum, a fractured vertebra and severe concussion. It was a simple accident: later lurid allegations that he was beaten up in a public house by a jealous husband have no basis in fact.

A week later, Jack Lynch visited him in hospital, where, according to

Haughey, the Taoiseach accused him of disloyalty in not informing him that he had given customs clearance for a consignment arriving into the country. Lynch sacked Haughey the following week after receiving information from the leader of the opposition, Fine Gael's Liam Cosgrave, that cabinet ministers were allegedly involved in illegal efforts to bring in guns for Northern nationalists.

Haughey always rejected this allegation. When asked at his trial had he given customs clearance knowing that a consignment of arms and ammunition was involved, he confidently stated 'no'. He did not know, he said, that customs clearance was directed to a specific consignment but thought it was rather a general arrangement whereby Army Intelligence would be absolved from customs examination for any consignment they wanted to bring in. He insisted it was a very normal routine procedure but did not exclude the possibility that the consignment might have contained arms and ammunition. The jury agreed with him.

On the night of his acquittal, Haughey hosted a huge party in Abbeville where the guest list included senior members of the judiciary, gardaí, civil service and RTÉ. But once the jubilation subsided, he faced an uncertain future. Politics was his life, yet his place at the centre of Fianna Fáil was now unceremoniously gone. Many people thought that Haughey should leave Fianna Fáil altogether and establish a new party, but he was wise enough to understand that it was only through the party that he could regain any prominence in Irish public life.

Over the next few years, he toured the country, giving talks to local Fianna Fáil constituencies. He topped the poll again in the 1973 general election with a massive personal vote of over 30 per cent of first preferences, but Fianna Fáil lost power for the first time in 16 years. The grass roots which he understood so well rescued him from political isolation, and, by January 1975, Lynch had brought him back onto the Fianna Fáil front bench. Two and a half years later, Haughey was returned to cabinet when Lynch made him Minister for Health and Social Welfare after Fianna Fáil's record 20-seat majority. The prodigal son was back.

For the next two and a half years, one question consumed Haughey:

how to become Taoiseach. He became a repository for back-bench complaints and bided his time. There were 57 backbenchers in Fianna Fáil after the 1977 election, and they would play the central role in Haughey's rise to the leadership of the party and to the office of Taoiseach. He became a vociferous advocate at cabinet for the allocation of more resources to the health and social-welfare services. Increased spending would also, of course, provide plenty of opportunities for Haughey to deliver largesse to Fianna Fáil backbenchers. Health spending increased at a rapid rate during Haughey's time as Minister, doubling between 1977 and 1980.

By late November 1979, Jack Lynch had tired of being Taoiseach and decided to retire. He wanted George Colley to replace him, and together they planned a short leadership campaign of just two days. Haughey was unprepared when Lynch announced his resignation on 5 December and declared that the leadership contest would take place less than 48 hours later. But Haughey's relationship with the backbenchers and the fact that Colley did not have such a relationship meant that his rival was on the back foot from the off.

The Haughey–Colley leadership contest of December 1979 pitted the maverick of the cabinet, and the darling of the backbenchers, against the candidate of the party's establishment, one seen by that establishment as epitomising its traditions. It was the quintessential contest between the outsider with no Fianna Fáil bloodline and the insider whose family was steeped in the party. The parliamentary party, with its massive backbench contingent, went for Haughey on a vote of 44–38. Fianna Fáil would never be the same.

Later that afternoon, Haughey gave a press conference during which he said he would leave the events of the Arms Crisis to historians, and also, when he was asked about his obvious wealth, that journalists should not assume he was a rich man. Haughey was hiding an uncomfortable truth. At this stage, he was in debt to the tune of 1.1 million Irish pounds.

Four days later, he was elected Taoiseach at a highly charged sitting of Dáil Éireann. In opposing Haughey, the Fine Gael leader, Garret FitzGerald, quite early in his speech, famously said that Haughey 'presents himself here, seeking to be invested in office as the seventh in this line, but he comes with a flawed pedigree.' For ever more, FitzGerald insisted that this referred to the fact that Haughey did not have the full support of the Fianna Fáil party, but to Haughey and his supporters, the phrase reeked of social snobbery.

For six hours on that most auspicious of days, Haughey listened to attacks on his character from the opposition. The veteran socialist Noël Browne stated that in his own nightmare Haughey was a dreadful cross between Richard Nixon and the Portuguese dictator António de Oliveira Salazar while the leader of the Labour Party, Frank Cluskey, implored Fianna Fáil deputies not to vote for a man who they knew, better than he did, was 'totally unfit for that position'. But Fianna Fáil stood behind their man, and Haughey was duly elected Taoiseach.

On taking office, Haughey had two main aims: he wanted to advance a solution to the Northern Ireland conflict, now a grisly and bloody decade old, and he wanted to get a grip on the state's finances. To that end, he went on television within a month of taking office to tell the Irish people that the country was living way beyond its means and would have to cut expenditure. In his private life, he was also living way beyond his means. He lived by his chequebook, and the banks – most principally Allied Irish Banks (AIB), although it knew he owed them over a million pounds – kept honouring his cheques. He had told the bank's leaders a few years earlier that he could be a very troublesome adversary, and, in effect, they refused to call his bluff.

His promises to both the Irish people and to his bankers to cut expenditure never materialised. Irish national debt continued to rise, and, by the time Haughey called an election in June 1981, the country was on the verge of bankruptcy.

Haughey had wanted to call the election a few months earlier and had planned to announce it during his party's Ard Fheis in February. But that event, the high point of Fianna Fáil's year, was cancelled after its first night when a catastrophic fire on Valentine's night at a nightclub in Haughey's constituency claimed the lives of 48 young people and left many more with life-altering injuries. Haughey knew the families of some of the victims and was traumatised by the tragic loss of life. He spent much of the following week visiting the families and attending funerals.

Haughey was desperate to call and win a general election. He had, to a very large extent, been living on his nerves since winning the Fianna Fáil leadership. His cabinet was divided, and his opponents within it, led by Colley, made little secret of the fact that they wanted him gone. He was trapped in a form of political insecurity that he believed he could only resolve by going to the country to win his own mandate. But June 1981 was a poor choice given that Ireland was engulfed by the republican hunger strikes taking place in the Maze Prison in Belfast. That strike had begun on 1 March when Bobby Sands refused breakfast. By the time it ended, six months later, 10 men had died, Haughey's hopes for a solution to Northern Ireland was in tatters, and he was in opposition.

One of the first things Haughey did on becoming Taoiseach was to reach out to the British Prime Minister Margaret Thatcher and propose a summit between the two leaders. They were of a similar age, were both elected in 1979, and both had something of the outsider in them when it came to their own parties. Haughey reckoned he could do business with Thatcher, and she was reportedly intrigued by him, although the British Embassy in Dublin reported back to her that he was 'no friend of ours, but not, perhaps, actively hostile' and that he kept his cards very close to his chest. After much discussion, a meeting was scheduled to be held in Downing Street between the two leaders in May 1980.

In the run-up to his historic meeting with Thatcher, Haughey was keen to get a sense of Britain's Iron Lady and how he should deal with her. He had been fascinated by the impact she had made in her short time as Prime Minister and what he saw as her almost quasi-religious mission to transform Britain. He was keen to make a similar impression on her. It also suited his own view of himself as Ireland's man of destiny.

Haughey decided that he would present Thatcher with a gift at their summit despite being strongly advised against such a gesture by his officials, who pointed out that gifts were usually something given by heads of state on official visits. Haughey dismissed their objections, and one of the secretaries in his office came up with the idea of a Georgian Dublin silver teapot and strainer. It was Haughey who decided to have the strainer inscribed with the famous words of St Francis of Assisi that Thatcher had quoted on the night of her election as Prime Minister: 'Where there is discord, may we bring harmony.' The quotation continues, 'Where there is error, may we bring truth. Where there is doubt, may we bring faith. And where there is despair, may we bring hope.' Haughey thought it an apt line for his discussion with Thatcher as he was correctly of the view that there was no conceivable possibility of any type of diplomatic breakthrough if she could not be convinced of a solution.

Haughey had faith that he would be the one to finally broker peace and pave the way to Irish unity. He was realistic enough to know that this was no short-term project, but he was determined to show Thatcher that he wanted to achieve something concrete. Thatcher was delighted with the gift, and the meeting passed amicably, with both leaders agreeing to enhanced cooperation between the states in the economic, political and security fields.

The return visit in Dublin in December 1980 did not go as smoothly. Haughey saw the meeting as a historic summit of the two leaders who could solve the Northern Ireland problem; Thatcher saw it as more of a routine discussion of Anglo-Irish relations. She was later furious at what she saw as Haughey's overselling of the summit's results as paving the way for potential new institutional arrangements in Northern Ireland. She felt she had agreed to no such thing, and relations went rapidly downhill. They reached a nadir during the hunger strikes when Haughey felt Thatcher's inflexibility contributed to the deaths of 10 men and cost him the general election as support for the hunger strikers diminished Fianna Fáil's vote in a number of marginal constituencies. The reality was that Haughey only had himself to blame for losing office.

He was only out of office for nine months because the Fine Gael–Labour government collapsed in February 1982 when it failed to pass its budget in the Dáil. After the subsequent election, Haughey scrambled together a minority government with support from a number of independents, particularly the socialist TD Tony Gregory, with whom he negotiated a deal for significant state largesse in his inner-city Dublin constituency.

He was only in power for nine months before his government ended after a shambolic period in which Anglo-Irish relations hit a new low. The cause of the enmity between Haughey and Thatcher on this occasion was the British–Argentinian war over the Falkland Islands in April and May of 1982. Despite initially supporting European Community economic sanctions against Argentina over its invasion of the Falklands and supporting the demand that it withdraw from the islands, the Irish government called for a ceasefire in the conflict in the aftermath of the sinking of the Argentinian warship the *General Belgrano*.

The statement on 4 May calling for a cessation of hostilities in the Falklands and for the withdrawal of sanctions against Argentina caused outrage in Britain. A senior Whitehall official described Ireland as 'a fair-weather friend turned disloyal in foul weather'. The decision was Haughey's alone and was taken against the advice of his officials although it was popular in Ireland. Haughey's volte-face poisoned relationships between himself and Thatcher for a number of years, although, as both were reaching the end of their tenures towards the end of the decade, a type of rapprochement was reached.

It certainly damaged Anglo-Irish relations in the short term when Thatcher basically shut down all communication with Haughey. It also ended any hope Haughey had for a diplomatic breakthrough on Northern Ireland. Haughey viewed the Falklands as a historical, colonial anachronism, as indeed did many other European leaders, but on the major international stage he had basically miscalculated the mindset of Thatcher, the Conservative Party and, indeed, the British people when he broke ranks with the rest of the European Community.

Haughey's 1982 government was given the moniker GUBU in the aftermath of the resignation of its Attorney General, Patrick Connolly, after a suspected murderer was found in his apartment. At a later press conference, Haughey rejected any suggestion that he had mishandled the affair, which he described as unprecedented, an unbelievable mischance, grotesque, bizarre and tragic, giving rise to the journalist Conor Cruise O'Brien's famous acronym. Haughey forced Connolly to resign, but the episode was symptomatic of the ineptitude that characterised that government.

Haughey survived a vote of no confidence in his leadership of the party tabled by the backbencher Charlie McCreevy in October 1982. His government ended a month later when it lost a no-confidence motion tabled by Garret FitzGerald after the Workers' Party with its three TDs withdrew its support. Weary and dispirited, Fianna Fáil lost six seats in the November 1982 election, and Haughey settled into opposition.

He was rocked in early January 1983 when the new Minister for Justice, Fine Gael's Michael Noonan, announced that the phones of two journalists had been illegally tapped at the instigation of his predecessor as Minister, Seán Doherty, and that there was no justification for such taps. Haughey denied all knowledge of the taps, but their revelation provided the background to yet another heave against him from within Fianna Fáil. On 27 January 1983, he woke up to read his own obituary in the Fianna Fáil-supporting *Irish Press*. Things were so bad for him that he was even taken out of the betting odds as to who would be Fianna Fáil leader by the end of the month.

A day later, the *Irish Independent* reported that Haughey was in his final days. Rather remarkably, Haughey held on and defeated a no-confidence motion by 40 votes to 33. Just the previous week, 41 members of the parliamentary party had signed a motion seeking a special meeting on the leadership. Eight of them had changed their minds and ensured that Haughey survived once more.

Opposition proved difficult for Haughey, who yearned to be in power. When Fianna Fáil opposed the Anglo-Irish Agreement negotiated between Thatcher and Garret FitzGerald in November 1985, with Haughey describing it as a very insubstantial document, it seemed to many that the party and leader had lost their way. Again, the decision was Haughey's alone, but he had miscalculated because the agreement, which was a serious attempt by the Irish government to represent Irish nationalist concerns, proved popular from the off. Haughey suffered no terminal damage, however, as voters were far more concerned by the worsening economic situation with unemployment, inflation and direct taxation all at historically high levels.

By February 1987, Haughey was back in power for the third time after an election fought principally on how to fix Ireland's ailing economy. Once again, he fell short of an overall majority but was able to lead a minority government. While he had campaigned in the election on a typically Keynesian platform with significant spending promises, his first day back in office awakened him to the reality that the Irish state was in significant economic peril. He was told by his incoming Minister for Finance, Ray MacSharry, that the only way forward was massive spending cuts and that if the state could not regain the confidence of the international markets, then its future would be very grim. MacSharry gave this news to a stony-faced cabinet at its first meeting but was met with serious opposition from some ministers. Haughey told them that if they did not sign up to massive cuts, they could walk out the door and he would replace them. None did.

Over the next two years, with the help of Fine Gael in opposition who supported the general thrust of economic retrenchment, Haughey and MacSharry painstakingly worked to revive the economy. The key to this was a Social Partnership Pact with the employers and the trade unions that brought industrial stability even though much of the agreement was unpalatable to the unions. It proved, however, to be the essential bedrock on which sound public finances and progressive fiscal, social and economic policies could be firmly based.

Two key achievements were the establishment of the International Financial Services Centre (IFSC) in Dublin with attractive tax incentives and the National Treasury Management Agency to manage the national debt. Haughey told the inaugural meeting of the IFSC committee that not only were they an unusual mixture of both the public and private sectors and one of the most high-powered committees ever established by any government, but that it was of national importance they succeed.

He became almost evangelical in his quest for public-spending cutbacks and was rewarded with large approval numbers for both himself and Fianna Fáil in various opinion polls. These led him to commit one of the greatest political blunders of his career when he needlessly called a general election in June 1989 in his quest to finally gain an overall majority. One of the difficulties of minority government was that it sometimes led to the government losing Dáil votes. These were relatively insignificant in the grand scheme of politics, but they gnawed away at Haughey, who never liked losing at anything. After the government's seventh defeat of its tenure over a compensation scheme for haemophiliacs who had become HIV positive as a result of having received infected blood products from the state, Haughey had had enough and called a snap election. Tired and jetlagged after a trade visit to Japan, Haughey could not be talked out of calling an election by calmer voices. While he was convinced he could win an overall majority, others, most notably MacSharry and Bertie Ahern, one of Haughey's closest political confidants, were not so sure.

As the campaign progressed, public support began to seep away, and, by polling day, it seemed inevitable that Fianna Fáil, far from winning an overall majority, would lose seats. So it proved. Haughey was distraught. His gamble had backfired disastrously, and he was now six seats short of a majority. Fine Gael told him that it would not support a minority government. Coalition, anathema to Haughey and indeed almost everyone in Fianna Fáil, or another election seemed the only options. The numbers added up for a coalition between Fianna Fáil and the PDs, which had been established in December 1985 by Desmond O'Malley after he had been expelled from Fianna Fáil earlier that year after refusing to support the party's position in opposing a government Bill on contraception.

O'Malley and Haughey had a visceral hatred of each other going back to the Arms Trial. A coalition between parties led by these two men seemed inconceivable, but Haughey's desperation to remain in power trumped everything else, and he quickly did a deal with O'Malley, who, although he distrusted Haughey, wanted to be in power himself. It was then sold to the Fianna Fáil parliamentary party as the only way for the party to stay in power. Many in the party were dismayed, particularly Albert Reynolds who was appointed Minister for Finance. While the deal with the PDs ensured that Haughey stayed in power, it also signalled the beginning of his political end.

Eighteen months later, he sacked his closest political friend, Brian Lenihan, as Minister for Defence, at the behest of the PDs, when Lenihan was the Fianna Fáil candidate for President, over a minor controversy about whether Lenihan had phoned Áras an Uachtaráin, the residence of the Irish president, on the night the Fine Gael–Labour coalition government fell in February 1982.

A feeling grew in Fianna Fáil that Haughey would do almost anything to stay in power. He fended off another heave against him in November 1991 led by the increasingly disenchanted Reynolds. But time was closing in on Haughey. He eventually fell in February 1992 when Seán Doherty revealed that Haughey had indeed known about the phone-tapping of journalists back in 1982. Haughey denied the allegation and said it was he who had been consistent on the issue for the past decade while it was Doherty who had changed his story, but few believed him. He resigned as Taoiseach and leader of Fianna Fáil on 11 February 1992, quoting Othello in the Dáil that he had done the state some service.

Haughey settled into a life of active retirement centred on his pastimes of sailing, horse riding and holidays in France and on his island, Inishvickillane. He was diagnosed with prostate cancer in late 1994 but was told that it would be manageable and that he would not need an operation.

Five years into his retirement, in April 1997, both RTÉ and the *Irish Times* named him as the politician to whom the businessman Ben Dunne had given over £1 million in a four-year period from 1987 to 1991 when he was Taoiseach. The extraordinary double life he had been leading was about to be exposed in the starkest of terms. Haughey was forced in July 1997 to give evidence to the McCracken Tribunal that was investigating payments by Dunne to politicians.

The months between April and July 1997 were Haughey's worst since his criminal trial in 1970. He had initially denied to his own legal team and the Tribunal that he had received any payments at all from Dunne. But when documentary evidence from Dunne's solicitor, Noel Smyth, emerged, Haughey was forced to admit that he had essentially been living a lie in relation to his finances. Dunne's sister, Margaret Heffernan, had visited Haughey in Abbeville in autumn 1993 to ascertain whether her brother had given Haughey over £1 million which, she insisted, was money that belonged to Dunnes Stores, the company, and not to Dunne himself. He told her that he did not know what she was talking about, but he must have had a gnawing feeling that his life could change dramatically for the worse. Four years later, it did.

The McCracken Tribunal uncovered the fact that for practically his whole political career, Haughey's financial and tax affairs had been handled by a close friend, the accountant Des Traynor. Traynor controlled the so-called Ansbacher accounts, a complex and extensive tax-avoidance system, from which Haughey himself benefitted. In his report, McCracken castigated Haughey's evidence as unacceptable and untrue, citing 11 instances in which the former Taoiseach's evidence was 'not believable', 'quite unbelievable', 'most unlikely', 'beyond all credibility' and 'incomprehensible'. He said he could not believe that Haughey was not aware of monies kept for him in the Ansbacher accounts by Traynor, who had died in 1994, or of the tax implications of the monies he received from Ben Dunne. However, he could find no evidence that Dunne had sought, or Haughey had offered, political favours. It did not matter. Haughey's reputation was ruined.

Concerned that Haughey's attitude to the Tribunal could have amounted to a criminal offence, McCracken sent his report to the Director of Public Prosecutions with a view to ascertaining if Haughey should be prosecuted for obstructing its work. For the second time in his life, Haughey was arrested, and charges were brought against him in October 1999. His prosecution was deferred and later abandoned by the state after the then Tánaiste and leader of the PDs, Mary Harney, stated that he should be convicted and sent to prison.

Haughey's legal woes were not over, and, between July 2000 and March 2001, he appeared a total of 33 times before another tribunal established to investigate yet more payments to politicians. He testified in two-hour blocks because of his advancing age and various medical issues.

In May 1999, the other great secret of Haughey's life was laid bare when the social diarist Terry Keane, with whom Haughey had been having a relationship since 1972, revealed it to Gay Byrne on Ireland's most watched television programme, *The Late Late Show*. A few weeks earlier, at their regular lunch at the exclusive Dublin restaurant Le Coq Hardi, Haughey had told Keane that he wanted to return various mementoes of their time together, including photographs and some correspondence. This upset her greatly as she felt she was being erased from his life.

It is more likely that Haughey was in fact putting his affairs in order. He was extremely conscious of the ambiguities of his life and highly sensitive to its ambivalences. The revelations about his finances had already sent his life reeling in a direction he could not control, and he did not want the same to happen with his extramarital affair. He was under investigation by the Moriarty Tribunal, which was seeking to account for all monies he was given and was looking at his various expenditures. It was certainly not beyond the bounds of possibility that money Haughey spent on Keane might have been investigated. Indeed, the Tribunal would later reveal significant payments to Le Coq Hardi and to the exclusive Parisian shirtmaker and designer store Charvet, to which Keane claimed she introduced Haughey.

On Thursday, 13 May 1999, Haughey and Keane met again for lunch at Le Coq Hardi where she told him she was publishing her memoirs, that they would be serialised in the *Sunday Times*, and that she was going to appear on *The Late Late Show* the following night. Haughey asked her not to go through with it, but she refused, although she would later tell Gay Byrne that Haughey had no issue with her doing the interview or, indeed, the newspaper serialisation. He most certainly had but could do nothing about it. The revelations of the affair pained all parties – Haughey, his wife Maureen and Keane herself – deeply. Two weeks after the revelation of the affair, Maureen Haughey told her husband that they would never speak of the affair but would just continue to live their lives. She remained steadfastly loyal to him over the remaining seven years of his life.

Those years were mainly spent in Abbeville as Haughey's health worsened. He died, aged 80, in his bedroom, at home in Abbeville, at 10 a.m. on Tuesday, 13 June 2006, surrounded by his wife and children. Six months later, on 19 December 2006, the Moriarty Tribunal reported that Haughey had received over £9 million from businessmen between 1979 and 1996, that his receipt of such gifts was unethical, and that he had engaged in corrupt favours for some donors including negotiating with the Revenue Commissioners to secure a tax write-off for Ben Dunne. His humiliation in death was complete.

From a young age, Charles Haughey wanted to be Taoiseach. After spending most of his adult life trying to achieve this goal, he was strangely hamstrung in the office, particularly during his first two terms. He was essentially a lonely man with few real friends in politics, and he trusted almost no one. Politics was his life, but from the time of his arrest in May 1970, he developed a siege mentality in his public life.

Although a decisive, charismatic and naturally dominant personality, Haughey was unable to assert authority in a party that was deeply divided over him. He was constantly on the lookout for enemies who he believed were trying to take him down. It was not until 1987, in his third term of office, that he finally had a united party behind him, but that unity frayed in the aftermath of the 1989 coalition with the PDs.

Despite his achievements in office, Haughey's legacy is that of a tarnished politician whose name has become a byword for corruption, venality and profligacy. The truth is more complex. There were many Charles Haugheys. Ultimately, he was a master compartmentaliser who, like Icarus, soared too close to the sun and burnt himself in a hubristic flight of fancy.

9

Garret FitzGerald
1981–2, 1982–7

Eoin O'Malley

Full name: Garret Desmond FitzGerald
Date of birth: 9 February 1926
Place of birth: Ballsbridge, Dublin
Date of death: 19 May 2011
Site of grave: Shanganagh Cemetery, Shankill, Co. Dublin
Education: Belvedere College; UCD
Married to: Joan O'Farrell (m. 1947)
Children: John, Mary and Mark
Assumed office: (1) 20 June 1981; (2) 14 December 1982
Date of resignation: (1) 9 March 1982; (2) 10 March 1987
Length of tenure: Four years, 11 months, three days
Quotation (apocryphal): 'That's all very well in practice, but how would it work in theory?'

As his first government collapsed upon losing a vote in Dáil Éireann on 27 January 1982, Garret FitzGerald looked almost elated; indeed, he claimed to be 'happy and exhilarated' because he could take his government's budget strategy to the people. His government's budget had fallen on the votes of a number of left-wing independent or minor-party TDs who were shocked at the austere measures the Fine Gael–Labour coalition was proposing. Famously FitzGerald joked (or, later, he claimed it was a joke) that the item that had seized most attention, the imposition of value added tax (VAT) on children's shoes, was because women with small feet were able to avoid the tax by wearing children's shoes. In fact, this was an argument used in the debate on the budget and earlier in the Department of Finance.

The budget and subsequent election exposed Garret FitzGerald at his best and his worst. His obsession with detail could paralyse him, and his passion and self-belief would energise those around him. FitzGerald's attempt at levity when his government collapsed on the toughest budget in living memory fell flat. He was taken literally, and voters sought to punish the government for the nature of the budget. Later, FitzGerald blamed his Minister for Finance, John Bruton, for the defeat. In the campaign, FitzGerald abandoned the harsher elements of the budget at which he had earlier enthused, but he threw himself into the campaign, working hard to deliver for his party.

It would take less than a year before Garret FitzGerald would be back in the Taoiseach's office. But he would never recover the passion or self-belief. His rivalry with Charles J. Haughey would define Irish politics for much of the 1980s. By the end of his career, he had defined himself in opposition to Haughey, and so the brilliant young public intellectual, whose mind fizzed with ideas on how to modernise Ireland, ended up bound by his fear of Haughey. He governed to restrain Haughey, and, while he has some genuine achievements to point to, a combination of a coalition with a divided Labour Party, a severe recession and the fear of Haughey meant he failed to deliver on the potential that voters had recognised in his first election as leader in 1981.

Garret FitzGerald's entry to politics had an air of inevitability about it. He was born into a prominent political family, and that upbringing shaped his politics. His father, Desmond FitzGerald, was a London-Irish would-be poet who found himself in the GPO for the 1916 Rising in an insurrection he opposed. Desmond's wife, and later Garret's mother, Mabel (née McConnell), was a more enthusiastic revolutionary. She was a Presbyterian from Belfast who met Desmond at Gaelic League classes in London. He was a conservative Catholic, whose involvement in the Rising led to his election as an abstentionist MP in the 1918 elections. He took the pro-Treaty side, eventually becoming Minister for External Affairs in the W. T. Cosgrave governments. Mabel was more sympathetic to the republican or anti-Treaty side.

Amidst this, Garret was born, in 1926, the youngest of Mabel and Desmond's four boys. It was an intellectual household, and Garret excelled at school, being put in a class with boys two years older than him. It was at Belvedere College that his teacher, Fr Burke-Savage SJ, suggested to him that he might aspire to becoming Taoiseach. He was not a typical student. He was not sporty, making it harder to make friends, but engaged in theological debates with Jesuit priests at school.

When he went to university in UCD, he studied languages and history, finding it all very easy. In the comfortable and close atmosphere of UCD at the time, he first came into contact with Charles Haughey, then a Commerce student. They were aware of each other but did not mix. FitzGerald was strongly pro-Allied Forces in the Second World War, not unusual in Ireland at the time, but it showed he lacked the visceral anti-Britishness some others held and was not willing to be contained by accepted wisdoms – such as that of neutrality.

This might have been due to his mother's influence. Mabel FitzGerald's Protestantism jolted a young Garret out of an unconscious reaction that many Irish Catholics held on the issue of Partition and the Union. It would define his politics, in particular, in his approach to the problem of the partition of Ireland. Garret FitzGerald held a greater appreciation for the position of unionists than would be normal in Ireland.

At university, Garret met the slightly older Joan O'Farrell. They were quickly enamoured, and the two arranged to get married when Garret was just 21. His father opposed the union, mainly on the grounds of their age, but Garret, characteristically impatient, went ahead anyway. If he might have been expected to engage in further study, his marriage meant he took a job in Aer Lingus, the national airline, where he tried to streamline the airline's timetables, and he later claimed to have hit upon the later Ryanair model of shorter turnaround times. He became interested in economics, and to supplement his income he wrote as an Irish correspondent for various international newspapers. He also started to lecture, at first part-time but later full-time, in UCD in economics, leaving Aer Lingus to concentrate on public jobs in preparation for politics. His column in the *Irish Times* and post in UCD gave the impression that he was an economist, though he actually had no training in the discipline. He did later publish a PhD thesis on economic planning in Ireland.

In this time, his politics shifted leftward, not least as a result of his exposure to his students' views. By the 1960s, he might have been described as a social democrat, though his patrician outlook was also consistent with Christian democracy. He was far too anti-authoritarian to be attracted by socialism. His instinctive liberalism meant he was an enthusiastic advocate of Ireland's application for membership of the EEC, and his position on Northern Ireland was more sophisticated than the Brits-Out nationalism typical at the time. He supported the Just Society document that later became Fine Gael's manifesto in the 1965 election. In the emerging division within Fine Gael between conservatives and social democrats, he was firmly in the latter camp.

FitzGerald was elected to the Seanad in 1965. Though this might be seen as a preparation for the Dáil, his prominence in Irish society meant he was already one of the better-known Fine Gael politicians at the time, thus securing himself a place on the party's front bench. By the time he was first elected to the Dáil in 1969, aged 43, he was relatively old. He was impatient, and one contemporary observer noted that 'it is difficult to imagine him being constrained within any strait-jacket'. He was not. He regularly spoke on all areas of policy, not just his area of Finance.

The party leader, Liam Cosgrave, disliked FitzGerald and was not afraid to show it. The feeling was mutual: FitzGerald was canvassing for Cosgrave's removal as party leader within two years of his entering the Dáil. It was clear that FitzGerald had leadership ambitions. The Offences Against the State Bill in 1972 almost delivered Cosgrave's head. Cosgrave supported the Fianna Fáil government's Bill, which would make it easier to secure convictions against IRA members. Fine Gael was split, with Garret FitzGerald one of the more vocal critics of the Bill. It was only massive bombs in Dublin that saved Cosgrave – so FitzGerald's ambitions would have to wait.

In the 1973 election campaign, FitzGerald's was a prominent voice. He was seen to have roundly defeated the Minister for Finance, George Colley, in a TV debate. Despite, or perhaps because of, his reputation as a cerebral economist, when Fine Gael and Labour formed a 'national coalition' after that election, FitzGerald was surprised and disappointed to be put in Foreign Affairs. However, it made him central on two issues he was deeply interested in: Northern Ireland and the EEC.

He expanded the Northern Ireland unit in the Department of Foreign Affairs and worked closely with Cosgrave, now Taoiseach, on the Sunningdale Agreement – an early version of the Good Friday/Belfast Agreement. It collapsed, in part because of the splits within Ulster Unionism, but also due to the lack of steel in the new government in London under Harold Wilson. FitzGerald enjoyed his role in the EEC where he travelled extensively and felt at home among the patrician elder statesmen of the EEC countries. He had been lucky to avoid the Department of Finance, as oil crises caused a recession that damaged the reputation and political career of Richie Ryan, the Minister for Finance.

An election in 1977 was badly mishandled by the government, and Fianna Fáil was returned to power with an unprecedented majority. FitzGerald's reputation was one of the few of those senior Fine Gael politicians not damaged. When Cosgrave stood down, FitzGerald was quick to declare. He negotiated with those in the conservative camp of the party and was then declared leader of the party unanimously – it was some achievement given how many privately disliked him.

FitzGerald set about modernising the Fine Gael party. Many of the party's TDs were part-timers, and the party organisation was more akin to an amateur club than a professional political party. The lack of ambition in Fine Gael enabled it to remain this way for decades, but FitzGerald's ambitions and energy were much greater than those of his predecessors, who seemed content to be available to serve when the country tired of Fianna Fáil rule. FitzGerald replaced and enhanced the professional staff in the Fine Gael head office, who did a survey of the party in each constituency. He empowered many younger professionals, such as Peter Prendergast and Ted Nealon, to take on the old guard in the party around the country. He knew how the media worked, and he worked it well. A new party constitution was drafted that diminished the power of sitting TDs. A youth organisation was launched, which successfully drew many more members, and women were actively encouraged to come into politics. The leader's more liberal politics, on contraception, divorce and Northern Ireland, attracted many new members and chimed with a changing politics in the country.

In late 1979, Charles Haughey replaced Jack Lynch as Fianna Fáil leader and Taoiseach – something that would fundamentally change FitzGerald. In some senses, FitzGerald was lucky to have Haughey as an opponent. Haughey's alleged involvement in the Arms Crisis – a plot to import arms to supply to the nascent Provisional IRA – made him a polarising figure, even within his own party. Because many distrusted Haughey, FitzGerald assumed a saintly air. One opponent, an *Irish Times* columnist, ironically dubbed FitzGerald 'Garret the Good'. For many of his supporters, it was this sense of honesty, especially in contrast to the seemingly malevolent Haughey, that boosted FitzGerald and Fine Gael.

But FitzGerald's distrust of Haughey also blindsided him. On the day of Haughey's nomination as Taoiseach, FitzGerald appealed to Fianna Fáil TDs to vote against him. That would never happen at the bidding of a Fine Gael leader. FitzGerald's speech included a reference to the new Taoiseach's 'flawed pedigree', which was seen as offensive and based on snobbery from the high-born FitzGerald.

Oddly, given his penchant for policy debate, FitzGerald's energy and enthusiasm in party organisation was not matched with policy development. He planned to run the election on the differences between him and Haughey on Northern Ireland, but most voters were more interested in the economy. If he was well able to criticise the Fianna Fáil government's performance, Fine Gael had developed few credible alternatives. Many of his front bench were cowed by FitzGerald, who made much of the running on all issues.

When the election came in 1981, Fine Gael struggled to explain how its tax credit for stay-at-home wives would be paid for. The Fine Gael campaign centred on Garret, but he struggled to be a man of the people. Instead of kissing babies, he shook their hands. Still, he had the advantage of a united party and of being in opposition to an unpopular government. Even though he was not a man of the people, people liked Garret. His image as a bumbling professor with uncontrollable hair and a motor mouth was one that many trusted and even warmed to. He delivered Fine Gael its best result since 1927, and, with Labour, the chance to form a government.

His social-democratic politics meant that compromising with Labour was easy for him. FitzGerald still needed the support of a small number of TDs from small parties or none. Their dislike and distrust of Haughey meant he was able to pick up this support, but the government was hardly secure. His choice of ministers indicated that FitzGerald was going to be a Taoiseach for change. Many of the more conservative ministers with whom he shared the cabinet table in the 1970s were not appointed, and, in their place, young men were promoted. But in doing this, FitzGerald was simply too busy to engage in the normal human pleasantries needed. His first few hours as Taoiseach left many bruised egos in his wake. This lack of caution would come back to bite him.

In the car, returning from his appointment by the President in Áras an Uachtaráin, the new Taoiseach was told by Dermot Nally, Secretary to the Government, that the state of the public finances was much worse than was publicly known. FitzGerald put John Bruton, an experienced, though still young, conservative TD in charge of Finance. Bruton's job was to deliver an immediate emergency budget. Given what they had just found out, he would have to introduce a deflationary budget that cut spending and increased taxes – something the agreed Programme for Government had weeks earlier said it would not do. None of the new government's economic plans were now viable.

FitzGerald was more concerned with the worsening situation in Northern Ireland. The hunger strikes brought rioting to the streets of Dublin. FitzGerald wanted to do something, but he had few options open to him beyond appealing to Margaret Thatcher. He decided on what would have to be a long-term proposal, a 'constitutional crusade', to make Ireland a more attractive place to Unionism by modernising many of Ireland's social laws and making Ireland 'a genuine republic'. The first piece of legislation was to abolish the death penalty, but it never got beyond the Seanad.

FitzGerald tried to engage with Thatcher, hopeful that his more nuanced Irish nationalism would have a better hearing in London than Haughey's greener rhetoric. If she was initially open to him, Mrs Thatcher soon tired of his loquacity. His secretary, Dermot Nally, had to urge him to slow down before his meetings with her. In any case, Thatcher needed time to come around to the idea of an agreement with the Irish.

Meanwhile, it became clear that the new government was not working very well. This was due to a number of factors. One was FitzGerald himself. He was prone to discussing items at great length. Meetings could last up to 14 hours as every detail was dissected. He tended to emphasise the urgent over the important and frustrated ministers with digressions and theoretical discussions not directly relevant to the decision at hand. It was in this government that FitzGerald was supposed to have reacted to a John Bruton proposal with, 'That's a very good idea. I know it will work very well in practice, but John, tell me, how would it work in theory?' It may not have been said, but it was the sort of thing that FitzGerald could have said. Another problem was the Labour Party leader, Michael O'Leary. He had a low boredom threshold and would go missing, even during cabinet meetings. O'Leary was increasingly disengaging from the debates within his party, the left of which was unhappy about budget proposals.

Despite these problems, the government signed off on a budget that would impose severe and sweeping cuts, ignoring warnings from the left-wing TDs that the government depended on for support. The government collapsed and faced an election with the least electorally promising budget possible. The subsequent election was indecisive, and FitzGerald harboured hopes of forming a government, but he was seen as out-of-touch by one of those TDs, Tony Gregory, on whose support he would depend. He met with Gregory, arriving with what Gregory regarded as a 'translator' to help him understand Gregory. It was unfair, but it put Haughey back in as Taoiseach, in what would be an extraordinary time in Irish politics.

The minority Fianna Fáil government was as insecure as the Fine Gael–Labour coalition it replaced. Internally, Haughey was fighting off heaves, but he also needed the support of some of those TDs who had abandoned FitzGerald a few months earlier. Other scandals erupted, which gave the Haughey government a whiff of sulphur. Its fall was inevitable, and, on 4 November 1982, that happened, giving Ireland its third general election in 18 months. This time, FitzGerald was better prepared, and in a head-to-head for preferred Taoiseach, he was more popular than Haughey. FitzGerald performed well in a TV debate, controlling his urge to use jargon and spit out statistics at a hundred miles an hour. Fine Gael did well, with nearly 40 per cent of the vote and 70 seats, just five seats behind Fianna Fáil.

With Labour and its new leader, Dick Spring, a young TD from Co. Kerry, in the rural south-west of Ireland, the two parties could form a government. Even though FitzGerald was old enough to be Spring's father, the two got on well, sharing the same basic social-democratic outlook and views on Northern Ireland and the position of the Catholic Church in the country. Having delivered a significant electoral result, FitzGerald was confident of the loyalty of his party and was willing to make significant concessions to Labour. Even these compromises were not enough for the left of the Labour Party, such as the party chair, Senator Michael D. Higgins. It campaigned against the proposed coalition agreement, but, despite this significant opposition, the proposed government was passed by the Labour Party's delegate conference.

Given the instability of the previous two years in Irish politics, and his distrust of Haughey, FitzGerald resolved that the government would last its full term. He decided that the government should not split on party lines and so gave each party a veto. It also meant that his habit of long cabinet meetings was retained, despite being warned by Dermot Nally that he could not run a government like he would a university seminar. FitzGerald was an inefficient administrator who struggled to deal with a number of issues at the same time. And wanting to hold the government together at any cost meant that he had to pay many costs.

It was his uncertain leadership, as he constantly tried to second-guess his nemesis Charles Haughey, that led to his maladroit performance as Taoiseach. If one of FitzGerald's aims had been to have a constitutional crusade that liberalised Ireland, one of his first mistakes had been to agree to hold a referendum to insert the prohibition of abortion into the Constitution. Labour refused to engage, recognising that it was a mistake. The Attorney General, Peter Sutherland, himself a committed Catholic, also opposed it on grounds that proved prescient: that the wording was ambiguous and unsatisfactory for both the medical profession and the judges who would have to interpret it. FitzGerald vacillated and eventually made a political decision to go ahead with a referendum on the unsatisfactory wording, a decision that would cause great problems in Ireland over the next 30 years.

His party hardly thanked him; one cabinet minister thought FitzGerald showed a lack of leadership. It was embarrassing for him that the Protestant church leaders came out against the referendum, given that his attempt to assuage the fears of Protestants was the basis for his so-called constitutional crusade. FitzGerald then changed his mind and voted against the Bill but could not bring his party with him on the alternative wording. The referendum went ahead, and FitzGerald made plain his opposition to the proposal that he had brought in. After a nasty campaign, the proposal passed by two-to-one. It was an episode that showed FitzGerald, who might have thought himself a conviction politician, lacking in both conviction and political acumen.

Divorce was also brought upon FitzGerald in a way he neither wanted nor was prepared for. Divorce had a constitutional bar in Ireland, regarded as one of the more sectarian elements of the 1937 Constitution. FitzGerald remained a devout Catholic but could see the offensiveness of this being in the Constitution. He hoped to bring the Catholic hierarchy around to his way of thinking. But the Church was still in its pomp, and it strongly opposed any change. Despite this, some early polling showed a majority in favour of change. Once again, FitzGerald led a lazy and half-hearted campaign that failed to deal with opposition lines on the financial security of divorcees. The result was a two-to-one defeat for the divorce referendum – yet another setback for FitzGerald and his faltering leadership.

The economy had been in severe trouble when FitzGerald took power. Inflation was at 23 per cent, unemployment at 12 per cent was suppressed only by rising emigration. The state's share of the economy had also increased, up to 60 per cent of gross national product when FitzGerald took office in 1982. A review of the performance of the Irish state noted 'Despondency seems to be on the increase, as though the intractability of our problems had at last sapped our will to solve them.' There may have been a will to solve the problems, but within FitzGerald's government there was no consensus on how to deal with them. Conservative members of Fine Gael felt that austerity was necessary to restore credibility to the Irish state and confidence for potential investors. Labour and FitzGerald worried of the impact of deflationary moves especially on the most vulnerable in society.

Neither side won out. Balancing the budget was a running battle between Finance, now under Alan Dukes, a young economist, and the Labour Party. Spring and Dukes became distrustful of one another, and FitzGerald struggled between them, failing to back up his finance minister on a few occasions. Added to this was that Spring's party was divided, and many agreements in cabinet were then second-guessed and sent back for revision by the Administrative Council of the Labour Party. So, a country with a severe economic crisis was led by a man who had made his name as an economist with no ideas as to how to solve it.

The economy drifted towards the rocks, as did the government. Disputes over the budget, over a national development plan – one of the government's few original ideas – and over Irish Steel, a loss-making state-owned company, spilled over into personal animosities between Labour and Fine Gael ministers. Meanwhile, FitzGerald withdrew. He withdrew mainly to the issue about which he was passionate: Northern Ireland. In government, he had said that he would run government policy on Northern Ireland himself, and, while he would countenance losing on any issue of government policy, on Northern Ireland he would have complete control. This was not difficult for many in government to agree to. If they did not necessarily share his instincts, they trusted his judgement. In any case, at least it kept him busy and out of their way.

Between his first government and his second, FitzGerald changed tack. FitzGerald held a deep abhorrence of the IRA, something shared by the UK Prime Minister, but Thatcher was also viscerally unionist in outlook. FitzGerald now regarded bringing the British on board as more important than anything he could do domestically. John Hume, the leader of nationalism in Ireland, suggested a Council for a New Ireland, where all interested parties, excluding Sinn Féin, the political wing of the Provisional IRA, could discuss the path to a peaceful settlement.

FitzGerald suggested a name change, aware that Hume's suggestion sounded too much like the failed Council of Ireland in the Sunningdale Agreement. Unionist parties, predictably, boycotted the New Ireland Forum – though a few spoke at it in a personal capacity. The Forum was a nationalist talking shop, whose three possible solutions to the conflict were a unitary state, a confederal state and joint authority between the British and Irish governments. FitzGerald had preferred not to include a unitary state as one of the proposed solutions, but others pointed out that if nationalists would not make a case for a united Ireland by peaceful means, then the IRA and Sinn Féin would do so by other means.

FitzGerald wanted to use the Forum report, which was published in May 1984, as a vehicle to restart meaningful talks with the British. A summit at Chequers that November at which he presented the main elements of the report was a public disaster. It was not helped that the IRA had attempted to assassinate Thatcher at the Tory party conference in Brighton six weeks earlier. There was confusion and disagreement over whether a press conference would be held. The Irish said they would have one, so then Mrs Thatcher decided she would too. She went through the suggested solutions and gave her famous 'out, out, out' response. FitzGerald, back in London, had not heard her and gave the worst press conference of his life. He felt that Mrs Thatcher had been 'gratuitously offensive'. Back home, Haughey exulted at FitzGerald's misfortune and felt vindicated for not supporting those solutions short of full reunification. FitzGerald bore the criticisms stoically and pushed on. Thatcher, too, might have felt she had gone too far. The support of Ronald Reagan for the Irish cause also helped.

However, a key relationship was that between FitzGerald's secretary, Nally, and Mrs Thatcher's secretary, Robert Armstrong. The two developed a close bond, a friendship based on mutual respect. An Irish diplomatic adviser, Michael Lillis, also developed relationships in the British system, in particular with David Goodall. Armstrong and Goodall were convinced that the British policy to treat Northen Ireland as a security issue was mistaken and were open to dialogue that would give the Irish government a formal role in Northern Irish affairs in return for a recognition of the Union, which meant amending Articles 2 and 3 of the Irish Constitution.

Thatcher's 'out, out, out' response had reassured unionists that any such development 'lay in a burial plot somewhere in Chequers'. Armstrong and Nally kept talking even when their principals found it hard to agree. By April 1985, the basis for an agreement was 'now discernible'. The Irish government would be given a consultative role in the running of Northern Ireland by way of a secretariat in Belfast in exchange for improved security cooperation and SDLP participation in any British proposal for a devolved assembly. (The party had boycotted the most recent attempt.) Talks were rocky, and Thatcher was not fully on board. When Tom King became the new Secretary of State for Northern Ireland, he asserted a security response again, setting the process back. Eventually, an agreement was found, and the Anglo-Irish Agreement, an international treaty, was signed at Hillsborough Castle outside Belfast on 15 November 1985. Unlike the previous year, both sides agreed a script, and stuck to it for press briefings.

The unionist response was united and unremittingly negative. It organised huge marches in opposition. Unlike Wilson and Sunningdale, Thatcher stuck to the agreement and did not flinch at the opposition – she might even have been steeled by it. Back home, Haughey also opposed the agreement, but it soon became clear that this was a political misstep since public support for the agreement was broad and strong. For FitzGerald, it gave a rare political win that saw Fine Gael get a temporary boost in the polls. But more than the political reward, FitzGerald felt the reward of having finally made progress. Although a consultative role might not have seemed much, it was the first significant change in the status of Northern Ireland since it was founded 60 years earlier. It also led to increased cooperation between the British and Irish officials that normalised relationships, gave constitutional nationalism a reward it badly needed and enabled the political process that would become the Good Friday/Belfast Agreement 13 years later. This political success was a relief from the incessant negativity of his government in Dublin.

FitzGerald tried to refresh his cabinet through a reshuffle in February 1986. It was another debacle. One minister, Barry Desmond, refused to move, which impacted all the other moves FitzGerald had planned. Another part of the reshuffle was unconstitutional, something he should have known himself, but that would have been pointed out had he consulted with Nally. No new ministers were promoted, which annoyed his backbenchers. The cabinet retained its jaded look. They were all exhausted.

The political landscape had also changed. A new party, the Progressive Democrats (PDs), was mainly a breakaway from anti-Haughey people in Fianna Fáil, but it seemed to be taking support from Fine Gael voters disaffected with the ineffectual government. The government lost its majority through resignations from both Fine Gael and Labour and depended on the PDs to pass legislation on the creation of the European single market and extradition. The PDs offered a liberal position on the economy, proposing to decrease the size of the state. This might have been a factor in Fine Gael's final budgetary response, which dropped any pretence to social democracy and asserted austerity. This predictably caused a rift with the Labour Party. But there were no fireworks. The energy was not there. The Labour Party quietly resigned, with letters that were appreciative of FitzGerald's efforts in the previous four years. Fine Gael did not even put the budget that would be the centrepiece of its election campaign to a vote in the Dáil. Instead, an election was called for 17 February 1987.

It would be a four-week campaign, which, FitzGerald reasoned, would give him time to chip away at Fianna Fáil's poll lead. It worked to some extent. FitzGerald tried to frame the election as him versus Haughey. He attacked Haughey's position on the Anglo-Irish Agreement and Northern Ireland. The problem was that Ireland had just had four years of FitzGerald. The economy was naturally the focus of the election. Little had improved. If anything, it seemed worse. Taking a chance on Haughey did not seem so bad. In any case, FitzGerald had lost much of the energy and enthusiasm of five years earlier, though he raised his game for a TV debate with Haughey in which he scored some successes. Beyond that, he seemed resigned to defeat.

That defeat came. Fine Gael dropped 12 percentage points and lost almost 20 seats. A consolation for FitzGerald was that Haughey was denied the overall majority he craved and that opinion polls at the start of the campaign suggested he would get. Fianna Fáil was close enough, though, to form a minority government. FitzGerald immediately resigned as leader of Fine Gael but not before tying the hands of his successor. He indicated that Fine Gael would support Fianna Fáil if it felt that the government party was behaving in the national interest. It was a final attempt to encourage Haughey to do the right thing.

Perhaps FitzGerald's successor, Alan Dukes, would have come to the same conclusion in any case. In a famous speech made in a south Dublin suburb, Dukes set out the 'Tallaght Strategy', which promised Haughey's minority government support if it worked to improve the financial state of the country. This Haughey did with surprising alacrity. Perhaps FitzGerald's lasting legacy would be to tame Haughey? He had little else to point to.

The Anglo-Irish Agreement was a clear achievement. But despite the difficult economic circumstances he inherited, FitzGerald also had an opportunity to do something in other areas. He had a united party and an almost obsequious media. While there was little unity in the government on how to deal with the economy, those other issues that FitzGerald dealt with, abortion and divorce, were ones on which he could have showed leadership. On abortion, he caved in to pressure, making a political decision. On divorce, he mishandled a strong position to deliver a defeat.

FitzGerald did not resign himself to a dotage out of the public eye. While he did not become an irritant to the new party leader, as some feared he might, he remained vocal in policy debates. He was re-elected for Fine Gael in the 1989 general election, staying a loyal backbencher. He was approached to run as Fine Gael's candidate for the Presidential election in 1990 but turned down the offer. Much of his extra time was devoted to caring for his wife, Joan. She was wheelchair-bound by severe arthritis during his premiership. He was now able to care for her, but physically she needed much more support. She died in 1999 after over 50 years of marriage.

FitzGerald also wrote a complete autobiography, becoming the first Taoiseach to do so. *All in a Life* was very long and detailed, though by some accounts it was cut by a third by the publishers, and it re-engaged in a lot of self-justification and detailed policy debate that he had had in government. FitzGerald borrowed a significant amount of money to invest in Guinness Peat Aviation (GPA), an airline leasing company of which he was a director. GPA went bankrupt, and FitzGerald lost a lot of money. He received a debt write-off by the bank of almost €500,000 in today's money, for which he was severely criticised, but a tribunal that considered the issue found no wrongdoing. In 1997, FitzGerald became the Chancellor of the National University of Ireland – a largely ceremonial office for the formal institution that oversees the independent constitute colleges that make it up.

But it was in policy debates that he continued to assert himself. He wrote a weekly newspaper column in the *Irish Times* throughout his retirement. It might be a stretch to say it was as influential as it once had been; one week, the paper failed to notice that it had reprinted an earlier column. He continued to write, publishing a new memoir in 2007, called *Just Garret*, which was largely lifted from his earlier autobiography. He was regularly invited on television and radio programmes to comment, which he did with force, defending a position on Northern Ireland and the EU that he had basically held since the 1960s. He canvassed actively in each of the referendums on the integration of the EU. When he died in 2011, aged 85, there was great warmth expressed for someone who ran two unsuccessful governments but who professionalised Fine Gael to become a real alternative to Fianna Fáil, with a degree of policy distinction that had never before been seen. He made it a competitive party, and while those governments might have been incoherent, they were free from corruption. His second government offered a degree of stability at a time it was needed. As his colleague and rival Conor Cruise O'Brien said, 'There [was] steel under all that pretty wool.'

10

Albert Reynolds

1992–4

Martin Mansergh

Full name: Albert Martin Reynolds
Date of birth: 3 November 1932
Place of birth: Roosky, Co. Roscommon
Date of death: 21 August 2014
Site of grave: Shanganagh Cemetery, Shankill, Co. Dublin
Education: Summerhill College
Married to: Kathleen Coen (m. 1962)
Children: Philip, Miriam, Leonie, Andrea, Cathy, Emer and Albert Jnr
Assumed office: 11 February 1992
Date of resignation: 15 December 1994
Length of tenure: Two years, 10 months, two days
Quotation: 'What Ireland needs now above all else is peace.'

The Reynolds family lived on Main Street, Roosky. John P. Reynolds engaged in multiple business activities: he was a farmer as well as a coach-builder, auctioneer, undertaker and later owned a ballroom. From early childhood, Albert Reynolds enjoyed dancing and was interested in horses but not farming. His parents inculcated a work ethic in their children and a strong religious commitment.

The Reynolds family were not politically involved but supported Fianna Fáil. A neighbouring family, the Hanleys, would be more influential, giving Reynolds his first experience of canvassing and learning more about the party. (During Reynolds's early life, from 1939 to 1954, the Fianna Fáil Roscommon TD was Gerald Boland, Minister for Justice in de Valera-led governments.) In the community, Reynolds also encountered families who had resettled from the North in the early 1920s to escape sectarian violence. He lived through the shortages and rationing of the war years.

Reynolds attended the national school in Roosky but transferred for his final year to Carrigeen, a one-teacher school with an inspiring teacher, Elizabeth McLaughlin, who tutored him outside school hours so that he could win a bursary to secondary school. He subsequently attended Summerhill College in Sligo as a boarder. He could not complete the Leaving Certificate because of a sporting accident, and that precluded teacher training. Subsequently, at work, he studied accountancy and completed his exams to intermediate level. He always knew how to read balance sheets. Like other leaders who started from a business background, such as W. T. Cosgrave and Seán Lemass, Reynolds's self-confidence and advancement came from varied and adventurous practical experience rather than academic qualifications.

After short-term jobs in a hardware shop in Pearse Street, Dublin, and the Pye factory in Dundrum, Reynolds found employment in Bord na Móna in Kildare, which allowed him to develop his bent for backing horses. He rented a plot and harvested turf for family use and local sale. He then moved to Córas Iompair Éireann, the semi-state public transport company, where he served as a railway clerk, starting at Dromod, Co. Leitrim, and then working at stations on narrow-gauge lines as far north in the county as Ballinamore. His job was to organise onward transport of goods and animals, including north of the Border. He encountered unionist farming and landed politicians from Fermanagh such as Harry West and Northern Ireland Prime Minister Lord Brookeborough.

He met his future wife, Kathleen Coen, when he was posted to Ballymote, Co. Sligo, and had to deliver parcels to the drapery store where she worked.

Recognised for his organisational ability, in 1955, Reynolds was invited by the parish priest of Roosky to take on the job of secretary of the Roosky Carnival Committee, which raised funds for church repairs. The dance bands in the marquee were a great financial success, and, with his brother, Jim, who returned from Australia, and support from other family members, a ballroom called Cloudland was opened in Roosky, followed by a chain of others. As the business developed, Reynolds gave up his career with CIÉ. One characteristic unusual in the business was that Reynolds was teetotal.

He hired showbands and singers, including Larry Cunningham, Joe Dolan, Johnny Cash, Roy Orbison, Jim Reeves, Brian D'Arcy (later a priest and family friend) and the ill-fated Miami Showband (three of whom were murdered on the Border in 1975). On one occasion, Reynolds hired the Ulster Hall, where Acker Bilk and Kenny Ball performed to a large crowd. He came to know people and performers north of the Border from both communities. His business dealings there with unionists as well as nationalists gave him a first-hand knowledge and experience that he was later able to put to good use in helping him to advance the Peace Process. He married Kathleen Coen in 1962, and the couple remained married for over 50 years until his death in 2014. They had seven children.

After the ballroom and showband era passed its peak, Reynolds embarked on other business ventures, including property companies and the development of a swimming pool in Longford with business associate Noel Hanlon under an urban renewal scheme. He parted commercial company with his brother Jim, owner of the Longford Arms Hotel. His business success gave him financial independence but not always freedom from disputes and controversy. While he had a genial manner, he could also be ruthless and unforgiving. From a bacon factory in Dublin's south inner city on Francis Street, where an early partner was John McShane from Portadown, and then an unsuccessful venture in fish exporting, Reynolds moved on to the major business venture of his life, what became C&D Foods, selling tinned pet food to the British market and in particular Sainsbury's from a premises outside Edgeworthstown,

Co. Longford. Although his son Philip took over the management after he became a minister, Reynolds remained the biggest shareholder. He was one of few Irish politicians to have personally created jobs.

His business background appealed both to his constituents and to those who favoured business experience in their politicians. In 1972, he was elected President of the Longford Chamber of Commerce. He also bought an ailing local newspaper, the *Longford News*, and turned it around. During elections of the early 1980s, it was a valued publicity vehicle for him. In the late 1960s, Neil Blaney, Minister previously for Local Government and then for Agriculture and Fisheries, took charge of by-election campaigns, six out of seven of which between 1966 and 1969 were won by Fianna Fáil. Reynolds volunteered to join his by-election team. He later acknowledged how much he learnt from Blaney's canvassing methods and how exciting those times had been.

While based in Dublin, overseeing his bacon factory, Reynolds assiduously attended the second Arms Trial in October 1970, in which former Minister Charles Haughey was charged with others with a conspiracy to import arms illegally. A similar charge against Blaney, another sacked minister, had been dismissed. Another defendant known to Reynolds was Flemish businessman Albert Luykx, who escaped prison. He had settled in Ireland after the war and had won the contract to supply and build the Longford swimming pool.

From 1971 to 1974, Reynolds was an elected member on the Fianna Fáil National Executive and Director of Elections for Longford in the 1973 general election. In 1974, he stood in local elections at the invitation of local TD Frank Carter, who intended to retire at the following election. Reynolds made plans to stand, but in early 1977 Carter changed his mind. Too committed at that point to withdraw, Reynolds won a nomination at the party's election convention. In the 1977 general election, when Fianna Fáil won a sweeping majority, the party returned two TDs in Longford–Westmeath, Seán Keegan and Albert Reynolds, then aged 45.

He made his maiden speech on the Industrial Development Bill, 1977. While praising the IDA, he urged it and the banks to be more adventurous with regard to small industry needing capital. He stressed the opportunities of an EEC market of 250 million people. He criticised the capital taxation policies of the previous National Coalition and spoke of the opportunity for canned foods, such as mackerel.

The Irish economy ran into difficulties in 1979, with the second oil crisis and a prolonged postal strike. Following Lord Mountbatten's assassination in Sligo in August, Taoiseach Jack Lynch came under heavy pressure from new British Prime Minister Margaret Thatcher to make security concessions impinging on sovereignty. Speculation grew about Lynch's imminent retirement, leading to jockeying for the succession between George Colley and Charles Haughey. Reynolds was a supporter of Haughey and an informal caucus, including Reynolds on the fringe, met to hasten the change in leadership, spurred on by two by-election defeats in Lynch's Cork heartland.

What Reynolds and others canvassing for Haughey during the leadership campaign wanted were a firmer grip on the economy and that Fianna Fáil in government would be 'the republican party' with more conviction. Lynch resigned after hosting the European Council in Dublin in early December, intending to give George Colley an advantage, but Haughey won a tight contest by 44 votes to 38 and became Taoiseach. He appointed Reynolds Minister for Posts and Telegraphs and then for Transport. After he became a minister, he and his wife acquired an apartment in Hazeldene in Ballsbridge, which could also accommodate family studying in Dublin.

Between 1979 and 1991, in four administrations led by Haughey, Reynolds always occupied an economics ministry. The late 1970s had seen a surge in inward investment, following Ireland's EEC entry. This exposed glaring infrastructural deficiencies, particularly the antiquated telephone system and poor transport connectivity. While plans had been drawn up to modernise the telecommunications system, political drive was needed to implement them. Reynolds received government backing for an investment programme costing over £1 billion. Over the next few years, the system was transformed.

After the prolonged 1979 postal strike, Reynolds had to restore confidence in the postal system, and he developed a problem-solving rapport with management, unions and workers. He rescinded a decree by a ministerial predecessor, Conor Cruise O'Brien, which refused permanent pensionable employment in the Post Office to any Sinn Féin member. At the request of Cardinal Tomás Ó Fiaich, he approved the installation of a television transmitter in the Cooley peninsula to boost RTÉ reception in Northern Ireland, as counterpart to increased reception of BBC NI and UTV in the Republic from their transmitters close to the Border. His other responsibility was public transport and air transport. He pushed through the first bus lanes in Dublin. Prompted by ministerial colleague Brian Lenihan, he restored a rail commuter service to Maynooth. A network of regional airports in addition to Monsignor James Horan's Knock Airport project was planned, to overcome long road journeys, not least for executives of multinational industries.

In the three general elections of 1981–2, a consequence of which were two governments that each lasted only nine months, Reynolds topped the poll and exceeded the quota. In June 1981, he could point to increased industrial employment and a new Telecom Éireann engineering headquarters in his constituency. During that election, standing in Longford–Westmeath, Reynolds was careful to show respect for the family of hunger-striker Martin Hurson held in the H-Blocks of the Maze Prison.

During opposition years in the 1980s, Reynolds returned to his business while remaining active politically. Under Haughey's leadership, statements by cabinet colleagues on the North were discouraged. Reynolds later admitted that he would have liked to comment on Owen Carron's election as MP for Fermanagh and South Tyrone as an anti-H-Block candidate and on Section 31 of the Broadcasting Act, which prohibited interviews with Sinn Féin He did strongly contest the charge made by Taoiseach Garret FitzGerald on Fianna Fáil's lack of contact with unionists and cited his own long-standing business contacts across the Border.

In January 1982, the Fine Gael–Labour government appointed a new front bench, and Reynolds lost his opposition responsibility for telecommunications. There was unrest within Fianna Fáil after backbencher Charlie McCreevy criticised the party's negativity on the economy, attacking the government for being 'monetarist' (i.e. Thatcherite). Reynolds, a friend of McCreevy, shared some of his reservations. The coalition's January 1982 budget, described by Reynolds as an economists' budget, was defeated and precipitated a general election.

Over the next year, Haughey faced three leadership challenges after his failure in three elections to win an overall majority, but Reynolds stayed in his camp. In the 1982 Fianna Fáil administration, Reynolds was appointed Minister for Industry and Energy. At the time, he regarded as his major achievement the attraction of the US forklift company Hyster, inclusive of R&D, to Ireland, where it established itself in Blanchardstown with generous IDA grants promising 400 jobs. However, the jobs never exceeded 300, and the company closed in 1987, when Reynolds was in America.

Reynolds had to decide immediately on nationalisation of the Whitegate oil refinery, which went through. He closely examined the proposed contract for building the Kinsale gas pipeline to Dublin and sharply reduced the cost to the state. It was completed on time and within budget. He directly negotiated a contract to supply gas to Northern Ireland. A deal was concluded, but a British treasury official privately complained that Reynolds had run rings round his minister of state. In 1984, Thatcher cancelled the deal, for financial and strategic reasons.

At the November 1982 general election, Albert Reynolds was joined in the Dáil representing Longford–Westmeath by party colleague Mary O'Rourke (née Lenihan, sister of Brian Lenihan). She was able, ambitious and competitive and was promoted to the front bench as Spokesperson on Education in February 1983. Reynolds became Spokesperson for Industry, but his faith in Haughey was eroding. The feeling was mutual; Haughey regarded Reynolds's instincts on the state sector as right-wing.

Reynolds was critical of the Fine Gael–Labour coalition and of the gulf between fiscal rectitude rhetoric and exponential growth in the national debt coupled with prolonged recession. His critique was summed up in his catchphrase, 'the paralysis of analysis'. Reynolds's reservations about Haughey's hard-line rejection of the 1985 Anglo-Irish Agreement became known, and Taoiseach Garret FitzGerald often praised Reynolds, reportedly to annoy Haughey.

In the 1987 general election, the party won three out of four seats in Longford–Westmeath, strengthening Reynolds's position in the party, and gave the Midlands constituency two cabinet ministers till 1991, though the third seat was lost in 1989. Reynolds insisted on being appointed Minister for Industry and Commerce. The economy had been in the doldrums for years.

The new government took office in March 1987 on a programme of national recovery, which developed into the first Social Partnership agreement with employers, trade unions and farmers that October. Reynolds made headlines by instructing oil companies to cut out their gift packages and lower the price of petrol by 10 pence. He challenged the Electricity Supply Board, which he discovered had substantial reserves tucked away in their accounts, to lower electricity prices. An accommodation was reached where they had to give ground. He also banned 'hello money', a practice that put new suppliers at a disadvantage when negotiating access for their products in supermarkets. He spent time in the USA and Japan on trade missions and promoting investment. As a minister speaking business language and with a developing range of pithy promotional aphorisms, he made a favourable impact at meetings and on business audiences abroad against the backdrop of an Irish economy taking off rapidly.

Reynolds was fertile in schemes, some derived from his business contacts. He was interested in selling Irish Steel to a German company, Korff AG, opposed by Desmond O'Malley, and the Whitegate oil refinery to a Nigerian state oil company. But he had difficulties persuading either his civil servants or his government colleagues, who were averse to such high-risk deals. Irish Steel was essentially gifted to an Indian company by the Rainbow Government in the mid-1990s and closed down shortly afterwards.

Reynolds sought to bring a businessman's approach to bear on the work of government and of the departments of which he was minister. At times this could be uncomfortable for government colleagues, civil servants and state agencies accustomed to a more conventional political and administrative approach. He believed in talking through problems and was resistant to voluminous and wordy written communications. He committed little to writing. He had a critical eye for balance sheets, especially those of state companies. He maintained his own independent channels of information, whether reliable or not, and he liked to clinch deals, some of which were undoubtedly advantageous and others which were or might have been unacceptably high-risk.

In November 1988, Reynolds succeeded the Minister for Finance, Ray MacSharry, who was appointed EC Commissioner. MacSharry had been tough but egalitarian. Reynolds's appointment represented some shift of emphasis towards the middle and business classes. In private, he expressed himself keen to bring the top rate of tax down to 50 per cent in two stages but was sceptical about social welfare increases. He believed poverty was often the result of financial mismanagement, but he was ready to increase payments to dependants. The budgetary redressment of 1987–8 had been so successful, aided by £500 million raised by the 1988 tax amnesty, together with the resumption of growth, that Reynolds was able in the 1989 budget to reduce the standard rate of income tax from 35 to 32 per cent and the top rate from 58 to 56 per cent. He announced his intention of means-testing child benefit but did not proceed with it. In March 1989, Reynolds went to New York to promote the IFSC, announcing that Chase Manhattan Bank was setting up an operation and proclaiming Ireland's commitment to free enterprise and the low 10 per cent rate of corporation tax for international traded business. He impressed the corporate elite, among them future key supporters of the Peace Process.

The minority government was prone to Dáil defeats on private members' motions. Reynolds opposed Haughey's decision to call the June

1989 election and try for an overall majority. Voters were unconvinced, and media campaign coverage concentrated on health cuts, which had borne the brunt of expenditure cutbacks, despite Fianna Fáil's 1987 general election advertisement that 'Health cuts hurt the old, the sick and the handicapped.'

The party dropped four seats in the 1989 election to 77, six short of a majority. Fine Gael declined to back the government from opposition by renewing the Tallaght Strategy. Its price for coalition was a rotating Taoiseach. However, the PDs, under Desmond O'Malley, after a bad election in which they lost eight seats, still had the missing number of six seats. As an alternative to another election and to salvage his leadership, Haughey met O'Malley, and negotiations started. The Fianna Fáil negotiating team was led by Reynolds and Bertie Ahern. Reynolds resented parallel back-channel discussions between McCreevy, reporting to Haughey, and Mary Harney of the PDs, while Minister of State at the Department of Agriculture and Food Joe Walsh also pursued direct informal PD contacts.

Reynolds regarded it as a high-stakes poker game, and, with Pádraig Flynn, at one point advocated going into opposition. On the number of PD cabinet ministers, Ahern and Reynolds held publicly there should only be one. Reynolds professed disgust when Haughey conceded two. Reynolds reflected a widespread party view that Haughey's leadership was the obstacle to an overall majority. At a party meeting in Kanturk, Co. Cork, in February 1990, Reynolds called the Fianna Fáil–PD coalition 'a temporary little arrangement', but, like so many developments initially thought of as temporary, coalition has proved a permanent feature of government ever since.

Reynolds introduced two more budgets, but this time PD influence was brought to bear on their priority of cutting taxes. The standard tax rate was reduced to 29 per cent while the top rate came down to 52 per cent, on the way towards a single higher rate converging on the middle rate at 48 per cent. Bands and exemptions were widened. The standard VAT rate was reduced in two equal steps from 25 to 21 per cent. In three budgets, the general welfare increase was 3.5 and 4 per cent. Reynolds was constrained on one side by the PDs, who constantly pressed for personal and corporate tax reductions, partly funded by indirect tax increases, and on the other side from 1991 by Social Partnership commitments under the Programme for Economic and Social Progress.

While Reynolds presented his budget as fulfilling the Programme for Economic and Social Progress, he was privately scathing about public service pay rises of 10 per cent over three years. Social partnership agreements were overseen and managed from the Taoiseach's office, sometimes leading to serious friction with Ministers for Finance. One structural change involved removing national debt management from the Department of Finance to the National Treasury Management Agency, the legislation steered through the Oireachtas by Reynolds. He had responsibility for distributing £3 billion in structural funds, negotiated with EC President Jacques Delors, to boost capital investment alongside completion of the single market.

During Ireland's 1990 EC Presidency, an informal EC finance ministers' meeting was hosted by Reynolds in Ashford Castle, Co. Mayo. Headway was made on defining budgetary criteria for membership of the single currency. This was when Reynolds first became friends with John Major, then British Chancellor of the Exchequer.

Internal party divisions were heightened by the debacle of the 1990 Presidential election. Acute controversy arose over the Fianna Fáil candidate Brian Lenihan's 'mature recollection' about attempts to speak to President Hillery to prevent a dissolution of the Dáil on 27 January 1982, when the Fine Gael–Labour coalition fell over the budget. Lenihan's ministerial dismissal for lying was demanded by the PDs. Reynolds stood by Lenihan, as he resisted pressure from Haughey's emissaries to resign. Mary Robinson was elected President of Ireland, but the campaign seriously damaged Haughey's leadership and increased the party's desire for a new leader before facing the electorate again.

The Goodman group, backed by the government in 1987–9 both with IDA grants and export credit insurance, went into examinership following the Iraqi invasion of Kuwait in August 1990 that led to the First Gulf War. Subsequent departmental investigations as well as media ones, following complaints by competitors, uncovered multiple irregularities, including the sourcing of non-commercial beef outside Ireland, leading to Dáil calls for a tribunal of enquiry into the beef industry, which had O'Malley's backing. Conceded by Haughey, it was a blow to his prestige. The Beef Tribunal caused collateral political damage that cut short one Reynolds administration and foreshortened the other.

Reynolds became the leading challenger to Haughey's hold on power. Time was seen as limited, with EC Commissioner MacSharry's term ending in December 1992. Two unremarkable speeches on Northern Ireland were seen as designed to bolster Reynolds's leadership credentials by Haughey. Against the background of an economic slowdown, in September 1991, the finance minister criticised public service pay increases under the Programme for Economic and Social Progress but was contradicted by a government spokesman. Renegotiation of the Programme for Government saw Reynolds dig his heels in on sweeping PD tax demands. While he successfully blocked 'big bang' tax reform, ministerial colleagues were unwilling to risk the fall of the government after four and a half years of economic progress.

That autumn, a wave of scandals broke over Haughey, relating to the privatisation of food company Greencore, a conflict-of-interest issue in the purchase of a telecom building in Ballsbridge and the purchase of Carysfort College. He came under intense pressure to wind up his leadership. Four backbenchers put down a challenge, which mustered the support of 22 TDs. They included Reynolds, Flynn and four ministers of state. During a prolonged parliamentary party debate, Reynolds alleged that his home was under surveillance by a white van. While this was ridiculed, the atmosphere of paranoia was general. All ministers who voted against the leader but did not resign were dismissed. Haughey's victory was short-lived. Jim McDaid, appointed Minister for Defence, had immediately to resign at the insistence of the PDs, when it emerged that he had attended an anti-extradition rally.

Haughey attended the Maastricht European Council in December, which concluded the Maastricht Treaty, paving the way for introduction of the single currency. In Dublin, he also briefed then British Prime Minister John Major on the early draft of a secret joint British–Irish declaration, agreed between John Hume and Gerry Adams, which was being further worked on by officials.

Reynolds returned to the back benches. His wife Kathleen was suffering from breast cancer, and circumstances now allowed Reynolds to be with her at a critical time. What was unclear as 1992 began was whether Haughey would shortly retire or seek to retrieve his position, as in the past. In mid-January, Seán Doherty implicated Haughey in the 1982 phone-tapping of journalists Bruce Arnold and Geraldine Kennedy. PD leader O'Malley made it clear that unless Haughey resigned they would leave government. Haughey stepped down as Fianna Fáil leader on 30 January and as Taoiseach on 11 February. With regard to how much Doherty's well-coached moves were concerted beforehand with Reynolds or some in his camp, Reynolds claimed to have kept his distance.

Reynolds was favourite to succeed Haughey, representing the hopes of those who had been out in the cold during the long Haughey years. He came to an understanding with his main rival Bertie Ahern that he would step down after six years. With metropolitan superiority, Reynolds supporters were dubbed 'the country and western' wing of the party. This referred to the Midlands and West of Ireland background of many of them, and to Reynolds former show business activity, illustrated by a clip of when he donned a cowboy jacket and a Stetson hat on the Mike Murphy show to sing Jim Reeves' 'Put Your Sweet Lips a Little Closer to the Phone'.

Reynolds was elected on 6 February with 61 votes. The two other remaining candidates, Michael Woods and Mary O'Rourke, received ten and six votes respectively. At his press conference that afternoon, Reynolds pledged to concentrate on ending the Northern conflict and indicated that he wanted repeal of the Government of Ireland Act, 1920, which created Northern Ireland, in return for changes to Articles 2 and 3 of the Constitution. He also pledged to develop the economy and reduce unemployment and emigration. He promised open government, and, in an early interview as Taoiseach, he promised 'to let in the light', seen as the genesis of a government commitment to bring in freedom of information legislation. Before the handover, Haughey briefed him on the secret peace initiative.

Reynolds's government formation involved an unprecedented purge. Senior ministers Gerry Collins and Ray Burke were dropped, while long-serving backbenchers, such as David Andrews and Charlie McCreevy, were brought in, along with John O'Connell, formerly of Labour. John Wilson became Tánaiste. Reynolds's political mentor was Pádraig Flynn. His chief adviser was Tom Savage. Ahern remained in Finance, and ministers dismissed in November 1991 returned. O'Rourke, demoted to Minister of State, refused to take on Women's Affairs but, after a stand-off, was given Consumer Affairs under O'Malley, and Labour Affairs under Ruairi Quinn. Reynolds later raised unnecessary doubt over his attitude to women in politics, when, on 9 December 1993, in noisy exchanges with Nora Owen, he expostulated, 'This is women now.'

The purge accentuated party divisions and left Reynolds dependent on his own support base in a crisis. When Brian Cowen became Taoiseach in May 2008, Reynolds doubted that his former protégé would follow his example. Reynolds's leadership style was that of managing director not chairman or partner, and this created difficulties. He had a preference for discussing problems, often till late, rather than on paper, to which, he told the Beef Tribunal, he had a 'one-sheet approach'. This was usually rendered as 'one-page man'.

Reynolds was media-friendly and spoke often to favoured journalists. He began holding weekly briefings which proved unsustainable and were not continued during his second administration. His openness to the media was qualified by his tendency to be litigious, in sharp contrast to his predecessor. No ideologue where history was concerned, he once said W. T. Cosgrave was right to force Fianna Fáil into the Dáil in 1927.

Reynolds had ambitious economic plans. Two initiatives came to fruition in 1993 and 1994. County and city enterprise boards were established to provide support to local small and start-up companies. The Strategic Management Initiative, borrowed from New Zealand, aimed to provide a framework for radical public-service reform. It did not achieve reduced costs or numbers. His hopes that McCreevy would streamline social welfare were dashed when cuts dubbed 'the dirty dozen' by Labour became an electoral disaster.

Reynolds found himself immediately under pressure on abortion. Within days of taking office, a storm of controversy, leading to street demonstrations, blew up over Attorney General Harry Whelehan's injunction to prevent a 14-year-old girl, raped by a family acquaintance, from travelling to Britain for an abortion (known as the 'X' case). Unknown to the public, the matter first arose during the interregnum between Haughey's resigning and Reynolds's assuming office.

When the High Court granted the injunction, Ireland was pilloried for 'interning' pregnant teenage girls. The family appealed to the Supreme Court on the grounds that the girl was suicidal and came under the mother's constitutional equal right to life. Their judgement upholding the appeal created huge shock in the pro-life movement and the Catholic Church, its authority about to be further undermined by the Bishop Eamonn Casey affair. The 1983 pro-life amendment needed urgent clarification. The attempted government policy compromise was to affirm the right to travel and information (i.e. to allow access to abortion services abroad) but to close the serious breach in the prohibition of abortion at home by removing suicidal intent as a legal ground for it.

Reynolds came into office an orthodox Catholic, having declined in his younger days an invitation to join Opus Dei. Because of his wife's illness, he had the opportunity of discussing practicalities of the issue with gynaecologists treating her. Not wanting a police state, he sought to steer a middle course between liberals and women's rights activists on the one hand and pro-life organisations and the Church on the other. After weeks grappling with a problem where the boat to Britain provided a safety valve, Reynolds protested privately: 'We are a nation of hypocrites, and we clearly wish to stay a nation of hypocrites. The government are not going to interfere with that wish.'

A looming complication was the referendum to allow ratification of the Maastricht Treaty, which had an Irish protocol ensuring that European law could not be invoked to overrule the constitutional ban on abortion. The protocol had a different meaning following the 'X' case. While the opposition and PD ministers wanted the abortion complications resolved before the Maastricht Treaty was ratified, Reynolds was determined to keep the issue separate and to give Maastricht priority. When the President of the Law Reform Commission, Justice Rory O'Hanlon, stated that he would rather Ireland left the EU than see abortion introduced, Reynolds dismissed him. He also removed the party whip from Senator Des Hanafin, chairman of the pro-life movement, for refusing to support the referendum legislation. Reynolds predicted to his press secretary that 'the people won't let abortion get muddled up with Maastricht. The Irish keep their money and their morals separate.'

Fastidious pro-EU Irish opinion deplored Reynolds's emphasis on the funds Ireland hoped to obtain rather than on more idealistic reasons. The Danish people rejected the Maastricht Treaty on 2 June. In the ensuing panic, Reynolds was urged, even in Brussels, to consider postponing the vote due on 18 June. He went ahead, the vote was won decisively by 69 per cent to 31 per cent, and Ireland was the toast of the EU. The Danish vote, however, lit the fuse for the currency crisis, which, three months later, ahead of a knife-edge French referendum, saw Britain exit the Exchange Rate Mechanism.

Market pressure intensified on smaller currencies, which Ireland withstood for four months. On occasion, overnight interest rates climbed to 100 per cent, and the Irish pound rose above sterling. The general election and delay in government formation meant that devaluation was deferred. Reynolds left the battle to Ahern and officials in Finance, the Central Bank and the National Treasury Management Agency. By January 1993, he was sceptical how long it could be sustained, on the adage 'you can't beat the markets'. A 10 per cent devaluation was agreed in the last weekend of January 1993 and sparked strong and sustained economic growth.

At an early meeting with John Major in London, the priority of peace in Northern Ireland was agreed. The two men established a rapport, both having climbed to head of government despite an unassuming background, and, particularly unusual for a British Tory Prime Minister, without the benefit of inherited wealth or a privileged education. The three-strand talks process chaired by Northern Ireland Secretary of State Sir Patrick Mayhew resumed after the British general election in April 1992 won by Major. Despite unionist parties coming to Dublin in the autumn, talks broke down in early November, just ahead of the Irish government's collapse. However, they did prefigure strand one institutional provisions for a power-sharing executive and assembly in the Good Friday/Belfast Agreement. Reynolds's main hope of progress rested, with Alec Reid acting as intermediary, on the draft declaration setting out principles for a peaceful settlement. To expedite this, in October, Reynolds authorised direct back-channel contact between his office and Martin McGuinness, leading figure in the republican movement designated as Sinn Féin's chief negotiator.

The contempt between Reynolds and O'Malley was mutual. Elements in the PDs wanted an election, convinced that, like the German Free Democratic Party, they could always be in office as a swing party. When O'Malley testified to the Beef Tribunal in July, he described Reynolds's ministerial decisions to keep increasing export credit insurance to Iraq as 'foolish, reckless and grossly unwise'. Three months later, Reynolds ill-advisedly retaliated by describing O'Malley's evidence as 'reckless, irresponsible and dishonest'. There was heated ongoing argument about the amount of public money put at risk and the estimated final cost. The coalition broke up, and an election was called.

The campaign went disastrously for Fianna Fáil, which, far from gaining an overall majority under a new leader, returned with nine fewer seats and a historically low 39 per cent of the vote. Reynolds was pilloried for using a four-letter word beginning with 'c', also used by Clinton and Major, and he was treated in the media as if he were Haughey Mark 2 or worse. Labour won 33 seats and became arbiters of the next government, Fine Gael having also lost many seats. Fianna Fáil lay low while Labour rebuffed what it considered presumptuous Fine Gael overtures and turned to construct a policy platform with the Democratic Left party. When that was circulated to other parties, Fianna Fáil's prepared response approved by Reynolds and Ahern was sent back by return, indicating a willingness to adopt Labour's priorities, including a third banking force (which was never proceeded with but still remains relevant).

Reynolds left to attend a European Council meeting in Edinburgh in Holyrood Palace that would determine the quantity and distribution of EU structural funds. The outcome was stunningly successful for Ireland, which was able to benefit from the hardball negotiating tactics adopted by Germany's valued partner Spain. A new cohesion fund was agreed, mainly for Spain, and Reynolds announced that Ireland would receive £8 billion in structural and cohesion funds to 1999. Critics claimed this was overstated, but it was still the largest package Ireland ever negotiated from the EU. Reynolds gave Chancellor Helmut Kohl an undertaking that IRA attacks in Germany on British Army barracks and soldiers would cease, on the basis of a contact made with the republican leadership in Derry by a personal intermediary of Derry origin living in the Midlands.

Back from Edinburgh, Reynolds met Dick Spring and briefed him on the secret back-channel Northern Ireland peace initiative. Coalition negotiations were initiated and a programme for a partnership government agreed. It included items previously not a priority for Reynolds such as an extra May Day bank holiday and the decriminalisation of homosexuality, which Minister for Justice Máire Geoghegan-Quinn steered through the Oireachtas in 1993. Later, Reynolds refused to seek the resignation of a Labour junior office holder stopped by gardaí in a car at night in ambivalent circumstances in the Phoenix Park, to avoid creating a precedent for open season on the private lives of politicians.

Despite last-minute opposition and media efforts to derail Reynolds's return as Taoiseach in a first Fianna Fáil–Labour coalition, it took office on 12 January. Labour expected to dominate, with Reynolds becoming an avuncular figurehead. Announcing his government, Reynolds recalled that in 1932 Fianna Fáil had taken power as a minority government with Labour support and that their leader, Tom Johnson, had said, 'We shall have to coalesce some day.' Labour had six cabinet seats, proportionately more than the nine for Fianna Fáil. Spring took Foreign Affairs, and Enterprise and Employment was filled by Ruairi Quinn. Otherwise, Labour chose mainly social ministries, with the exception of social welfare, where Michael Woods was reinstated to repair the 'damage' left by McCreevy. Michael D. Higgins became the first Minister for Arts, Culture and the Gaeltacht, responsibilities removed from the Taoiseach's office. Reynolds remained personally committed to the film industry. To Labour's relief, Flynn, perceived by them to be a reactionary figure on social and family issues who was the strongest political influence on the Taoiseach, left to become EU Commissioner, where he reinvented himself as socially progressive, to the point of causing serious alarm in boardrooms.

In 1993, Reynolds nominated Gordon Wilson to the Seanad, where he was a strong witness for peace. The nation had been deeply moved at the time of the Enniskillen Remembrance Day bomb in 1987, which killed 12 people, by the poignant, deeply moving and dignified manner in which Gordon Wilson described the last dying moments of his daughter, Marie.

Reynolds retained Dermot Nally, who retired as Cabinet Secretary in December 1992, on a consultancy basis, for his experience in dealing with the British Cabinet Office. Reynolds met new US President Bill Clinton, who was eager to support Irish peace efforts, in March and asked him to defer his campaign commitment to appoint a special envoy. He also met Senator Edward Kennedy, his sister Jean Kennedy-Smith, who was nominated US Ambassador to Ireland, and leading New York businessmen and opinion-formers such as Chuck Feeney, Bill Flynn and Niall O'Dowd. Reynolds returned to Boston and New York that April.

On 20 March 1993, an IRA bomb exploded in Warrington, England, killing two boys. In April, another bomb exploded in the City of London at Bishopsgate, killing one and causing hundreds of millions of pounds worth of damage, a year after a similar bomb at the Baltic Exchange. These acts caused soul-searching about pursuing peace by back channels. Reynolds believed the city bombs ultimately made the British government amenable to negotiation, but, against that, combined with inflexible republican political messages, it made the British back channel more cautious and ultimately sterile.

Controversy arose over President Robinson's plan to visit community groups in West Belfast, where she would also meet Gerry Adams without cameras present. Despite British Government and Labour Party pressure, Reynolds let the visit proceed so as not to undermine the Peace Process. Work in the Irish back channel on the draft joint declaration had reached an impasse, but Reynolds was anxious to transmit it, even in an unsatisfactory state, to the British. Cabinet Secretary Robin Butler travelled to Baldonnel airport to receive it.

The British, whether at political or senior official level, where they met Nally and Seán Ó hUiginn of the Department of Foreign Affairs, were unwilling to negotiate on the draft, especially after John Hume and Gerry Adams went public in joint statements. In late September, Hume handed to Reynolds a short paper that nationalists were led to believe was 'Hume–Adams', in an attempt to pressurise both governments and retain control of the initiative. Unrealistic expectations and fears were raised that British acceptance of their offer would bring immediate peace.

Autumn 1993 was tense and turbulent on both security and political fronts. On 13 October, an IRA bomb based on faulty intelligence about the presence upstairs of the Ulster Defence Association leadership, detonated in a Shankill Road fish shop killing nine civilians, all Protestant, and one IRA bomber. Adams carried his coffin to much public outrage, but Reynolds understood he had to do it. First at official level, then *en marge* of a European Council in Brussels on 28 October, Major made it clear that he could not proceed with a document bearing the fingerprints of Hume and Adams. Reynolds came away believing that if the declaration were sufficiently distanced from them, it might still work. Three days after the

Brussels meeting, in the Greysteel massacre, loyalist gunmen killed eight people in a Co. Down pub.

At the subsequent Fianna Fáil Ard Fheis on 6 November 1993, he came under pressure for distancing himself from Hume–Adams. Among his catchphrases were that he was seeking a formula for peace, taking risks for peace, 'opportunity comes to pass and not to pause' and, the pointed challenge, 'Who is afraid of peace?'

The leak of an early Irish draft of a joint framework document designed to revive the talks process between constitutional parties had the opposite effect. In late November, the existence and content of secret back-channel talks between a British emissary and McGuinness, facilitated by intermediaries – former priest Denis Bradley and businessman Brendan Duddy – were exposed.

Briefed in his office by British Cabinet Secretary Robin Butler, Reynolds expressed indignation at not being informed. Two versions of documents exchanged were published: the first by the British government, then a fuller one by Sinn Féin. Partially inaccurate reports also appeared in the British press about a secret Irish back channel to republican and loyalist paramilitaries. In both countries, surprisingly, there emerged cautious support for unapproved roads to peace.

Reynolds made it clear that he was ready, if necessary, to pursue his initiative without the British government, which tabled, then withdrew, a Northern Ireland Office pro-unionist counter-draft that had no prospect of persuading the republican movement to renounce violence. Over the autumn, the draft declaration had been amplified and made more inclusive to meet British objections. Reynolds obtained paragraphs from Archbishop Robin Eames, who was in regular touch with Ulster Unionist Party leader James Molyneaux, and principles from Revd Roy Magee agreed with the Combined Loyalist Military Command. For Major, two of three avenues for progress had closed. The talks process remained in abeyance. The British back channel had ended in public acrimony.

The remaining way forward was the joint declaration. Following a stormy meeting in Dublin Castle on 3 December, when famously John

Major broke a pencil in frustration, intense negotiations on the joint declaration began, which, henceforth known as the Downing Street Declaration, was published by Major and Reynolds following a meeting on 15 December. Major later acknowledged it would not have happened without the drive and political courage of Albert Reynolds. In summary, the declaration committed the two governments to be persuaders for an agreed Ireland while outlining how a united Ireland could be achieved peacefully, using the mechanism of concurrent self-determination.

History showed that majority rule where minority consent was refused did not work. Irish unity would only be achieved by those who favoured this outcome peacefully persuading those who did not. The Taoiseach promised a balanced constitutional accommodation, fully reflecting the principle of consent in Northern Ireland. With a permanent end to violence, democratically mandated parties that established a commitment to exclusively peaceful methods would be free to participate fully in democratic politics. The Irish government would establish in their jurisdiction a forum for peace and reconciliation.

The declaration did not contain any time limit to reach agreement that could be misrepresented as a timetable for British withdrawal. It was widely welcomed and was a catalyst for peace. Among unionists, only the Democratic Unionist Party denounced it, without loyalist backing. Molyneaux sent Reynolds a friendly cautionary letter. Hume supported it with some regrets. Sinn Féin temporised, as it went well beyond what they agreed in June 1992, and sought clarification. Whereas Major adopted a peremptory approach to reassure unionists, Reynolds sought to persuade, and was willing to supply all clarification required, not involving renegotiation. He embarked on other confidence-building measures, notably lifting Section 31 of the Broadcasting Act that prohibited interviews with Sinn Féin, where his pragmatism matched Michael D. Higgins's anti-censorship zeal.

Reynolds supported Adams's US visa request, Clinton's granting of which for 48 hours caused an Anglo-American rift lasting a week. Reynolds considered the appearance of nationalists winning an argument with the British, with American support, very important. The British later accepted that they had overreacted. Reynolds wrote on a draft March 1994 letter to Adams: 'You will be amazed at the level of international support all of us can muster to assist in bringing about a political settlement. Your recent visit to the US must have convinced you of this.'

Reynolds experienced this himself on his St Patrick's Day visit to New York, Chicago, Washington and Connecticut. But IRA violence continued, including mortars fired at Heathrow Airport, which infuriated him. Reynolds rejected a temporary Easter truce. He helped the British clarify 20 Sinn Féin questions. He gave similar clarification to loyalists. In interviews, he was a tireless persuader for peace.

While waiting, the two governments reverted to trying to restart the talks process. Major pressed for changes to Articles 2 and 3 of the Constitution, asserting *de jure* jurisdiction over the island, with Reynolds, like Lemass in 1968, only willing to modify Article 3. In mid-July, when an increasingly isolated Reynolds indicated that he would have to draw negative conclusions if there were no movement by the end of the summer, his message crossed with a signal that there would be. Covering their tracks, Sinn Féin rejected the Downing Street Declaration at its Letterkenny Ard Fheis in late July. Reynolds again rejected a temporary ceasefire, proposed to him by an Irish-American delegation. A precondition of a ceasefire was that veteran republican Joe Cahill receive a US visa so as to brief IRA supporters there. Strongly urged by Reynolds, it was very reluctantly granted by President Clinton. The case put to republican activists by the leadership included their assessment that 'Dublin's coalition is the strongest government in 25 years or more' and that Reynolds had no historical baggage to hinder him.

The IRA ceasefire was announced on 31 August. A week later, Hume, Adams and Reynolds shook hands outside Government Buildings. Demilitarisation began, with border crossings gradually restored and all road-closure orders lifted by Mayhew and phased prisoner releases in the Republic. Clinton pledged a Washington investment conference in 1995. The Forum for Peace and Reconciliation opened in October.

Reynolds embarked on a tour of Australia and New Zealand. On his return, he secretly met Gusty Spence and other loyalists in Dublin, shortly before their announced ceasefire on 13 October. The British wanted movement on decommissioning weapons, made more urgent after the IRA murder of a Newry post-office worker on 10 November. The joint frameworks document, mainly drafted by Ó hUiginn at Foreign Affairs on the Irish side, was virtually complete and was published in February 1995 after the change of government. Reynolds went to America again in late October.

Success in the Peace Process did little to arrest rapidly deteriorating relations between the coalition leaders. There had been controversy over passports for sale to an Arab investor in C&D Foods, although examination of the file did not show any personal intervention by Reynolds, over tax residency rules, and in 1993 over a second tax amnesty opposed by Labour and Ahern that Reynolds pushed through. Tensions erupted over publication of the Beef Tribunal Report just before the IRA ceasefire. Before Labour had time to study the report, and without any consultation, Reynolds pre-emptively claimed vindication, which in terms of integrity was true, but not with regard to the wisdom of his conduct of the export credit insurance scheme. His informal decision-making style, businessman to businessman, without adequate regard to procedures or safeguards, especially when the rules were being flouted, won him no credit, even if in the end taxpayers were less exposed than they might have been.

A stand-off was brewing over the vacancy of President of the High Court, to which Reynolds wished to appoint then Attorney General Whelehan. Spring was opposed, wanting a more liberal nominee. There was hostile briefing from Labour sources against Reynolds while he was abroad. This, along with material later that year, led to a celebrated libel suit against the British edition of the *Sunday Times* that made legal history, in which Reynolds was at first awarded nominal damages but later won a settlement where the damaging allegations were completely withdrawn.

Reynolds failed to pin down a decision on the presidency of the High

Court appointment when he met Spring on his return. The gravity of revelations of delays in the Office of the Attorney General in processing warrants for extradition from Northern Ireland of paedophile priest Brendan Smyth was not properly grasped, and, when Reynolds pushed through a government decision, Labour withdrew from cabinet.

Whelehan's appointment proceeded in a frigid atmosphere. There was cliff-edge drama in the Dáil, with Reynolds first justifying the appointment and then, the next day, apologising abjectly for it. Claiming alleged dishonesty about an abstruse legal precedent as a justification, Labour resigned from government. Quinn told Reynolds, 'We've come for a head, Harry's or yours – it doesn't look like we're getting Harry's.' They got both.

Reynolds resigned the following day, reflecting sadly, 'It's amazing. You cross the big hurdles, and when you get to the small ones you get tripped.' Having lost the confidence of the Dáil, he did not seek a dissolution, which, under the Constitution, the President could have refused. He resigned as leader of Fianna Fáil but remained Taoiseach in a caretaker capacity while Ahern attempted to re-form the Fianna Fáil–Labour government. Labour explored all options before forming a Rainbow Coalition under John Bruton with Fine Gael and Democratic Left, for which a series of by-elections had improved the arithmetic.

The unexpected fall of Reynolds caused consternation in the republican movement. Intermediaries warned of blood in the streets. Reynolds momentarily considered a fightback but was dissuaded. Spring pronounced that the Peace Process was bigger than one man. On 15 December, Reynolds left office and then attended a party in his honour that night at the residence of US Ambassador Kennedy-Smith. The editor of the *Irish Times*, Conor Brady, later accepted that they had been unfair to Reynolds in judging his departure to be no loss. Early in 1995, a Dáil subcommittee took evidence on events leading to the fall of the Reynolds government but refrained from forming conclusions. Subsequently, more emphasis was placed on the breakdown of relations, especially between leaders, as the explanation.

As ex-Taoiseach, Reynolds continued to be a member of the Council of State. He remained a TD till 2002 and was in international demand for his unique blend of political and business achievement. In October 1995, he talked to the Basque parties seeking a similar peace process to end the ETA campaign in Spain. He disputed the British contention that the decommissioning precondition to talks was signalled prior to the IRA ceasefire. He received an honorary doctorate from the National University of Ireland in 1995, and was honoured by universities in North America, Europe and Australia. In 1998, he was elected Grand Marshal of the New York St Patrick's Day parade.

At Ahern's suggestion, he offered himself as party nominee for President in 1997, but the nomination was won by Mary McAleese. After bruising revelations concerning Haughey, there was nervousness in the parliamentary party that old controversies concerning Reynolds would resurface and that his unconventional habits of operation might create problems in a Presidential role, which he promised to use to promote business. (He was later criticised for inappropriate solicitation of a party donation from developer Owen O'Callaghan in the Mahon Tribunal Report.)

Reynolds felt betrayed by Ahern and sometimes made political interventions unhelpful to his successor. Ahern invited him to the reopening of Stormont in May 2007. Some were astonished to see Ian Paisley Jnr crouch beside Reynolds to obtain his autograph. Reynolds claimed he had helped advise the Democratic Unionist Party how to navigate Sinn Féin negotiating tactics. Internationally, after talks with President Pervez Musharraf of Pakistan, Reynolds persuaded Bill Clinton to meet Musharraf when visiting the region. Reynolds also had discussions with Colonel Muammar Gaddafi on compensation to the families of victims from the Libyan bomb on an aircraft that exploded over Lockerbie in 1988.

In 2006, the C&D factory burnt down, but the business was kept going by Philip Reynolds. Between 2008 and 2019, ownership transferred in stages to the Goodman group. Reynolds's autobiography with Jill Arlon was published in 2009. In 2010, during the financial crisis that led to the

IMF/EU bailout, he conveyed to government what he believed was an alternative offered by the Chinese.

A last public appearance was in May 2011 at the state banquet in Dublin Castle for Queen Elizabeth II. At that stage, he had been diagnosed with Alzheimer's disease, and within a short time his condition deteriorated drastically. Years previously, he and Kathleen had moved to a penthouse apartment in the Four Seasons Hotel in Ballsbridge. John Major visited him and his family there on the 20th anniversary of the Downing Street Declaration in December 2013. Albert Reynolds died on 21 August 2014, and was buried in Shanganagh Cemetery in Shankill, Co. Dublin.

Reynolds came to politics late, in mid-life, without any strong party background, and, unusually for a Fianna Fáil leader, other than Jack Lynch, without earlier family involvement in the War of Independence. He prided himself on his pragmatism and made a significant contribution towards bringing Ireland's economic performance and living standards up to European levels. He negotiated a transformative EU aid package. Nevertheless, his business-style approach to government had a mixed reception at home and created for him a controversial and contested reputation. However, combined with success in peace-making, it was very attractive to the American investment community. While not good at holding governments together, nor a strong party leader, Reynolds pioneered a highly productive, if short-lived, Fianna Fáil–Labour partnership. He was the shortest-serving Taoiseach till then, but not subsequently. His lasting achievement, despite one breakdown in the ceasefire, was his decisive role in persuading the republican movement to bring to an end the 25-year IRA campaign.

This is an edited version of the Albert Reynolds entry in the *Dictionary of Irish Biography*, reproduced by kind permission of the Royal Irish Academy. For the original, see www.dib.ie.

11

John Bruton

1994–7

Matthew Dempsey

Full name: John Gerard Bruton
Date of birth: 18 May 1947
Place of birth: Dunboyne, Co. Meath
Married to: Finola Gill (m. 1978)
Children: Matthew, Juliana, Emily and Mary-Elizabeth
Education: Clongowes Wood College; UCD; King's Inns
Date of death: 6 February 2024
Site of grave: Saints Peter and Paul's Church, Dunboyne, Co. Meath
Assumed office: 15 December 1994
Date of resignation: 26 June 1997
Length of tenure: Two years, six months, 12 days
Quotation: 'The economy is not an abstraction. The economy consists of people, and it will only grow if people feel secure and are reasonably free.'

The road as the darkness descended was lit by a continuous line of candles and phone torches as people spontaneously came out to pay their respects to their constituency's long-serving TD and the country's former Taoiseach, John Bruton. A small group of cars followed the coffin and the state funeral army outriders from the house and farm where John and Finola lived and reared their family for the few miles to the parish church in Dunboyne – a Dunboyne which had during John Bruton's lifetime grown from a country village to a commuter town on the outskirts of an expanding Dublin.

John Bruton had represented the Meath constituency since 1969 when, at the age of 22, he was elected as a Fine Gael TD. It was inconceivable that he could have stood for any other party. Fine Gael, in his and his family's view, stood for an Ireland that would make its own way in the world but as part of a European family and with good relations with Britain the former colonial power. He once described Fine Gael as being made up of the 'coping classes', people who would want to stand on their own feet and make their own way by their own efforts in the world. These basic tenets of self-reliance and a sense of duty to society were to shape his attitudes and set the tone for his career as a member of the Dáil, as Minister, as Taoiseach and, finally, as the EU Ambassador to the USA. It was the range of experiences that gave him an unusual blend of the local, national and international.

The family background of John Bruton was graphically encapsulated in Raymond D. Crotty's seminal work, *Irish Agriculture: Its Volume and Production*. In the aftermath of Catholic Emancipation, the Land Wars and the resultant Land Acts that were passed in Westminster, there emerged a group of well-off Catholic farmers who, in Crotty's memorable phrase, 'were not pushed by poverty nor pulled by Noblesse Oblige to the mud and dirt of Flanders'.

With the increasing industrialisation and growing wealth and population of Britain, the demand for agricultural produce, especially meat and, during the First World War, cavalry horses, was vibrant. With capital and good land, this group of farmers prospered. John's father, Joe, was sent to the Jesuit boarding school at Clongowes Wood College. John was to follow him in 1959 and completed his Leaving Certificate in 1965.

At Clongowes, he thrived. Intelligent and good-humoured, he honed his skills at debating as well as taking part in the school plays and rugby, while his natural interest in history was encouraged by the presence of an excellent collection of history volumes overseen by a committed Jesuit priest. Even at that stage, he was enthusiastic at the possibility of EEC entry. In UCD, as well as doing Economics and Politics, John did the Bar at King's Inns but never practised as a barrister.

UCD had an active Fine Gael branch -- there was never a question of joining any other party – and in 1969, at the age of 22, he secured a nomination to contest the Meath constituency. He was narrowly elected, unseating the existing Fine Gael TD. He was to serve as TD for Meath until his retirement from politics in 2002. There followed three years as an opposition TD with Liam Cosgrave as party leader.

In 1973, the Fine Gael–Labour coalition came to power in the aftermath of the dismissal of three Fianna Fáil ministers accused of gunrunning by Jack Lynch. With Liam Cosgrave as Taoiseach, Bruton was promoted to the junior ministerial ranks, or Parliamentary Secretary as the office was then termed, in the Department of Education. He had particular responsibility for coming up with policies to encourage underprivileged children to remain in education. He was particularly conscious of the intergenerational cycle of lack of education and resultant poverty.

The 1977 election came as a nasty shock to Fine Gael. The country had joined the EEC in January 1973. After the oil shock later that year, and the collapse in cattle prices in 1974, the economy was improving, and there was a growing confidence that the coalition would be re-elected. But in what was widely seen as fiscally irresponsible pre-election promises, Fianna Fáil, under Jack Lynch, won a landslide victory but one which, with the benefit of hindsight, reinforced Fine Gael's reputation for fiscal prudence.

It was with Cosgrave as Taoiseach that the Sunningdale Agreement had been signed, and John Bruton, with his close relationship with Cosgrave, was fully au fait with the negotiations that led up to it. Cosgrave resigned as leader after the election defeat in 1977 and was replaced by Garret FitzGerald. In some ways, Cosgrave was a father figure to the young John Bruton. He was also deeply interested in farming and rural families. FitzGerald, however, was much more urban in his outlook and upbringing.

John Bruton formed a close friendship with Garret's wife, Joan. Born in

Liverpool, her father, though of Irish extraction, had served in the British diplomatic service in Africa, and this cosmopolitan broad experience as well as her Economics degree from UCD made her an unusual political wife in the Irish firmament.

Despite the deeply contrasting characters of Cosgrave and FitzGerald, Bruton got on well with both men and was highly regarded by both, but his relationship with each of them proved to be very different. FitzGerald had incorporated Declan Costello's Just Society document as Fine Gael policy, and John Bruton accepted the thrust towards equality and social inclusion in Costello's proposals.

On becoming leader, FitzGerald promoted Bruton to the opposition front bench as Spokesman for Agriculture, a job he took to with gusto. His father, Joe, had been Chairman of the Livestock Committee of the Irish Farmers' Association as well as on the Executive Committee of the Royal Dublin Society where the main agricultural show, the Spring Show, as well as the National Bull Sales were held. He worked hard at his brief and was naturally at home with Fine Gael's important agricultural constituency.

But politically the period was dominated by the bitter infighting within Fianna Fáil between Jack Lynch and Charlie Haughey as well as a developing national financial crisis. When Garret FitzGerald won the 1981 election and was elected Taoiseach, he promoted the 34-year-old Bruton Minister for Finance. It was a baptism of fire. It was a coalition government taking over a country with a large budget overspend as well as inflation and interest rates that were sending businesses into bankruptcy and indebted farmers into penury. Unemployment soared as did the balance of trade deficit.

As Bruton presented his first budget in January 1982, the need for increased government revenues was all too apparent. He proposed to levy VAT on clothes and shoes, including, critically, children's shoes. The budget and the government fell as a key independent TD voted against it.

The early to mid-1980s were chaotic for the national finances. Garret FitzGerald as the new Taoiseach initially demoted Bruton to Minister for Trade, after the third election in two years, Fianna Fáil were again in opposition and Garret again became Taoiseach. As Taoiseach, he was unable to control the petulant leader of the Labour Party, Dick Spring, but in 1986 made John Bruton Minister for Finance for a second time.

After the 1987 election, Haughey again became Taoiseach, and Alan Dukes became leader of Fine Gael. While Dukes and Bruton had a mutual respect for each other, they were too different to be close friends. Bruton replaced Dukes as leader in 1990. In the election of 1992, Fine Gael recovered much lost ground, and Bruton seemed to be in pole position to head a new coalition government, but Dick Spring, instead of joining with Labour's traditional ally Fine Gael, joined up with the new Fianna Fáil leader, the amiable, blunt-spoken businessman, Albert Reynolds from Longford.

Consigned to the opposition benches, with no visible route to government, John Bruton's leadership of the party came under intense internal pressure. Prominent colleagues went on television to talk of his 'charismatic deficit'. As party leader, he not only faced disloyalty in his own party ranks, he also faced a party that was so short of money that it considered selling its own national headquarters, a modest Georgian townhouse on Dublin's Mount Street. These problems did not deflect him from developing policies in which he believed deeply: the European ideal, a strong ethical base founded on clear religious convictions and an abhorrence of violence to achieve political goals.

During these early years of his leadership, it became clear who his friends and supporters were. Chief among them were Phil Hogan, his brother Richard, Enda Kenny and Ivan Yates. Michael Lowry, with his financial fundraising skills, totally transformed the party's finances. An amusing footnote and an indication of the party's financial recovery is that the Fine Gael Christmas drinks reception moved, under Enda Kenny's leadership, from soggy sandwiches and carafe wine in the down-at-heel garden at the back of the house on Mount Street to delicate finger food and an open bar in the main first-floor suite of the Shelbourne Hotel.

Bruton's wife, Finola, formerly Gill, from Westport, whom he married in 1981, provided unwavering support as he pursued his political career with its long hours and varying prospects. A devout Catholic of strong faith and beliefs, she provided a stable and principled home for the rearing of their four children.

In February 1994, there was a proposed party vote of no confidence in Bruton as leader. The rebels were defeated, and he stamped his authority on the party by sacking the ringleaders from the front bench. They included Michael Noonan, Alan Dukes and Frances Fitzgerald. Also during 1994, Fine Gael unexpectedly won a crucial by-election in Mayo caused by the promotion of Pádraig Flynn to the European Commission. The favourite to take the seat was Pádraig Flynn's daughter, Beverley (Cooper) Flynn, running for Fianna Fáil. However, the seat went to the flamboyant Fine Gael candidate and Westport native Michael Ring. Ring's victory marked a turning point for John Bruton personally as his delight at the stunning victory was as infectious as it was visible.

On the same day, at a by-election in Dublin South Central, Fianna Fáil also lost a seat, this time to Democratic Left candidate Eric Byrne. Democratic Left had emerged in 1992 after a split in the Workers Party. During the years in opposition, Bruton had, despite holding ostensibly very different views, developed a respect and liking for the Democratic Left leader, Proinsias De Rossa. Their election victory now gave them four Dáil seats which were to prove crucial in future discussions.

With the loss of two Fianna Fáil seats, the Dáil arithmetic was changing, and, after a reasonably good European parliament election in 1994, when the party held on to its four seats and secured 24.5 per cent of the vote, John Bruton was in a stronger position.

Meanwhile, the long-running Beef Tribunal, essentially an inquiry into the close relationship between Larry Goodman and Albert Reynolds and the granting of export guarantees to Goodman's firm, Anglo Irish Beef Processors, trundled on. Labour had pushed for the inquiry, and, after months of exhaustive probing and a less than conclusive conclusion by the presiding judge, and subsequent Chief Justice, Liam Hamilton, Albert Reynolds declared that he had been vindicated.

Labour leader Dick Spring did not see it quite the same way, and, after a furious row over the botched extradition of a paedophile priest and the subsequent short-lived appointment of the Attorney General, Harry Whelehan, to the presidency of the High Court, Albert Reynolds, under intense pressure, resigned after losing a vote of confidence.

On the electoral front, Fianna Fáil lost two more seats in Cork. The new leader Bertie Ahern assumed that the coalition with Labour could be put back together again. But, following an RTÉ interview with John Bruton and strong media comment in the *Irish Times*, Dick Spring was forced to reconsider his proposed alliance with Fianna Fáil and Bertie Ahern. On 6 December, just a day before the Dáil was due to elect a new government, Spring informed Ahern that he would not continue in coalition with him and instead rang John Bruton and asked for a meeting.

Suddenly negotiations with Labour were back on, and the friendship that had formed between Bruton and De Rossa of Democratic Left bore fruit. While Lowry was the main negotiator and adviser, Bruton also relied on the grand-niece of Michael Collins, Nora Owen, to reflect a balanced view of party feeling. Ostensibly, Dick Spring drove a hard bargain in securing the position of Tánaiste and Minister for Foreign Affairs for himself and the Finance portfolio for Ruairi Quinn. The demand for a rotating Taoiseach was dropped.

While it was the first time a Labour minister was in charge of the finance ministry, Quinn proved able, far-seeing and balanced. He led the negotiations that resulted in the 12.5 per cent corporate tax rate being accepted by Brussels, an achievement that was to have a long-term beneficial effect on Ireland's prosperity. Quinn also abolished the levying of Capital Acquisitions Tax on assets passing between husband and wife.

As Taoiseach, one of Bruton's key challenges was the handling of the Peace Process in Northern Ireland. Having seen at first hand how the Sunningdale power-sharing agreement had been undermined, he treaded carefully. It is hard to overestimate the difference between Bruton and the then Sinn Féin leader, Gerry Adams. Bruton believed to his core in non-violence to achieve political ends and was never slow to refer to the success of John Redmond (the leader of the Irish Parliamentary Party) in achieving Home Rule for Ireland by peaceful means only to see its implementation delayed by the outbreak of the First World War. He viewed the Easter Rising as a misjudgement, and one of his first acts as Taoiseach was to hang a portrait of John Redmond in his office. He also hung one of Seán Lemass, one of his predecessors as Taoiseach.

Gerry Adams was visibly more comfortable with Fianna Fáil and was conscious that John Bruton never hid his belief that not only was Gerry Adams prominent in the leadership of the IRA but that he was also a member of its Army Council. Nevertheless, he was Taoiseach, and peace was a prize worth fighting for. Bruton is quoted by Stephen Collins of the *Irish Times* as saying 'I put a high priority on protecting the institutions of this state and ensuring that there was no tolerance for private armies or arms dumps. My first responsibility was to the people of this state. Others had different views and probably believed that other objectives were more important.'

Bruton met Gerry Adams, accompanied not by his former special adviser and former Irish Ambassador to the USA, Seán Donlan, who was well known to share Bruton's views, but by Paddy Teahon who was later to become Secretary General of the Department of the Taoiseach. Teahon was a key figure in Irish political and economic life for decades, and he acknowledged with some admiration that Bruton recognised his own limitations in dealing with republicans.

The Peace Process itself took an enormous amount of John Bruton's time and energy as Taoiseach. He himself estimated it took 70–80 per cent of his time with endless talks around the crunch issue of decommissioning weapons. The disappointment of the abandonment of the IRA ceasefire and the bombing of Canary Wharf were setbacks, but the discussions continued. The unionists viewed Bruton as the first Taoiseach who understood their point of view, and, slowly, a framework emerged that was ultimately to result in the Good Friday/Belfast Agreement.

There were other significant challenges. Bruton operated to an extremely high standard ethically. To an extent, it was self-imposed, and the leaking of budget details a few hours before its delivery led to the sacking of Phil Hogan as Junior Minister at the Department of Finance, though it did not in the longer term prevent him from being nominated by Enda Kenny as Ireland's Commissioner in Brussels. Hugh Coveney, as Minister for Defence, was forced to resign having casually mentioned that his quantity-surveying firm was available to undertake contracts. It was ironic that Coveney was sacked in John Bruton's own home on his way to the Union Day at Clongowes where both had been at school and John Redmond had become President of the Past Pupils' Union during the school's centenary year of 1914. John Bruton was to become the President for the bicentenary year of 2014.

Hugh Coveney's son, Simon, inherited his father's Cork seat and became a minister in a later Fine Gael government, but Hugh Coveney himself died in an unfortunate accident while out walking along the coast near his home in Cork.

John Bruton had agreed in the Programme for Government that a second referendum on divorce would be held, and, despite his strong religious views, he believed that the constitutional ban on divorce was inappropriate. He campaigned strongly, and a radio interview he gave on the Sunday before the referendum date was seen as crucial in securing the result, the tightest in Irish referendum history: 50.2 per cent voting yes, 49.8 per cent no – a margin of just 9,114 votes.

The removal of the claim to the six counties of Northern Ireland was a long-standing objective of Bruton who steadfastly maintained that unification could only come by peaceful means and with the consent of both parts of the island. Both he and the British government under John Major insisted that the decommissioning of paramilitary weapons had to be an intrinsic part of any peace agreement. Eventually, a framework document was agreed which was an essential prerequisite for the Good Friday/Belfast Agreement and was formalised in April 1998 by Tony Blair and John Bruton's successor as Taoiseach, Fianna Fáil's Bertie Ahern.

John Bruton estimated that Northern Ireland and the Peace Process took up 70–80 per cent of his time as Taoiseach, but he was spared the odium that comes from a faltering economy. On the contrary, under his competent Finance Minister, Ruairi Quinn, the economy continued to improve, and it was confidently expected that as the preparations continued for the official introduction of the euro, Ireland would be able to meet the entry conditions.

Domestically, however, there were some hiccups. Bruton's long-term adviser and confidant, Michael Lowry, had to resign following the revelation of a dubious tax arrangement with Dunnes Stores with whom his refrigeration company did business. Ironically, the revelations led to the setting up of the McCracken Tribunal, which led to the discovery of large payments from Ben Dunne to Charlie Haughey.

There was also embarrassment from the discovery that women who had received blood from the state Blood Transfusion Service were affected by Hepatitis C infections, some fatally. While a full compensation scheme eventually emerged, the Minister for Health Michael Noonan's handling of the issue was strongly criticised. The issue affected the government's standing with the public.

On the law-and-order front, the public was horrified at the murder on the public highway at Newlands Cross, just outside Dublin, of Veronica Guerin, a senior journalist with the *Sunday Independent*. John Bruton's close friend and colleague Nora Owen, as Minister for Justice, led a reappraisal of how organised crime should be combatted. The Criminal Assets Bureau was established in response to the outrage. This is now seen as one of the outstanding and long-lasting achievements of the Rainbow Coalition.

Nevertheless, the constitutional imperative of a Dáil election within its five-year period was coming into focus. John Bruton and his party had come into office without an election. The omens looked favourable: the economy was doing well; the Northern Ireland Peace Process was visibly making progress; and even though bovine spongiform encephalopathy (BSE) was affecting farming and particularly the markets for beef, the blame was not attributed to government failure, and significant financial support was provided by Brussels.

Ivan Yates had been appointed Minister for Agriculture by John Bruton and served as Minister for Agriculture during John Bruton's entire time as Taoiseach. He was a popular minister with the important agricultural constituency. Despite various problems in the sector, he was widely acknowledged as being committed and hard-working. In fact, at one stage, he was ordered to rest because of exhaustion brought on by overwork. He continued to back John Bruton until the end of his time as Taoiseach. Yates backed Bruton's establishment of a specialist agricultural policy unit.

Never lacking in moral courage or a willingness to acknowledge past omissions, John Bruton initiated, on the 50th anniversary of the end of the Second World War, an official commemoration of the many Irish who had fought with Britain in the two world wars. The impressive Irish National War Memorial Gardens, designed by Sir Edwin Lutyens in Islandbridge, Dublin, so long neglected, were restored, and there is now an official annual commemoration of all those Irish men and women who died in wars in the form of a National Day of Remembrance. Bruton also apologised for the failure of de Valera's government during the Second World War to admit into Ireland Jews fleeing Nazi Germany.

The year 1997 had to be an election year, and making a decision when to hold an election was not easy. However, with favourable opinion polls on the government's performance, John Bruton opted for June rather than waiting until the autumn as some advised. The Rainbow Coalition of Fine Gael, Labour and Democratic Left campaigned on a joint platform while Fianna Fáil entered a formal alliance with the PDs, led by Mary Harney. Fine Gael had an excellent election, gaining 10 seats, but Labour lost 17 seats going from 33 to 16. Fianna Fáil's partner, the PDs, also lost, going from 10 seats to four. At the end of the day, it was Fianna Fáil, with Bertie Ahern as leader, with the PDs and support from miscellaneous independents who formed the next government.

In August, the McCracken Tribunal provided riveting details on Charlie Haughey's lifestyle, the cost of it and the source of the money. The Fianna Fáil Minister of Foreign Affairs, Ray Burke, had to resign and serve a prison term. The revelations came after the election, and whether they would have had any effect on the result can only be a matter of conjecture. Despite wobbles, the Fianna Fáil–PD coalition hung together, and Fine Gael and John Bruton faced an indeterminate period in opposition – a role which John Bruton found difficult. Stephen Collins quotes Bruton calling 'leader of the opposition' the most difficult job in politics: 'Party activists want you to be unremitting in attacking the government and floating voters want you to act responsibly in the national interest. Navigating these contradictory pressures is almost impossible.'

It was only a matter of time before discontent flowed over, and, in November, Waterford TD and Garret FitzGerald's Minister for Agriculture in the mid-1980s, Austin Deasy, proposed a vote of no confidence in John Bruton as leader. While he was expected to get only five or six votes, in fact Deasy got 24 members of the parliamentary party to back his no-confidence proposal; while Austin Deasy's motion failed, the size of the vote against Bruton meant that he had become vulnerable. Three months later, there was another effort to unseat him, this time with Michael Noonan and Jim Mitchell leading the rebellion. Despite a strong speech widely acknowledged as one of his best ever, Bruton was defeated by 39 votes to 33.

He stayed on as a TD representing Meath until the 2002 general election which he did not contest and in which Fine Gael, under Michael Noonan, returned with just 31 seats, a loss of 23 seats. Fianna Fáil, with Bertie Ahern as leader, were to continue in power until another tribunal forced his resignation, to be replaced by Brian Cowen and the effective financial collapse of the state. In fact, Fine Gael's best days lay ahead of it.

One of the strengths of the European system is that former prime ministers' talents can be assessed and made use of. With Bruton's training and experience recognised, he served as a leading member of the committee that drafted the proposed European Constitution, which was signed in Rome in October 2004. While it failed to be ratified by some key member states, the main provisions were incorporated into the Lisbon Treaty.

Because of his impressive role on such a key European project and his prominence in the European People's Party (Christian Democrats),

Bruton was appointed as EU Ambassador to the USA in 2004. He was the first politician to fill this post and was extremely active in explaining and representing the EU across America, as well as addressing a joint session of Congress. After five years in Washington, he and Finola returned to Ireland convinced that Europe needed to increase the democratic visibility to its public by implementing a system of directly electing the President of the EU Commission.

He returned to Ireland deeply concerned about the growing polarisation that was becoming apparent in American politics – a polarisation that has become more extreme in the intervening period and a system which he described as 'dysfunctional'. He formed a close friendship with leading American figures and took up the chairmanship of the IFSC in Dublin as well as board membership of Ingersoll Rand.

Along with Bertie Ahern, he gave evidence to the UK House of Lords on the damaging implications of Brexit and the harm a hard border on the island of Ireland would do to the Good Friday/Belfast Agreement. In his retirement, he kept closely in touch with Fine Gael and never wavered in his strong religious convictions, publicly opposing, with his wife, the introduction of abortion in Ireland.

His state funeral took place on Saturday, 10 February 2024, four days after his death on 6 February 2024. Taoiseach Leo Varadkar gave the graveside oration and recalled that when John Bruton became a TD, there were 1 million people employed in Ireland; by that time there were 2.7 million. He had lived through a time of momentous change in Ireland and in Europe and had played an important part in influencing some of the key events.

12

Bertie Ahern

1997–2008

Mick Clifford

Full name: Bartholomew Patrick Ahern
Date of birth: 12 September 1951
Place of birth: Drumcondra, Dublin
Married to: Miriam Kelly (m. 1975; sep. 1987)
Children: Georgina and Cecilia
Education: St Patrick's National School, Drumcondra; St Aidan's Christian Brothers, Whitehall; Rathmines College of Commerce
Assumed office: 26 June 1997
Date of resignation: 7 May 2008
Length of tenure: 10 years, 10 months, 11 days
Quotation: 'The reason it's on the rise is because probably the boom times are getting even more boomier.'

To begin at the end. On the afternoon of 26 March 2008, a Ministerial Mercedes pulled into a leafy estate off Griffith Avenue on Dublin's Northside. Emerging from the car was Brian Cowen, the Minister for Finance – the man, many observers claimed, who had saved Bertie Ahern's bacon at the general election nine months earlier. The previous day, Cowen had returned from an extended St Patrick's Day break in Vietnam and Malaysia, and this was the first opportunity for him to meet with his leader in over a week. Cowen went inside the Taoiseach's home where Bertie Ahern was waiting.

What transpired between them has never been fully revealed. In all likelihood, the obvious went unspoken. Both men knew what was required. The past had caught up with Bertie. A tribunal examining his finances had heard some startling evidence – to the point where what was tumbling out could no longer be ignored, brushed off, ascribed to overeager lawyers. So soon after the peak of the greatest triumph of his career, in June 2007, he had arrived at the nadir.

We can envisage the two men conversing, maybe over a whiskey or two, a little reminiscence, a few serious thoughts on gathering economic clouds. But no rancour. This was not Cowen making a grab for power. Far from it. He had long been anointed to be Ahern's successor, to the point that Bertie had publicly declared it on radio the previous year.

When the meeting ended, Cowen left to begin preparing for the change to come. Inside his home, Bertie had a little time to reflect on an extraordinary journey in which he had overseen transformative change for his country.

When Ahern was first elected Taoiseach, in 1997, the last remnants of a theocratic state were dissolving. Economically, the country was in the early years of speeding towards the ranks of wealthy, developed nations. By the time he left, in 2008, the Republic of Ireland was transformed. Under his premiership, the place grew up, matured, acquired wealth and ultimately lost the run of itself. Decades of emigration were swapped for the advantages and challenges of immigration. The perennial scourge of unemployment was erased. A liberal, secular state emerged from the theocracy, and, crucially, the north-east of the island had arrived at a point where internecine violence would never again be contemplated.

His tenure was also marked by a national awakening as to the secrets and lies that had kept a respectable veneer on the state while many, usually the most vulnerable and weakest, suffered in silence. The inquiries into the past were cathartic. Most had to do with the crimes of the Church, but there were also examinations of how those at the upper echelons of business and politics had abused their positions. It was in the latter that lay the seeds of Ahern's own downfall.

Inevitably, in light of all he did and all he did not do, opinion on his role in Irish politics tends to be divided. In essence, there are three prongs to his legacy: his stewardship of an economy that boomed and then went bust; his role in silencing the guns in Northern Ireland; and his personal financial conduct when he first held high office.

Bertie Ahern was born in 1951 and grew up in a family of five siblings in Drumcondra, on Dublin's Northside. His parents were from Cork – his father, Con, a farm manager in the All Hallows seminary, his mother, Julia, a homemaker. Con was a veteran of the War of Independence and the anti-Treaty side of the Civil War. As such, Fianna Fáil was in the family blood.

Bertie showed an early interest in politics and was reputedly shimmying up lamp posts to apply posters during the 1965 general election. Twelve years later, he had completed his education and was working in the Mater Hospital as an accountant when the opportunity came up to get on the party ticket in the Dublin Central constituency. One of the party grandees told Frank Dunlop, who was serving as Government Press Secretary, that there was a 'young fella called Ahern' in the reckoning but added, according to Dunlop, 'I don't think he'll amount to much.'

Ahern was elected in the 1977 landslide win for Jack Lynch's Fianna Fáil which yielded a majority of 20 seats in the Dáil. Once in, he was determined he would never be found wanting in minding his constituency. He quickly developed a ward system in which the whole area would be assiduously covered for canvassing right throughout the Dáil term. That system, peopled by a group with which he surrounded himself – Ahern hacks rather than party hacks – led to the moniker of 'the Drumcondra mafia'.

Ahern quickly hitched his wagon to Charlie Haughey, the outsider, the fellow Northsider, who won leadership of the party in 1979 on Lynch's forced retirement. In 1982, Haughey appointed him Chief Whip and a Junior Minister at the Department of Defence. Haughey's political instincts were suspect in many ways, but in this choice for his chief whip he was certainly astute.

Ahern was a man who went out of his way not to make enemies. He got along with people, and he was an excellent negotiator. Some of his attributes in this respect were down to a personality that many perceived – erroneously – as non-threatening. He was Bertie, the cuddly guy in the anorak from the Northside of Dublin. That was how he projected himself, and those who were not as clever as him often initially underestimated his intelligence and resolve as a result. It was not all a designed front, but the projected persona served him well. Years later, in his autobiography, Bertie would reveal, 'With me, what you saw was what you got.' Many among those who would have collided with him during his career might react to such a declaration with a wry smile.

Haughey was a hugely divisive figure in the party, prompting steely loyalty from some and disdain, often bordering on hatred, from others who saw him as a person of low morals. It would be many years before the extent of his corruption would come to light, but his enemies within Fianna Fáil sensed that his character was hugely flawed. Ahern was vital during a series of heaves against Haughey, managing to marshal support for his boss until such time as the disaffected retreated into the long grass.

The party was out of government between 1983 and 1987, but when it returned, Ahern's status had grown. In 1987, he was appointed Minister for Labour, an ideal vehicle for his talents. He oversaw the establishment of the social partnership in which employers, unions and farmers came together to agree a broad outline for the way forward for a fixed term. (A community and voluntary pillar would be added in the mid-1990s.) This was to be the start of a system that persisted right until the end of Ahern's premiership, one for which he was a competent midwife but which grew to be more problem than solution during the years of the Celtic Tiger as far as some were concerned.

Haughey called a snap general election in 1989, which he hoped would return his party to power with a comfortable majority. It did the opposite. Fianna Fáil were left short and required, for the first time in its history, a coalition partner. In stepped the PDs, the entity established four years earlier by refugees from Haughey's rule in Fianna Fáil. Ahern was crucial to the coalition negotiations, managing to be trusted by both sides at a time when large numbers in both parties were appalled at the idea of coalescing with the other.

He was credited with bringing the final deal home in the early hours of 18 October 1989. Later that day, while Ahern was briefing reporters, Haughey stuck his head in the door and pointed to his protégé. 'He's the man', Haughey said. 'He's the best, the most skilful, the most devious and the most cunning of them all.' It was a description that would be referenced many times over the remainder of Ahern's long career.

In late 1991, there were attempts to unseat Haughey. Ahern stuck by his man, but the Taoiseach sacked his Minister for Finance, Albert Reynolds, who had been behind one of the heaves. Ahern was appointed as the new Minister, an effective imprimatur that he was the incumbent's designated successor.

The following January, two months ahead of his first scheduled budget, Ahern went on an RTÉ chat show and revealed that his marriage had broken down. On a political level, this was designed to pre-empt issues around his budget, a day when the Minister is customarily accompanied by his wife for a photocall. On a human level, the revelation from the father of two daughters that he 'had my own domestic difficulties for a couple of years and will continue to have them' was a departure for any public figure. He also voiced support for a change in the law to allow divorce. While the breakdown of a marriage barely registers a footnote with most public figures in the developed world, a public acknowledgement of it by a prospective Taoiseach was unprecedented in Ireland at the time. Fianna Fáil was the conservative force in the country, yet here was one of its top figures publicly acknowledging that the edifice around marriage was susceptible to human frailty.

Ahern's domestic circumstances cast a very long shadow over his career. Some of his political opponents would use it against him when later that year Haughey resigned and a battle to succeed him ensued. Much later, when the Mahon Tribunal investigated his finances, Ahern would claim – implausibly, according to the Tribunal Chair – that a whole range of irregular actions and the accumulation of money were all associated with his marriage breakdown.

In January 1992, Haughey was forced out under the welter of political scandals. Ahern and Reynolds were the front-runners to succeed him, but, even before the campaign got under way, one of Reynolds's key supporters told a local newspaper that Reynolds was the 'envy of politicians in terms of his family life'. Reynolds himself said in one interview that 'people want to know where their Taoiseach is living'. Dragging in Ahern's entirely normal family circumstances was low but may not have been the only factor to prompt Ahern to decline to run against Reynolds, who won the subsequent leadership battle easily. Reynolds appointed Ahern as the Minister for Finance.

The early 1990s were a busy time for Ahern. He went from being an upcoming Minister to taking over the Finance portfolio and, ultimately, in 1994, being elected leader of his party. Many years later, it would emerge that it was also a period during which he was involved in highly unorthodox financial dealings. He would claim, consistently, that all of this had to do with the breakdown of his marriage. For much of his tenure as Minister for Finance between 1991 and 1994, he did not have a bank account. This, he would say, was attributable to his domestic circumstances, although he had been separated in the mid-1980s and was in a new relationship once the money started flowing in.

Between December 1993 and December 1995, a total of £147,500 was lodged in accounts associated with him or his partner at the time, Celia Larkin. There was also another £30,000 sterling – which may have actually been $45,000 – lodged in another account. Much of the money was acquired through what came to be known as whip-rounds and dig-outs. On two occasions, the Tribunal was later told, friends of his got together and collected money to give him a handout as he was allegedly having financial difficulties. At the time, he was the Minister for Finance.

He did not have an ostentatious or extravagant lifestyle – far from it. As a separated father, he obviously had the extra expense that arises with supporting himself and his wife and two children, but at the time he was living in an apartment above his Drumcondra constituency office. During this period, there was also a 'whip-round' for him among UK-based Irish businessmen in a Manchester hotel following a match at Old Trafford. Ahern says he did not solicit any of this money. The Tribunal did not identify any favours which were asked for or received by any benefactor.

Some of the explanations given by Ahern and others about how the money was acquired were bizarre. One man told the Tribunal of bringing £30,000 sterling in a suitcase over to him from the UK. Ahern himself would at one point claim that he won a lot of money at the time gambling on horses. At least one individual who was alleged to have contributed to a dig-out at the time had a recollection of being asked to make a political donation.

In 2012, the Tribunal ruled that Ahern did not truthfully account for £165,000 (€220,000) which had arrived in various bank accounts associated with him. 'Much of the explanation provided by Mr Ahern as to the source of substantial funds identified and inquired into in the course of the Tribunal's public hearings was deemed by the Tribunal to have been untrue', the Mahon Report stated.

The whole narrative around how Ahern acquired the money – the explanations, the myriad accounts, the absence of any personal bank account for the Minister for Finance – left a sour taste among the public. This was not the Bertie of the anorak, the working man who was trying to do his bit for his community and his country. This was what might be described as a poor man's Haughey.

A separate tribunal determined that Haughey received around £8 million over the course of his time in politics and that on a couple of occasions he appeared to be providing favours for a benefactor. Ahern, or the few other senior Fianna Fáil figures who came into big sums of money, were nowhere in that league. But it might well be posited that some who observed the party leader, the great chief, hoovering up money all over the place might have concluded there was no big deal in acquiring a bag of cash here or there as a little bonus for their public service.

In December 1994, Reynolds resigned, a casualty of his inability to treat his junior coalition partner with due respect. The ostensible reason was a hasty judicial appointment under the shadow of the state's apparent shoddy handling of a clerical sexual-abuse scandal. Ahern's ascent to the top job was a given. However, there was one sting in the tail. Further revelations about the scandal prompted the Labour Party to walk away from the coalition with Fianna Fáil and form an alternative one with Fine Gael and the Democratic Left party.

Just as Ahern had arrived at his party's summit, his crowning hour of glory as Taoiseach was further delayed. That was rectified in the general election two and a half years later. Running on a campaign of tax cuts, Fianna Fáil increased its seat complement by nine to 77 in the 166-seat Dáil. The PDs, led by Mary Harney, won four seats, and a deal was hatched with four independents for their support. The outgoing government had also promised tax cuts, but their plans were wrapped up in credits and bands. Fianna Fáil provided a simple message of rates, easily digested and appreciated. It was a victory against the odds, the first in which Ahern was to demonstrate his personal appeal to the electorate.

The following year, the relatively new Taoiseach was a central figure in the Good Friday/Belfast Agreement, an achievement that posterity is likely to rank as his greatest in politics. The Provisional IRA had stopped killing in 1994 but broke its own ceasefire 18 months later due to the intransigence in the opening up of an alternative political path.

In 1997, talks got under way for a new dispensation between nationalists and unionists, under the joint auspices of the two sovereign governments. Senator George Mitchell from the USA was drafted in to chair the talks. In the UK, the 1997 election of the bright, shining Tony Blair added further momentum. Ahern, however, was crucial to it all. His personal political skills, his comprehensive knowledge of history, his innate feel for the disenfranchisement and sense of abandonment experienced by Northern nationalists all ensured he would be a central figure in the negotiations.

One of his key skills had always been negotiating, and this came to the fore in dealing with unionists. Initially, they regarded him with suspicion, considering him the de facto leader of a pan-nationalist front, but he won them around with a combination of charm and a capacity to absorb their insults and suspicion and keep ploughing on, eyes fixed firmly on the finish line rather than any bruised ego on his part. This, to him, was personal and something he was determined to see through, leaving his stamp on an ancient quarrel that had bedevilled relations within the island and with the Republic's nearest neighbour. 'I always learnt to watch first, get my bearings and try not to attract too much in the way of attention', he wrote in his autobiography. 'Then when I had got the lie of the land, I would have my say.' The approach was precisely what was required in the talks.

His commitment to the cause was most notable in the week in which the negotiations rumbled towards an endgame. In Holy Week 1998, Ahern's mother Julia died. He left the negotiations in Belfast and returned to Dublin. While he was gone, things began to falter. A frantic call was made to the bereaved Taoiseach, gathered with his immediate family to grieve a highly significant passing. He did not hesitate but decided to make his way back up, even before the full funeral rite had been completed. His effort in this respect was captured in the diaries of Alastair Campbell, Blair's communications guru:

> We were also a bit stuck without Bertie but he came back around 6.30, looking even more knackered than before. I felt really sorry for him. It was obvious the way he talked about her that he was close to his mother, and she was barely buried and he was back taking a whole lot of grief from the [Ulster Unionists]. They talk to him and about him, with something close to contempt, and it was terrific the way he took it.

The prize was finally achieved in the early hours of Good Friday 1998. Some observers have asked whether the deal could have been done without Ahern. The answer is probably – but at further cost. The Provisional IRA's campaign was running out of steam. Even among the sections of the nationalist community that supported the Provos, major questions were arising as to the purpose of continuing to kill people for an island that was simply unattainable. The world was also in flux. Just three years later, 9/11 would change everything, particularly in relation to tolerance of terrorism of any form.

So, change was coming. However, the skills that Ahern – and others like Mitchell – brought to the table ensured that there would be no more killing and that a framework was in place through which the peace could be held to a point where it would be the norm. For that, Bertie Ahern is entitled to all the plaudits he has received for his role.

In terms of domestic politics, fortune favoured Ahern's timing in coming to power. By 1997, the Celtic Tiger economy was trotting along nicely. Had the outgoing government waited an extra four or five months, they may well have been re-elected.

Once in power, the Fianna Fáil–PD coalition set out its task. Ahern's first priority was stability in government. The brief history of coalitions in the Fianna Fáil party had been turbulent. In the late 1980s, Haughey and the PDs' leader, Desmond O'Malley, could barely stand the sight of each other. A similar frostiness informed the relationship between Albert Reynolds and Dick Spring, culminating in the collapse of the Fianna Fáil–Labour government. Ahern was determined that interpersonal relations would not be a trigger to stymie his shot at the big time.

His immediate predecessor, Fine Gael's John Bruton, had shown how to manage these things. As head of a three-party coalition, he had emphasised to aides that the other two party leaders must be kept in the loop at all times and, to the greatest extent possible, must be kept happy. Such an arrangement was an implicit acknowledgement that coalition would mean the junior partner or partners would have an influence beyond the strength of their representation.

The first real test of inter-party harmony came within months of taking office. There had long been suspicious allegations and rumours about planning corruption, particularly in the greater Dublin area. One name continued to crop up: Ray Burke, a close Ahern associate whom he had appointed Minister for Foreign Affairs. Although it only became public knowledge later, Burke had been investigated three times over the years by An Garda Síochána, but each time no charges were brought.

In autumn 1997, a series of newspaper reports alleged that Burke had been in receipt of large sums of money associated with planning decisions. This time, there was a whistleblower: a man who had been present when £30,000 had been handed over to Burke. Initially, Ahern was slow to move against his old pal, declaring he had been 'up every tree in North Dublin' trying to uncover the facts behind the allegation. But, under pressure from further revelations and particularly from Harney, he agreed to set up a public tribunal into planning corruption. Burke resigned, and there were a few wobbles in the coalition, but Ahern demonstrated that he would not be stubborn when the time came to make a tough call. The forecast was that the tribunal would finish its work by Christmas. In fact, it persisted for 15 years and was the instrument that ultimately led to Ahern's own downfall.

For the greater part, the 1997–2002 government's economic policies were dominated by tax cuts. The key person in this, and the wider economic policy, was the Minister for Finance, Charlie McCreevy. Legend has it that on the Sunday before budget day, McCreevy would call to St Luke's, Ahern's Drumcondra base, leave his boss with a draft of the budget and go for a walk. When he returned, if there were any issues, they would thrash it out. That was the extent of the Taoiseach's input into a succession of McCreevy budgets. In contrast, McCreevy's consultations with Mary Harney were reputed to be much more detailed.

McCreevy set the tone with his first budget in which he wanted to reduce capital gains tax (CGT), which stood at 40 per cent. The officials in the Department of Finance explained patiently that this would deliver a huge blow to the £131 million in receipts from CGT in 1997. McCreevy ignored the advice, pointing to his belief that receipts would increase because asset-holders saw that the rate was not so punitive. He wanted a new rate of 20 per cent, which had the officials nearly choking on their cornflakes. McCreevy introduced the measure to the sound of loud opposition from both the political arena and trade unions. He was proved right on one point. The receipts from CGT for the following year increased nearly by half to £193 million.

McCreevy's habitual disdain for official advice was to be both a strength and a weakness during his tenure as Ahern's money man. That the boss let him have his own way, to a huge extent, ensured that McCreevy and his PD kindred spirits were the real powers on economic policy. Over the lifetime of that government, the effective income-tax rate of a couple on €60,000 went from 37 per cent to 20 per cent. For a single earner on €25,000, it went from 34 per cent to 16 per cent. Meanwhile, the boom times, as Ahern himself went on to note, just got boomier. The public at large had money in their pockets and appreciated the extra few bob in pay packets courtesy of tax cuts. As is the way with these things, the fruits were not spread evenly. Those in the upper echelons, both employed and entrepreneurs, saw their lifestyles heading north at a rate of knots. Bling was everywhere in the country, particularly in Dublin, years before bling was even invented.

A small, open economy is disproportionately vulnerable to world shocks, and so it was to be in the early 2000s. The tech boom collapse and the war in Iraq rippled onto the shores of Ireland, but there was enough credit on the domestic economic ledger to keep a recession at bay. The euro was introduced as the new currency, but, again, the strength of the Irish economy ensured there was little turbulence.

That is how things stood when the 2002 general election came around. 'A lot done, more to do' was the Fianna Fáil election slogan, and every poster had Bertie's mug smiling down. The country had taken to Ahern, his combination of apparent quiet competence along with the retention of his image of bonhomie. He was a man you could send out to represent the country with world leaders but once he got home you might find him in the local pub dissecting the Dublin GAA team's latest loss or the secret of Manchester United's success.

His luck held. Fine Gael was in some disarray, having gone through two leadership changes since the previous election. The new leader, Michael Noonan, was not setting the world alight. Also, by polling day, the Tribunal had yet to issue any report of substance. There had been plenty of dark revelations, credible allegations of corruption and drama, but no report. When the first major report did issue, in autumn 2002, it showed how some Fianna Fáil politicians had been up to their necks in the business of 'money for planning' and how in the wider sense a culture of impunity and heads in the sand from the hierarchy of mainly Fianna Fáil governments had allowed corruption to flourish. Whether or not the publication of a report before the election would have made a difference remains a moot point.

On the whole, though, the election was a victory march for the man from Drumcondra. At one point, it looked as if Ahern might be in a position to retrieve the Holy Grail that was once the preserve of Fianna Fáil: an overall majority. It was left to a PD stalwart, Michael McDowell, to stymie such a prospect. In a high-profile stunt, he went up a ladder on a telegraph pole to affix a poster with the legend 'One-Party Government? NO thanks!' The message was loud and clear: you need somebody in there with them to keep Fianna Fáil honest. The coalition returned, with the PDs doing particularly well in capturing eight seats – an increase of one on their outgoing complement of four.

Once the election was out of the way, McCreevy set about reverting to the prose that had been shelved for the poetry of campaigning. Cutbacks were necessary; spending could not continue as it had, and there would be no question of increasing taxes to meet the shortfall. A few months later, the *Sunday Tribune* broke the story that the cutbacks had all been laid out prior to the election but kept quiet. The government's popularity began to plunge. This was writ large at an event in Croke Park to mark the opening of the Special Olympics in 2003. Ahern was booed at the event, an extremely unusual occurrence in the country at the time, not to mention it being directed at a leader who had always enjoyed high levels of popularity. Ahern's response was out with the old. McCreevy was dispatched to take up the role of EU Commissioner. (By his account, he requested the move.) He was replaced by Brian Cowen, who would have been identified with the left of the party and who turned out to be far more malleable than McCreevy.

The new change of direction was symbolically installed at a

pre-legislative term get-together in West Cork in 2004. Attending the event by invitation from Ahern was Fr Sean Healy, a renowned campaigner for the underprivileged. The message went out: 'Bling is dead, baby. From here on in, this is a government for all the people.' What ensued was a further building boom from which transactional tax receipts kept the show on the road. Spending was increased hugely, but there were no corresponding tax increases. Total public spending, including current and capital, went from €37 billion to €62 billion between 2002 and 2007. With stamp duty from home-dwelling purchases taking up a huge amount of the slack, the economy was balanced precariously, but economists and the media were full of reassurances that any landing would be soft.

As the government entered the home strait to a general election in early 2007, storm clouds were gathering around the global economy, starting out in the US housing market and heading east rapidly. The 'soft landing' mantra was trotted out with greater frequency, but the omens were all there. And while Ahern and his government talked up the economy, down in Dublin Castle, at the Planning Tribunal, the low hum of the past being excavated was slowly rising to an ominous rumble.

By 2007, Ahern had been in power for 10 years, but at no point did he elucidate any kind of vision for the country. There was no grand plan at a time of transformative change. He appears to have taken his Catholic religion seriously, but he never attempted to stem the various scandals emerging from the Catholic Church. Like most Irish politicians of the day, he was wary any time the abortion issue came into the public domain. The public in general were unsure as to where he stood on the great issues of the day, other than that he showed commensurate compassion when it was called for without committing to any vision.

What defined him as a Taoiseach probably more than anything else was his work ethic. Public-affairs consultant Gerard Howlin, who worked as an adviser to Ahern when he was Taoiseach, later described his erstwhile boss as 'a meticulous, grinding slogger'. Howlin told the *Irish Times*, 'Briefcases full of cabinet papers, letters to be read and signed personally, material for cabinet subcommittees and more was dispatched every Friday afternoon to Drumcondra. These were read, signed and annotated by Monday morning. And of course he had personal sources nesting across government, the better to verify official accounts.' According to Howlin, Ahern was never one to lose the run of himself in terms of his elevated position in public life:

> Unfailingly polite, he never forgot to say please and thank you. He had an appetite for gratuitous goading from his opponents that was apparently insatiable, and on the stormiest days remained outwardly completely calm.
>
> That composure was aided by a capacity for compartmentalisation of multiple crises, not just on the same day but in different meeting rooms within the same hour. He could switch back and forth from the relatively trivial, to the politically life-threatening, remembering that the insignificant was important to someone.

Despite his hectic lifestyle, Ahern always found time to spend with his two daughters, Georgina and Cecilia. Georgina married Nicky Byrne, a member of the pop group Westlife. Cecilia went on to have a highly successful career as a novelist. Ahern himself was not one for reading novels. Interviewed in 2005 on an RTÉ arts programme, he nominated his favourite books as a history of the GAA and biographies of a Dublin GAA player, Dessie Farrell, and one of his predecessors, Seán Lemass. His favourite songs included 'You Raise Me Up' – a recent hit at the time for … Guess who? Westlife! – and 'How Much Is That Doggy in the Window?', the latter a choice he shared with none other than Margaret Thatcher. Quite obviously, Ahern was not one for high culture, but, on the other hand, he avoided the affectations or pretentions that some politicians were guilty of when casting themselves as being far more culturally aware than they actually were.

His political compass was, to put it plainly, bland. He led a government that cut taxes as a primary policy instrument yet also increased spending hugely. To that extent, he was not wedded to a political ideology, although he once declared himself a socialist – a positioning that was greeted with a mixture of mirth and ridicule. To some extent, he was true to his Fianna Fáil creed: a 'something for everybody in the audience' old-style populist, with one eye affixed on social justice and the other firmly focused on fostering an entrepreneurial culture. He was a man of the people yet also in thrall to the wealthy sections of society that funded both his party and his spending priorities in government.

Had political cards fallen differently, and Fianna Fáil gone into government with the Labour Party in 1997, Ahern would have been just as at home, if not more so, with a left-leaning administration as he had been with the economically ringht-wing PDs. It could equally be posited that his popularity owed a great deal to the fact that people were comfortable with him, who he was and what he represented. Like Tony Blair, he was a new kind of leader for a buttoned-down generation, breaking with the past when such figures were remote. There was an informality about him that a young, more educated public found reassuring and comforting.

By the time the 2007 election came around, the rumble from the Castle was unmistakeable. Serious questions were being raised about the sums of money Ahern had received and his explanations for them. Ahern was due to give evidence. Then, early on Sunday, 30 April, a few days before his scheduled appearance at the Castle, he travelled to the Áras to ask President Mary McAleese to dissolve the Dáil. Even though an election was imminent, the move was seen as an attempt to get re-elected before he gave evidence about his money. Once the election was called the tribunal suspended hearings, as had happened prior to the previous election in 2002.

The first week of the election campaign was dominated by Ahern's finances. At one event, in Dublin's Henry Street, a reporter asked him a direct question about evidence at the tribunal in relation to his money. Ahern did not answer. He stayed silent for seven seconds until another question was posed. It was the longest seven seconds of any election campaign. By all standards, Bertie, the man of the people, the Teflon Taoiseach, was foundering.

This was where Cowen stepped in to take the bull by the horns. He came out with all guns blazing, decrying the attempted assault on his leader. This election was about 'the issues' rather than some long-ago contortions about money of which nobody but a few journalists were across. Michael McDowell, the leader of the PDs by then, initially expressed himself concerned at what was coming from the Castle, but he quickly sniffed the wind and declared that he was happy with Ahern's answers so far. The public, largely fed up of a decade of lawyers creaming it at the tribunal, and uneasy at the gathering economic storm clouds, came on board.

In the main leaders' debates, Ahern went head to head with Fine Gael's Enda Kenny and won the tussle, hands down. He got his mojo back. In the final, crucial days of the campaign, he was in his element. The electorate saw what was before them. Ahern had been at the helm in the good times. He knew his stuff, appeared to be capable of steering the economy, and now, as the good times rolled to a halt, he was the man to trust. Why take a chance on the untried Kenny?

In the end, Fianna Fáil lost one seat from the extraordinary high of the 2002 election and actually increased its share of the vote by 0.1 per cent to 41.6 per cent. It was Ahern's greatest moment of triumph. Against the odds, he had fought his way out of his personal morass and delivered yet another victory for Fianna Fáil, taking his place next to the party's founder, Éamon de Valera, as the only other leader to win three general elections.

The honeymoon was short. An awful economic reckoning was rippling across the Western world, and Ahern still had that date in the Castle. In July 2007, the pressure showed in an uncharacteristic manner when he addressed a trade-union conference. Bertie was fed up with the naysayers who would not stop going on about what was approaching. 'Sitting on the sidelines, cribbing and moaning is a lost opportunity', he said, at the event in Co. Donegal. 'I don't know how people who engage in that don't commit suicide because frankly the only thing that motivates me is being able to actively change something.' Strangely, he received some applause for the remarks. Pretty quickly, the criticism began to flow in, and he apologised. But there was huge symbolism in the mild-mannered Bertie lashing out Canute-style against the rising tide of doom.

The remainder of his premiership was inevitable. He gave evidence about how he had acquired all those bags of cash, but it did not add up. Pretty soon, his ministers ran for cover when asked to bat for him on the whip-rounds and dig-outs. Things came to a head the following March when a former secretary of his was in the witness box and broke down under the pressure. The general reaction was one of disgust, informed by the perception that Ahern had sent this innocent woman out to do his dubious bidding while he looked on from afar. There would be no coming back from it. After a brief period when he was unavailable, and following his summit with Cowen, he announced his intention to resign on 2 April 2008.

Within months, the country fell apart through the banking collapse, the decision to guarantee the banks and, ultimately, the request for assistance to the IMF. In 2012, after the report of the Planning Tribunal was published, Ahern resigned from Fianna Fáil ahead of a move by his successor, Micheál Martin, to expel him. It was an ignominious end to a career that had for so long been successful. By then, however, the state he had led for so long was grappling with a deep recession which many attributed directly to the stewardship of the economy when he was Taoiseach.

He has never come to terms with what emerged in the Tribunal about his financial activity. In his autobiography, he lashed out at his political opponents. 'The Opposition could not beat me fair and square in a general election, so it was time to play dirty instead', he wrote, adding that he was disappointed they used his personal affairs for political gain. 'They condemned me because I had only partial recollection of events in my life almost two decades previously.' The reality, however, was he simply had no credible explanations as to how he came into huge sums of money when he was one of the most powerful politicians in the state. His positioning on the issue was entirely self-serving. The Tribunal had been charged to investigate allegations of 'money for planning'. That led it to

Mr Ahern's finances and his bank accounts, or lack thereof. While there was no finding that Bertie had given favours for anything, his explanations for the money he received, as a full-time politician, simply did not stack up. That presented a major problem with credibility and whether his evidence, given when he was a serving Taoiseach, was factually based.

Life after high office was not always smooth for Bertie Ahern. After resigning as Taoiseach in 2008, he enjoyed a period capitalising on the public-speaking circuit and earned a lot of money over the following years. Following the economic collapse, his appeal tightened. No longer was he asked to talk about the economic miracle, but he was still in demand for his thoughts on the Peace Process. After the Planning Tribunal ruling, his appeal as speaker or counsellor slipped further.

For a decade on from 2012, he was in the wilderness in terms of the elder statesman role he no doubt coveted. During that period, two interviews he conducted, both outside Ireland, created waves – for different reasons. In 2015, on BBC Radio 4's *Today* programme, he suggested that the economic crash in Ireland was all down to the availability of credit and 'Joe and Mary Soap' losing the run of themselves. 'Anyone could walk into any institution and seem to get any amount of money, and this is where the cocky bit came in', he said. 'Unfortunately ... Joe Soap and Mary Soap, who never had a lot, got the loans for the second house and leveraged the third house off the second house and the fourth on the third, and you know, what are you having yourself.' The interview was not well received in an Ireland that was still wrestling with austerity, the blame for which many, including economic commentators, felt rested with Ahern-led governments.

In 2018, Ahern was interviewed on German public broadcaster Deutsche Welle by journalist Tim Sebastian. After dealing with his role in the Peace Process, Sebastian began asking Ahern about the rulings from the Planning Tribunal around his finances. Ahern quickly became irritated at the line of questioning. 'I've dealt with that issue and I'm not saying anything more about it again', he said. 'That'll be for another day. I agreed to meet you on the Good Friday Agreement. We've done that, so

I'm finished.' He then got up, took off his microphone and walked out of the studio.

In 2023, he was readmitted to Fianna Fáil and became a more frequent commentator in the media. Speculation was rife for a while afterwards that he would consider a run for the presidency in 2025, but that still appears to be unlikely.

Bertie Ahern's legacy is thus complicated, more so than that of the vast majority who came before and after him. He did the state some positive service, of that there is no doubt. His legacy on the North is unimpeachable. He failed to make the most of an opportunity to put society at large on a better financial footing in the 2004–7 period because of his focus on the next election to the exclusion of most other considerations. And his financial activity in the 1990s left a stain on his political character that many find difficult to stomach. Above all, perhaps, in terms of the evolution of politics and the economy in the state, it could well be posited that he was a man of his time.

Brian Cowen

2008–11

Theresa Reidy

Full name: Brian Bernard Cowen
Date of birth: 10 January 1960
Place of birth: Offaly
Married to: Mary Molloy (m. 1994)
Children: Sinead and Meadhbh
Education: Cistercian College, Roscrea; UCD
Assumed office: 7 May 2008
Date of resignation: 9 March 2011
Length of tenure: Two years, nine months, 30 days
Quotation: When asked about coalition government with the Progressive Democrats, Cowen famously said, 'When in doubt, leave them out.'

Brian Cowen was nominated for appointment as Taoiseach on 7 May 2008. His nomination won a comfortable majority of 88 votes to 76, and he assumed leadership of the Fianna Fáil, Green Party and PDs coalition government.

Cowen served as a TD for 27 years. He was a Minister for almost 16 of those years, and he served as Taoiseach for just under three years. There was never any doubt that Brian Cowen would succeed Bertie Ahern as leader of Fianna Fáil and Taoiseach. He became deputy leader of the party in 2002, and, in 2007, Bertie Ahern described Cowen as his 'natural successor'.

In the 24-hour period after Bertie Ahern announced his resignation, every senior Fianna Fáil minister declared they were supporting Cowen for the party leadership. It quickly became apparent that he would be elected unopposed, and, on 4 April 2008, the *Irish Independent* headline read, 'Cowen Gets Crown'. Brian Cowen was elevated to the top of Irish politics, fulfilling a long-ordained plan.

However, his term as Taoiseach coincided with the onset of the global financial crisis that quickly engulfed the Irish economy. His leadership skills were found wanting at an early point in his premiership, the economy descended into crisis, and his term as Taoiseach ended in early resignation and an electoral defeat for Fianna Fáil from which it has never fully recovered.

Cowen was born in Offaly in 1960 and is a member of a well-established political dynasty. His father, Bernard (Ber), served as a Fianna Fáil TD and Senator, and his grandfather, Christopher Cowen, was a founding member of Fianna Fáil and a local councillor. After Brian's retirement from politics in 2011, his brother Barry followed him into national politics, taking the family seat at that general election, and he was later elected as an MEP.

Cowen came from a typical, if affluent, Fianna Fáil background. He was the middle child of three boys, and the family had a number of small businesses which included a pub, butcher's, auctioneering business and undertaker's. The family were deeply rooted in their local community through politics and sport. Cowen was educated locally in Clara National School before he proceeded to second level at the Cistercian College in Roscrea. The well-known boarding school for Catholic boys has educated several government ministers and has always had a strong reputation in sport, an area in which Cowen also excelled. He played hurling and rugby at school and later played Gaelic football at county level for his native Offaly. He has retained a lifelong interest and affiliation with the GAA, and he became an avid golfer, especially after his retirement from national politics.

Cowen also has a musical ear and a keen interest in traditional Irish music. His flair for music followed him into adult life, and, during his political career, he was well known for breaking into song at social and political events. In 2022, he was awarded a lifetime recognition award by the traditional music body Comhaltas Ceoltóirí Éireann for services to Irish music. He is also a fluent Irish speaker. A talented mimic, he was known to entertain colleagues and friends from his early time in secondary school.

Having studied law at UCD, Cowen qualified as a solicitor before he entered politics in 1984. His interest in politics developed during his time in university, both through his involvement in local politics in his native Clara and also through his time in Ógra Fianna Fáil, the youth wing of the party. But it was the sudden death of his father, from a brain haemorrhage in January 1984, that propelled Brian into national politics at a very young age. As the most politically active and interested of the three Cowen sons, Brian was the natural successor to his father's career in politics. He was co-opted to Offaly County Council in early 1984, and he won the by-election caused by his father's death in June 1984.

Sometimes known by the unpleasant acronym BIFFO (Big Ignorant F***** From Offaly), Cowen developed a reputation as a serious and engaging politician. He was widely regarded as a sharp and intelligent minister, but, equally, he developed a reputation for being impatient and at times brusque. At one stage, he was described in the *Irish Times* as 'Fianna Fáil's Gurrier in Chief'.

Like many politicians of his generation in Fianna Fáil, Cowen was not overtly ideological in his approach to politics. In office, he tended towards the conservative side on social policy and exhibited classic Fianna Fáil statism in his approach to many aspects of economic policy. He was a big spender as Minister for Finance and generally pragmatic in his approach to policy. A traditionalist on institutional matters, despite a long career in the Dáil, he showed little interest in political reform. He disagreed with the abolition of the dual mandate that allowed TDs to simultaneously serve as councillors, and he did not agree with often widespread criticism of the large constituency workload of TDs.

Indeed, Cowen was himself an assiduous local politician. He served on Offaly County Council until 1992 when he was first appointed to cabinet. In several interviews, he spoke of the importance of working with constituents to resolve personal and local issues. And, while serving as Minister for Foreign Affairs, he was known to be particularly concerned that his constituents should continue to receive a comprehensive constituency service. In this regard, he very much fits the mould of a rural, localist Fianna Fáil TD.

He was a Fianna Fáil party man, hugely popular with party supporters, and it is his deep loyalty to the party that to a great extent defined his political life. With a grandfather and father in politics, he was deeply interwoven with the fabric of Fianna Fáil politics from an early age, and he came from a strongly nationalist and localist tradition within the party. The unexpected death of his father shaped some of his approach to political office, and he spoke occasionally about how it inclined him to value each ministry as he found it and not to plan his political career too extensively into the future. Nevertheless, he was spoken of as a future leader of the party from an early point in his career as a TD.

Noel Whelan, an *Irish Times* columnist, described how his 'combative orations' at ard fheiseanna (party conferences) endeared him to the party faithful. A powerful public speaker, when he was on form he could be incisive and engaging. He was regularly given the role of energising the crowd in the slot before the party-leader address on a Saturday evening. Cowen would give barnstorming orations, playing to the deep-rooted values and preferences of party members. It is some of these contributions that provide Cowen's more memorable public speeches.

Fianna Fáil made an uneasy peace with the need to enter coalition government in the 1990s, and Brian Cowen was one of those reluctant to embrace the electoral reality that Fianna Fáil could no longer form single-party majority governments. Speaking at the 1992 ard fheis, he famously declared, 'What about the PDs? When in doubt, leave them out', referring to that party's continuing role in a coalition with Fianna Fáil.

Cowen was a pragmatist in politics and, some decades later, admitted to having changed his views on coalition government. Nevertheless, his skills as a manager of a coalition government were later called into question during his term as Taoiseach when relations with the remnants of the PDs and the Green Party reached a nadir. He was also on the Fianna Fáil negotiating team to form a series of coalition governments and was described by an *Irish Times* columnist as having the role of 'bad cop' in the discussions.

Cowen was invested in the politics of Fianna Fáil at all levels. He put considerable effort into party organisation, and the Laois–Offaly constituency structures were considered among the most effective in the country. This is all the more significant because it is generally agreed that while Fianna Fáil local constituency organisation atrophied during the leadership of Bertie Ahern, this was not the case in Laois–Offaly.

Cowen's interest in party organisation extended beyond his own patch. He served on a commission exploring the aims of the party in the 1980s and was heavily involved in candidate selection processes and campaigns while a back-bench TD and minister. These interests persisted and endured when he was Taoiseach. He initiated a review of party financing very early in his term and later a series of organisational evaluations after the party's poor showing at the local and European elections in 2009.

Loyalty to Fianna Fáil is a dominant theme in Cowen's political career. In a documentary about the economic crisis that started in 2008, his party colleague John McGuinness described him as having a 'loyalty to [Fianna Fáil] tribalism that was unequalled'. Indeed, 'loyalty' was a theme picked up by several TDs on the day of his election as Taoiseach. Enda Kenny (leader of the opposition) and Mary Harney (PD party leader and Minister for Health) congratulated him and spoke of how strong his 'political loyalty' was. This loyalty was, first and foremost, to Fianna Fáil, and ultimately it contributed to his political downfall as he struggled to separate being Taoiseach and his obligations to the state from his loyalty to Fianna Fáil and deep inclination to preserve the party at all costs.

Cowen was a back-bench TD for the first eight years of his 27-year career in national politics. He was an opposition TD from his election in 1984 until 1987 and then a back-bench government TD until 1992. He was not close to the party leadership during the Haughey years but had a strong working relationship with Albert Reynolds, before and after he took up the leadership of the party in 1992.

From an early stage, he developed a reputation as a strong performer in parliament, and he delivered cogent and informed speeches, but he continued to work as a solicitor until he was first appointed to cabinet in 1992. This practice was not uncommon at the time, but it is interesting to note that it took some years for Cowen to commit to full-time politics, and he did not give up his legal interests until he was required to do so through ministerial appointment.

Following the acrimonious collapse of the Fianna Fáil–Labour coalition government in 1994, Cowen returned to the opposition benches. He was appointed Fianna Fáil spokesman on agriculture, food and forestry in 1994 by the new leader of Fianna Fáil, Bertie Ahern, and in 1997 he was moved to shadow the health portfolio. The first government minister from Offaly, he would serve in five portfolios during his long ministerial career. He was assiduous, an especially effective negotiator but unimaginative in his approach to policy. Indeed, he has few standout achievements from his ministerial terms.

The lack of innovation from his early years is not all that noteworthy. First, he was Minister for Labour and, later, Minister for Transport, Energy and Communications at times of ongoing economic turmoil. Firefighting was often the primary concern of ministers in perilous times, and there were few resources available for creative new policies. But later in his ministerial career, the Celtic Tiger boom was well under way, and, while Cowen carefully implemented Fianna Fáil policy, he rarely delivered innovative change.

His early ministerial terms coincided with a period of transformation in some of the most protected and sheltered sectors of the Irish economy. But the impetus for change came in the neo-liberal shift at EU level and the drive for deregulation and privatisation. He was not as ideologically committed to the policy shift as his coalition partners, the PDs, in some of those governments, but he was an effective implementor of government policy and, for example, oversaw significant liberalisation in the Irish aviation sector.

Cowen's ideological flexibility mirrors that of Fianna Fáil more generally. After the collapse of the Fianna Fáil–Labour coalition, the party returned to government in 1997, in the first of three coalitions that included combinations of non-party TDs, the PDs and, later, the Green Party. Cowen had been a member of the coalition negotiating team for the establishment of the Fianna Fáil–Labour coalition in 1992, and, while he was responsible for ensuring Fianna Fáil policy was given sufficient space in the programme for government, the team was able to easily reach agreement on a policy programme that accommodated the social-democratic preferences of Labour. He also governed mostly without difficulty with the neo-liberal PDs and supported the ideological shift to the right in Fianna Fáil from 1997. In 2004, he moved leftwards once more as a change in ideological orientation was spearheaded by Bertie Ahern following poor election results. By 2007, he was instrumental in establishing the coalition that included the Green Party albeit that Cowen's environmental turn might best be described as 'greenwashing'!

Bertie Ahern appointed Cowen as Minister for Health in his first coalition government in 1997. Cowen had been the health spokesperson for a few months in early 1997 and had been an effective critic of the Rainbow Coalition government led by John Bruton. Although he served in the Health portfolio until 2000, he was widely considered to have been unenthusiastic about his appointment, and he famously referred to the Department of Health as 'Angola'. He often elaborated later that he was not suggesting that Ireland had a Third World health service, rather that the Department of Health was prone to multiple simultaneous crises. The budget for the health service expanded substantially during Cowen's term as Minister, but many indicators showed no sign of improvement, and, indeed, there was disimprovement in certain key areas such as waiting lists for treatment. But this exact scenario has been the outcome for a great many of his successors as Ministers for Health.

Cowen did have some important successes, especially in capital development. There were changes to the management of capital budgets and also investment in key health facilities. Negotiating workable solutions to protracted industrial-relations matters was a feature of his terms in many ministries, and this was also the case in Health when he eventually achieved resolution to a prolonged nurses' strike. He had also dealt with a bank officials' strike and a postal strike during his tenure in the Department of Labour, and, later, he managed several complex industrial-relations matters during his term in the Department of Transport.

Cowen's well-honed negotiating skills were undoubtedly an asset on his appointment as Minister for Foreign Affairs in 2000. He served in the department until 2004, during a delicate period in the Peace Process in Northern Ireland. He developed strong relations with interlocuters on all sides in Northern Ireland although he was initially considered to have a poor relationship with the British Secretary of State for Northern Ireland Peter Mandelson and to have tepid tolerance for certain unionist sensibilities.

In an offensive incident early in his term, Ian Paisley derided and jeered at Cowen for his appearance although Cowen later spoke favourably about how he developed a good working relationship with Paisley. Embedded in the republican tradition in Fianna Fáil, the constitutional status of Northern Ireland was a matter of sincere principle for Cowen, but he was not considered an ally of Sinn Féin. He remained actively suspicious of the party and, along with Ahern, was concerned to ensure that Sinn Féin would not use its peace credentials in Northern Ireland to advance its electoral ambitions in the Republic. Cowen is generally credited with having navigated the immediate years after the signing of the Good Friday/Belfast Agreement with the care and creativity needed in a delicate post-conflict context. Although he had a personal reputation for being gruff and sometimes short-tempered, he was an effective negotiator and administrator.

Cowen has a variable track record on Europe. The first referendum on the Treaty of Nice took place in June 2001 while he was the Minister for Foreign Affairs. He was heavily criticised for the poor government campaign which he had also overseen as the Fianna Fáil Director of Elections. The 'No' vote was attributed to the insertion of extraneous and irrelevant issues such as abortion, a European army and neutrality into the debate. Cowen faced further criticism less than a year later, while still Minister for Foreign Affairs, for the decision to re-run the referendum in November 2002 when it eventually passed.

Ireland held the presidency of the European Council in 2004, and Cowen was deeply involved in the large EU expansion as well as in the negotiations leading up to the Lisbon Treaty. But, ultimately, the Lisbon Treaty would also take two referendums to pass, and, again, Fianna Fáil and Cowen were personally critiqued for lacklustre campaign efforts. This time, however, he was the Taoiseach.

Cowen had shown limited interest in international affairs prior to taking up his role in Foreign Affairs. While Northern Ireland took up much of his time, he made a number of valuable contributions because of specific roles held by the Irish state during his tenure. Ireland secured a seat on the UN Security Council and was elected to the chair on 1 October 2001. Cowen addressed the UN General Assembly for the first time in October 2001, just weeks after 9/11, and he delivered a three-point plan to combat terrorism along with directly criticising the UN for an insufficient approach to ensuring anti-terrorism laws were enforced.

The foreign-affairs posting took Cowen out of his natural terrain and provided him with some important statecraft credentials that would be necessary to position himself strategically in the eventual post-Ahern Fianna Fáil leadership contest. He had some achievements in Northern Ireland, but luck and the hard work of his predecessors contributed to his elevated international profile. In a television interview on TG4 in 2013, he declared the foreign-affairs posting to have been his favourite.

His final ministerial position was in the Department of Finance where he served until his appointment as Taoiseach. It is perhaps this ministerial term that is most controversial for him. He was a profligate Minister, overseeing large increases in public spending, especially in his later budgets when economic clouds were already beginning to gather on the international horizon. To an extent, he continued the policies of his predecessor, Charlie McCreevy, cutting taxes and providing sectoral incentives, especially in the property market, but without McCreevy's deep ideological conviction.

With McCreevy moved to the European Commission, there was a decided change on the expenditure side under Cowen. Large increases in the health, education and social-protection budgets became the pattern in his four budgets. Although reports from the 2007 Fianna Fáil ard fheis suggest that Cowen did not favour promises of large budgetary giveaways before the general election, he fell in line with Bertie Ahern's plan for an election auction. Once back in office, he assiduously delivered on the Ahern agenda. Public spending increased to €51 billion, and, in his last budget, delivered in December 2007, current expenditure increased by 8.2 per cent and capital spending by 12 per cent.

Cowen was a 'giveaway minister'. Public-sector pay increased rapidly, and he reduced tax rates, raised tax thresholds and abolished stamp duty on second-hand homes. Budgetary policy was highly expansionary and deeply inappropriate for the Irish economy where there were serious concerns about potential overheating as well as signs of problems in the housing market driven by tax incentives, rapid credit growth and poor regulation. But the tax cuts and spending increases were hugely popular.

In practice, Cowen's approach to making budgetary policy also differed from McCreevy's. Pat Leahy in his book *Showtime: The Inside Story of Fianna Fáil in Power*, about Fianna Fáil governments during the Celtic Tiger economic boom, reported that Cowen engaged much more extensively with Bertie Ahern than his predecessor, and also with his ministerial colleagues.

The research on budget institutions is clear: the more stakeholders and personnel involved in decisions, the more likely it is that loose fiscal outcomes will occur, and so it was under Brian Cowen. The great difficulty for him was that in the very near future his policies would come under intense scrutiny. A narrative became firmly established that his budgets contributed to the economic bubble that would be the undoing of his government when the crash came in 2008.

As he approached the end of his ministerial career, Cowen had a well-established reputation for competence but a less well-deserved reputation for achievement. Reviewing his time in each portfolio demonstrates that he was an effective, adaptable and skilful minister. He had good political antennae, and his combative political style delivered for Fianna Fáil in media debates. He took no prisoners and was at times unrelenting in his criticism of opponents. But, unlike some of his contemporaries, he has few policy changes of note with which he is directly associated, and his performance in referendum campaigns was below par. In important respects, his reputation was not especially well explained by his just about 'above-average' performance.

Cowen was elected unopposed as leader of Fianna Fáil. He was immensely popular with grass-roots Fianna Fáil members, and he was also popular with the wider public. He was a regular poll-topper in his Laois–Offaly constituency, where jubilant scenes of public celebration greeted his election as Taoiseach.

In many ways, Cowen was a very welcome clean sheet in the leader's seat after the final murky years of Bertie Ahern's tenure when his personal finances were under intense scrutiny and the party seemed to be mired in eternal financial scandals. Cowen's reputation was as a politician of great ability and integrity.

The party experienced a small bump in the opinion polls following his nomination as Taoiseach, described as the 'BIFFO bounce' in the *Sunday Business Post*. Reflecting the widespread confidence in Cowen's abilities, the same article described him as a 'formidable opponent' and some weeks into his term pronounced that the situation was 'looking good so far'. The optimism did not last long, and the government faced a series of early challenges.

The first of these was the defeat of the Lisbon Treaty referendum on 12 June 2008. Described as a 'bad beginning' for Cowen's leadership, the government was criticised for another poor EU campaign and several missteps by senior Fianna Fáil figures. Cowen himself was entangled in a controversy about whether he said he 'never read the Treaty' or he 'never read it cover to cover'. There was an unedifying war of words with opponents that did little to persuade voters to give a 'Yes' vote.

As the campaign progressed, there were also tensions with Fine Gael and Labour about whether their party campaigns were sufficiently active. The parties took umbrage at a throwaway remark by Cowen, and he began to reap some of the consequences of his reputation for being dismissive and brusque. Charlie McCreevy (by this time well established as a European Commissioner) also made unhelpful comments about how complicated the treaty was. It was a poor start to Cowen's term. One of his first tasks on the international stage was to attend a European Council meeting and explain to his fellow EU prime ministers what had gone wrong. It was evident fairly quickly that some guarantees would be provided for Ireland, and, at a second vote in 2009, the treaty was passed.

Within weeks, the Lisbon Treaty debacle had been replaced by a looming collapse in the Irish property sector. Cowen and his government persisted with a communication strategy that emphasised the core strength of the Irish economy and that a 'soft landing' was possible for the property market. As summer 2008 progressed, problems also started to emerge in the banking system. The government was faced with the global financial crisis that was swamping Ireland's small open economy.

A large shortfall in tax receipts was publicly acknowledged, and Minister for Finance Brian Lenihan Jnr announced a series of expenditure cutbacks on 8 July 2008. The plans were greeted with much criticism, but they were minor in comparison to the swingeing adjustments that would become the norm over the coming years. Almost as soon as the announcements had been made, it was obvious that the cuts were far too small. Problems for the Cowen government escalated rapidly thereafter. The national wage-setting agreement, known as Social Partnership, which had been central to industrial peace in the Republic since the late 1980s, collapsed in stages.

Recognising the serious malaise throughout the economy, the annual budget usually presented in December was brought forward to October. The growing economic crisis led to greater scrutiny of the senior ministerial team. As Taoiseach, Cowen officially appointed the entire cabinet, but in practice he only had complete influence over the Fianna Fáil team, where he opted for close friends and confidants. His choices of Brian Lenihan and Mary Coughlan were especially critiqued. Lenihan was an exceptional communicator with a very successful legal background but no experience in economic or financial affairs. His appointment to the finance portfolio on the cusp of a catastrophic economic crisis led to questions about Cowen's judgement and whether he valued loyalty and friendship too much. Mary Coughlan was appointed as Tánaiste and Minister for Enterprise and Employment. She had more ministerial experience but again was not well versed in economic matters and was heavily criticised for missteps as the crisis advanced. Like Cowen, Lenihan and Coughlan were both dynasty politicians and could identify long and loyal family lineage in Fianna Fáil. This too contributed to an eventual sense that the Taoiseach was not prioritising state interests sufficiently over the priorities of Fianna Fáil.

On 15 September 2008, Lehman Brothers investment bank collapsed. Almost immediately, it was apparent that Irish banks were devastatingly exposed to the turmoil in global financial markets. An immediate credit squeeze left Irish banks on the verge of collapse as September drew to a close. Irish bank shares collapsed in value, but there was also emerging domestic panic that deposits in Irish banks were vulnerable, and people started moving their personal savings around various financial institutions. There were grave fears that a run on an Irish bank was imminent and that the entire financial system was vulnerable to collapse.

Just months into his term, on 29 September, Brian Cowen and his government took the extraordinary step of introducing a state-backed guarantee of all Irish bank deposits and borrowings. Formally the Credit Institutions Act (2008) but known universally as the 'Bank Guarantee', this decision would define Cowen's term as Taoiseach. The obligations of the Irish banks were understood to be somewhere in the region of €400 billion. There was absolutely no possibility that the Irish state could stand over the cost if called upon to do so. The decision was taken overnight in Government Buildings through an incorporeal cabinet meeting. The rationale for the decision was rooted in the belief that the pillar banks (AIB and Bank of Ireland) in the Irish system were mostly sound and experiencing liquidity problems in part driven by global banking problems. There was awareness that a smaller bank, Anglo Irish Bank, which had been at the forefront of aggressive property-focused lending, was potentially insolvent, although proposals to nationalise Anglo at that stage were rejected.

Cowen and his government have been criticised vociferously for the bank guarantee decision, most particularly on the basis that they did not grasp the enormity of the decision they were taking and its implications for the state's solvency. No serious advance investigation of the scale of the banking problems was undertaken prior to the decision, and there was a notable absence of specialised expertise on banking crises at crucial points in the discussions on the guarantee. A solvency crisis was mistaken for liquidity problems.

In interviews after his retirement, Cowen continued to maintain that the decision to guarantee bank deposits and borrowings was the right one and the only serious policy option open to the state at that point given the precarious position of the banks and the information that was available. It remains one of the most contested and consequential policy decisions in Irish history.

Brian Lenihan Jnr delivered his first budget in October 2008. It was to be the first of a sequence of 'hair shirt' budgets. Most controversially, the budget included a measure to withdraw universal access to free GP medical care for everyone over the age of 70. The decision sparked massive protests widely known as the 'grey revolt'. Ultimately, there was a U-turn, but the episode was hugely damaging for Fianna Fáil, which drew disproportionate support from older voters. Cowen's political appeal with the party faithful evaporated, and Fianna Fáil support began to drop sharply in opinion polls.

The economic news went from bad to worse through 2009. Gross domestic product (GDP) fell by 11.3 per cent. Chaos in the banking system was marked first by the resignation of the financial regulator and then by many senior leaders throughout the banking system as the year progressed. In January, Anglo Irish Bank was nationalised, and, in February, AIB and Bank of Ireland were bailed out to the tune of billions of euros.

Crisis contagion became an enormous issue as banking problems worldwide spread into the real economy. In Ireland, unemployment rocketed, and the state's finances grew increasingly fragile. The end-of-year projected deficit was close to €20 billion (14.3 per cent of GDP). It was the largest deficit in any euro-area economy. The communication and leadership capabilities of the Taoiseach were scrutinised fiercely. Cowen often failed to explain precisely what was happening in the economy and exactly how his government was planning to address the multiple concurrent crises.

An emergency budget was delivered in April 2009 as the Finance Minister struggled to maintain order in the public finances. Cuts to public spending were small, but income taxes were increased for all, and a levy on all public-sector salaries basically operated as a pay cut of between 3 and 9.6 per cent. The government had begun to take the steps to bridge the gap between the revenues the state was generating and its ballooning cost base.

The budgetary measures in 2009 and in each subsequent year had horrendous consequences for the lives of Irish citizens. Social supports were greatly reduced, and, inevitably, it was the most vulnerable citizens who were hardest hit. Post-crash evaluations have argued cogently that Cowen and his government took the right steps to address the crisis. The budgetary adjustments were inevitable, but, even if Brian Cowen had been more effective at making his arguments to the public, cutbacks are never popular. Fianna Fáil was to reap this consequence of its variable stewardship of the economic bust, first at the local and European elections in 2009 and then in a much more devastating way at the 2011 general election.

The budget for 2010 was delivered in December 2009 and contained further tax rises, public-sector pay cuts and spending cuts. The austerity pattern had become established by this point, but Cowen, in particular, had become no more effective at communicating the situation to the Irish public. His often-tetchy relationship with the media deteriorated further, and he was frequently abrupt and abrasive.

There was no respite for the government in 2010. Much of the early part of the year was spent establishing the National Asset Management Agency (NAMA) which would effectively operate as a bad bank. Fifty-four billion euros was to be pumped into NAMA to deal with the problems in the banking system. The initial costs that had been suggested for the bank guarantee decision proved to be a gross underestimation. The growing burden being posed by the banking system on a weakening Irish economy was causing financial jitters across Europe. Irish government borrowing costs soared on international bond markets. The Irish public became intimately informed about bond yields and interest rates.

A new mantra emerged in public contributions to national debate with the Taoiseach and multiple ministers asserting that the state was 'fully funded into the middle of next year'. This was used to explain why the government withdrew from the bond market. The truth was that the Irish state was now being charged an exorbitant price to borrow money; it was priced out of the market. Rumours abounded that the state would need to access the newly created EU Bailout Fund. In parallel, the Minister for Finance was also working on a four-year budgetary plan that would include €15 billion of austerity measures in addition to those already implemented.

The Taoiseach personally became a political story in September 2010 when he gave an early-morning radio interview in which he was hoarse and less fluent than usual. Commentary online very quickly accused him of being hung-over on air. Earlier, in a 2009 *Late Late Show* interview, Cowen had been asked about his drinking habits. He vociferously denied the charge and described the questioning as a 'new low in Irish politics'. It did not prevent international headlines that read 'Irish Premier Denies Being Drunk, Hung Over on Air'. In the greater scheme of things, it is an irrelevance whether the claim that he was hung-over was true or not, but the incident highlights the lack of care that Cowen paid to curating his personal image. After his accession to the leadership of Fianna Fáil, private concerns were aired by some of his colleagues that images of celebration including the Taoiseach participating in public singalongs and drinking were not the image the party wanted to project.

Brian Cowen had become a very unlucky general, and, as his term progressed, he came under pressure from every direction. The government entered its final act as 2010 was closing. The Irish state was no longer able to secure finance on international markets, and, even with extreme cuts and tax rises, it would take years to close the deficit. The banking crisis had financially torpedoed the state, but the massive increases in public spending promulgated by Cowen himself while Minister for Finance created a second strand to the crisis. The spending had been partially based on temporary revenues from the construction boom, which had evaporated in 2008. The state might have managed a banking crisis, but it could not overcome the dual banking and public finance calamities.

Cowen and his ministers continued to insist that there was a plan to deal with the crisis in the public finances. But there were serious problems in the government, and it became apparent that there were inner and outer circles of ministers. Successive senior ministers appeared in public to deny that the government would apply for financial assistance from the EU Bailout Fund or that any discussions were taking place behind the scenes. But the reality was that the IMF had already arrived in Dublin to assist with the negotiations.

Ultimately, it was the Governor of the Central Bank, Patrick Honohan, who communicated this information to the nation in an early-morning radio interview. Cowen's government was pushed into admitting that Ireland was likely to need a large loan. It was the Minister for Finance, Brian Lenihan, who negotiated the agreement. He described travelling to Brussels for the discussions as standing at 'the gates of hell'.

The application for bailout loans was endorsed by the government on 28 November 2010. Brian Cowen and Brian Lenihan appeared on national television to provide details of the €85 billion loans from the EU, IMF and neighbouring European states. The interest rate on the loans was 5.83 per cent, and the deal was finally agreed on 16 December 2010 for a programme that would run for three years until December 2013.

The bailout was a near fatal blow for Fianna Fáil. Republicanism and commitment to national sovereignty were, and are, defining strands in the identity of Fianna Fáil. From its earliest days in government, led by Éamon de Valera in the 1930s, the party had emphasised the independence of the nation and its unique spirit. Following the bailout and the abdication of national financial sovereignty, even some of the party's most loyal supporters abandoned it, and opinion-poll support for the party dropped to just 17 per cent. The party has never returned to its pre-crisis support levels of over 40 per cent. The bailout was also catastrophic for Cowen personally. As Taoiseach, he led the state to the verge of bankruptcy. He was accused of 'economic treason' in the Dáil. Cowen rejected the assertions, but they took a toll. Fianna Fáil republicanism and national sovereignty were deeply meaningful for him.

As the economic crisis was briefly staunched through the economic bailout, the political crisis deepened, and the Green Party announced that it would withdraw from the coalition government. As Taoiseach, Brian Cowen insisted that it was imperative that the government should pass the budget for 2011 before proceeding to a general election.

Contacts between Brian Cowen and senior banking leaders dating back to 2008 were revealed between 9 and 12 January 2011 in the national newspapers. Cowen's personal probity was not questioned, but it was the final nail for many in relation to his political judgement. Background rumblings about his position as leader of Fianna Fáil moved centre stage. Combative and forceful to the end, he sought to meet the challenge head on and called a vote of confidence in his own leadership. Senior ministers publicly backed him, apart from Micheál Martin, who withdrew his support. In a critical move, Brian Lenihan, who had been diagnosed with cancer, announced that he would support Cowen, and the Taoiseach won the vote. It was at this point that the government descended into chaos.

As discussions were under way with the Green Party to expedite the passing of the Finance Bill and arrange a date for the general election, Cowen attempted a dramatic reorganisation of his cabinet. Several senior Fianna Fáil ministers had already announced they were to retire from politics. Cowen devised a plan to replace almost half of the cabinet with Fianna Fáil junior ministers and back-bench TDs who would be contesting the election. The Green Party was notified of some details of the scheme, but there is disagreement about the extent to which the Greens advised Cowen that they 'absolutely would not' support the strategy.

In any case, Cowen proceeded, and a series of government ministers announced they were stepping down from cabinet for an array of reasons. Pandemonium ensued as some of the proposed new ministers declined the offers of cabinet appointment, remaining cabinet ministers were appalled, and the Greens publicly declared that they would not vote for the new arrangements in the Dáil. Cowen was left with a barely constitutional government. Responsibility for the vacant portfolios was reassigned to the remaining ministers. The failed reshuffle was the final and perhaps most ignominious decision of Cowen's tenure. It was an example of the flawed judgement that defined his last years in politics. Enthralled to Fianna Fáil tribalism, he was unable, at the nadir of the economic crisis, to put Ireland first. In the lexicon of Irish politics, it was an old-style Fianna Fáil stroke.

Having won a vote of confidence in his leadership a week earlier, all support for Cowen ebbed away, and he resigned as leader of Fianna Fáil on 22 January 2011, while remaining in place as Taoiseach until the election of a new Taoiseach following the 11 March election. Following a contest, he was replaced by Micheál Martin as leader of Fianna Fáil. Fianna Fáil lost 58 seats in the ensuing election. It secured just 20 seats and was left with just one TD in Dublin. Willie O'Dea, a former Minister and close ally of Cowen, described the election as a 'near-death experience' for the party.

Cowen's legacy is dominated by the economic crisis that befell the state in 2008 and the grave consequences of a decade of austerity for millions of Irish people. The bank guarantee was a calamitous financial decision, and responsibility for it has been squarely placed at Brian Cowen's door. His immediate pre-crisis term as Minister for Finance means that he has culpability for the poor economic strategies that contributed to the scale of the economic crash. His tax cuts, spending increases and property-market incentives inflated the construction boom and grew the size of the state on the back of volatile revenues.

Like so many other finance ministers around the world, he gave almost no attention to banking system stability and probity. On his pathway to the top job, he had not been tested sufficiently, his leadership style was unsuited to deep crisis, his communication skills were inadequate, his relations with the media strained, and his relationship with his partners in the coalition government quickly soured.

But equally, it is also true the Irish crisis cannot be separated from the global context. The Lehman Brothers crash led to a global financial catastrophe. The Irish case was among the most acute, but it was by no means unique. Ultimately, the corrective actions taken by the Cowen government have been judged favourably. Very early, NAMA was deemed to have delivered the 'most expensive bank bailout in world history', but it did work. The system eventually stabilised, and the cost to the taxpayer was much less than projected in the early years. The catastrophic cuts in spending, increases in taxes and public-sector pay cuts were the only options open to the state given the policy preference for austerity in the EU and the response of global bond markets to the crisis. By the time the election was called in 2011, Cowen's government had implemented much of the required fiscal adjustment and agreed the plan that would be followed closely by the government that followed his.

Brian Cowen was a tribal Fianna Fáil TD. He was a product of the nationalist and localist strands of Fianna Fáil politics. These influences provided the foundations for his early success in politics and his path to the party leadership. However, he would later become a victim of these influences as he struggled to adequately distinguish between his obligations to the state and Fianna Fáil. It may be true that he was an unlucky general, but, equally, he was unprepared for the intensity of leadership in a crisis. He showed poor judgement at critical moments. His administration was overwhelmed by the economic crisis, and his government ended amid chaos and recrimination.

He should appear towards the end of any ranking of Taoisigh. However, to be fair, his personal commitment to public service was sincere. His integrity and probity in public life have never been questioned. For these reasons, he does not deserve to be placed on the bottom rung of the ladder.

Brian Cowen suffered a serious illness in July 2019. His period of rehabilitation was long, but by 2023, he had begun to attend a small number of public occasions. He is fully retired from national politics and does not comment on current events.

14

Enda Kenny

2011–17

Harry McGee

Full name: Enda Kenny
Date of birth: 24 April 1951
Place of birth: Castlebar, Co. Mayo
Married to: Fionnuala O'Kelly (m. 1992)
Children: Ferdia, Aoibhinn and Naoise
Education: St Gerard's College, Castlebar; St Patrick's College, Dublin; University College Galway
Assumed office: 9 March 2011
Date of resignation: 14 June 2017
Length of tenure: Six years, three months, five days
Quotation: 'I don't take myself too seriously, but I take the job very seriously, and I expect people to do the job that they're given because this is about all our people, young and old, and it's an enormous responsibility.'

If there was an antithesis of the cruel epitaph of the Roman historian Tacitus on the life of the Emperor Galba, its subject would be Enda Kenny. Tacitus's verdict on Galba was, 'Would have been thought by all to have been capable of ruling, had he never ruled.' With Kenny, it was the other way around. It would need to be rephrased thus: 'Would have been thought by all to have been incapable of ruling had he never ruled.'

Kenny is one of a small subset of Taoisigh composed of those who somehow stumbled into the job without necessarily seeking it. The others are John A. Costello of Fine Gael, who was Taoiseach in the First Inter-party Government, and Jack Lynch of Fianna Fáil, who served two stints as Taoiseach between the mid-1960s and 1979. Unlike Kenny, they were compromise choices.

Uniquely in the Irish context, Kenny became leader of Fine Gael almost by happenstance at the moment of the greatest crisis in the party's history. He became leader because there was nobody else in the parliamentary party with the requisite skill and experience to fill the role. 'What is different about Kenny is that he has been around for a lifetime yet we don't know him at all', wrote the *Irish Times* editor, Geraldine Kennedy, in 2011, just as he was about to be elected Taoiseach.

He was the classic case of a leader who had risen without trace. The corollary of Tacitus's comment in an Irish context is that you do not know how well a politician will be suited to being Taoiseach until they actually assume the role. Kenny's immediate predecessor, Brian Cowen, had been the dauphin prince of Fianna Fáil for a decade. True, Cowen was dealt a very difficult hand when he was elected to the office in 2008, but even taking that into consideration, he was not a successful Taoiseach.

There were few expectations in relation to Kenny, and, as time would tell, he surpassed them easily. He was the first Fine Gael Taoiseach to be re-elected to the role. His term in office, which lasted more than six years, exceeded those of his more illustrious Fine Gael predecessors. All in all, his period in office was a successful one, though there were failures, and he himself had flaws.

If you were analysing why Kenny made a success of the role, there would be three broad themes. The first was he was a late bloomer: an undistinguished 25 years followed by 15 years of focus and application. The second was he lacked some of the skills people associate with the position. He was a mediocre orator, struggled in live debates and on television, and his grasp of economics and figures was not of honours standard. Against that, he had other skills in abundance: energy, a tactile personableness, ruthlessness when required and the modesty to defer and delegate to others who had more skills, expertise or nous in a particular policy area. The third theme was that fortune favoured him at crucial times in his career even though he might not have realised it at the time. He was one of Napoleon's lucky generals.

Take the extraordinary general election of 2002 from which he emerged as leader. That could have had a very different outcome. In the seventh count, Kenny was hanging on by a thread, lying 400 votes behind his running mate, Jim Higgins. Fianna Fáil Senator Frank Chambers was eliminated and transferred 600 votes to Kenny and only 120 to Higgins. It put him 87 votes ahead of Higgins, who was then eliminated. Chambers was from Newport, which was closer to Kenny's base of Castlebar than to Higgins's, who was from Ballyhaunis. The irony is that the high-profile Higgins, then a front-bench spokesman, would have become leader had he survived.

Though Fine Gael complained bitterly that they had actually 'won' the 2007 general election (Bertie Ahern struck a deal with the Greens and became Taoiseach for the third time), that, too, was a lucky break when viewed through a longer lens. If Kenny had become Taoiseach then, he would have arrived just in time to feel the first harsh winds of the banking, housing and financial crises that brought the once-imperious Fianna Fáil to its knees.

How did Kenny become Taoiseach? Was it happenstance, or a Damascene conversion at mid-career when he was 50, or was his journey to the top a slow burn? Like many others, the reason why Enda Kenny became a politician was that it was a family profession. There is a famous cartoon from the magazine *Dublin Opinion*, in the 1950s, which depicts a TD on his deathbed, telling one son he will get the pub, another he will get the undertaking business and the farm, and the third he will get his Dáil seat. It was not unusual for the son or daughter of a TD to essentially 'inherit' their parent's seat, especially if that parent died in office.

Enda Kenny's father, Henry Kenny, had been a TD in Mayo South (and later Mayo West) for Fine Gael since 1954. A schoolteacher and a farmer, he had little knowledge of politics when he was first approached to stand for the Dáil that year. He did have another attribute, however. He was a GAA hero, part of an All-Ireland winning team from the 1930s. Upon his election, Henry made a short speech in which he admitted, 'I know nothing about the Dáil, but you can rest assured I will do everything I can for the people, and all they have got to do is ask me, and I will do my best for them.' Kenny Senior was very much a constituency politician first. He made few speeches in the Dáil during his career and was not involved in drafting legislation. He was known for being courteous, modest and punctilious. He attended all functions and meetings across his constituency.

When Fine Gael finally returned to power in 1973, in a coalition with the Labour Party, Taoiseach Liam Cosgrave appointed Kenny Parliamentary Secretary (essentially a Minister of State) for the Office of Public Works. By this stage, he was battling an illness that would lead to his death in 1975, at the age of 62. There were five children in the family. The eldest were three boys, of whom Enda was the third.

Born in 1951, he trained as a primary-school teacher at St Patrick's College in Drumcondra and returned to teach in schools near Westport. He was also hugely involved with sport, as his father had been, and was a star forward with his local GAA club of Islandeady. When his father died, his older brother Henry (also a teacher) and Enda were seen as the most likely successors. Henry passed on the opportunity, leaving it open to Enda, who was 24 years of age.

Fair-haired and fresh-faced, he had a common touch, a trait he shared with his father. In the by-election that November, he won over 50 per cent of the vote and was elected on the first count. 'I have grown up with an understanding of what the life of a politician is really like. After all, I was only a few years old when my father was elected for the first time', he said at the time.

Those who criticise hereditary TDs sometimes miss the point that the children of politicians have themselves grown up in politics and have an innate appreciation and understanding of the qualities and responsibilities required. Indeed, in the same year that Kenny was elected, 1975, two others were elected in by-elections who were the children of TDs who had died in office. Máire Geoghegan-Quinn, in Galway West, was the daughter of Johnny Geoghegan, a long-standing Fianna Fáil TD. Michael Kitt was the son of another Fianna Fáil TD, in Galway East, Michael F. Kitt. All three would have careers that eclipsed those of their parents – Geoghegan-Quinn would become Minister for Justice and a European Commissioner.

In his early career, Kenny followed the pattern of his own father by focusing on the constituency and being a near-anonymous presence in the Dáil. It would take two years for him to make his first major Dáil speech. In his early years in the Dáil, he was known as a socialiser, who frequented pubs and nightclubs with political acquaintances, mostly TDs and Senators. Some of his colleagues shared the impression during those years that the Mayo TD could not be fully relied upon and lacked the necessary focus to be given additional responsibility.

His first decade was undistinguished. Kenny did not come in the frame for Cosgrave's successor, Garret FitzGerald, and spent his time on the back benches, in opposition and in the 1982–7 Fine Gael–Labour government. There were useful experiences. He was a delegate to the New Ireland Forum, where he was able to develop an understanding of the complexities of the Northern political situation. It was there that he also struck up a friendly relationship with Fianna Fáil leader Charles Haughey, who had shared Castlebar roots with him. In the twilight months of FitzGerald's government, some 10 years after Kenny's election, he was appointed Minister of State for Youth Affairs, a relatively minor junior ministerial position.

Alan Dukes, who succeeded FitzGerald in 1987, did not appoint Kenny to his front bench. Duke's appointment was the beginning of a long period of internal tension and disruption within Fine Gael that would take over a decade to finally resolve. Kenny was a strong supporter of John Bruton and backed him strongly when Dukes stood down in 1990 after a heave. However, Bruton was the third leader in a row not to sufficiently rate Kenny. He was not included in Bruton's front bench. Instead, Jim Higgins, a TD since 1987, became education spokesman.

One of Kenny's big flaws, which he never fully came to terms with, was that his natural bonhomie and conversational skills did not translate to radio or TV. In interviews, he would assume a very formal persona that made him look stiff and awkward. He also struggled sometimes to think on his feet when confronted with awkward questions. In contrast, Higgins was a smooth commentator and was relaxed in 'red light' situations.

However, there was a partial reprieve. Kenny was appointed Party Whip in September 1992, just two months before an unexpected general election. He was involved in negotiations for government formation with Labour and the PDs. But Dick Spring of Labour could not overcome his antipathy to Bruton, with whom he had had a difficult relationship in a previous government. In opposition, Kenny was one of Bruton's loyal lieutenants when the Fine Gael leader successfully faced down a heave in 1994.

When the Fianna Fáil–Labour government of that year unexpectedly collapsed, Kenny, as whip, was centrally involved in negotiations with the Labour Party and Democratic Left. He was particularly friendly with Pat Rabbitte, from Ballindine, Co. Mayo. He was awarded by Bruton with his first senior government position, Minister for Trade and Tourism. He had been a TD for over 19 years. Still, even after his promotion, he was seen as personable, energetic and easy-going … in other words not a heavyweight or serious contender.

In yet another heave, John Bruton was deposed in 2001. The party's long-time finance spokesman Michael Noonan was the clear favourite, but TDs and Senators were taken aback when Enda Kenny announced he would be standing for the position. He was well liked by colleagues, but few saw him as leadership material. He insisted that some colleagues had pressed him to stand. 'They wanted me to stand on the basis that I provided a fresh face with long political experience, somebody who had the energy and the stamina to re-energise and revitalise the Fine Gael electorate', he told the broadcaster Sean O'Rourke on the *News At One*. 'I'm going to electrify the Fine Gael party.'

O'Rourke put it to him that some considered him to be a lightweight.

'I don't know where the notion of [me] not having dealt with the substantial issues over the years has come from', he replied. 'Just because one has a sense of humour and is not weighed down by the troubles of the world does not mean that one doesn't have a conviction, a commitment or a competence to do the job in a proper manner', he added.

However, the view was not widely shared in the media. Writing in the *Irish Times*, Vincent Browne argued that Kenny was a nice fellow but that his name 'would not have been the first, or the second, or even 23rd that would have occurred to me as a future leader of Fine Gael'.

Any hope that Kenny had of challenging Noonan was undone in a televised leadership debate between the candidates on RTÉ's *Prime Time*. Kenny struggled to articulate why he wanted to be leader of Fine Gael. In the end, he was Noonan's only rival and performed creditably, winning 28 votes compared to the Limerick TD's 44. Ungraciously, Noonan did not select Kenny for his front bench, even though he was his only rival.

Noonan's term as leader was short-lived and disastrous. He shipped a lot of political damage from a fictionalised TV drama of the experience of a Donegal woman called Brigid McCole who died from Hepatitis C caused by infected blood products. The 'fictional' Minister in the series was very like Noonan, who had been Minister for Health at the time. His image, personality and energy levels were also unsuited to leadership, and he was unable to match the traction his Fianna Fáil rival, Bertie Ahern, had with the public.

In the 2002 general election, Fine Gael ended with only 31 seats, its worst electoral performance in its history. Noonan promptly resigned. After narrowly avoiding defeat in the Mayo constituency, Kenny easily won the leadership contest, beating Richard Bruton by 29 votes to 20 in the final count. In one sense, it was a poisoned chalice. With Fianna Fáil in such a powerful ascendancy, questions were being asked about the future of Fine Gael.

Kenny may have been a 25-year veteran at that stage, but he had two attributes that were essential for the task in hand: energy and optimism.

'Fine Gael's political mourning is over. This party is getting up off the floor and we are determined to demonstrate all over Ireland that we are a force to be reckoned with in the future', he told colleagues that night.

What political columnist Miriam Lord wrote about him the previous year encapsulated his attributes adroitly: '"Indakinny," they shout. "Young and blonde and will keep his mouth shut. He's the boy for us." And so it came to pass that a mere stripling of 50 years of age, with 25 years of Dáil experience emerged as the fresh youthful face of Fine Gael.'

Kenny's project to revive the party was driven by a number of key supporters. The Kilkenny TD Phil Hogan was to become his closest ally and was his chief strategist. He asked a long-time adviser to the party, Frank Flannery, to head a committee charged with revitalising the party. It came up with a hard-hitting 42-page report that recommended root-and-branch reform.

'The truth is that while Ireland has changed beyond recognition over the last generation, Fine Gael has stood still', the report stated. 'Fianna Fáil is essentially a pragmatic, populist party and, by definition, is perpetually renewing itself.' The report concluded that Fine Gael's way forward was not simply to offer itself as an alternative to Fianna Fáil but to project 'an alternative and better version of the modern political organisation which is needed to win votes in today's Ireland'. It was also to use the triangulation used by Tony Blair's New Labour and Bill Clinton's Democratic Party to appropriate the more attractive facets of Fianna Fáil as its own while setting out its alternative ideals.

Arising from the report, the party made key appointments at senior levels in policy, communications and economics to professionalise the operation. Given the churn of leaders the party had over the previous decade, Flannery also cautioned TDs and Senators to give Kenny time as leader and to allow him space to play to his strengths. It was a long game, but Flannery shared his fellow Mayo man's optimism, predicting the party could win 60 seats in the next general election.

Kenny spent the following months traversing the country, visiting each constituency, in an effort to revitalise the base. His natural bonhomie and common touch lent to this effort: the party's grass roots (especially in rural Ireland) regarded him as one of their own. He repeated a 'single transferable' speech designed to re-energise the party's base.

Another attribute was that he was willing to embrace the changes that had been suggested. Many of his new appointments, for example, were younger TDs, including John Deasy from Waterford, who he promoted to the Justice portfolio. He also displayed a steeliness from early on. Part of the party's revival plan provided for the replacement of 'career' Senators with candidates who could win seats in the Dáil next time around. All of them were replaced with the exception of two: his close Castlebar ally, Senator Paddy Burke, and Paul Coghlan, a redoubtable and larger-than-life Kerry Senator who is reputed to have retained his seat by garnering votes from councillors from all parties in Kerry (including Sinn Féin).

In another relatively early show of straight, he fired Deasy as justice spokesman after the Waterford TD insisted on smoking in the Dáil bar soon after the smoking ban was introduced.

His flaws were also evident. He was constantly bested in Dáil exchanges by Bertie Ahern and even by the new Labour leader Pat Rabbitte. His unfortunate penchant for making careless remarks, recollections of conversations (that sometimes strayed from the facts) and off-colour anecdotes would come to haunt him more than once during his leadership. At a private event close to the Dáil, he told the audience a story about an occasion when a friend of his visiting Portugal had asked about a cocktail named after a Congolese leader. The barman had used the 'N' word in describing the political leader, and Kenny had repeated the phrase he used. His comments were reported in Sunday newspapers, prompting an apology from Kenny.

In opposition, Fine Gael began to develop new policies and stances, based on research. One of the more successful was finance spokesman Richard Bruton's campaign against benchmarking, where public servants' pay was compared to what was being earned in the private sector. It was an artificial bidding war, with steep pay hikes being awarded, which Bruton argued were unsustainable. He was also one of the first to ask if the ever-expanding housing sector was in danger of becoming a bubble.

There were other policies that were more questionable. Despite being a fluent Irish speaker, who spoke with an authentic Connemara Gaeltacht accent, Enda Kenny was never a fan of state backing of the language and suggested it no longer be a compulsory subject in schools. He also, along with Hogan, suggested there was no need for Seanad Éireann, the Upper House, and that it should be scrapped.

The party threw all its resources into the 2004 local and European elections. The well-known broadcaster Mairead McGuinness was recruited in the East constituency, much to the displeasure of sitting Member of European Parliament Avril Doyle. The internecine warfare yielded a great result for the party. It won two seats in the constituency and five out of the 13 nationally, outpolling Fianna Fáil.

The revival was under way. The party's prospects for the general election in 2007 seemed to have greatly improved after it emerged that Taoiseach Bertie Ahern had been questioned by the Mahon Tribunal into planning corruption about unexplained payments that had been made to him. The opening week of the campaign was dominated by Ahern's personal finances, with journalists questioning him wherever he went. However, the election turned on a number of key events during the campaign. Fianna Fáil Minister for Finance Brian Cowen gave a barnstorming press conference where he cast doubt on Fine Gael's ability to manage the economy. To reinforce that doubt, in the live televised debate between Kenny and Ahern on RTÉ, where the Fine Gael leader struggled on figures and the economy, Ahern came across as the more competent.

In the event, Fine Gael won 51 seats, a gain of 20, but far short of Fianna Fáil, which won 78 seats and went into coalition with the Green Party, which had won six seats. There were some very impressive new young TDs in the intake, including Leo Varadkar and Lucinda Creighton. Speaking bullishly on the day the new coalition was formed, Kenny said he was preparing for the next election: 'Anything could happen with this government', he said.

It was prescient. And even though he did not realise it at that moment in time, he and Fine Gael were lucky not to have crossed the line. Within a year, Bertie Ahern, unable to shake off the continuing allegations about his personal finances, had resigned. His successor Brian Cowen started off poorly, losing the Lisbon Treaty, which all the bigger parties supported. It was to go downhill from there for the unfortunate Cowen. Within weeks, the new Minister for Finance, Brian Lenihan, observed wryly that he had become Minister just as the building boom was coming to a 'shuddering halt'. He was right. All hell was to break loose. The economy collapsed like a house of cards as the housing bubble deflated. Within months, an emergency budget was drafted. Anglo Irish Bank collapsed and had to be nationalised. NAMA was established to buy and manage the bad debts of the banks. Fianna Fáil's popularity plummeted.

Fine Gael, in contrast, began to gain support in opinion polls. In the local and European elections in 2009, it easily outpolled Fianna Fáil, winning 340 seats in local authorities, a high-water mark. However, Labour's new leader, Eamon Gilmore, was a very effective communicator, and the party was polling well. By 2010, Labour was breathing down Fine Gael's necks in the support stakes, and Gilmore seemed to be scoring more points in Dáil exchanges. The party also mounted a campaign 'Gilmore for Taoiseach', which was, in retrospect, hubristic, but spooked TDs in Fine Gael.

Questions about Kenny's leadership, his ability and his pedigree began to re-emerge. The catalyst for the leadership heave was a poor opinion poll in the *Irish Times* that showed Labour ahead of Fine Gael. When Richard Bruton effectively declared his hand to Kenny by asking him to step aside, Kenny promptly tabled a motion of confidence in himself as leader and sacked Bruton from the front bench. Phil Hogan quickly rallied to Kenny's side: there was nobody in the party better equipped to run the numbers, orchestrate a campaign and rally the troops.

Many of the front bench were in the rebel camp, and they planned to confront Kenny at its next meeting and tell him one by one that he could not stay as leader. This group included Michael Creed, Leo Varadkar, Simon Coveney, Denis Naughten, Lucinda Creighton, Brian Hayes,

Billy Timmins and Olwyn Enright. Kenny short-circuited the process. He began the meeting by excoriating the nine TDs, accusing them of treachery. He then informed them he was standing down the entire front bench before marching out of the room.

What looked bad for Kenny turned out to be entirely good. In a fractious campaign, Hogan and his deputies cajoled a majority of back-bench TDs and Senators to back Kenny. One of the ploys they used was that there was innate snobbery at play, the Brahmins of Fine Gael turning their noses up at a leader who came from rural Ireland. After winning the vote, Kenny buried the axe quickly with some of the protagonists including Bruton, Coveney and Varadkar, bringing them back to his front bench. For some others, such as Naughten, Timmins, Hayes and Creed – to whom he had been very close – there would be no forgiveness.

When the dust settled, it could not have worked out better for Kenny. The question of his leadership was now conclusively settled. He had also proved that he had the required steeliness to lead. There was also another bonus. He needed a new finance spokesperson, and he recalled former leader Michael Noonan, who had played no part in the contest. Whatever failings Noonan had as leader, he was the perfect choice for the Finance portfolio, through his vast experience, skills as a communicator and cool authority. He settled into the job just as the country was losing its sovereignty and the IMF and EU were coming in to oversee the running of the economy.

The party's Five Point Plan to recover the economy had resonance with voters. Gilmore's Labour, so effective in the Dáil, did not perform so well in the early part of the campaign. As polling day loomed, the odds of Kenny winning an overall majority shortened. In response, Labour put out a spoiled ad that parodied the Tesco supermarket slogan, 'Every Little Helps.' Labour's attack ad read, 'Every Little Hurts' and listed a number of Fine Gael actions that would hurt the voter, including water charges, VAT and Deposit Interest Retention Tax increases and extra duty on wine. It halted the gallop a little. Fine Gael won 76 seats (a huge haul), Labour won 36, and the Fianna Fáil seat numbers collapsed from 78 to 20.

The task facing Kenny and his new government was daunting. To achieve control of the public finances, there would be a need for very stringent cuts in welfare, in pay levels and in pensions. Hundreds of services would need to have their budgets slashed. The scale of it unnerved ministers, especially on the Labour side. Kenny's first speech was characteristically optimistic. 'I believe that for Ireland this current crisis is the darkest hour before dawn', he said in his first Dáil speech. 'Together and for our country let us believe in our future. For Ireland and each other, let us lift up our heads, turn our faces to the sun and hang out our brightest colours. This is the first day of a journey to a better future.'

At the first cabinet meeting, in a symbolic gesture, the new ministers agreed to swingeing cuts in their own salaries. Privately, Kenny was concerned. He confided that within a year he expected there would be tens of thousands of people on the streets baying for his blood. Moreover, he was thrown into the deep end within days. At his first European summit, he tried to get agreement from other EU leaders to reduce the interest rate on the loan of €67 billion that had been extended to Ireland in the bailout. However, he was rounded upon in private by German Chancellor Angela Merkel and French President Nicolas Sarkozy, who told him they would only agree to it if Ireland changed its corporate tax policy. Despite the intense pressure, Kenny resisted, knowing that compromising on a cornerstone of Irish foreign direct investment policy would be hugely damaging to Ireland and to his authority as Taoiseach. Facing down such intimidatory rivals in the rarefied atmosphere of a Brussels summit was an important moment for him.

If one were to assess Kenny as Taoiseach using a uniquely Irish metric, he was more chairman than chief. He was happy to delegate responsibility to colleagues with more expertise and knowledge of the area than himself and then defer to them. That was especially true for Finance, where he gave Michael Noonan free rein. In addition, Richard Bruton was also given freedom to develop new policies to kickstart the economy. Unemployment rates had peaked at 15 per cent after the crash. Kenny said he was determined to get people jobs. Bruton set out the comprehensive but easily understandable Action Plan for Jobs with over 200 targets. By the time the government's term came to an end, the unemployment rate had halved.

It was a strange period. While the Troika – as the European Commission, European Central Bank and IMF were known – was associated with the austere policies adopted during that time, there was high public support for what it was doing. But it was not the Troika that was formulating policy. Its memorandums of understanding were agreed with the government, and it was the government that had the ultimate say on which policies to implement. In a sense, the Troika provided political cover for non-crowd-pleasing policies.

It was a signal sign of the success of the plan that the government was able to announce in December 2013, well ahead of schedule, that Ireland was exiting the EU–IMF bailout. Kenny delivered his second televised speech to the nation during his term (the first had been right after his election to the role). He was bullish. 'Ireland is now moving in the right direction. Our economy is starting to recover. While there are still far too many people out of work, jobs are being created.'

Public perceptions of Kenny had also changed. At the end of 2011, within a three-week period, he welcomed both President Barack Obama and Queen Elizabeth II to Dublin for what can truly be called historic visits. His impassioned speech in College Green as he welcomed the American President, which actually borrowed some phrases from Obama's own speeches, was particularly memorable.

For much of his career, too, Kenny, a practising Catholic, would have been regarded as socially conservative, but he began to negate the image in government. When the Cloyne Report, which showed suppression of sexual abuse of children by clergy, was published, he made damning criticism of the Vatican. 'The Cloyne Report excavates the dysfunction, disconnection, elitism and narcissism that dominate the culture of the Vatican to this day. The rape and torture of children were downplayed.' Equally, in 2013, he made a highly emotional speech to the Dáil during his state apology to the survivors of Magdalene Laundries, choking back tears. 'We put away these women because for too many years we put away our conscience', he said.

The death of a young woman, Savita Halappanavar, during pregnancy in late 2012 refocused attention on Ireland's restrictive abortion laws. There was also a case from the European Court of Human Rights that ruled that the absence of access to abortion where a woman's life is at risk violated the European Convention on Human Rights. The government published the Protection for Life During Pregnancy Bill 2013, which legislated for such cases. Kenny argued that the legislation would provide only for such cases and that there would be no abortion on demand. However, despite being a Catholic, crucially, he distinguished his responsibility as a politician. 'My book is the Constitution', he said. 'That's the people's book, and we live in a Republic.'

In the event, five Fine Gael TDs voted against the legislation, and all of them had the parliamentary party whip removed. The most high-profile, Lucinda Creighton, went on to form a new party, Renua, which failed to take off electorally.

Kenny's strong support for the 2015 marriage-equality referendum was another indication that a party that was once divided between a liberal wing and a Christian democrat wing was reflecting the big changes that were happening in society and the relationship of people with its institutions. This was only 23 years after homosexuality was decriminalised. One of Kenny's senior ministers (and future Taoiseach) Leo Varadkar gave a radio interview at the start of the year and said, 'I am a gay man. It's not a secret. Not everyone would necessarily know.'

Elsewhere, there were undertows, missteps and misjudgements, some of which landed at Kenny's door. Hogan was a great strategist and campaigner and also had an ambitious reform agenda. Kenny backed him on all of them. Some worked well, including the gender quota for candidates (to improve representation of women). Others did not. A referendum was called to abolish the Seanad, but it was defeated in 2013.

The government might have considered itself lucky not to have faced mass street demonstrations and public unrest over austerity, as had happened in Greece and in Spain. But that was not to say it got all its measures over the line seamlessly. The government introduced a Local Property Tax (a Troika ask) through the Minister for the Environment, Phil Hogan. However, there was considerable resistance, with some opposition parties using people to boycott it. Ultimately, the Revenue Commissioners were asked to collect that tax, which had the effect of increasing compliance.

There was no such luck with water charges. The government began an ambitious programme to install water meters outside every home in the country. But a nationwide campaign, which had the strong backing of Sinn Féin, attracted substantial support, with mass rallies and protests attracting thousands of people. It would become one of the major issues in the 2016 election and would be a millstone around the neck of the coalition in the latter stages of its terms.

There was a series of controversies involving senior garda management and allegations made by whistleblowers, primarily Sergeant Maurice McCabe. The most serious moment came in 2014 when Kenny effectively forced Minister for Justice Alan Shatter to resign on the back of premature judgement by Kenny based on a report by Senior Counsel Seán Guerin. Shatter took cases to the superior courts against Guerin's report, which ultimately backed up his version of events. In other words, there was no justification for Kenny to seek his resignation.

In the run-up to the 2016 election, Fine Gael could point to the success it had in turning the economy around from the verge of bankruptcy to real growth and quickly growing employment. However, while recovery was happening, it was not felt everywhere. Fine Gael's slogan 'Let's Keep the Recovery Going' grated with certain sections of the electorate. Some of Kenny's old failings also resurfaced during the campaign. In the opening press conference, he showed a very poor grasp of the figures. In a weak attempt to ward off further questions, he said, 'I'm not going to get into economic jargon here because the vast majority of people don't understand.'

His habit of unthinkingly coming out with a gaffe also appeared. At a rally in Castlebar, he told the crowd that some people were complaining about the lack of economic activity in Mayo. 'These people are

All-Ireland champions when it comes to whingeing', he exclaimed to his stunned audience. He later had to apologise to the people of Castlebar, having tried to say he was referring to Fianna Fáil supporters.

The lingering effects of austerity, water charges, plus a growing housing crisis conspired to negate the huge gains made in the economy. The party lost 26 seats in the 2016 election and finished with 50. It was still the largest party, but Fianna Fáil was only five seats short, and Sinn Féin was also growing. Moreover, Labour had been annihilated, losing 30 of its 37 seats.

There was success, but it had to be judged in context. Enda Kenny was the first Fine Gael Taoiseach to be selected for a second term. Against that, for the first time in six years, there were doubts expressed about his leadership. By this stage, Varadkar was seen as the most likely to succeed him. Within hours of the election result, he nonetheless gave Kenny strong backing. 'The vast majority view even from those who have fallen out with Enda Kenny is the election was a defeat but not a rout.'

A convoluted 'confidence-and-supply' agreement was put in place with Fianna Fáil, and a government was scraped together composed of Fine Gael ministers and a number of ministers drawn from the independent benches. In the more fetid atmosphere of the new Dáil, critics of Kenny began to emerge, possibly as stalking horses. The first to publicly challenge his leadership was Brendan Griffin, in mid-2016. Later, others followed. Kenny deflected the criticism and vowed that he would continue as leader.

It was his habit of the unguarded and unfocused comment that cost him dearly in the end. In February 2017, there were shocking revelations that Tusla, the Child and Family Agency, had made false accusations against garda whistleblower Maurice McCabe. McCabe had briefed Minister for Children Katherine Zappone on the allegations when he met her in her department. In a radio interview, Kenny recalled having a conversation with Minister Zappone before she met Mr McCabe and his wife in her department. He recalled purporting to give her advice on how to deal with the meeting. However, his version was contradicted by Minister Zappone who recalled no such conversation.

The bombshell, and the implication that he had essentially recalled a conversation that had not happened, created a substantial crisis for the government, undermined Taoiseach Kenny's status within his own party, and forced him to issue a mea culpa at a fraught parliamentary party meeting, and in the Dáil several days later. Ultimately, it was to lead to his stepping down.

On the eve of his departure, Kenny met his friend Senator Paul Coghlan, and brought up the subject of Kerry football legend Colm 'The Gooch' Cooper. Coghlan recalled, 'Enda said to me, "The Gooch knew that the time was right to go." I replied to him, "That's not a fair comparison. The Gooch was grounded by a bad injury, and you are fit and full of energy."'

It was one of his old flaws that grounded Kenny in the end. But, against that, any balanced judgement of his six years as Taoiseach would be that he grew in stature, grew into the job and will be remembered as a leader who was well capable of ruling.

After stepping down as Taoiseach, Kenny returned to the back benches of Fine Gael. In keeping with the tradition of former Taoisigh stepping away from active politics, he was not an active parliamentarian, voting on only a handful of occasions for the rest of the Dáil term. He retired from politics in 2020.

He was named European of the Year in 2019 by European Movement Ireland in recognition of his lifetime pro-EU political outlook. In February 2023, he disclosed that he had received treatment for cancer but was expected to make a full recovery. During US President Joe Biden's visit to Ireland in 2023, Kenny (whom Biden described as a 'good friend') accompanied him throughout the Co. Mayo portion of the visit.

In the intervening years, he was appointed to the board of several international companies, including an Irish-based venture-capital company, a public-relations company and an environmental company. He also presented a six-part series for the Irish-language TV station TG4, about railroads. The series, titled *Iarnród Enda (Enda's Railways)*, was loosely based on the format of the long-running *Great Railway Journeys* presented by former Conservative politician Michael Portillo. In his spare time, Kenny plays golf and is also involved in the GAA in Co. Mayo, where he has been President of his home club, Islandeady.

15

Leo Varadkar

2017–20, 2022–4

Philip Ryan

Full name: Leo Eric Varadkar
Date of birth: 18 January 1979
Place of birth: Dublin
Education: The King's Hospital; Trinity College Dublin
Civil partner: Michael Barrett
Assumed office: (1) 14 June 2017; (2) 17 December 2022
Date of resignation: (1) 27 June 2020; (2) 9 April 2024
Length of tenure: Four years, five months, three days
Quotation: 'Geographically, we are at the periphery of Europe, but I don't see Ireland in that way. The way I see us is as an island at the centre of the world'.

Leo Varadkar did not fit the mould of a Taoiseach. Due to his Indian heritage, he did not look like any of the Taoisigh who predated him, who had all been white Irish men. He also did not act like former Taoisigh nor, indeed, any party-aligned politicians of the time. He had a habit of speaking his mind even if it did fit with the party line. On 18 January 2015, while a cabinet minister, he became even more unique when he announced he was gay. Two years later, he would become the first openly gay Taoiseach.

In the same interview with RTÉ broadcaster Miriam O'Callaghan in which he announced he was gay, Varadkar also told the nation he did not intend on remaining in politics beyond the age of 50. This was a promise he kept, and, on 20 March 2024, he announced his resignation as Taoiseach. Ironically, he made the announcement just a couple of days after returning from a week-long state visit to Washington DC, where he attended a number of events with President Joe Biden, who would ultimately pull out of the race for the White House a few months later.

Undoubtedly, Varadkar's distinct characteristics helped propel him to the very top of Irish politics, but there is an argument that they may have ultimately led to his downfall. However, his tenure saw him tackle significant challenges that other Taoisigh could never have envisioned and introduce political and social reforms which have had and will have a lasting impact long after his resignation.

Varadkar's story begins in a West Dublin suburban housing estate where he lived with his father, Ashok, and mother, Miriam, along with his sisters, Sonia and Sophie. His parents met while working in a UK hospital where Ashok, an Indian migrant, was working as a doctor and Miriam, an Irish migrant, worked as a nurse. They spent a short period in India before settling in Dublin in the 1970s where Ashok set up a GP practice in the family's home.

Leo Varadkar did not look like a lot of his neighbours and friends due to his heritage, but, surprisingly, he suffered very little racism growing up in 1980s Dublin. Speaking to me for the book *Leo: A Very Modern Taoiseach*, he said he could only really remember a couple of incidents when bigoted comments were made towards him. Varadkar suggested his family was warmly accepted into their community because his father was the local doctor. Neighbours and classmates would be regular visitors to the family home for appointments with his father while he and his sisters watched television in an adjoining room.

They were not an overly religious family, but Varadkar was brought up in the Catholic rather than Hindu tradition and would irregularly attend Mass at the weekends. Varadkar has always insisted neither his Indian heritage nor indeed his sexuality ever defined him as an individual or a politician.

He is not the only member of the Varadkar family to take on political causes. Ashok's brothers, Madhu and Manohar, took up the cause of Indian independence from British rule during their university days and ended up spending a year in gaol for their parts in protests against colonialism. Their imprisonment was considered a badge of honour by their middle-class family and by most Indians at the time. They would perhaps be proud of the role their nephew would later play, decades later, in taking on the British government once again following Britain's exit from the EU.

Leo Varadkar's relationship dynamic with his father is complex. In a rare interview, Ashok once described himself as a 'champagne socialist' and urged his son to focus his political work on the more vulnerable in society. He also noted his son had 'matured' since his early years in politics when he held highly conservative right-wing views on abortion, LGBTQIA+ rights and welfare support for the poor. During an interview for his biography, Varadkar dismissed his father's comments as 'total rubbish', adding that his father is 'quite right-wing' in his views on taxes, welfare and distribution of wealth. Varadkar also spoke about the 'weird experience' of being hugged by his father when he was elected leader of Fine Gael. However, family friends say the two men are quite alike in their work ethic, political outlooks and mannerisms.

Varadkar followed his father's footsteps in studying medicine. Third-level education was liberating for the academically driven young Varadkar. At Trinity College, he met people who shared his interest in politics and debate, which led to him joining Young Fine Gael and the college debating society. It was not long before he was asked to get actively involved in politics and run for a seat on Fingal County Council in the 1999 local elections.

It was a baptism of fire, with party headquarters designating him a working-class electoral area where the right-leaning Fine Gael was far from the go-to political organisation. He received just 380 votes, but he was not deterred and remained active in Fine Gael until the next local elections, in 2004, when he defied the opinion polls and received almost

5,000 votes in an election in which Fine Gael did not perform well.

The local polling figures meant that Varadkar was destined for a run at national politics three years later when Bertie Ahern called the general election. Again, Varadkar defied the odds and saw off experienced competition to become a member of Dáil Éireann at just 26 years old. With the Celtic Tiger economy still thriving under Fianna Fáil, Fine Gael performed poorly in the general election, and Varadkar was one of their few success stories. Fine Gael leader Enda Kenny appointed him as his enterprise spokesperson and let him loose on the government in the Dáil chamber. He quickly made a name for himself as Fine Gael's attack dog and regularly made headlines for his no-holds-barred criticisms of Ahern who was engulfed in a scandal over his personal finances.

Bertie Ahern ultimately stepped down and was replaced by Brian Cowen as Taoiseach. Not long after, the 2008 financial crash saw the Irish economy nosedive into the abyss. Unemployment skyrocketed and was followed by mass emigration. The IMF and the EU were forced to intervene, and the Fianna Fáil-led government was instructed to impose an unprecedented series of austerity measures on the people of Ireland. This was red meat to Varadkar who continued his attacks on the government.

The Cowen administration struggled on for a couple of years despite daily calls for a general election from Fine Gael. The election would come, but not before Fine Gael became embroiled in a leadership heave against Enda Kenny in the summer of 2010. Varadkar sided with the Richard Bruton-led coup seeking to oust Kenny. The heave failed after a vote was finally held on Kenny's leadership, and the debacle resulted in a lot of bad blood in Fine Gael. Kenny reshuffled his front bench but, despite his treachery, reappointed Varadkar.

The 2011 general election resulted in Fine Gael and the Labour Party forming a coalition, and Kenny appointed Varadkar Minister for Transport, Sport and Tourism. There was a new government, but the austerity continued with new charges and taxes introduced to comply with the terms of the bailout Ireland received from the so-called Troika of the IMF, European Commission and European Central Bank.

Despite the political challenges the economic crash presented, Varadkar still had some political successes in his first ministry. The hospitality and tourism industry were especially thankful for his commitment to reducing VAT on their services, and he introduced the Gathering initiative, which encouraged wealthy emigrants to visit Ireland.

His reputation at this time was of a minister who could appear simultaneously aloof while also being unafraid to speak his mind on contentious issues. Colleagues were equally intrigued and baffled by the young minister. He could end up on the front pages accidentally as much as by design. He was also increasingly becoming a media darling and was a regular on current-affairs shows, waxing lyrical about the events of the day. Along with his team of advisers, he built up contacts across the media where his views could be briefed privately, especially when it involved internal party or cabinet issues.

However, his public comments could rankle with his party colleagues. There was the incident when he raised questions about Minister for Health James Reilly's allocation of a primary care centre to his own constituency. He also publicly praised garda whistleblowers who lifted the lid on the practice of senior gardaí squashing penalty points given to friends and colleagues for road-traffic offences despite the two officers being in conflict with the then Minister for Justice, Alan Shatter. These conflicts with his own party colleagues made him stand out as a politician in a political system that was more accustomed to ministers always toeing the party line. His standing among some of the more experienced members of Fine Gael may have been low, but he was seen as something of a messiah to an increasing number of disillusioned backbenchers who were dissatisfied with the Enda Kenny regime.

In 2014, Varadkar ended up in the Department of Health, replacing Reilly who had become too prone to controversy. It was another big challenge, and a lot was expected of him, given his medical background.

Possibly the biggest personal political test ever faced by an Irish Taoiseach came a few months later when Varadkar came out as a gay man ahead of the 2015 marriage-equality referendum. At this point in his career, there was increasing speculation about his sexuality, and some tabloid newspapers were making queries. The RTÉ interview mentioned above was well received domestically and internationally, and the LGBTQIA+ rights referendum passed overwhelmingly. It was a weight off Varadkar's shoulders, and he could now enjoy life without the burden of hiding his sexuality from the public.

He remained in the Department of Health until the 2016 general election after which Fine Gael returned to power but only as part of a complex confidence-and-supply arrangement with Fianna Fáil and the direct support of a small group of independent TDs. Enda Kenny remained Taoiseach and asked Varadkar to continue serving in the Department of Health. However, Varadkar made a series of what were seen as unreasonable demands for his department, and he was instead given the Department of Social Protection. The move suited Varadkar as it meant far less work and controversy than the Department of Health; also, he could travel the country meeting Fine Gael politicians and members.

He always denied that he forced Enda Kenny from office, but, over the course of a year, pressure mounted on the Fine Gael leader to step aside while his heir apparent not so quietly developed a support base for leadership bid. During this period, Varadkar and a team of close confidants were actively working the numbers on who would support his leadership bid once a contest was announced, and the figures were good. Kenny eventually stepped aside as Fine Gael leader in May 2017, and the race to replace him started immediately. But the contest was over before it started because Varadkar's only competition, Minister for Housing Simon Coveney, had put in none of the preparatory work and was left with few high-profile supporters.

On 2 June 2017, Varadkar was elected Fine Gael leader and, in his victory speech, said his elevation in politics, given his background and sexuality, showed 'prejudice has no hold in this Republic', adding, 'Around the world people look to Ireland to be reminded that this is a country where it doesn't matter where you come from but rather where you want to go.' He also talked about building a 'republic of opportunity' in which all citizens can realise their potential and share in the prosperity of the country. The comments came as Ireland's economy was rebounding strongly in the aftermath of the 2008 recession, with the government unveiling a series of progressive giveaway budgets which had equal amounts of income-tax cuts and welfare increases.

A couple of weeks later, Varadkar was elected Taoiseach by the Dáil and he began his first stint as Ireland's leader. While the economy was beginning to thrive once again, there were dark clouds on the horizon. A year earlier, on 23 June 2016, UK voters shocked the world by voting to leave the EU in a divisive referendum that would have lasting impacts for Britain and Ireland. There were few at the highest levels of Irish politics who believed the British public would vote to leave the EU. Perhaps they were blinded by the significant levels of financial supports Ireland had enjoyed since joining the Union. Regular opinion polls also showed the Irish public was well disposed to the technocrats and politicians in Brussels passing down legislation to be implemented locally. Years of petty and not-so-petty corruption involving Irish politicians meant that people were happy to have some oversight from abroad on how the country was managed.

In Britain, it was different. The Conservative Party used Brussels as a punchbag for difficult decisions especially when EU directives were not well received by their electorate. Brexit campaigners played on voter fears developed over decades coupled with advanced social-media advertising targeting techniques that ultimately resulted in the public voting to leave. British Prime Minister David Cameron, who proposed the referendum and campaigned to remain in the EU, resigned immediately and was replaced by Theresa May.

On both sides of the Irish Sea, no one appeared to have given serious consideration as to what would happen to the border between the Republic of Ireland and Northern Ireland should Britain leave the EU. The British Army gun towers of the Troubles were long gone from the border, and there was complete free movement of people and goods on the island of Ireland. But now what? There were genuine fears of a return to sectarian violence if a new border or customs checkpoints were established. The EU was also insisting that Britain could not leave the Union and continue to enjoy access to the customs union.

Much of Enda Kenny's last year in office was focused on ensuring a border did not return to Ireland. He travelled the continent meeting counterparts, making the case and attending European Council summits in Brussels where Brexit was, naturally, top of the agenda. Ultimately, Kenny achieved his objective in no small part due to the relationships he built at the most senior levels of the EU as he navigated Ireland out of the economic mire following the financial crash. Theresa May agreed with Kenny in principle, and both countries also wanted to maintain the Common Travel Area between the islands. Kenny's big win was the commitment from the European Commission President Jean-Claude Juncker that ensuring the border did not return would be a key principle in all Brexit negotiations.

A year on, the situation had not changed, but the Taoiseach had. Varadkar was buoyed early on in his tenure by the support he received from other EU leaders who echoed the commitment Enda Kenny received on the border. A marked difference in the lengthy Brexit negotiations under Varadkar came in how Brexiteers and Unionists viewed him. He quickly became a bogeyman in Britain and was regularly targeted by the Brexit-supporting media. There may have been no place for prejudice in the Republic of Ireland, but Varadkar soon found that this was not the case in Britain. He was called a 'typical Indian' by Ulster Unionist MP Lord Kilclooney while then Foreign Secretary Boris Johnson was alleged to have said, 'Why isn't he called Murphy like the rest of them?'

Brexit negotiations were not helped by the collapse of the Northern Ireland Assembly in early 2017, or by Democratic Unionist Party MPs propping up May's embattled Tory government. To his credit, Varadkar held firm and ensured the relationships developed by Kenny in Europe were maintained and strengthened. Despite attempts from the British government to establish back-channel negotiations with Ireland, Varadkar, along with his Minister for Foreign Affairs Simon Coveney, insisted all talks had to be run through Brussels. The view was that any side-dealing with Britain would put at risk the solidarity built up around the EU.

Months turned into years as all sides struggled to find compromise on an orderly exit. Meanwhile, relations between Ireland and Britain collapsed to a low not seen since the Troubles. Brexit became all-encompassing for both governments. Emergency legislation and contingency plans were drafted in Ireland in case of talks between the EU and Britain collapsing. There were endless numbers of meetings with the Brussels negotiating team led by Michel Barnier who would prove to be a huge ally to Ireland.

During this period, Varadkar's personal popularity surged with voters who appreciated his steadfast determination to face down Britain and protect Ireland's interest in the negotiations. However, he faced accusations of leaning into the appearance of taking on the British and Unionists for the sake of his own political advancement rather than focusing on finding a solution to the Brexit quagmire.

The circus that was British politics at the time eventually resulted in Theresa May resigning and being replaced by Boris Johnson who called an election and campaigned to 'Get Brexit Done'. Unlike May, Johnson secured a stunning majority that significantly strengthened his hand in Brexit talks with Brussels. There was extreme nervousness about how talks would proceed with the reliably unpredictable Johnson, and it would be the first true test of Varadkar's negotiating skills. There were open hostilities between Britain and Ireland at the time, but, with the potential of a no-deal Brexit fast approaching, Varadkar and Johnson agreed to meet in Liverpool in October 2019. Dublin insisted they clear the meeting with Brussels despite the impression they eventually succumbed to Britain's advancements for a side deal.

The meeting would eventually result in what became the Northern Ireland Protocol, which essentially put a border in the Irish Sea rather than on the island of Ireland. It certainly did not happen overnight, and talks would rumble on for a number of years, with the collapse of the Northern Ireland Assembly for a second time exacerbating matters further. The final deal had the potential to make the North a very prosperous region with access to both the European and British markets. The arrangement is still in its infancy, and sectarian divisions still plague the North, but the Irish government believe the deal could eventually be hugely attractive to international businesses seeking to invest in both markets.

Varadkar's first stint as Taoiseach was dominated by Brexit negotiations, but it was not the only challenge he had to overcome. The Programme for Government agreed with independent TDs committed to holding a referendum on Ireland's restrictive abortion laws, and time was ticking down on the administration's term in office.

A couple of years earlier, following the tragic death of Indian woman Savita Halappanavar, who died in hospital after being refused an abortion, the Fine Gael and Labour Party government passed laws allowing for pregnancy terminations in certain circumstances. The passing of legislation in 2016 led to several Fine Gael TDs quitting the party as they could not support the introduction of any form of abortion in Ireland. In the early days of his political career, Varadkar was vehemently pro-life. In an interview, he even compared the plight of women travelling to Britain for abortions to tourists flying to Amsterdam to smoke cannabis. But he did vote with the government on the 2016 legislation and had come on a journey in the preceding years.

The referendum was on repealing the Eighth Amendment of the Constitution and introducing legislation that would allow for abortions up to 12 weeks of pregnancy. Varadkar allowed his party members to vote with their consciences on the divisive referendum but fully supported the constitutional change himself. Fine Gael deputy leader Simon Coveney personally struggled with the referendum but eventually supported the vote.

The referendum was supported by a landslide, and, for the first time, abortions were permitted in Irish hospitals. It was a huge social change for the country, and, while it was an activist-driven campaign, it was notable that a Fine Gael leader, who not long before was staunchly anti-abortion, oversaw the government's campaign and brought the legislation underpinning the constitutional change to the Dáil.

The passing of the referendum, along with the marriage-equality vote, is an example of how depictions of Varadkar as a right-wing ideologue can be somewhat unfair. Granted, it was the Labour Party who pushed for marriage equality, and it was independent TD Katherine Zappone who championed abortion rights. However, Varadkar threw his weight behind both campaigns and ensured the Dáil passed legislation introducing the historic changes to an Irish society that had well and truly moved on from being ruled by the Catholic Church.

In 2018, Fianna Fáil leader Micheál Martin committed to extending the confidence-and-supply agreement until the end of the following year. This gave Varadkar the choice of holding an election in late 2019 or early 2020. The Fine Gael leader went for the latter despite many in his party urging him to go earlier. Under the guidance of Minister for Finance Paschal Donohoe, Fine Gael brought forward an expansionary but cautious budget before the election on 14 January 2020. They also centred much of their campaign on addressing the threats posed by Brexit rather than focusing on the more bread-and-butter issues of interest to voters.

Meanwhile, Fine Gael's plan to increase the pension age to 67 dominated the campaign and handed an easy election strategy to Sinn Féin who wanted to lower the age to 65. Sinn Féin leader Mary Lou McDonald was excluded from some election debates, which gave the impression of Varadkar and Martin seeking to squeeze her out. However, this only resulted in public sympathy for McDonald, whose party made historic gains once the ballots were counted.

Varadkar went into the campaign expecting to make gains but ended up losing seats. This was hugely disappointing for Fine Gael members who had enjoyed success in the local and European elections a few months earlier. It was almost a dead heat between Fine Gael, Fianna Fáil and Sinn Féin when all the votes were counted, and lengthy Programme for Government talks followed.

There was an impression among some in his party that Varadkar failed his first true test as leader in steering Fine Gael to such a dismal general-election result, but there was no challenge to his leadership. It was not long before opinion polls showed public trust in the Taoiseach rising as he faced down a once-in-a-lifetime global pandemic. Varadkar was in Washington, DC meeting US President Donald Trump in early March 2020 when he announced the first series of lockdown measures due to rapid spread of the deadly COVID-19 virus.

The virus was being monitored by a high-ranking team of Department of Health civil servants at this point, but it was clear that it was now out of control and presenting a serious threat to public health. The same was happening all around the world. Varadkar took the decision to put his trust fully into a team of medical professionals led by Chief Medical Officer Tony Holohan and regimentally followed their advice on social-distancing restrictions. Ireland had some of the strictest regulations during the pandemic, but Varadkar's sure-footed public announcements meant there was widespread adherence to rules even if they were challenged by the opposition at times.

There was no rule book on how to deal with a global pandemic, but Varadkar's leadership throughout the crisis meant that lives were saved. However, business, especially hospitality and tourism, suffered due to the restrictions, and state supports continued to be needed long after the virus subsided.

The only misstep Varadkar made during the pandemic was his televised attack on Tony Holohan after he had advised another full lockdown. Varadkar suggested that it was easy for senior civil servants to suggest lockdowns because they were well paid and their salaries were unaffected by COVID. The Taoiseach later apologised to Holohan. The pair had previously crossed paths during the horrific CervicalCheck scandal that resulted in the deaths of 20 women who were not told about abnormalities in their smear tests. Holohan always defended his role during the crisis and was critical of the government's rush to judgement in the scandal, which stemmed from a court case taken by cancer victim Vicky Phelan.

While dealing with COVID, the Fine Gael leader and his senior team were also locked in government-formation talks with Fianna Fáil. After months of negotiations, a partnership between the two Irish Civil War adversaries was agreed, and a so-called grand coalition was formed, along with the Green Party. A historic rotating Taoiseach arrangement was also established which would see Fianna Fáil leader Micheál Martin serve as the country's Taoiseach for the first two and a half years, followed by Varadkar. The Green Party was a minor coalition party and only received cabinet positions. However, the Greens, led by Eamon Ryan, secured significant climate-action commitments in the Programme for Government.

Despite a shaky start, which was overshadowed by distrust between Fine Gael and Fianna Fáil, the coalition would go on to be one of the most stable administrations to govern the country. Fianna Fáil were especially distrustful of Varadkar due to his propensity to indulge in political spin when serving as Tánaiste under Taoiseach Micheál Martin. Varadkar always faced accusations of being more focused on style over substance and would go out of his way to gazump Martin when the government had positive news to share, especially when easing COVID restrictions.

During his first stint as Taoiseach, Varadkar was forced to shut down the Strategic Communications Unit, which aimed to promote government messaging, due to public backlash over what was seen as the introduction of a propaganda machine. In some ways, the grand coalition exposed the naked political ambition of Varadkar when it was seen in contrast to Martin. The Fianna Fáil leader gave the impression of an apolitical politician who appeared almost happy to let his party flounder for the good of the country. Meanwhile, Varadkar seemed to be always politicking and seeking to advance his own personal political ambitions along with those of Fine Gael. This is perhaps an unfair charge, made by some of his detractors, especially when considering the selfless way he resigned as Taoiseach to give his successor Simon Harris time to bed in ahead of a general election.

Despite past differences, Varadkar and Martin, along with Ryan, worked effectively as a leadership team while faced with major challenges such as a refugee crisis sparked by the Russian invasion of Ukraine, which, in turn, was followed by record levels of inflation. There appeared to be little division between the trio when taking serious decisions on these major controversies such as providing all Ukrainian refugees with full welfare payments and housing on arrival or unveiling billions of euro worth of cost-of-living measures to households hammered by skyrocketing inflation.

That is not to say they got everything right. The hospitality shown to Ukrainians was far more generous than other EU states and soon resulted in more than 100,000 people arriving in Ireland. The government was already scrambling to deal with a near-decade-long housing crisis, and a further spike in the population meant they could barely manage to house many of those fleeing the war. This was coupled with a rise in people seeking asylum in Ireland from other parts of the world.

Despite the global rise of mass migration, Varadkar appeared to have a blind spot to the consequences of having a weak asylum system. Ireland was seen as a soft touch to economic migrants seeking a better life, and they began arriving in Ireland in their thousands. Immigration had never been a serious social issue in Ireland where most people were welcoming, and there was an acknowledgement that our health service would not function without migrants. But after the pandemic it was clear that the number of people seeking asylum was greatly increasing.

The government did not take the issue seriously until a migrant attacked a number of children outside a school in Dublin city centre. This resulted in a night of rioting and looting in the heart of the capital, which finally woke up the government to the public unease over the lack of state controls around migration. Perhaps blinded by the success his family enjoyed from migration, Varadkar was near dismissive of concerns about the number of people arriving in Ireland. Opposition TDs who raised concerns were dismissed as racists, but when migrant encampments began popping up around Dublin, the government was forced to act. However, real action on the issue was only taken after Varadkar left office.

On the international stage, Varadkar and Martin were world leaders when it came to challenging Israel's approach to the war in Gaza. The Dáil was one of the first parliaments in the world to call for a ceasefire in the war sparked by the Hamas attack on innocent Israelis. Ireland also chose to formally recognise Palestine as a state as Israel bombarded Gaza in an attempt to bring an end to the violence. Varadkar and Spanish Prime Minister Pedro Sánchez even wrote to European Commission President Ursula von der Leyen questioning an EU–Israeli trade agreement. Varadkar also used his annual visit to the White House to put pressure on US President Joe Biden to bring about a ceasefire. While Ireland is not a world superpower, Varadkar and Martin certainly used any political capital they had to seek a truce in the bloody war that has led to the deaths of up to 55,000 Palestinians at the time of writing.

Back home, the economy under Varadkar was always strong and led to record levels of employment, but there were fears that tax revenue was overly reliant on a small number of international firms paying corporation tax. The budgets Varadkar introduced were always aimed at encouraging people to work and make the most of their lives. Income taxes were reduced while welfare supports for those who needed them were increased.

Varadkar also insisted on reducing costs for working people around health and childcare in the hope that this would ensure more could work. This harks back to his commitment to make sure Ireland was a country where everyone had the opportunity to fulfil their ambitions. However, he never got a handle on the housing crisis, and when he left office, home-ownership continued to remain out of the reach of many young people. Despite Ireland being a wealthy country, homelessness levels remained at crisis point throughout his tenure, and the number of people without homes rose steadily while he was Taoiseach.

Naturally, as a senior political leader, Varadkar was regularly in the public eye. But, with time, it became increasingly difficult for him to lead a normal life. With the rise of social media, the Taoiseach often found himself on the other end of a camera phone lens as someone shouted obscenities at him or threw a milkshake at him. Protestors even targeted his family home where he lived with his partner, Dr Matthew Barrett. The crescendo of the invasion of the Taoiseach's privacy came when he was photographed kissing another man, who was not his partner, in a gay nightclub. The video went viral on social media with millions of views while traditional media debated how to address the controversy. In my own organisation, the issue was debated for a week before it was decided such was the level of disquiet within Fine Gael over the video that it meant it was worth reporting on.

One of his final acts as Taoiseach was a botched attempt to remove archaic language in the Constitution around the role women play in the home and the definition of a family. A referendum had long been called for by women's rights activists, and it appeared a vote on the issue would be an easy win for the government. However, the wording proposed to replace the constitutional clause was badly communicated to the public, and the referendum was overwhelmingly defeated. Voters had supported a lot of social change under Varadkar but were not convinced by his arguments on this referendum.

It would be unfair to suggest his tenure did not bring significant changes to Ireland – not only on abortion rights but also on LGBT rights and child poverty. The conservative views on social issues shifted over time, and his more right-leaning views on the economy were tempered with significant increases in welfare rates while reducing the cost of state services.

On 20 March 2024, Varadkar made the shock announcement to step down as Fine Gael leader and Taoiseach. The announcement caught many people, including his would-be successors, off guard, and there was lots of rumour and speculation over why he took the decision. However, his political stock was falling at this point, and, with local and European elections approaching, stepping down made sense for himself and Fine Gael. Besides, he had said he did not intend remaining in politics after he was 50 years old. He stayed in office while Fine Gael chose his successor, Simon Harris, who took over the seals of office on 9 April.

16

Micheál Martin

2020–2; 2025–

Gavan Reilly

Full name: Micheál Anthony Martin
Date of birth: 16 August 1960
Place of birth: Cork
Married to: Mary O'Shea (m. 1990)
Children: Micheál Aodh, Aoibhe, Ruairí, Cillian and Léana
Education: Coláiste Chríost Rí, Cork; University College Cork
Assumed office: (1) 27 June 2020; (2) 23 January 2025
Date of resignation: (1) 17 December 2022
Length of tenure: (1) Two years, five months, 20 days; (2) incumbent at time of writing
Quotation: 'Spring is coming – and I don't know if I have ever looked forward to one as much as I am looking forward to this one.'

I have two personal anecdotes from encounters with Micheál Martin that might illustrate his interests in public life. The first is from November 2017, during the period when Fianna Fáil supported a Fine Gael-led government through a confidence-and-supply deal. Martin's party had lost confidence in the Minister for Justice, Frances Fitzgerald, over her handling of complaints by a high-profile whistleblower within Ireland's police force. I was dispatched to Martin's office in Leinster House to record a clip for the TV news, after which we made small talk about the realpolitik of defusing a crisis that threatened to cause a general election.

Well, I surmised, three things would have to happen: first, Fitzgerald would have to offer her resignation, which she might not do; second, Leo Varadkar would have to accept it, which he might not be minded to do; and, third, the repair of the seemingly broken trust between Varadkar's party and Martin's. Martin stopped me mid-flow. A Minister offering their resignation, and a Taoiseach declining it? Come off it, that will never happen. It appeared that the Fianna Fáil leader, who had already served in cabinet himself for 13 years, had forgotten how his own ministerial tenure had ended: with a challenge against the leadership of Brian Cowen and a resignation that was offered but temporarily declined.

The second occasion was in 2021 during a relative lull in Ireland's COVID-19 restrictions, when again I was meeting the now Taoiseach to record a TV clip about the government's reply to some of the latest public-health advice. The previous night, I had been helping my wife, who was working as an academic at the time, on research for some turn-of-the-millennium policy on IT in schools. This gave me cause to tell Martin that I had spent the previous night looking at his written replies to parliamentary questions from 1999, when he served as the Minister for Education and Science, about a scheme providing a PC to every primary school. 'Oh', he said, quick as a flash, 'the beauty of that IT2000 scheme was that we were also able to partner up with [the then national telecoms provider] Telecom Éireann and get them to do the same, so we got two for the price of one. It really made a difference in terms of getting the computers out to schools to get them going, you know?' The ins and outs of his own actions in a genuine political crisis seemed to elude him, but the minutiae of a ministerial scheme from almost a quarter of a century earlier were instantly accessible in the recesses of his mind.

Little in Micheál Martin's background suggested he was destined for high political office. Born in August 1960, he and his twin brother, Pádraig, were the second and third children in what would become a family of five. The terraced council house rented by his family in Turner's Cross was happy but cramped; it was not until his youngest sister, Mairéad, turned

14 that the house was fitted with a bathroom. Otherwise, as was common in many local-authority houses until the 1970s, the family shared a toilet at the bottom of the stairs and bathed in a portable tin bath in front of the fireplace.

Also typical of the Martin household was its single-income status, in an era where even if Lana Martin had time or a desire to work, Ireland's ban on married women taking jobs in the public service still prevailed. The breadwinner, Paddy, the father of the house, was a city bus driver, a tireless hard worker and assiduous saver, consistently putting money aside for the children's education. Education served Martin well: long before the abolition of tuition fees, he was able to attend University College Cork, first to study for a Bachelor of Arts degree, then a first-class MA in political history and finally a higher diploma to qualify as a secondary-school teacher. As someone proud of both his party and his home county (as all Corkonians are), Martin's master's thesis discussed party politics in Cork in the Civil War era and was published as a book in 2009.

Paddy also neatly illustrated the family's sporting interests: a multidisciplinarian, he played Gaelic football at St Nicholas' GAA club, alongside the likes of Jack Lynch, who was dipping his own toes in Fianna Fáil politics at the time. Despite the ban on GAA figures playing 'foreign games', he also played soccer with local outfit Free Booters, where he was a contemporary of Frank O'Farrell. Martin would become a fan of Manchester United largely because his dad's teammate was chosen to succeed the legendary Matt Busby as its manager in 1971.

Paddy's greatest sporting prowess was in boxing, regularly claiming county and Munster titles at light heavyweight. His crowning achievement was in 1951 when, before a home crowd in Cork's City Hall, he defeated Joe Bygraves. Jamaican-born Bygraves would subsequently become the Commonwealth heavyweight champion, retaining the title against Henry Cooper, who in turn would later knock down Muhammad Ali. Being able to proclaim himself their equal, Paddy was nicknamed 'The Champ'.

Becoming a history teacher was a predictable career path. Decades later, on the day he became Taoiseach, Micheál Martin would tell the Dáil that his parents had not only taught him the importance of community spirit and of mutual support, the virtues of optimism and persistence, but also the efforts of Ireland's revolutionary leaders. The Martins were not political in a partisan sense but had a strong sense of practical republicanism. Micheál, his oldest brother, Seán, and his elder twin Pádraig were taught about the leaders of 1916. They were taught that those who strove for independence were 'visionary and brave – not just physically but, far more importantly, in their willingness to question themselves and embrace change'.

The Martins' republicanism, with a small R, was practical in several ways. Paddy's family included several who had fought on the anti-Treaty IRA side of the Civil War, yet his own brother, Philip, enlisted in the British Army in the late 1930s in pursuit of a stable income. Philip served in the Royal Engineers during the Second World War, was taken captive by the Japanese in 1942, and held in the prisoner-of-war camp at Changi in Singapore for three years. His family at home, with no news of his welfare, presumed him dead. It was only when the island was liberated at the end of the war, and the list of prisoners catalogued, that they learnt he had survived, emaciated from hunger and weighing eight stone. Martin visited Changi as part of a diplomatic trip to Singapore in 2022. I was able to show the then Taoiseach his uncle's name on a touchscreen database of former prisoners.

Pragmatism was part of Martin's outlook in politics too. While lofty principles had their place, they were useful only if they translated into practical improvement in people's lives. And, in a purely practical sense, the family's anti-Treaty republicanism meant the practical way of getting involved in party politics was to join Fianna Fáil, as Micheál did in university. Doubtless, the choice of party was also eased by the fact that its leader, now in his second term as Taoiseach, was his father's former Gaelic football teammate Jack Lynch.

As a young man in a hurry, Martin's career as a secondary-school history teacher was short-lived. He taught for only one year at Cork's upmarket Presentation Brothers College before election to Cork Corporation, the then city council, a role with pitiful pay but which he took on (as many do) as a full-time job. A tilt at national politics followed not long afterwards in the election of 1987, but as the fourth Fianna Fáil candidate in the four-seat constituency of Cork South Central, election was always unlikely. Far from being a spoiler, though, Martin won enough of the vote to warrant being given a second try in 1989, and, second time round, polled second overall in what had then become a five-seater.

Martin joined Dáil Éireann aged 28, a back-bench TD in what was Fianna Fáil's first ever coalition government alongside the PDs. The dual mandate had not yet been abolished, so Martin retained his seat on the corporation, was re-elected in 1991, and became Lord Mayor of Cork in 1992. The profile might not have done any harm: he grew his own vote in the general election that same year and emerged from the crowded back benches to become Fianna Fáil's education spokesperson when Albert Reynolds's government collapsed and Bertie Ahern led Fianna Fáil into opposition during the mid-term transition of 1994.

By the time of the 1997 election, Martin was a recognisable member of the front bench, and, when coalition with the PDs was re-formed in 1997, he became Minister for Education, the baby of the cabinet at 36. The values instilled in Turner's Cross were put to good use. The previous government had abolished tuition fees for third-level students, but Martin oversaw a significant increase in funding for education at all levels, and the first introduction of special-needs assistants into Irish classrooms.

A particular hallmark achievement was the adoption of a new primary curriculum in 1999, replacing the previous edition from 1971, and incorporating the first formal teaching of Science, Visual Arts, and Social, Personal and Health Education in primary schools. There was, too, an initiative to begin supplying all schools with at least one internet-ready PC – something, this author would later discover, over which Martin pored over the details.

He was also among the first ministers to have to contend with a far darker corner of Ireland's legacy: abuse within so-called 'industrial schools' (in practice, juvenile detention centres) where children from troubled homes or with behavioural issues would often be sent as boarders. Under his watch, a formal state inquiry was set up. It would take nine years, from 2000 to 2009, to uncover sustained physical, sexual and emotional abuse.

The command of detail and preparedness to tackle long overdue reforms may have been why Martin was given the rather less attractive posting as Minister for Health in 2000. At the time, Ireland's public-health services were run by a patchwork of regional health boards. All independently responsible for services in their fiefdoms, each had the possibility of throwing up a political grenade for a minister several degrees removed from its operation. Brian Cowen, Martin's predecessor, had famously quipped that the Department of Health was like Angola, given the quantity of landmines ready to go off at any moment.

Martin's big idea was to merge them into a single administrative territory under the governance of a new singular Health Service Executive (HSE). No fair analysis could label this project a success. The HSE has become a singular bloated mess, which subsequently broke the country back into administrative health-care regions and organised hospitals into regional groups – two federal maps which are not quite contiguous with one another. Rather than driving synergies from removing internal barriers between territories – though the specialisation of some services such as cancer care did result in better outcomes, albeit requiring patients to travel further distances – the HSE was not made any more efficient. Instead, the retention of existing staff, mashed into a new administrative structure that may not have necessarily needed them, led the HSE to become a national byword for ineffective bureaucracy.

There was, however, one other project during Martin's tenure for which he is better recalled: the landmark move to ban smoking in workplaces, including pubs. When first announced, over a year ahead of its planned introduction, the ban was derided as a nonsensical joyless overreach of nanny-stateism and encroaching on the fabric of Ireland's primary venue for socialising. But, by giving a year's notice of its introduction, pubs had plenty of opportunities to invest in beer gardens, and the public was quickly won over when it turned out that the clothes worn to a pub might not smell of smoke the next day. It remains, arguably, Martin's crowning ministerial achievement – a ban which was quickly mimicked in cities and countries across the world.

It may largely have been drawn from Martin's own personal outlook on health: he is a fitness fanatic, partial to sea swimming and, even as Taoiseach, would make time for an outdoor walk to reach his regulation 10,000 steps per day. (I have regularly been sitting on the phone in Dublin's Merrion Square, close to the parliamentary complex, and been interrupted by Martin offering a passing greeting as he scuttled by, garda protection in tow.) He also keeps a strict diet, inheriting his father's pugilistic need to watch his weight, favouring salads and eschewing coffee in favour of green tea – something a press officer had to fetch at short notice from a nearby supermarket on the day of his installation as Taoiseach.

During his time as Minister for Health, he intervened to ban biscuits from the breakfasts at cabinet meetings, ordering that fresh fruit be served instead. Even still, not all fruits met his approval. One reporter, who had been playfully scolded for having a takeaway during a recent election campaign, stopped him to point to their own lunch in the Leinster House canteen: 'Hey, Micheál, look! Grapes! Good and healthy!' Martin tutted dismissively: 'Balls of sugar.'

Just before the HSE came into existence, in September 2004, the appointment of Charlie McCreevy as EU Commissioner necessitated a cabinet reshuffle. Martin moved to the relatively safer territory of the Department of Enterprise. At a time when corporate Ireland was booming, it was a far less demanding brief. Its only skirmish with negative publicity was during a time when the surging economy began to trigger a surge in the cost of staple foods. After pressure from an RTÉ TV series, *Rip Off Republic*, Martin revoked legislation that forbade foods from being sold below their cost price. Consumers were pleased; farmers less so. Several trace the squeeze on agricultural incomes back to Martin's popular/populist decision.

Otherwise, his tenure in Enterprise was largely benign, a series of visits to new industrial developments where foreign investors were creating hundreds of new jobs at a time. The largest headaches came from legacy issues from his time in Health, with controversy over his failure to act on a 2001 Ombudsman's report highlighting that many older citizens had been illegally charged for their time in publicly run nursing homes. The political furore escaped Martin's tenure and only caught fire when the Supreme Court struck down an attempt by his successor, Mary Harney, to retroactively legalise the charges. Martin told an Oireachtas committee he bore no responsibility for the changes; his profession of ignorance was dismissed by many, and the respected *Irish Times* columnist Fintan O'Toole called for his resignation.

The departure of Bertie Ahern in May 2008, a year into his third term, left a vacuum at the helm of Fianna Fáil. Though touted as a prospective candidate in his own right, Martin backed the candidacy of Minister for Finance Brian Cowen, who took the job unopposed. Martin was given the relatively plum job of Minister for Foreign Affairs, a job Cowen himself had previously held. The first task at hand was June's referendum to approve the Lisbon Treaty, on constitutional reforms of the EU. As a broadly Europhile country, the task should have been a simple one, but Cowen's government – taking a far longer honeymoon period than the public was prepared to countenance – mounted a lacklustre campaign and allowed insurgent opposition upstarts to voice concerns about increasing Eurofederalism and also to link the broadly impenetrable treaty, which made wholesale changes to EU structures but did not itself amount to a consolidated rewriting, to sensitive Irish issues like tax independence, abortion and an EU army. The referendum was duly defeated, 53 per cent to 47 per cent.

Just four weeks into its tenure, the government was plunged into crisis. At a remove, however, it is curious to see how the political blame was placed on Cowen and not on Martin, the government minister nominally responsible for the campaign. While Cowen took the public beating, Martin busied himself with the response, trying to ascertain exactly what could be done. He looked to the fallout from a similar earlier calamity – the defeat of Ireland's original referendum on ratifying the Nice Treaty, by a similar margin, in 2001 – for inspiration. Then, a European Council summit had issued a declaration assuring Ireland of its continued military neutrality, paving the way for a second referendum a year later. This time, a similar model was pursued: the binding wording of Lisbon could not be reopened, but Martin and Cowen negotiated an additional protocol once again asserting that Ireland's positions on militarism, abortion and tax would remain untouched.

A larger concession was a commitment to abandon a slimming down of the European Commission itself. Where previously all member states were entitled to nominate one Commissioner, Lisbon proposed that the jobs would rotate among member states, two-thirds at a time. The loss of 'Ireland's voice at the table' was cited as a reason for the referendum's rejection. Brussels, which had wanted to undo the creation of superfluous portfolios after the EU's eastern expansion in 2004, hoped to consolidate the jobs into beefier briefs. Reluctantly, member states agreed to retain an enlarged commission so that Ireland (and everyone else) would be guaranteed a portfolio for their own nominee. The pseudo-revised treaty was put to a second referendum and passed in October 2009. Should any reader become the underemployed European Commissioner responsible for 'Promoting the European Way of Life', they can thank Micheál Martin for their position having survived the cull of 2009.

Much as he loves the party, the manner in which Martin became its leader would never sit comfortably with him. Having reached the end of his patience with Brian Cowen's handling of a crashing economy in 2010, and disillusioned with Cowen trying to paper over the cracks by tabling a motion of confidence in himself, Martin broke ranks and announced he would oppose the Taoiseach's continued leadership – tendering his resignation from cabinet in the process, feeling he could not serve under Cowen as Taoiseach given his public dissent in his party leadership. Cowen accepted the resignation only after his victory in the subsequent vote, but Martin's departure opened a floodgate: five of the other 11

Fianna Fáil ministers, all of whom intended to retire at the next election, quit the cabinet.

The wound was voluntary, yet fatal: the Green Party, having stood aside for Fianna Fáil's internal machinations, refused to comply with the transfer of the vacant cabinet jobs to newer personnel. A week later, with the government on the ropes, the Greens walked anyway. Cowen resigned as party leader, remaining on as an interim caretaker Taoiseach while an election was called, with Martin defeating three of the loyalist ministers to become the new party leader.

It was a baptism of fire. Given the catastrophic loss of fiscal sovereignty, Fianna Fáil would be fighting not just for a mandate but for its very existence. With the national political outlook as cold and dark as the February weather, Martin's newly inherited party was reduced to a shell: it returned with just 20 TDs, one of whom (the outgoing Finance Minister Brian Lenihan) was to pass away that summer. It was the first time since the late 1920s that Fianna Fáil had not been the largest party in the Dáil; now it would lead a shallow opposition in the face of a behemoth Fine Gael–Labour coalition.

Opinions differ as to the motivation – whether it was a perceived duty to the party, a sense of personal ego or a clannish desire to bind everyone together – but the following years were notable for Fianna Fáil becoming a one-man show. At every point in which the party would face the media (which was regular, given its continued status as the larger opposition party and its control over some parliamentary time), every outing was dominated by Micheál Martin. No matter the topic, no matter the brief and no matter its lead spokesperson, Martin led the campaign.

The likelihood is that the simple calculus showed Martin to be more popular than the party he led and the need to harness that popularity for all its worth. As the first figure from the previous cabinet to call time on Cowen, Martin at least enjoyed some public goodwill. It might not have always been shared by those who sat behind him in parliament: so central was Martin to Fianna Fáil's fortunes that the parliamentary party was tamed and its meetings became rigid, dull affairs. Only a couple of TDs, Timmy Dooley and Billy Kelleher, could claim to have the leader's trusting ear. His most trusted advisers were the back-room duo of his long-time Chief of Staff Deirdre Gillane and his Head of Communications Pat McParland.

Martin took to the task with energy and duty, taking on as many pre-election engagements as possible. And slowly but surely it seemed to work: only three years after the demoralisation and near-oblivion of 2011, Fianna Fáil won the most votes and seats in the nationwide local-authority elections, making gains, while Fine Gael slipped back into second place. With this reasserted electoral mandate, there was no need to change a winning formula. Martin remained the party's sole dominant figurehead into the election of 2016, where it returned with 44 seats (of 160), only about one percentage point behind Fine Gael, who won 50.

If Fianna Fáil's drubbing in 2011 was the 'earthquake' election, 2016 was the tsunami: Fine Gael, damaged by the rebound of the austerity era, and Labour, the junior coalition partners elected to soften the human edge of austerity, were punished for the perception of doubling down on it. Martin's understated but clear personal positioning had helped Fianna Fáil to begin its recovery, such that there was no obvious way for any parties to cobble together what might look like a stable majority in the Dáil.

Martin understood that Fianna Fáil and Fine Gael were increasingly competing for the same voters and quickly rebuffed Enda Kenny's straightforward offer of coalition talks, for fear the dividing lines between the parties might be irrevocably eroded. Moreover, Martin's antipathy towards Sinn Féin, and the Provisional republican movement, left him unwilling to cast upon them the status and platform of 'lead opposition party'. Nonetheless, Martin's pragmatic streak kicked in: the country needed a government, and a second snap election would only punish the parties who were seen as refusing. Some kind of arrangement would have to be made.

Eventually the realisation dawned that Fianna Fáil, while unwilling to join a coalition, could use its Dáil weight to facilitate a government through a confidence-and-supply arrangement in exchange for certain policy commitments. Nine weeks of torturous negotiations eventually led to an unprecedented deal with Fine Gael: Fianna Fáil would abstain on matters of constitutional business but would allow Fine Gael to form a government on a 'no surprises' basis of ongoing advance consultation. Kenny found a caucus of independents to fill out his own numbers, and Fianna Fáil became kingmakers, governing from without. The arrangement, so novel in Ireland, seemed to suit neither party. Fine Gael saw itself as having authority but no power; conversely, Fianna Fáil had some power but no authority to leverage it.

Nonetheless, the robustness of the measure was quickly tested: just seven weeks after taking office, the government was hit with the shock of the UK's unexpected vote to leave the EU. Again, pragmatism was the order of the day. Protecting the openness of the Irish Border was not a partisan priority but rather a national imperative and a universal desire within the Irish body politic; Martin illustrated early on that it would not be an issue on which Fianna Fáil would play politics. So sensitive was the situation that, loveless though the partnership was, Martin (unilaterally, without seeking formal agreement from his parliamentary party) extended the confidence-and-supply arrangement for an additional year so that the Enda Kenny administration – helmed at this stage by Leo Varadkar – was free to focus on securing Ireland's national post-Brexit objectives without looking over its shoulder at an election.

While his frontbenchers grew into the dual roles of counterparts and collaborators with government, Martin himself sought to reposition the party, remodelling its republicanism as inherently liberal on social issues, notwithstanding the conservative backgrounds of both the party and many of its prominent members. One key illustration came in early 2018, ahead of a referendum (instigated by a citizens' assembly) on the lifting of a near-total constitutional ban on abortion.

Martin had previously spoken of his broadly pro-life beliefs, in particular as Minister for Health in 2001–2 when he proposed an unsuccessful referendum seeking to remove the threat of suicide as grounds for an abortion being available. It was a surprise, then, when he announced to the Dáil in 2018 – alongside a carefully curated bunch of unsuspecting colleagues – that he favoured the lifting of the constitutional ban entirely. While no whip would be placed on party members (pragmatism?) as abortion was a matter of conscience, he would personally vote to hold a referendum and would back its approval.

To this day, there remain some who believe it was a cynical ploy by Martin to curry popular liberalism, that he knew which way the political wind was blowing and that being a dominant voice in a campaign would be damaging were his side to be defeated. There are others who thought Martin was broadly agnostic and had nothing to lose: Fianna Fáil could credibly claim both sides of the argument when Martin had taken the relatively rare decision not to whip his TDs on either side.

Though he has always been reserved about his personal reasons, there are also some who think his personal experience weighed on him. Micheál and Mary Martin were sadly familiar with family tragedy and the pain of losing a child: they lost their third child, Ruairí, to cot death in early 2000 when he was just five weeks old and their youngest, Léana, to an unexpected cardiac condition in October 2010 shortly before her eighth birthday. While some wonder if the loss of Léana jolted Martin into a 'carpe diem' mode that resulted in his eventual challenge to Cowen, many imagine that the grief in his personal life allowed him to better relate to those undergoing the trauma of an unviable pregnancy and their differing views on whether Irish law ought to have required such pregnancies to be carried to term. Martin was in the minority within his party – the majority of TDs and Senators voted against the referendum even going ahead – but was closer to the public mood. In 2018, 66 per cent of voters backed the lifting of the ban.

The confidence-and-supply deal was due to last for three budgets, meaning immediate speculation in October 2018 about the timing of the poll to come – speculation put to bed by Martin soon afterwards with his unconditional offer to extend it for a further year in the midst of the ongoing Brexit tumult. The next election was ultimately called in January

2020, when by-elections had left the Dáil arithmetic inhospitable to Varadkar's continued administration.

The same 'coalitionology' arguments from 2016 were rehashed in 2020. Martin appeared opposite Varadkar in the first head-to-head debate of the election campaign, somehow trying to present himself as an agent of change, having supported Varadkar's government from the outside for the previous four years. Sinn Féin was able to present itself as such a plucky upstart outsider that Mary Lou McDonald won her way into another planned two-day debate on RTÉ in the week before polling.

The eventual outcome was an unprecedented three-way split. Only three seats separated the three largest parties, and the Dáil was so fragmented that no obvious path to a coalition was evident. Varadkar and his outgoing cabinet (some of whom had lost their seats entirely yet were constitutionally required to remain) kept the seats warm while waiting for some other configuration of parties to emerge.

While the remaining parties dithered and danced around each other, each waiting for others to make a conclusive move, a novel coronavirus from Wuhan in China began to show up in Ireland, and partisan politics took a back seat. After all, it was impossible to have any meaningful talks on a possible Programme for Government when it was impossible to even share a meeting room.

The pandemic did at least create a sense of urgency. Once the first national lockdown was relaxed in May 2020, there was an obvious impetus to address the democratic deficit. Fine Gael and Fianna Fáil, lifelong rivals descending from opposing sides in a bitter civil war that lived on in many hearts, agreed to talk as soon as the public-health advice allowed sufficient numbers to meet up for talks. The Green Party was brought on board not only to make up the parliamentary majority but also to grease the wheels between two parties that might not otherwise have been hospitable to each other. A draft coalition deal was struck and approved by each party's members in a pandemic-proof postal vote. The deal included a constitutional novelty in Ireland: the premise of a rotating Taoiseach, where Martin (as head of the larger party) would get to serve for two and a half years before resigning on an agreed date and facilitating the reappointment of Varadkar for the remainder of the term.

On a novel Saturday sitting, in the novel setting of the main auditorium of the Convention Centre on Dublin's north quays, chosen so as to allow a full attendance of TDs amidst Social Distancing, Micheál Martin was elected Taoiseach on 27 June 2020. The seals of office, ordinarily presented at Áras an Uachtaráin, were 'handed over' (deposited on tables) in the airy halls of Dublin Castle. So severe were the COVID-19 rules on the day that Martin's wife and children were forbidden from attending and watched on TV in Cork.

It was not an easy mantle to take up. Varadkar's outgoing administration, though politically unpopular, had garnered immense respect for the level-headed and clear response to the pandemic's arrival. On the day of Martin's installation, the most recent poll had put Fianna Fáil on just 13 per cent, down from 22 per cent on election day, while Fine Gael had rebounded from 20 per cent to 37 per cent.

Martin and the new government (in which nine of 15 were new to cabinet) had the harder prospect of managing a graduated reopening of society. Where lockdown was a uniform national act, reopening would require the occasional regional imbalance, and explanations that were not quite as readily received. One illustration came on 15 September when, unable to commit to a one-way timetable for lifting restrictions, the government adopted a five-tier framework for COVID restrictions, with different counties placed on different tiers as the situation required. On the very day of its introduction, though, it was immediately undermined by advice to place Dublin somewhere between two tiers. What should have been a clear programme incentivising sensible behaviour, telling the country what freedoms would come or go on Levels 1 through 5, resulted from its very first day with over a quarter of the population at neither Level 2 nor 3.

It was a publicity debacle that the new ministers found tough to shake off. One reason for this was the rise to prominence of figures such as the Chief Medical Officer, Tony Holohan, who found public favour with his calm demeanour and capable handling of delicate questions at everyday press briefings. Varadkar and his outgoing caretaker cabinet were acutely aware of having lost the previous election and their lack of a political mandate to undertake such drastic moves – sometimes holding round-table briefings with opposition parties to secure broad buy-in for measures and consistently couching decisions on the direct advice of Holohan and the National Public Health Emergency Team (NPHET). Holohan had therefore become such a powerful figure that even when a new government was formed it was hard to regain the perception of political responsibility. So, if Holohan and NPHET recommended that pubs stay shut in Dublin, the government felt little option but to comply, even if it erred from the five-tier model that ministers had adopted for themselves.

One other cause for difficulty was the fact that, upon taking office, Martin seemed suddenly weighed down by the significance of his own words. The Martin who had dragged Fianna Fáil back from the precipice through fluent performances in the Dáil and televised debates gave way almost overnight to a Taoiseach who, while not dithering, sometimes seemed afraid to finish a sentence for fear that his words would be interpreted as settled government policy. Journalists quickly noticed how subclauses were inserted inside subclauses, so that some sentences were never actually completed, abandoned in favour of a safer thing to state.

Of growing prominence was a new verbal crutch, 'in terms of', which became a foundational building block of many sentences and mimicked with relish by the leading political satirist Oliver Callan. Add in the fact that Pat McParland was no longer his communications chief, having become Deputy Chief of Staff in the kitchen cabinet, beside Deirdre Gillane, and the sense of flux was compounded. McFarland's deputy as Director of Communications, Lisa-Dee Collery, was flung into the role of Government Press Secretary – an extraordinarily demanding role at the very best of times and even more all-consuming in a time of constant crisis and firefighting.

As if the situation were not fluid enough already, there was always the prospect of ministers themselves becoming ill. On 15 September, just a few hours after the publicity debacle of the not-quite-five-tier framework, the Minister for Health Stephen Donnelly became unwell and went into precautionary isolation. Given he had attended a cabinet meeting only a few hours earlier, the entire cabinet were considered close contacts and were also therefore expected to self-isolate – news which was shared so abruptly in the Dáil that even some ministers themselves (including Helen McEntee, doing a live radio interview at the time) were unaware of it. Donnelly, thankfully, tested negative later that evening.

On top of struggling to assert itself over the fluid circumstances, Martin faced the added complication of Varadkar himself. In ordinary circumstances, no party seeking power on a mandate of change and transformation would ever choose to share power with the very party they sought to remove, but circumstances meant that Martin was now sitting in cabinet with the very same figures his party had spent the campaign bemoaning. The Housing and Health portfolios, two crunch issues that had largely decided the election, were now in Fianna Fáil's hands, but the former Taoiseach, and the former Minister for Health, was still sitting at cabinet. The usual get-out clause for a stuttering new government – to appeal for patience as the poor work of the previous administration was undone – could not be invoked when the leaders of the previous cabinet were still at the table.

Nonetheless, though his electoral record was underwhelming, Varadkar remained an excellent and concise communicator, already at ease with the import his own words would carry as a government leader. Liberated to some degree by his own demotion to Tánaiste, Varadkar was able to simultaneously model himself as an ersatz co-Taoiseach ('co-*teesh*', as Oliver Callan put it) and separately as the leader of Fine Gael with influence, but not final control, over the coalition.

Moreover, there were some early instances where Varadkar's new Department of Enterprise would formally spill the beans on a government announcement, issuing finer details of some new business supports, before Martin had had an opportunity to announce the measures himself.

The biggest of those challenges came in early October 2020, little over three months into Martin's tenure.

Having taken some time away to care for his terminally ill wife, Holohan returned as Chief Medical Officer and unexpectedly recommended the country move immediately from Level 2 to 5 and enter a second full nationwide lockdown. Martin, obviously uneasy about the social, economic and political cost of such a sudden move, was at least prepared to keep his counsel in private until other ministers were formally consulted. Varadkar, though, emerged on *Claire Byrne Live*, one of RTÉ's flagship current-affairs programmes, to launch an unqualified broadside against Holohan and NPHET, complaining that they were personally detached from the employment and fiscal consequences of their own advice.

Though fiscal and social advice was hardly the job of a public-health advisory team, the prominence of Varadkar as a government figure left Martin's government seemingly in open dispute with its own, more popular, public-health advisers. The government rebuked the advice, moving instead to Level 3, but eventually relented only a fortnight later. Ireland became the first country in the world to adopt a second nationwide lockdown.

Though never testing positive himself during the primary waves of COVID-19, as Taoiseach, Micheál Martin remained personally unfortunate. One of the few perceived perks of the Taoiseach's job is an annual audience in the Oval Office with the President of the United States on St Patrick's Day, an audience which Martin could not pursue in person in 2021 given ongoing travel restrictions. Destined to give up the job before the 2023 instalment, 2022 marked the only opportunity for Martin to press the flesh with Joe Biden. Unlucky, then, that on the night before his 2022 visit, Martin failed a routine COVID test administered by the US State Department. If 2021 saw him present a virtual bowl of shamrock from across an ocean, 2022 saw him present it from across the street, holed up in the President's official guest house.

If there was to be a change of tack as a result of Varadkar's TV intervention, it was the move to start taking other advice before future decisions on lockdowns. For the lifting of the second lockdown, alongside the public-health advice from NPHET, the government was also presented with economic advice from Ernst & Young. That might well have influenced the most consequential decision of Martin's tenure as Taoiseach: the decision to go back to Level 3 from the end of November and tout a 'meaningful Christmas' as an uplifting end to a torrid year.

NPHET had recognised how quickly the benefits of the second lockdown could be lost and recommended against allowing both household visits and the reopening of pubs and restaurants. Ministers, though, knew the Christmas season was a vital one for the hospitality industry and that the spirit of an Irish Christmas was the idea of being able, even on a limited basis, to visit friends and family. Consequently, both were allowed. 'We are going as far as we believe is possible to achieve the best balance of health, economic and social considerations, but no further', Martin said in a televised address (a once-novel feature that was quickly becoming tiresome). 'The government and I are satisfied that this combination of new arrangements strikes a safe balance between maintaining the pressure on the disease and creating space for families, friends and loved ones to be together this Christmas.'

The volume of mingling quickly saw infection rates balloon – and surge even more dramatically when the new 'alpha' variant was brought home from London by waves of young emigrants on Christmas visits. Less than a month after the second national lockdown, Ireland entered a third lockdown, on Christmas Eve 2020, which would endure for four months. Though the advice in November 2020 could never have accounted for a newer and faster-spreading version of the coronavirus, the departure from the public-health advice had been punished mercilessly. There would be no repeat for the remainder of the pandemic.

The pandemic's effects were not just limited to the trickiness of opening, or closing, the country; it threw up more traditional political scandal too. Martin's government was barely two months old (and had just curtailed the number of people permitted to attend indoor gatherings) when the

Minister for Agriculture, Dara Calleary, attended a dinner organised by the Oireachtas Golf Society, a pseudo-official golf group made up mostly of former parliamentarians. News of the event took barely a day to break and kicked off an overwhelming political firestorm; at the tail end of a lost summer, the public were apoplectic that a largely elitist grouping was having the sort of knees-up expressly forbidden for others. It took only hours for the controversy to become a full-blown '-gate': Golfgate.

Calleary had attended the dinner only to make an after-dinner speech in honour of his recently deceased political mentor but resigned from cabinet (and as Martin's deputy leader of Fianna Fáil) the morning after the story broke. Six Senators from Fianna Fáil and Fine Gael also had the party whips suspended, while the Chief Justice instigated an inquiry to the presence of Séamus Woulfe, the newly appointed Supreme Court judge who had been Varadkar's Attorney General.

A further, novel problem was thrown up by the attendance of Phil Hogan, Ireland's European Commissioner responsible for trade (and, thus, ironically, best placed to defend Ireland's interests in the midst of the fractious Brexit talks). Hogan became embroiled in a tangled series of disclosures about his transit across Ireland, across county boundaries when some had local Level 3 lockdowns in place. Adding further complication was the piecemeal way in which his movements had become public, in seeming contradiction of the itinerary he had given Ursula von der Leyen when the controversy kicked off.

The controversy left Martin and Varadkar with a quandary. Hogan's brief in Brussels made him a national asset; his cavalier approach to the COVID-19 rules and dismissive approach to the resulting scrutiny also made him a political liability. Though not directly answerable to the Irish government, it was intolerable that a domestic cabinet minister would resign for attending but a European equivalent would not. The leaders eventually chose to breach usual protocol, directly calling on Hogan to resign, something he eventually did a few days later. He would later grumble that his resignation was enforced to maintain equality, and equal culpability, between his own Fine Gael and Calleary's Fianna Fáil.

Especially embarrassing in the whole affair was the fact that Calleary was not even Martin's first appointment as Minister for Agriculture. Barry Cowen, the original pick, quickly found controversy of his own when it emerged he had previously been convicted of drink-driving and had been accused of trying to evade the garda checkpoint at which he was caught. While Cowen disputed the latter allegation, and complained to the Garda Ombudsman about how the press had got hold of the records, Martin – only a fortnight into the job – insisted on maximum transparency and on Cowen's presence in the Dáil for questioning. When Cowen refused, arguing it was a matter of live inquiry, Martin sacked him. It was a dramatic and unexpected move, a pointed gesture of transparency and of the highest political standards – a demonstration that Fianna Fáil was worthy of trust.

Yet the immediate high standards became a stick with which Martin could later be beaten. Only four months later, Leo Varadkar himself faced more grievous allegations when it emerged he had personally posted a copy of a sensitive draft contract, struck with the official representative body of GPs, to a personal friend who was also the President of a rival doctors' group. The allegations were politically explosive and, for almost two years, a matter of active criminal inquiry. Varadkar, who claimed he had shared the document in a bid to win broader support for the draft, conceded that he had been overtly casual in doing so.

For the Taoiseach, the problem was that Varadkar was too big to fail – a load-bearing pillar of government, who needed to be shown more forbearance than others in cabinet would be shown. Fianna Fáil backbenchers fumed that Cowen had been sacked for what, while serious, was a far lesser allegation. Varadkar was now facing a criminal investigation for alleged corruption and breach of the Official Secrets Act, yet Martin was obliged to support him. It would take until summer of 2022 for the Director of Public Prosecutions to drop the official inquiry.

While there were strong grounds to believe Martin was holding Fianna Fáil's ministers to higher standards than their own cabinet peers, Martin was not beyond certain accusations of making rules as they suited him. Some complaints were raised about Martin attending an indoor event

– marking the presentation of the Paddy Martin 'Champ of Champs' cup – at his father's former boxing club in Cork during Level 3 restrictions limiting indoor gatherings to six people. Twelve were in attendance, though when the recipient was also a serving garda, it was argued that many of those present were there for work reasons.

There were other grievances about preference being shown. At one point, outdoor socialising was still frowned upon while (amateur) Gaelic football and hurling were permitted. Many in other outlawed sports, such as golf, openly wondered whether Martin had organised for his personal preferred sports to continue; his retort was that, as the country's most popular and widely played games, televised sport would be a useful national distraction. The Taoiseach certainly did not make personal use of the distinctions: while his own son Micheál Aodh played in goal as the Cork footballers scored a surprise win over Kerry in the 2020 Munster football final, Micheál Senior was in his office in Dublin, watching with a chickpea salad.

Eventually, as with much of Europe, January 2022 brought relief. Ireland had enjoyed one of the Continent's fastest and most popular vaccine roll-outs, and the spread of the relatively milder Omicron variant meant the old adversaries of Holohan and NPHET were happy to recommend the lifting of all restrictions. 'None of us will be fully safe until we are all safe. There is much to do', Martin said, in the final televised address of the pandemic. (To this day, civil servants still cannot comprehensively count the number of times Martin addressed the nation from the steps of Government Buildings.) 'But today is a good day, and we should all take a moment to appreciate how far we've come.'

It was 21 January 2022; the anniversary of the date in 1919 on which the first independent Irish parliament had gathered. 'Spring is coming', the Taoiseach said, offering a rare smile, 'and I don't know if I have ever looked forward to one as much as I am looking forward to this one.'

Though he was not to know that he would spend a week of that spring holed up in quarantine in Washington, it would be a turning point in the national mood.

To one extent or another, lockdown had robbed three-fifths of Martin's term, and it might have been hoped that the final year would be a clean break to pursue other priorities. Geopolitics would get in the way. A month later, Russia invaded Ukraine, unleashing a wave of refugees across the Continent. While the EU collectively activated a directive that gave Ukrainian citizens certain automatic entitlements in member states, Ireland went a step further and waived visa requirements for citizens fleeing the war while also offering direct accommodation and elevated social-welfare assistance. The generous offering, and Ireland's status as the EU's predominant English speaker, was generously taken up: 70,000 had arrived by the end of 2022.

The immediate arrivals were broadly supported, but the rush to find suitable accommodation did begin to prompt social strain. Ireland was already short of housing; the number of full-time residents in emergency accommodation was already higher than 10,000, and fringe elements began to question the urgency of housing so many new arrivals when similar impetus was not shown to others. The rush for alternative venues also meant the repurposing of the likes of community halls, raising concern from those who felt dormitory accommodation was inappropriate for the victims of war – and from those who wondered if ordinary communities should lose their own amenities in exchange. It was a social sore that would continue to fester after Martin had handed back to Varadkar.

The events of 2022 may have influenced Martin's own political future. The 'rotating Taoiseach' arrangement technically entailed the mass resignation of all cabinet members, allowing Martin to take his pick of the jobs when he became Tánaiste. He chose to return to Foreign Affairs, a job that allowed him to retain an active presence in Brussels, to continue asserting Ireland's position on Ukraine and, perhaps, to bolster his credentials should he want to become a European Commissioner himself when the jobs next arose in 2024.

On the morning of Saturday, 17 December, a day later than scheduled so that he could attend a European Council summit, Martin resigned.

That afternoon, the Dáil reappointed Leo Varadkar as Taoiseach. 'I want to take this opportunity to commend Micheál Martin on the leadership that he showed as Taoiseach', Varadkar said, 'for putting the country before politics and for providing reassurance and hope during difficult times.' He continued: 'In 2020, the incoming Taoiseach was unable to have his wife and family with him at the Convention Centre as he received the greatest honour of his life. That, too, was leadership, and I am glad that they are with us today.'

If Martin's return to the Department of Foreign Affairs originally came under the cloud of war in Ukraine, the bulk of his tenure came to be defined by renewed hostility in the Middle East. In September 2023, Martin visited Israel and the West Bank, in the hope that he could redivert European attention back to the stalled peace process between Israel, Fatah and Hamas. The Tánaiste had barely returned before Gaza-based Hamas militants launched a scale of attacks and hostage-taking within Israel, prompting a merciless wave of Israeli military retaliation.

While Ireland had something of a historical affinity with Israel, identifying with a nomadic people seeking an independent and recognised homeland, more recent sympathies had sided with the Palestinian people for whom the quest of unfinished nationhood struck a chord. (Sinn Féin and others in the Provisional republican movement, who equally believed Irish independence to be an unfinished project due to the partition of the island, felt this even more so.) Taking what was originally a minority view at European level, Ireland began to more forcefully argue for a two-state solution and for a distinction to be drawn between the actions of Hamas and the overall treatment of Palestinian civilians. This included increasing, at Martin's behest, Irish funding for UNRWA, the UN body charged with delivering public services to displaced Palestinians, after Israel accused some of its staff members of being complicit in the terror of 7 October and prompted other countries to suspend their own funding.

The denouement of relations came in May 2024 when Ireland, along with Spain and Norway, announced a formal recognition of Palestinian statehood. Israel portrayed this as a reward for Hamas's attacks and recalled its ambassador. When Martin's department later intervened in a case at the International Court of Justice accusing Israel of genocide in Gaza, the embassy in Dublin was formally closed entirely. The terse relationship with Israel, given its closeness to the USA and the return of its sympathiser Donald Trump, would prove to be an important dynamic as the next general election came into view.

The coalition originally led by Martin was entitled to run until March 2025, but Varadkar's abrupt retirement in March 2024 and the resurgence of Fine Gael under Simon Harris at the subsequent local elections, coupled with a dismal outing for Sinn Féin, created internal momentum for the general election to be brought forward. The delivery of a comparatively giveaway budget that October, with buoyant corporate tax receipts allowing for spending hikes and tax cuts as well as deposits to national savings funds, only increased the internal appetite. Rather than risk a change in political climate or give the lead opposition party a chance to rebuild, the election was brought forward to November 2024.

That election itself was a relatively drab one; the darker winter evenings placed greater emphasis on broadcast set-pieces of which there were few. The buoyant economy reduced the campaign to discussion about how to spend the country's future billions, thus replaying the same pre-budget arguments in the coalition's favour. The unremarkable campaign suited Martin fine; the few notable moments on the campaign focused on Simon Harris's stilted engagement with voters, leaving Fianna Fáil as the marginally more popular of the outgoing pair. The eventual gap in seats (48 versus 38 in a 174-seat house) was boosted by the fruits of previous compromise: where Fianna Fáil had missed out on seats through a shortage of vote transfers in 2020, outperforming Fine Gael meant gathering bountiful transfers from their coalition colleagues. Government formation, punctuated only by the Christmas break, was relatively routine: continuing in power alongside Fine Gael was a no-brainer, and the only bump in the road was having to recruit a minority partner.

A deal was eventually struck with a self-organised caucus of seven independent TDs, led by controversial Tipperary TD Michael Lowry.

Lowry had previously served as Fine Gael Minister for Communications but had resigned – from both the government and the party, under John Bruton in 1996 – over contentious relationships with several businessmen. One of them, Ben Dunne, had bankrolled an extension at Lowry's home; Lowry, a later tribunal found, had used his ministerial office to influence the rate of rent paid by the national telecoms provider for a premises owned by Dunne. The Moriarty Tribunal, eventually reporting in 2011, described this arrangement as 'profoundly corrupt to a degree that was nothing short of breathtaking'. When that report had been published, Martin was to the fore in pursuing an all-party motion of censure calling on Lowry to resign entirely. Three elections later, Martin found himself insisting that Lowry's continued electoral mandate had to be respected and a stable government formed. The Tipperary TD had taken the lead in corralling the miscellaneous independents into a negotiating bloc and had to be respected as their interlocutor. That respect was not shared on the opposition benches: when the Dáil was scheduled to meet and ratify his return as Taoiseach, a vocal and rowdy protest over the arrangement with Lowry – and the proposal to grant him Dáil speaking time as if he were an opposition leader – resulted in the chaotic abandonment of proceedings. The family who watched Micheál Martin first become Taoiseach on television now watched in impatient horror as his second appointment was deferred by another day.

Was this deal with Lowry the most vivid illustration of Martin's pragmatism? Or was it, like the change of position on abortion, naked opportunism for the sake of political gain? Was breaking the habit of a century to govern with Fine Gael an act of noble public sacrifice to ensure stable government, or a connivance to get into power? The answer likely depends on the person being asked. Though Martin is commonly labelled simply as a 'decent' man, survival at the highest levels of politics for three decades cannot simply be a matter of decency. Then again, nor can anyone stand still and expect to move forward. Critics inside his party believe he treats the positions of other members as an afterthought; allies believe he is simply a canny analyst of public mood and nudges the party towards the more politically savvy centre. Whatever the truth, he is a man blessed with both longevity and patience. He has survived many scrapes and skirmishes, seen off many challenges and tolerated infinitely many crises when finally ensconced in power. Yet, setting out on a second term as head of the Irish government, he remains visibly energised in the pursuit of politics, power and progress. Six decades on, the work ethic instilled in Turner's Cross remains undiminished.

17

Simon Harris

2024–5

Pat Leahy

Full name: Simon Francis Harris
Date of birth: 17 October 1986
Place of birth: Greystones, Co. Wicklow
Married to: Caoimhe Wade (m. 2017)
Children: Saoirse and Cillian
Education: St David's Holy Faith; Dublin Institute of Technology
Assumed office: 9 April 2024
Date of resignation: 23 January 2025
Length of tenure: Nine months, 14 days
Quotation: 'It is the honour of my life to become leader of Fine Gael. I promise I will work hard, with responsibility, humanity and civility. I love this country, and will work night and day to keep it safe and deliver for people.'

On 9 April 2024, Simon Harris was elected Taoiseach by the Dáil, by 88 votes to 69, relying on the support of Fine Gael, Fianna Fáil, the Greens and some independent deputies to command a handsome majority. A couple of hours later, he was formally appointed by President Michael D. Higgins to be the youngest ever leader of his country. At 37, he was a year younger than his predecessor as party leader, Leo Varadkar, whose shock resignation had created the vacancy Harris had seized with both hands.

The two men had a sometimes uneasy relationship. Harris had managed the campaign of Varadkar's rival for the leadership, Simon Coveney, back in 2017 after which the victorious Varadkar had toyed with the possibility of dropping him from the cabinet. In the event, Varadkar kept Harris as Minister for Health in his minority government – a move interpreted in some circles as a greater punishment than sending him to the back benches. It was suggested by observers at the time that Varadkar might be better off keeping an ambitious potential rival in a job where he would be kept busy. That it certainly did.

Relations between the two men – never personally close – improved in subsequent years, Harris would tell confidants. Certainly, he was the beneficiary of Varadkar's bolt from the blue when the Taoiseach and Fine Gael leader announced his shock resignation on 20 March. Harris's apparent readiness for a leadership contest would raise some suspicions among his colleagues, but perhaps it was just that chance had favoured the prepared mind.

Either way, seven years after Varadkar assumed the mantle of youngest Taoiseach ever, Harris now stepped into the role in very different circumstances. Varadkar became Taoiseach just one year into that government's lifespan, giving him potentially four years to make his mark before he faced the voters in a general election. Harris, by contrast, became leader with, at most, 11 months to go before a general election would be required. For no recent Taoiseach has the electoral clock ticked so loudly or, perhaps, so threateningly.

The task facing Harris was not just to lead the country but to revive the stuttering fortunes of his party. If he did not, he would become not just the youngest Taoiseach ever, but also the shortest-serving. 'Time is short', the new Taoiseach-elect told the Dáil when accepting its nomination, 'and there is much to do.'

Simon Harris was born on 17 October 1986 in Greystones, Co. Wicklow, a prosperous commuter town on the coast, 20 miles south of Dublin. His father, Bart, was a taxi driver and his mother, Mary, a special-needs assistant. Simon was their eldest; two more children would follow: Gemma, three years younger than Simon (she shares his birthday) and Adam, nine years his junior. It was a close family, modest and hard-working. 'They [my parents] have been my driving force, making many personal sacrifices for their three children', Harris said in his Dáil speech after winning the vote to become Taoiseach. 'I hope they can be proud of their eldest son because I know I would not be standing here were it not for them. I thank my sister, Gemma, and my brother, Adam. They are my best friends, and we are each other's biggest supporters.' He also thanked his grandmother: 'my nana, who is here today.'

Also there were his wife, Caoimhe Wade, a nurse, and their two small children, Saoirse (aged five) and Cillian (two), both of whom were visibly excited to see Daddy. They enlivened the solemn parliamentary occasion by enthusiastically and repeatedly waving at him. He responded by promising them that his most important job would remain 'being your dad'. Glimpses of the Harris family life were often featured on the new Taoiseach's social-media accounts; his prolific use of one platform for political communication caused the satirist Oliver Callan to dub him the 'TikTok Teesh'. It is a backhanded compliment of sorts.

The teenage Harris had already come to notice as a writer – writing and directing a play called *On the Run* which ran in the local community hall – but it was as a disability-rights activist that his entry into politics would come. His brother Adam was diagnosed with Asperger syndrome, a condition on the autism spectrum. Angered at a lack of supports for people with autism, Harris began to campaign – and to get noticed. He founded an autism awareness group, the Triple A Alliance.

But he had a sense even then that it was in politics where he could make his mark and exert influence. He campaigned for local Fianna Fáil Minister Dick Roche. The association with Fianna Fáil – it is a constant delight for members of that party to remind each other of it – did not last long. By the age of 16, Harris had joined Young Fine Gael, the party's youth wing. Fianna Fáil's political hegemony under Bertie Ahern might have seemed impregnable, but Fine Gael was rebuilding after electoral disaster, and for an ambitious young would-be politician, there were opportunities in that party to be grasped.

Wicklow voters had been 'misled' by the county's two Fianna Fáil TDs, he told a local newspaper in 2003 – already being described as a 'well-known local activist'. 'With job cuts, a lack of hospital beds, inadequate schools, not nearly enough public amenities, a high rate of crime and an ailing economy, is this what the public voted for?' he asked. 'When the electorate voted for Dick Roche and Joe Jacob, is this what they expected? No, the voters were misled, and the voters were given lists of promises, all broken. Broken promises seem to form the backbone of the Fianna Fáil party.' Urging people to join the 'Fine Gael revival', Harris promised 'a new politics, for a new time, for a new generation', concluding, 'Let's bring honesty and integrity back to politics and let's bring politics back to the people.'

He was already becoming a name in Young Fine Gael. He would, one activist later told the *Irish Times*'s Jennifer Bray, 'turn up to meetings in suits three times too big for him'. But he 'already knew how to work a room'. A few months later, he became the youngest ever member of the Young Fine Gael national executive. The following year, having distinguished himself as a competitive debater, he was his school's student of the year. 'He is a talented student who always displayed qualities well beyond his years', the school said.

Harris registered as a student of Journalism and French at the Dublin Institute of Technology, but the pull of politics proved irresistible, and he dropped out after three years. He began work for Frances Fitzgerald, a Fine Gael grandee who was the leader of the party's group in the Seanad. To its great good fortune, Fine Gael had lost the 2007 general election. The financial crisis that was even then beginning to stir on the US housing market would upend Irish politics and transform Fine Gael's fortunes, offering opportunities for a bright, young and hungry would-be politician.

Fitzgerald became a boss, a mentor and a political ally. Later she would recall her first meeting with Harris to the *Irish Times*. 'He was dead keen to work in Leinster House', she recalled. 'I asked him if he was going to finish his journalism course and he said, "No, I really want to work here." I was very struck by him. He was motivated. He liked the business of politics even at that age.'

Inevitably, Harris ran in the local elections in 2009, seeking a seat on Wicklow County Council. He topped the poll in Greystones, winning over 3,000 votes, almost double that of the next highest candidate. When the Fianna Fáil–Green Party coalition collapsed in early 2011, after Ireland had slid into near-bankruptcy and a bailout financed by the EU and the IMF, Harris was one of three Fine Gael TDs elected for Wicklow. He was just 24, and on his way.

In her speech nominating Harris as Taoiseach in April 2024, the Fine Gael Minister Heather Humphreys recalled her first day in the Dáil back in 2011, one of 76, the largest number of TDs the party ever saw elected.

> Like any first-time TD, I was nervous. I was finding my feet and trying to get used to this place and all the new faces around me. I saw this young lad walking around the place, and I said to myself, 'Ah sure, he must be on a school tour or on work experience.' So you can imagine my surprise a few moments later when I saw him standing up to nominate Enda Kenny for the position of Taoiseach. It took me a few weeks to make my maiden speech. He did it on day one. Anyone who heard him that day would have known from the start that he would go far.

Echoing a letter of consolation sent by George Bernard Shaw to the grieving sister of Michael Collins after his death, Harris – the baby of the house – declared, 'Today, the period of mourning is over for Ireland. Today, we hang out our brightest colours and together, under Deputy Kenny's leadership, we move forward yet again as a nation.'

The period of mourning may or may not have been over, but the period of austerity was just getting into its stride. The Fine Gael–Labour government, bolstered by a super-majority in the Dáil, implemented a harsh EU/IMF-mandated programme of austerity, cutting spending and increasing taxes. Slowly and painfully, the country's economy began to stabilise and, eventually, to recover. But that would come at a fearsome political price for the new government parties.

If Fine Gael and Labour were to experience a grindingly difficult few years in office, though, the Dáil's youngest deputy was making progress and making plans. He secured a spot on the powerful Public Accounts Committee and also became a fixture in the media, always willing to defend the government against a growing band of enemies. Affable and insidery, he developed good relations with a large number of political journalists, always keen to hear their take on events, which they loved.

When Fine Gael found itself short a candidate in the 2014 European Parliament elections for the Ireland South constituency, Harris was prevailed upon to run as a 'sweeper' candidate – even though he did not see his future in Europe. The plan almost worked too well: Harris ran a typically energetic campaign across the sprawling constituency, with a strong social-media element to it, and was less than 4,000 votes behind Fine Gael colleague Deirdre Clune at the final count. Impressed, Enda Kenny made him a Junior Minister, in charge of the Office of Public Works, at the post-election reshuffle.

If Harris was by now clearly a man on the up, the Fine Gael–Labour coalition seemed to be going in the opposite direction. When spooked backbenchers put down a no-confidence motion in Tánaiste and Labour leader Eamon Gilmore after a shellacking by voters at the 2014 local and European elections, he had resigned, to be replaced by Joan Burton after a contest. Burton did not prove to be the party's salvation.

By 2016, the country's economy had turned the corner, and recovery was well under way. Unemployment was down, growth was up, and the sense prevalent five years earlier that the country was teetering on the brink of collapse was no longer present. But the years of austerity had left deep scars and a legacy of anger and resentment on the part of many voters against those who had administered the tough medicine. Both coalition parties were flayed by the voters. In Wicklow, Harris was comfortably re-elected.

After months of negotiations, Kenny pulled together a curious minority government, including several independent TDs, and supported – or at least facilitated – from the outside by a rejuvenated Fianna Fáil through a confidence-and-supply arrangement. Fianna Fáil leader Micheál Martin guaranteed to maintain a Dáil majority for the government by abstaining on key votes, subject to agreed criteria. 'This new departure for Irish politics is a major challenge', Martin told the Dáil, while announcing the decision.

A new departure and a major challenge were on the way for the young Wicklow deputy, too. 'He was nearly shaking when he was told he had the job', a colleague later told the *Irish Times* of Harris's reaction when he was offered the job of Minister for Health in the Fine Gael-led government formed in May 2016. His rise to 'great political heights has been meteoric, dazzling', the *Irish Independent* remarked. 'But will he fulfil his early promise', the paper wondered, continuing,

> or will the man once dubbed 'the White Obama' by his Fine Gael colleagues prove in the long run to be, instead, the Icarus of Irish politics – the career politician who rose too fast to the top, never given the chance to gain vital experience along the way but sent plummeting – his wings prematurely singed by the searing sun of ambition, too much piled on his relatively young shoulders far too soon?

If the metaphors were somewhat breathless, the question was not an unreasonable one. It is not the case, as the conventional wisdom frequently averred, that the Department of Health is the graveyard of political careers. Of the last five people to serve as Taoiseach, four are former Ministers for Health. What is true is that the Department often confronts its ministers with severe political difficulties, rooted in failures that impact – sometimes catastrophically – on people's lives. Brian Cowen famously called it 'Angola', where landmines can go off underneath you at any time. To survive, to get out alive, ministers need to understand a vast system whose constituent parts are often at war with one another, they need to have an ability to communicate directly with the public, and they need political instincts that can detect danger a mile off.

Harris survived, just about. After years of austerity and uncertain leadership – Fine Gael first dropped plans for a system of universal health insurance and then did a U-turn on abolishing the HSE that runs the health-care system – the politics of health was a cauldron for the young minister. There were protests over the conditions at hospitals; waiting lists were soaring; staff were threatening strikes over pay. Health budgets were starting to increase again after the years of austerity, but to nothing like what was necessary to keep up with demand. There was constant pressure on services; Harris frequently found himself explaining and promising to address the system's shortcomings.

But he got to talk about other things, too. By 2018, a long-awaited referendum to repeal the Constitution's almost blanket ban on abortion was being planned. Harris himself had moved from a strong anti-abortion position – he had written guarantees to pro-life groups when first running for election assuring them of his anti-abortion views – but, like many politicians and others, he would come to change his mind on the issue. Conscious that there was a majority – the polls said, anyway – for change in the country but that it was a majority nervous of moving too far, too fast, Harris and his colleagues resolved to outline in detail the legislation that would provide for relatively restricted legal abortion in the aftermath of a successful repeal referendum. It was a softly, softly approach that was both well judged and smartly executed. And Harris was central to it. This is about women and about taking care of Irish women who need health care, he repeated endlessly. The women of Ireland approved; on the day of the results, when a large crowd gathered in Dublin Castle to celebrate a landslide victory, Harris was cheered to the echo. One waved a placard that read, 'I fancy Simon Harris.'

But celebrations in the sun were the exception rather than the rule in the period. When cervical-cancer patient Vicky Phelan refused to sign a confidentiality agreement as part of a legal settlement, she shed light on a scandal that would see over 200 women being told that their smear tests may not have been correctly read previously. Many went on to develop cancer.

Harris quickly took Phelan's side, making contact with her immediately and staying in touch with her throughout the controversy. He was critical of the health authorities' handling of the cases, and, while some officials resented his willingness to blame the system, his ability to align himself with the victims, rather than the state, would serve as a sort of political prophylactic. Yet he looked panicky at times: his offer of an extra smear test for any woman who wanted one put enormous pressure on an already creaking system. The then HSE Chief Executive, Tony O'Brien, would later accuse Harris of behaving 'like a frightened little boy' during the controversy.

There were other controversies, too. The costs of the new National Children's Hospital ballooned, with neither the Minister nor his officials apparently able to control them, accurately predict where they would end up or explain the reasons for them. 'The National Children's Hospital under construction at St James's in Dublin is well on its way to becoming the most expensive hospital in the world, yet the taxpayer has been given no explanation for the massive cost overrun', wrote Paul Cullen in the *Irish Times* at the end of 2018.

Harris survived a motion of no confidence in the Dáil in February of 2019, but Fianna Fáil backbenchers and independents – this was a minority government, remember – were getting jumpy in the face of long waiting lists for treatment and overcrowded emergency wards.

On housing, the government's other Achilles heel, the Minister responsible, Eoghan Murphy, barely survived a confidence vote in December 2019. The government's majority was just three; with another confidence motion in Harris threatened for February, Varadkar decided he had had enough. On 14 January 2020, he called a general election for 8 February. Harris was re-elected in Wicklow on the 15th count, the sole Fine Gael TD for the county. Elsewhere, the party had a dreadful day, dropping 12 seats from its 2016 result. The promise of Leo Varadkar to Fine Gael TDs back in 2017, that he would open up new seams of support for the party in a modernising Ireland, seemed hollow now.

With Fianna Fáil also despondent after a deeply disappointing result

– Sinn Féin won the largest share of votes if not Dáil seats – the two old rivals eyed one another with little enthusiasm as possible coalition partners. But there would be one final twist for this unique administration. An unprecedented global pandemic was about to hit. And the Minister for Health would be front and centre in managing it.

By convention, ministers who remain in place after a general election pending the formation of a new government are 'caretaker' ministers. Though legally they are just as much ministers as ever, the loss of their political mandate means that they do not generally initiate any new policies or initiatives. Like much else, that went out the window during the pandemic. From the outset, Harris made a virtue of the fact that he was following the medical and scientific advice. Politicians are not the ones making the decisions, he would say. We are following the public-health advice. There would come a time, later in the pandemic, when politicians would be called on to make decisions, to weigh up the impact of imposing or lifting lockdowns on social and economic life, on the mental health of people. But not yet.

For the first few months of 2020, Harris's deference to the doctors reassured people. The government, which was, after all, waiting to be ejected from office, saw its approval ratings soar. Harris's ability to communicate and reassure, and to project empathy (vital for any modern politician) were important factors. 'Two months ago, Simon Harris was one of the most unpopular health ministers in living memory', the *Irish Independent*'s Hugh O'Connell wrote. 'Now children write to him telling him they miss school, while his growing Instagram following swoons over his every word in daily video updates on the government's response to an unprecedented pandemic.'

Progress towards forming a new government was slow, retarded further by the lockdown. Martin and Varadkar also needed to allow their party organisations to become psychologically attuned to the momentous step of sharing power with the old enemy. Both knew the alternatives were sharing power with Sinn Féin or another general election. Neither was very attractive. Eventually, a Programme for Government was hammered out with the Greens, and, on 27 June, a unique three-party coalition was approved by a vote of the socially distanced Dáil.

Micheál Martin became Taoiseach and Leo Varadkar Tánaiste, with the commitment that the two would swap roles in December 2022. Not being a masochist, Harris had no desire to stay in the Department of Health. But when Fine Gael portfolios were handed out, he secured neither an economic department nor the Department of Justice, as he might have hoped. Instead, he would take charge of the newly created Department of Further and Higher Education. It might have looked like a demotion, but at least he was still in cabinet. Several others were not.

Though something of a political backwater, Harris used the platform of the higher-education job to deepen his ties in the organisation. He spent time travelling around the country visiting colleges and universities (a programme of upgrading institutes of technology to university status was popular, if academically questionable), often meeting the local Fine Gael TDs, councillors and party bigwigs. He secured budget funding to cut the costs of third-level education for students and their parents and promoted the status of apprenticeships. But on the biggest question facing the university sector – the lack of a sustainable funding model – he faced criticism throughout the sector. He appeared to enjoy a stint as stand-in Minister for Justice (Helen McEntee was on maternity leave) at least as much, and possibly more, than his day job. He never tired of making announcements; as ever, some observers questioned the follow-up.

Harris never made any secret of his ambition to lead party and country, but his private view was that Varadkar would not make any decisions on his future until after the local and European elections in June 2024. Like all his colleagues, he wondered why Varadkar had not really seized on his return to the Taoiseach's office in December 2022 to assert himself and his party again. The Fine Gael leader seemed, they told one another quietly, oddly disengaged.

Unlike the others, though, Harris was making preparations. Just in case, just in case. When Varadkar in March 2024 decided he had had enough, Harris was ready to move. While others discussed and digested the move, and pondered their own futures, Harris and his aides and supporters hit the phones. That evening, with Leinster House still slightly reeling from the unusual sight of a Taoiseach wilfully giving up his office and an air of deep uncertainty in Fine Gael, Harris's old stomping ground of Young Fine Gael made its voice heard. 'He has been a great friend to both me and YFG, and would make a great leader of Fine Gael & Taoiseach', the Young Fine Gael President Eoin Gallagher posted on X.

When Harris managed Coveney's leadership campaign against Varadkar in 2017, he learnt the hard way the value of generating momentum early in the contest. Then, the Varadkar campaign blew its opponent away with a steady stream of endorsements at the start, leaving Coveney (and his campaign manager) chasing to keep up. Harris now executed a similar manoeuvre. His key adviser Sarah Bardon left Leinster House at about 1 a.m. but was back at her desk by 7 a.m. the next morning when the first members of the parliamentary party began making public declarations of support, the *Irish Examiner* reported in a detailed reconstruction of the events.

Dublin Senator Barry Ward was first out, followed by Junior Minister Neale Richmond on RTÉ's *Morning Ireland*. Then Peter Burke declared, and then, at brief intervals – remember, it was not yet 9 a.m. – a succession of endorsements arrived on news desks. By 10 a.m., when nominations officially opened, Harris had the backing of 15 members of the parliamentary party. By lunchtime, Helen McEntee, Heather Humphreys and Paschal Donohoe had ruled themselves out, and the contest was over almost before it had begun.

The following Sunday, Harris attended a party event in Athlone, where he delivered a barnstorming speech to a packed hotel ballroom heaving with ecstatic Fine Gaelers. Two weeks later, just a few days before he was due to become Taoiseach, Harris went to Galway for his party's Ard Fheis, quickly refocused on the theme of 'A New Energy'. The excitement and optimism at the venue was palpable, for the first time in a long time at a Fine Gael conference. 'I'm gonna hit the ground running!' the new leader told delirious delegates.

In truth, his early weeks as Taoiseach did indeed display a new energy in the Taoiseach's office, as announcements and initiatives arrived in a flurry. But they were also dominated by the issues that had proved so intractable for his predecessor: housing, health care, immigration. He had an early skirmish with the British government, trading barbs over Dublin's concerns that a large proportion of its asylum-seekers (over 80 per cent, Helen McEntee told an Oireachtas committee) were arriving into the state over the border with Northern Ireland, apparently scared out of the UK by Prime Minister Rishi Sunak's promised deportations of illegal migrants to Rwanda. Sunak seized on the concerns of the Irish government as evidence that his migrants policy was working. Harris promised emergency legislation to facilitate returns. The early polls showed little sign of any bounce for Fine Gael; politically, all eyes were on the upcoming local and European elections, due in early June.

As Taoiseach, Harris made good his 'new energy' promises, dashing around the country and giving his party organisation – depressed by falling poll ratings and shocked by Varadkar's early departure – a desperately needed shot in the arm. In a remarkably short time, the mood of his party was completely transformed. Its allies in government, knowing they were soon to be rivals in the election, looked on with a bit of concern and tut-tutted about how much time the new Taoiseach was spending campaigning rather than governing.

Harris displayed a bias towards action; one of his first actions was to order the clearing of tents pitched by asylum-seekers seeking accommodation around the International Protection Office near Leinster House – they were moved on to local-authority land south of the city. It didn't solve the problem of accommodation for asylum-seekers. But it removed it from the streets of the city. It displayed Harris's feel for how gestures work as political communication.

Soon the Fine Gael poll numbers started to recover. At the local and European elections, where the big story was the collapse of Sinn Féin, Fine Gael performed credibly, virtually neck and neck with Fianna Fáil in local-authority seats won. On to the general election. Despite months of insisting that the government would wait until early 2025, a combination of a big giveaway budget in October and Sinn Féin's continuing political weakness made a late 2024 poll irresistible.

Fine Gael began the election campaign with a clear lead in the polls, but the trajectory would be downward. Harris continued his high-octane style in the campaign, but Fine Gael – as it had done in all recent general election campaigns – started to stumble as soon as the starting pistol was fired. Ryanair boss Michael O'Leary made some disobliging comments about teachers when launching a Fine Gael candidate's campaign in Mullingar; there was a renewed focus on a Fine Gael candidate in Louth who had been successfully sued for assault and who promptly disappeared from public view; at an early Harris press conference, the 'new energy' sign fell off the front of the podium – all grist to the mill of a critical media on the lookout for mishaps. Most serious of all, Harris, clearly exhausted from all the haring around the country, had a snippy exchange with a woman in a supermarket in Kanturk, Co. Cork. He immediately apologised, and kept apologising, but the story ran for days. Harris and his party were well and truly rattled.

When the votes were counted, the results showed that Sinn Féin had staged an impressive recovery in the second half of the year, and the picture of three large parties – Fianna Fáil, Fine Gael and Sinn Féin – competing for the top spot remained unaltered. But it was Fine Gael that was, by a tight margin of a single seat, in third place with 38 seats, behind Sinn Fein on 39 and Fianna Fáil well ahead on 48 seats.

Fianna Fáil's clear victory meant that when the inevitable coalition government was formed in January between the two parties and a group of independent TDs, it was Micheál Martin who would return to the Taoiseach's office. Harris moved to the Department of Foreign Affairs, also taking responsibility for the Department of Defence. The election result was disappointing for Harris and his party for sure – and yet, they were returning to government for the fourth time in a row. He is due to move back into the Taoiseach's office on 16 November 2027.

After only nine months in the job, and with another stint in the

Taoiseach's office due under the agreement between Fianna Fáil and Fine Gael, it is perhaps too early to judge the premiership of Simon Harris. He brought to the office youth and energy, that much is clear. But he faced, probably, the greatest step up of anyone who has come to the role. He had not held any of the finance or economic portfolios, or Foreign Affairs, nor had he led the opposition. However, inexperience is not a barrier to success. The great generation that founded the independent Irish state was almost impossibly young. Michael Collins was 31 when he died; Éamon de Valera was President of the First Dáil at the age of 36 – a year younger than Harris is now. More than half of the first cabinet of the Free State was under the age of 35. Furthermore, perhaps the most qualified man ever to occupy the office, Brian Cowen, had the most miserable time in it.

But just as experience is no guarantee of wisdom, so youth is not, in itself, a virtue. The qualities that Harris will need to be a successful Taoiseach and successful leader of his party are the same as they would be at any age: an even temperament, self-belief and strength of character; the courage to take on problems and make decisions and the judgement to make the right ones; mental and physical stamina; and, maybe, a fair dollop of luck. Harris is undoubtedly a brilliant communicator and an instinctive politician. He has risen through the ranks irresistibly. He has proved adept at avoiding problems and at managing the politics of them. But being Taoiseach is unlike any other job in Irish politics. There is no escaping problems when you are in the Taoiseach's office: they will surely come and find you.

Index of Names

Adams, Gerry 209, 216–17, 219, 230–1
Adenauer, Konrad 63
Ahern, Bertie 12, 14, 22, 133, 175, 206, 209–10, 212, 214, 221, 222, 230, 232, 234–256, 258, 261–5, 284–8, 299, 316, 319, 342
Ahern, Cecilia 251
Ahern, Con 239
Ahern, Georgina 251
Ahern, Julia 245
Aiken, Frank 65, 87, 115, 120, 130
Ali, Muhammed 314
Andrews, David 210
Andrews, Eamonn 165
Arnold, Bruce 102, 117, 209
Armstrong, Sir Robert 192
Attlee, Clement 78

Baldwin, Stanley 55
Ball, Kenny 199
Bardon, Sarah 350
Barnier, Michel 304
Barrett, Dick 31
Barrett, Matthew 310
Behan, Brendan 107
Berry, Peter 120
Bewley, Charles 74
Biden, Joe 295, 297, 310, 329
Bilk, Acker 199
Blair, Tony 232, 244, 251, 285
Blaney, Neil 115, 120–1, 123–4, 127-9, 143, 200
Blythe, Ernest 33–4
Bodkin Thomas 87
Boland, Freddie 79
Boland, George 120
Boland, Gerald 198
Boland, Harry 120, 160, 162, 166
Boland, Kevin 66, 115, 120–1, 123–4, 128–9
Böll, Heinrich 11
Bradley, Denis 217
Brady, Conor 221
Bray, Jennifer 342
Brookeborough, Lord 198
Browne, Noël 64, 82–6, 169
Browne, Vincent 284

Brugha, Cathal 46
Bruton, Finola 224, 228, 236
Bruton, Joe 225
Bruton, John 23, 144, 181, 186–7, 221, 224–36, 246, 263, 282–3
Bruton, Richard 284, 286, 288–90, 299
Burke, David 129
Burke, Paddy 286
Burke, Peter 350
Burke, Ray 210, 234, 246–7
Burke, Thomas 27
Burke-Savage, Father 182
Busby, Matt 314
Butler, Robin 216–17
Byrne, Eric 229
Byrne, Gay 178
Bryne, Nicky 251
Bygraves, Joe 314

Cahill, Joe 219
Callan, Owen 327–8, 341
Callaghan, Rose 72
Calleary, Dara 331–2
Cameron, David 302
Campbell, Alastair 245
Carron, Owen 202
Carter, Frank 200
Casey, Charles 84
Casey, Eamon 211
Cash, Johnny 199
Ceannt, Éamonn 28
Chamberlain, Neville 58, 101

Childers, Erskine 63
Churchill. Winston 60–2, 85, 101
Clinton, Bill 213, 215, 217, 219, 222, 285
Clune, Deirde 344
Cluskey, Frank 169
Coghlan, Paul, 286, 295
Coll, Kate 42
Collery, Lisa-Dee 327
Colley, George 119–21, 130, 134, 156, 160, 165, 168, 170, 184, 201
Collins, Michael 17, 19, 27, 30, 35, 45, 47, 73, 160, 230, 235. 343, 353
Collins, Gerry 210
Collins, Stephen 39, 150, 231
Connolly, James 94
Connolly, Patrick 172
Coogan, Tim Pat 120
Cooney, Patrick 143
Cooper, Henry 314
Cooper, Colin 295
Cooper, Beverley 229
Cosgrave, Bridget 27
Cosgrave, Ciarán 139
Cosgrave, Liam 12, 20, 27, 38, 86, 113, 137–52, 167, 183–4, 226–7, 281–2
Cosgrave, Liam T. 139, 150
Cosgrave, Louisa 138
Cosgrave, Mary 139
Cosgrave, Miceál 27
Cosgrave, Thomas 27
Cosgrave, W. T 17, 26–40, 49, 52, 54, 74, 138–40, 150, 182, 198, 210

Costello, Declan 89, 227
Costello, Eavan 91
Costello, John 91
Costello, John A 19, 39, 63, 69–92, 103, 279
Coughlan, Mary 269
Coveney, Hugh 232
Coveney, Simon 232, 288–9, 301, 303, 305, 340, 350
Cowen, Barry 332
Cowen, Bernard 258, 313
Cowen, Christopher 258
Cowen, Brian 135, 210, 235, 237–8, 249, 252, 254, 257–77, 279, 287, 299, 317, 320, 353
Cox, Arthur 77–8, 85
Creed, Michael 288–9
Creighton, Lucinda 287–8
Croker, Richard 73
Crotty, Raymond D. 224
Cullen, Paul 347
Cunningham, Larry 199

D'Arcy, Brian 199
Dale, Iain 93
Dalton, Charles 35
de Gaulle, Charles 63, 110
De Rossa, Proinsias 229–30
de Valera, Éamon 10, 16–18, 20, 29–30, 36–7, 41–68, 74, 76, 85, 87, 90, 92, 95–6, 98–9, 105–06, 108–09, 115–17, 120, 122–5, 133, 234, 274, 353

de Valera, Juan 42
Deasy, Austin 235
Deasy, John 286
Deasy, Richard 164
Delors, Jacques 207
Desmond, Barry 193
Dillon, James 38, 87–8, 122
Dockrell, Henry 75
Doherty, Seán 173, 176, 209
Dolan, Joe 199
Donlon, Sean 231
Donnelly, Stephen 327
Donohoe, Pashal 350
Dooge, Jim 38
Dooley, Timmy 322
Doyle, Avril 287
Duddy, Brendan 217
Dukes, Alan 190, 194, 228–9, 282
Dukes, James 117
Dunlop, Frank 239
Dunne, Ben 176–7, 179, 337

Eames, Robin 217
Eden, Anthony 101
Edward VIII, King 55–6
Egan, John 72–3
Eisenhower, Dwight D. 86
Elizabeth II, Queen 223, 291
Enright, Olwyn 289
Esmonde, Sir John 78, 84

Farrell, Brian 18, 34
Farrell, Dessie 251

INDEX OF NAMES

Farrell, Mel 39
Faulkner, Brian 131, 151
Feeney, Chuck 215
Finlay, Thomas 74, 92
Finucane, Marian 138
Fisher, Desmond 122–3
FitzGerald, Alexis 81, 91
FitzGerald, Desmond 181
FitzGerald, Frances 229, 312–13, 342
FitzGerald, Mabel 181–2
FitzGerald, Garret 12, 14, 18, 21–2, 38, 90, 143, 150, 168–9, 173, 180–96, 202, 204, 226–8, 235, 282
Fitzgerald, Joan 195, 226
Flanagan, Louise 27
Flanagan, Michael 138
Flannery, Frank 285
Flynn, Bill 215
Flynn, Pádraig 208, 210, 215, 229
Fox, Billy 149

Gaddafi, Muammar 222
Galba, Emperor 278
Gallagher, Eoin 349
Geoghegan, Johnny 282
Geoghegan-Quinn, Máire 214, 282
George VI, King 55, 76
Gibbons. Jim 126, 128
Gillane, Deirdre 322, 327
Gilmore, Éamon 232, 288, 344
Goodall, David 192
Goodman, Larry 229

Gray, David 61–2
Gregory, Tony 172, 188
Griffith, Arthur 17, 27, 30, 45–6
Griffin. Brendan 294
Guerin, Veronica 233

Halappanavar, Savita 292, 305
Hales, Seán 31, 36
Hamilton, Liam 229
Hanafin, Des 212
Hanlon, Noel 199
Harney, Mary 177, 206, 234, 247, 261, 319
Harris, Adam 341
Harris, Barr 340
Harris, Cillian 341
Harris, Gemma 341
Harris, Mary 340
Harris, Saoirse 341
Harris, Simon 311, 336, 339–53
Haughey, Charles 12, 18, 21-2, 105, 113, 119–21, 123–4, 129, 130, 133–4, 143, 153–79, 181–2, 185, 188, 191, 193–5, 200–01, 203–11, 213, 222, 227–8, 233–4, 239–42, 243, 246, 262, 282
Haughey, Eoghan 158
Haughey, Sarah 157–8
Haughey, Seán 157–8, 160
Hayes, Brian 288
Hayes, Michael 30
Healy, Sean 250
Healy, John 119

Heath, Edward 131
Heffernan, Margaret 177
Hempel, Eduard 62
Heney, Michael 129
Herrema, Tiede 149
Higgins, Jim 280–3
Higgins, Michael D. 188, 215, 217, 339
Hillery, Patrick 107, 119, 127–8, 131–3, 207
Hitler, Adolf 62
Hogan, Phil 228, 231, 285, 287, 288–9, 292–3, 331
Hogan, Richard 228
Holohan, Tony 307, 326–8
Honohan, Patrick 273
Horan, James 202
Howlin, Brendan 22
Howlin, Gerald 250–1
Hughes, Peter 31
Hume, John 190, 209, 216–18
Humphreys, Heather 343, 350
Hurson, Martin 202

Iveagh, Lord 71

Johnson, Boris 303–04
Johnson, Tom 214
Jordan, Anthony J 39, 71
Juncker, Jean-Claude 303

Keane, Terry 178
Kearney, John D 62

Keegan, Seán 200
Kelleher, Billy 322
Kelly, James 126, 166
Kennedy, Edward 215
Kennedy, Geraldine 209, 279
Kennedy, Hugh 72–4
Kennedy, M J 63
Kennedy-Smith, Jean 215, 221
Kenny, Enda 22, 228, 231, 252, 261, 278–95, 299-301, 303, 323, 343–4
Kenny Jr, Henry 281
Kenny Sr, Henry 280–1
Kilclooney, Lord 202
King, Tom 192
Kitt, Michael 282
Knirck, Jason 39
Kohl, Helmut 12, 214

Laffan, Michael 28, 39, 150
Larkin, Celia 242
Lavery, Cecil 74, 77, 84
Leahy, Pat 266
Lemass, Frances 96
Lemass, Herbert 92–3
Lemass, John 95
Lemass, Maureen 105, 161, 178–9
Lemass, Noel 93, 96
Lemass, Seán 11, 20, 39, 48, 63–7, 88, 90, 92–111, 117-18, 120–2, 162–3, 165, 198, 219, 231, 251
Lenihan, Brian 120, 176, 202–03, 207

INDEX OF NAMES

Lenihan Jr, Brian 268, 269–70, 273, 288, 321
Leo XIII, Pope 99
Leyden, John 100, 106
Lillis, Michael 192
Lloyd George, David 46, 52
Lord, Miriam 285
Loughnane, Bill 134
Lowry, Michael 228, 230, 233, 336–7
Lutyens, Edwin 234
Luykx, Albert A. 166, 200
Lynch, Dan 113
Lynch, Jack 20-1, 66-7, 112–36, 143, 148, 155–6, 165–6, 168, 185, 201, 223, 226–7, 239, 279, 31–5
Lynch, Liam 48
Lynch, Máirín 114, 116, 126
Lynch, Norah 113
Lynch, Patrick 81

McAleese, Mary 222, 251
MacBride, Seán 78–9, 81, 83, 87
McCabe, Maurice 293–4
McCole, Brigid 284
McCreevy, Charlie 173, 203, 206, 210–11, 215, 247–9, 265, 268
McCullagh, David 71
McDaid, Jim 208
McDonald, Mary Lou 306, 325
MacDonald, Malcolm 58
MacDonald, Ramsay 52, 58
McDowell, Michael 249, 252

McEntee, Helen 327, 349–51
MacEntee, Seán 51, 53, 64–5, 120, 130
MacEoin, Sean 128
McGee, Mary 143
McGilligan, Patrick 34
McGrath, Pa 115
McGuckin, Basil 74
McGuinness, John 261
McGuinness, Mairead 287
McGuinness, Martin 213, 217
McKelvey, Joe 31
McLaughlin, Elizabeth 198
Macmillan, Harold 109–10
MacNeill, Eoin 95
McParland, Pat 322, 327
McQuaid, John Clarke 57–8, 82, 86, 102
McShane, John 199
MacSharry, Ray 174–5, 205, 208
McWilliams, Owen 159–60
Maffey, Sir John 61
Magee, Roy 217
Major, John 207, 209, 213, 217–19, 223, 232
Mallon, Seumas 152
Mandelson, Peter 264
Martin, Léana 324
Martin, Mairéad 313
Martin, Mary 324
Martin, Micheál 23, 254, 274–5, 306–07, 313–38, 345, 348, 352
Martin, Micheál Aodh 333

Martin, Paddy 314, 333
Martin, Philip 315
Martin, Ruairi 324
Martin, Seán 315
May, Theresa 302–04
Mayhew, Sir Patrick 213, 219
Meehan, Ciara 144, 150
Mellows, Liam 31
Merkel, Angela 290
Mills, Michael 165
Mitchell, George 244, 246
Mitchell, Jim 235, 246
Molyneaux, James 217-18
Morrissey, Daniel 141
Mountbatten, Louis 124, 201
Mulcahy, Richard 18, 35, 78, 85, 88
Murphy, Gary 129
Murphy, Michael 209
Musharraf, Pervez 222
Mussolini, Benito 54

Nally, Dermot 21, 186–7, 189, 192, 215, 216
Naughton, Denis 288–9
Nealon, Ted 185
Nixon, Richard 169
Noonan, Michael 22, 173, 229, 233, 235, 247, 283–4, 289, 290
Norton, William 78, 86

O'Brien, Conor Cruise 150, 152, 172, 202
O'Brien, Tony 347

O'Brien, William 114–15
O'Byrne, John 73–4
O'Callaghan, Miriam 296
O'Callaghan, Owen 222
O'Carroll, Patrick 88
O'Casey, Seán 107
O'Connell, Daniel 17, 113
O'Connell, Hugh 348
O'Connell, John 210
O'Connor, Charles 73
O'Connor, Rory 31
O'Dea, William 275
O'Donoghue, Martin 131, 133
O'Dowd, Niall 215
O'Duffy, Eoin 37, 54, 75
Ó Faoláin, Seán 86–7
O'Farrell, Frank 314
O'Farrell, Joan 182
Ó Fiaich, Tomas 202
O'Gowan, General Dorman 85
O'Hanlon, Rory 211
O'Higgins, Kevin 18, 27, 29, 35–6, 49, 104
O'Higgins, Tom 66, 86–7, 143
Ó hUiginn, Seán 216, 220
O'Kelly, Seán T 66, 74, 86
O'Leary, Michael 187, 352
Ó Máille, Pádraig 31
O'Malley, Desmond 108, 129–30, 132–3, 135, 175, 204, 206, 208–10, 213, 245–6
O'Malley, Donogh 107, 120
O'Malley, Ida 72

Ó Moráin, Micheál 128
O'Neill, Terence 108
O'Rourke, Mary 203, 209–10
O'Rourke, Sean 283–4
O'Toole, Fintan 319
Obama, Barack 291
Orbison, Roy 199
Owen, Nora 210, 230, 233

Paisley, Ian 264
Paisley Jnr, Ian 222
Parnell, Charles Stuart 17
Pearse, Patrick 94
Phelan, Vicky 347
Portillo, Michael 295
Prendergast, Peter 185

Quinn, Ruairi 210, 215, 221, 230, 232

Rabbitte, Pat 283
Reagan, Ronald 192
Redmond, John 115, 231–2
Reeves, Jim 199, 209
Regan, John M 39
Reid, Alec 213
Reilly, James 300
Reynolds, Albert 14, 22, 176, 197–223, 228–9, 241–3, 246, 262, 316
Reynolds, Jim 198-9
Reynolds, John P. 197
Reynolds, Kathleen 198, 209, 223
Reynolds, Philip 200, 222
Richmond, Neale 350

Ring, Michael 229
Robinson, Mary 207, 216
Roche, Dick 341
Roche, Stephen 114
Roosevelt, Eleanor 61
Ryan, Eamon 307
Ryan, James 65
Ryan, Richie 144

Salazar, António de Oliveira 169
Sánchez, Pedro 310
Sands, Bobby 170
Sarkozy, Nicolas 290
Savage, Tom 210
Sebastian, Tim 255
Shatter, Alan 293, 300
Shaw, George Bernard 343
Shawcross, Sir Hartley 85
Simpson, Wallis 55
Smyth, Brendan 221
Spence, Gusty 220
Spring, Dick 214–5, 221, 228, 230, 246, 283
Sunak, Rishi 351
Sutherland, Peter 189
Sutton, Ralph 91
Sweetman, Gerard 86–8, 90

Teahon, Paddy 231
Thatcher, Margaret 134, 157, 170–1, 187, 190–2, 201, 203, 251
Thomas, J. H 53
Timmins, Billy 289

Tobin, Liam 35
Traynor, Des 177
Trump, Donald 307
Truss, Liz 16

Varadkar, Ashok 297
Varadkar, Leo 14, 23, 236, 287–9, 292, 294, 296–311, 313, 325–8, 331–2, 335–6, 339–40, 347–51
Varadkar, Madhu 298
Varadkar, Manohar 298
Varadkar, Miriam 297
Varadkar, Sonia 297
Varadkar, Sophie 297

Wade, Caoimhe 341
Walpole, Sir Robert 14
Walsh, Brian 91

Walsh, J. J 27
Walsh, Joe 206
Ward, Barry 350
West, Harry 198
Whelahan, Harry 211, 220–1, 230
Whelan, Noel 260
Whitaker, T. K. (Ken) 65, 87, 106-7, 118, 124–5, 135
Wilson, Gordon 215
Wilson, Harold 110, 184, 193
Wilson, John 210
Woods, Michael 209, 215
Woulfe, Séamus 331

Yates, Ivan 228, 234

Zappone, Kathleen 294, 306